Studies in Philosophy
and the
History of Philosophy

Founded in 1960 by John K. Ryan

Volume 2

STUDIES IN PHILOSOPHY

AND THE

HISTORY OF PHILOSOPHY

Edited by

JOHN K. RYAN

THE CATHOLIC UNIVERSITY OF AMERICA PRESS
Washington, D. C.
1963

Paperback Edition Copyright © 2018
The Catholic University of America Press
All rights reserved

The paper used in this publication meets the minimum requirements of the American National Standards for Information Science – Permanence of paper for Printed Library Materials, ANSI Z39.48-1984.
∞

Cataloging-in-Publication Data available from the Library of Congress

ISBN 978-0-8132-3110-5 (pbk)

Nihil obstat:
    Peter J. Rahill
    Censor Deputatus

Imprimatur:
    ✠ Patrick A. O'Boyle
      Archbishop of Washington
    February 7, 1963

    The *Nihil obstat* and the *imprimatur* are official declarations that a book or pamphlet is free of doctrinal or moral error. No implication is contained therein that those who have granted the *nihil obstat* and the *imprimatur* agree with the content, opinions, or statements expressed.

                Acknowledgement is made of assistance received from
The Very Reverend Ignatius Smith, O.P., Fund in defraying publication costs of *Studies in Philosophy and the History of Philosophy,* Volume 2. This fund was established at The Catholic University of America by the Reverend James P. Counahan, O.P., M.A. (School of Philosophy, 1953), from a bequest left by his uncle, Mr. Charles A. Counahan of Pittsburgh, Pennsylvania, "to publish works and susbsidize studies which [will] produce a greater knowledge and appreciation of the thought of St. Thomas Aquinas in America."

TABLE OF CONTENTS

		page
1.	A Protreptic: What Is Philosophy? *by Thomas Prufer*	1
2.	The Concept of Personality in Greek and Christian Thought *by C. J. de Vogel*	20
3.	Philosophy, Education, and the Controversy on St. Augustine's Conversion *by Eugene Kevane*	61
4.	St. Thomas Aquinas and the Doctrine of Essence *by Gilbert B. Arbuckle*	104
5.	The Question of the Validity of the *Tertia Via* *by Thomas G. Pater*	137
6.	The Metaphysical Crisis in Physical Theory *by Leo A. Foley, S.M.*	178
7.	Private Property and Natural Law *by Felix Alluntis, O.F.M.*	189
8.	The Political Thought of Tommaso Campanella *by Bernardine M. Bonansea, O.F.M.*	211
9.	Two Instances of the Tripartite Method in Machiavelli *by John K. Ryan*	249
	Notes on Contributors	257
	Index	259

1

A PROTREPTIC: WHAT IS PHILOSOPHY?

by

Thomas Prufer

"Philosophy with problematic foundations . . . is no philosophy, it contradicts its very meaning *as* philosophy. Philosophy can take root only in radical reflexion upon the meaning and possibility of its own scheme."[1]

* * *

The philosophical life cannot be the unexamined life,[2] least of all unexamined with respect to the foundations of philosophy itself. We must think about what we are doing, that is, we cannot philosophize without reflecting on the nature of the philosophical experience. We must ask the question: "What is that posture or use of the mind which constitutes philosophy?". Philosophy is perennial, but it is also ephemeral; it is continually being blurred and destroyed[3] and transformed into something not itself, and so if we wish to philosophize, we are continually faced with the task of rediscovering and restoring philosophy.

In attempting to answer the question "What is philosophy?", we cannot ignore the history of philosophy. Other minds are the condition of the possibility of our own minds; we do not think *ab ovo* or alone. We possess our minds as a sharing of insight.[4] History is the past which is not over and done with, but present and rele-

---

[1] Edmund Husserl, *Ideas*, trans. W. R. Boyce Gibson (New York: The Macmillan Co., 1931), 27. Cf. Descartes' *Meditatio Prima* (Adam and Tannery text): a primis fundamentis denuo inchoandum, si quid aliquando firmum & mansurum cupiam in scientiis stabilire . . . quia, suffossis fundamentis, quidquid iis superaedificatum est sponte collabitur, aggrediar statim ipsa principia.

[2] Plato, *Apology* 38a5-6.

[3] "Both (Plato and Aristotle) have given us an account of philosophy, but not without giving us also an account of the ways to it and of the ways to reestablish it when it becomes confused or extinct." Alfarabi, *Philosophy of Plato and Aristotle,* trans. Muhsin Mahdi (Glencoe, Ill.: The Free Press, 1962), 49-50.

[4] Plato, *Gorgias* 506a4; *Meno* 86c5; *Protagoras* 336b2; *Symposium* 176e8; ep. VII 341c6-7. Aristotle, 1170b10-12; 1245b5.

vant, present and relevant to such a degree that we would not be what we are, if the past were not. Philosophizing is always a re-grasp, a re-petition, of the history of philosophy, where we find the forms of philosophical experience, the paradigms of our own philosophical life.[5]

When we turn to the history of philosophy, we find it divided into three periods: ancient, medieval, and modern. What is the principle of this customary division? Is the periodization simply the application of a general division of "cultural forms" to philosophy considered as one among other such forms? If so, then the division is not *philosophically* explained and it reduces philosophy to *Weltanschauung*. Or is this division extrinsic to philosophy because philosophy is always the same, so that it has no differentiation of forms at all? (One could hold that classical philosophy is the only form of genuine philosophical experience.) Or finally, is there an *intrinsic* periodization of philosophy, that is, a division of philosophy into epochs or forms which is *philosophically* intelligible? This view would distinguish itself from the two previous views in refusing to reduce philosophy to one "cultural form" among others, considering philosophy an ascent from the cave (which other human activities are not or with a radicality which is not found in other human activities) and in holding that there is a plurality of forms of philosophical experience which are different from each other without ceasing to be genuinely philosophical.

Let us say that ancient, medieval and modern philosophy are the beginning, middle and end of philosophy. The beginning is that which is preceded by nothing but followed by something, the middle is that which is preceded and followed by something, the end is that which is preceded by something, but not followed by anything; the succession is not fortuitous or merely temporal.[6]

Philosophy as a form of experience fully differentiated from the ancestral, *techné,* magic and myth begins with the Greeks.[7] Those do not philosophize who do not live with each other in justified speech about the whole and the first; philosophy does not seek to use or placate; the myth is not subject to discussion or verification.[8] Philosophy for the Greeks is phenomenological ontology: speaking

[5] Plato, *Symposium* 207c8-208b6.
[6] Aristotle, *Poetics* vii.
[7] Cf. Aristotle, *Metaphysics* I, 1-2; Plato, *Theaetetus* 172c-177b. In justification of the identification of Greek philosophy with Plato and Aristotle: Aristotle, 1252b31-34.
[8] διαλέγεσθαι; βασανίζειν.

about the totality of being and the fundamental sense of being by speaking about being in so far as it is a phenomenon, in so far as it shows itself—and being shows itself to man primarily through man himself: man is the only being which concerns itself with being as being; only man questions being as being;[9] man is the phenomenal locus of being. (Socrates differentiates himself from the *physiologoi* by concerning himself with the *anthropina,* and Plato was a Socratic Parmenidean.)

Greek philosophy is the beginning of philosophy because, being the first differentiation of the philosophical experience, it is philosophy experienced in a form which is followed by another form which both remembers it and differs from it: philosophy in a theological context. By "theology" we mean the *logos theou,* the speech of God: "of" understood both as a subjective and objective genitive: it is God who speaks and God who is spoken about. These two meanings are inseparable because God is the only one who can speak about Himself as He is in Himself: *auctor nobis de Deo, Deus est.*[10] God is the only one to whom God's life is manifest, and man can speak of God as He is in Himself, that is, theologize, only in so far as he is elevated by God to a participation in God's speech about Himself: to a participation in the Word of God.

Phenomenological ontology is not theology, because God is not manifested as He is in Himself by means of the world, where man, the phenomenal locus of being, has his being and discovers the meaning of being. Not that Plato and Aristotle do not speak of the nonworldly ground of the world, but they speak of it only in so far as it is available or manifests itself through the world; they speak of the nonworldly from a worldly viewpoint. For Plato the ecstatic *bios theoretikos,* the life of the silent stranger, is complemented by the return to the cave, by speaking of the *cosmos* and *polis.* The Good as it is in itself is unspeakable, but philosophy must present itself in speech:[11] Socrates frequented the *agora* and *palaestra,* living in the exchange and *agon* of words. For Aristotle the human mode of contemplation is "timely" and "passionate."[12] The world implies

---

[9] Aristotle, 1028b2-4; Plato, *Sophist* 244a5. Cf. Martin Heidegger, *Kant and the Problem of Metaphysics,* IV, trans. James S. Churchill (Bloomington, Ind.: Indiana University Press, 1962).

[10] St. Hilary, PL X, 143.

[11] Plato, *Symposium* 211a7; ep. VII 341c5-6; *Phaedo* 99e4-100a3.

[12] 1075a7-10 and N.E. X, 8; the Platonic ὁμοίωσις θεῷ and the Aristotelian ἀθανατίζειν are qualified: "in so far as it is humanly possible." See *Republic* 613b1; *Theaetetus* 176b1-2; *Phaedrus* 253a4-5; *Symposium* 212a5-7; *Republic*

God, but it does not manifest Him as He is in Himself. If God is creator, then He is the most fundamental sense of the word "being" and the world is through participation in Him; theology will not destroy the validity of phenomenological ontology's understanding of the meaning of word "being," because if the world is totally the effect of that being which is in the most fundamental sense, then a knowledge of being reached through a knowledge of the world will be a way toward reaching an understanding of the most fundamental sense of the word "being": God. But the existence of a theology implies that an adequate understanding of the most fundamental sense of the word "being" cannot be reached through phenomenological ontology or through an understanding of being as it shows itself through man in the world. *Ipse solus seipsum nominavit, Verbum coaequale sibi generando.*[13] The fact of a Word of God implies that phenomenological ontology does not have the last word to say about the meaning of the word "being."

The Greeks did not philosophize in a theological context; they did not have a double vision of being: seeing being as it shows itself in the world, and seeing being as it is seen by that being which is in the most fundamental sense. The Greeks did not philosophize in a theological context because no theological mode of knowledge was available to them: God did not speak to them about Himself. The Greek form of philosophical experience was neither influenced by theology nor anti-theological, although it was open to a *theologia ventura.*

The middle form of philosophical experience (Jewish, Christian and Muslim) remembered the Greek form but differentiated itself from it by taking place in a theological context. Medieval philosophy is a genuine philosophical experience (and not merely a pseudo-philosophy or crypto-theology), but it co-exists with another view of being, the theological, which is nevertheless philosophically relevant in so far as it includes truths about the world, man, and being which are discoverable by a phenomenological ontology but which in point of fact were not discovered by Greek philosophy, by philosophy outside a theological context.[14]

500c9-d1; Aristotle, 1177b22 & 27; 1178a10 & 20-21; 1178b5 & 35. See Leo Strauss, *Natural Right and History* (Chicago: The University of Chicago Press, 1953), 124 and *What Is Political Philosophy?* (Glencoe, Ill.: The Free Press, 1959), 92-94.

[13] Aquinas, *Commentary on the Sentences,* I, 22, 1, 1.

[14] Averroes denied the philosophical relevance of theology, trying to return philosophy from its medieval or middle form to its Greek or beginning form.

Modern philosophy as the end-form of philosophy has been preceded by both Greek and medieval philosophy; it remembers them both and differentiates itself from them both; as end-form it is the form of philosophy which, although being philosophy, nevertheless destroys philosophy. Modern philosophy is like Greek philosophy in so far as it is not philosophy in a theological context (it is not the work of philosophizing theologians or of philosophers who acknowledge a non-philosophical view as higher or dominant), but it is differentiated from Greek philosophy because it absorbs or rejects this context, an absorption or rejection which are un-Greek. Modern philosophy is like medieval philosophy because it knows of a God-like view of the world, man, and being, but it is unlike medieval philosophy because it attempts to achieve this view philosophically or as the human view and not theologically or as a view held by gracious participation in God's view.

It is now our task to explain in greater detail what we mean by "a God-like view of the world, man, and being, held as the human or non-gracious view" and to see this view as fundamental to modern philosophy; to show how the modern positions which do not seem to be characterized by this view are nevertheless dominated by it, because they react against it without regaining a Greek or medieval position; to see why this view destroys philosophy; and then to examine the attempts of Husserl and Heidegger to re-ground philosophy after its destruction.

Beginning with Cartesian non-worldly mind, modern philosophy is concerned with mediating mind to world (and world to mind). This endeavor reaches the fullness of its form in Hegel, who conceives the end-point of philosophy as that state in which the self has become identified with the totality of being and in which the totality of being has become self-possessed or reflexive. The starting-point to be overcome is an alienation of mind and world; but world-alienation is not the natural condition of man's mind; it presupposes a theological experience of mind; we may call this presup-

---

But this is an un-Greek manœuvre because the Greek has no theology to reject; the Averroists therefore assimilated theology to mythology: quod sermones theologi fundati sunt in fabulis, Condemnation of 1277, prop. 152. "To think Greek" [see Heidegger, *Holzwege* (3d ed.; Frankfurt a/M: Vittorio Klostermann, 1957), 308ff.] cannot mean to return to the Greeks, because the Greeks as philosophers did not return to anyone. "It is precisely that contemporaneity of philosophic thought with its own basis which no longer exists in modern philosophy, and whose absence explains the eventual transformation of modern philosophy into an intrinsically historical philosophy." Strauss, *What Is Political Philosophy?*, 76.

position the theological *apriori* of the modern world-alienation of mind.

St. Augustine is paradigmatic for the theological experience of mind in contrast to the Greek experience; here is an interiorization of the self toward the transcendent *Deus Creator,* who is independent of all world, who is Himself without world, and who makes the world to be because He knows and wills it in nonnecessitated fashion. The being of the world is grounded in a non-worldly intellect and will not necessitated to this grounding, and the human intellect and will are fundamentally ordered toward this non-worldly free ground of the being of the world out of nothing. The *Confessions* are a dialogue of the self and God; they have the form of prayer, not of speech with other men about being as it shows itself in the world. The Psalms are the origin of the literary genre of the *Confessions,* whose form[15] is most adequate to *caritas: mutua redamatio cum quadam mutua communicatione et familiari conversatione.*[16] The self is constituted in listening and speaking to God; it is no longer primarily constituted as a being in the world. The best thing in the world is the self as transphenomenal abyss,[17] hidden to others and to itself and constituted through its manifestness to the eyes of the *Deus Creator.*[18] The controlling position is no longer the *logos* of *phainomena,* but the *homo abyssus* as image of the *Deus absconditus.* The Greek shining-forth and manifestness to others has become hidden in the transcendent: *Deus conscientiae testis maxima est gloria.*[19] No longer "that which appears to all, that we call being,"[20] but "the hermitage of the hidden heart."

"If by abyss we understand a great depth, is not man's heart an abyss? For what is more profound than that abyss? Men may speak,

---

[15] Dante, ep. XIII, 9 (*Opere,* Firenze: Società Dantesca Italiana, 1921): forma tractatus et forma tractandi.

[16] Cf. Aquinas, *Summa Theologiae,* I-II, 65, 5.

[17] Johannes Philoponos criticized the Aristotelian principles "man is not the best thing in the world" (1141b1; 1141a21-22) and "the visible god" (1026a18; 286a11; 196a33); cf. S. Sambursky, *The Physical World of Late Antiquity* (London: Routledge and Kegan Paul, 1962), chap. VI.

[18] *Conf.* 13, 38, 53: nos itaque ista quae fecisti vidimus, quia sunt; tua autem quia vides ea, sunt; *De trin.* 15, 22: non quia sunt, ideo novit, sed ideo sunt, quia novit; *De civ. Dei* 11, 10: iste mundus nobis notus esse non potest, nisi esset; Deo autem nisi notus esset, esse non potest.

[19] *De civ. Dei* 14, 28; see also 5, 12-20; note the interpretation of Matthew 5, 16 in 5, 14.

[20] Aristotle, 1172b36.

may be seen . . . may be heard speaking: but whose thought is penetrated, whose heart is seen into? What he is inwardly engaged on, what he is inwardly capable of, what he is inwardly doing, or what purposing, what he is inwardly wishing to happen or not to happen, who shall comprehend? Do not you believe that there is in man a deep so profound as to be hidden even to him in whom it is? . . . For now, since thou seest not my heart, and I do not see thine, it is night. . . . Every man is a stranger in this life, in which we are girt round with flesh, through which the heart cannot be seen. In the sojourning of this carnal life each one carries his own heart, and every heart is closed to every other heart. . . . The good heart lies hid, the evil heart lies hid, there is an abyss in the good heart and in the bad. But these things are bare to God's sight, from whom nothing is hid. . . . Within in the consciousness. A great solitude which is not only not passed through by any one, but also not seen. There let us dwell in hope, since we do not yet in reality. It is an interior hermitage. There where no man can see is this hermitage, where we rest in hope."[21]

This interiorization of the self toward the transcendent ground strikes us in an incident in the *Confessions*;[22] Augustine goes to Milan and sees Ambrose: "when he was reading, he drew his eyes along over the leaves, and his heart searched the sense, but his voice and tongue were silent." For Plato and Aristotle the human mind is constituted in speaking with others about the world, although for them this speaking would be impossible without an openness to the unspeakable. But in a theological experience of mind, the heart can search the sense while the voice is silent, because it is ultimately God speaking who is the sense of things. An ontology centered around creation implies an epistemology centered around illumination, because the truth of worldly being is its relation to the divine

---

[21] *In Ps.* 41, 13; 100, 12; 55, 9; 134, 16; *Sermo* 48, 14, 23; cf. *De magistro* 11, 38: non loquentem qui personat foris, sed intus ipsi menti praesidentem consulimus veritatem; *Conf.* 7, 10; 10, 25.

[22] *Conf.* 6, 3; the Platonic parallel to the *intravi in intima mea et ad ipsius animi mei sedem* is found in *Symposium* 174d4-5, but it is balanced by an ἀγορεύειν and πολιτεύεσθαι, whose Augustinian parallel is citizenship in the City of God. On Greek "interiority," see A.-J. Festugière, *Personal Religion Among the Greeks* (Berkeley and Los Angeles: University of California Press, 1954), chap. IV. The Good (*Republic* 509b6-10) as *sol res illustrans, mentem illuminans* is not the *Pater Omnipotens Factor* in spite of Augustine, *De civ. Dei* 8, 7. Cf. *Theaetetus* 173e1-5 and *Phaedrus* 249c8-d1 with *Gorgias* 521d6-8. Plotinus 1, 2, 7 *ad fin.* is not balanced by a *bios politikos*, which is never lacking in Plato and Aristotle.

intellect. The human intellect is constituted by participation in the mind of the creator. "All knowledge of a creature is more certain and more pure and more manifest in the most lucid eternal reasons of creatures in the divine mind (which reasons are the most lucid exemplars of creatures) than in the creature itself."[23] St. Thomas rejects the illuminationism of the avicennizing augustinians, but he does it by drawing out the deepest implications of the fact that the world is created. For him worldly being and truth are convertible: everything is because of a relation to God's intellect[24] (and will), whereas for Aristotle to be true or related to an intellect is not constitutive of worldly being. Aristotle's God does not know the world.[25]

In St. Augustine's *De trinitate*[26] we find the *mens ab aliis secreta quaerens quid sit mens: mens secreta ab aliis* or non-worldly mind.[27] What the self is, is hidden in its constituting relation to the hidden God. There is a cleavage between the phenomenal and the noumenal, between the self in so far as it can appear and be seen, and the *homo abyssus,* who is a noumenon of God and who is what God knows him to be.

Non-worldly human mind or *mens secreta* will remain as a residue after the rejection of the theology which made it possible, and since the self had been identified in grace with world-constituting intellect and will, if it experiences itself as naturally in this Archimedean point outside the world (the image is from Descartes' *Second Meditation*),[28] it will face the temptation of constituting its world out of itself, remembering its gracious identification with transcendent world-constituting intellect and will. Man makes himself and his world, or as Heidegger (not speaking *in propria persona*)

---

[23] Robert Grosseteste in *Selections from Medieval Philosophers,* ed. R. McKeon, (New York: Scribners' Sons, 1929), I, 280; cf. Josef Pieper, *Wahrheit der Dinge* (Muenchen: Koesel Verlag, 1947).

[24] *De veritate* 1, 2.

[25] The thesis that God knows the world follows from the thesis that he is the *dator essendi* and not only moving cause as final cause. See Aquinas, *Comm. in meta.* #2614; #2616; #1164; #1215; #233 (ed. Cathala) and Franz Brentano, *Die Psychologie des Aristoteles* (Mainz: 1867), Beilage, 234-250; *Aristoteles Lehre vom Ursprung des menschlichen Geistes* (Leipzig: 1911), 26-33, 121-141 (against Zeller's critique); see Simplicios, *in phys. lib.* (in 267b17), *Comm. in Aris. gr.* X, 1363.

[26] IX and X *passim;* esp. X, 4, 6; X, 8, 11.

[27] Cf. Aristotle, 1178a22; the reconciliation of "separateness" and "humanness" is one of the fundamental Aristotelian *aporiai.*

[28] Cf. *Husserliana* VIII, 69, 10-17.

says: "all being has become material for work."[29] Descartes' theory of the creation of the eternal truths is the theory of the presuppositions of a technological view of the world.[30] World is what has been willed; world can become whatever can be willed; "this" world is not the only world which can be willed. Man's relation to himself and his world is that of a master, legislator, technocrat, creator. And this relation is not theoretical or contemplative. "The increase in the power of man over the things of this world springs . . . from the distance which man puts between himself and the world, that is, from world-alienation."[31]

And, we can add, the world-alienation of mind has a theological *apriori*. Let us hear John Scotus Erigena, thinking of the transformation his position undergoes in modern philosophy: "Where beings are known, there they are; indeed they are nothing more than their being known. . . . What is there astonishing, if the idea

---

[29] *Brief ueber den Humanismus* (2d. ed., Berne: Francke Verlag, 1954), 87.

[30] Ferdinand Alquié, *La découverte métaphysique de l'homme chez Descartes* (Paris: PUF, 1950), chap. V. The condition of the possibility of the historico-technological transformations generating the new man and the ultimate earth: (creatoris) voluntas rerum necessitas (Augustinus, PL 34, 350); voluntas conditoris conditae rei cujusque natura (PL 41, 721); Deus praeter infinita individua harum specierum finitarum potest facere infinitas alias species, et in singulis speciebus infinita individua (Aquinas, *De veritate* 20, 4, ad 1); qualibet re a se facta potest Deus facere aliam meliorem (*Summa Theologiae* I, 25, 6). *Corruptio optimi* (i.e. of the principle of Ephesians 5, 1: imitatores Dei estote) *pessima:* ". . . (the human) destiny is to be the agent of the evolutionary process on this planet, the instrument for realising new possibilities for its future. The picture of the universe provided by modern science is of a single process of self-transformation, during which new possibilities can be realised. There has been a creation of new actualities during cosmic time: it has been progressive, and it has been self-creation . . . the self-creation of novelty . . . that man is only at the beginning of his period of evolutionary dominance, and that vast and still undreamt-of possibilities of further advance still lie before him. . . ." Julian Huxley, *Religion Without Revelation* (New York: The New American Library, 1958; Mentor Book), 190-191, 193. See Leibniz' *De rerum originatione radicali* (ed. Erdmann, 147, 150): primum agnoscere debemus eo ipso, quod aliquid potius existit quam nihil, aliquam in rebus possibilibus, seu in ipsa possibilitate vel essentia, esse exigentiam existentiae, vel (ut sic dicam) praetensionem ad existendum et, ut verbo complectar, essentiam per se tendere ad existentiam . . . semper in abysso rerum superesse partes sopitas adhuc excitandas et ad majus meliusque et ut verbo dicam, ad meliorem cultum provehendas. Nec proinde unquam ad terminum progressus perveniri. See also Bruno, *De l'infinito universo e mondi* (*Op. italiane*, ed. Lagarde), 314.

[31] Hannah Arendt, *The Human Condition* (Chicago: The University of Chicago Press, 1958), 252, n. 2. See J. Klein, "Die griechische Logistik und die Entstehung der modernen Algebra," *Quellen und Studien zur Geschichte der Mathematik*, B-3 (Berlin: 1934), esp. "Ueber die Differenz antiker und moderner Begrifflichkeit," pp. 122-129.

of things which the human mind possesses . . . be understood as the substance of the very things of which it is the idea, that is, in the likeness of the divine mind in which the idea of the whole created universe is the substance of that whole."[32] We remember Augustine's "the world is, because God knows it," when we hear Vico's "we only know what we make" or Nietzsche's "world must first be created" or Novalis' "we know the world only is so far as we are God and create it" or Marx' "the earth itself is of no value; it does not represent objectified labor." Kant's famous remark in the *Preface to the Second Edition of the Critique of Pure Reason* that "reason is a pupil of itself alone and knows only what it has put into its object" is a true statement about the relation of God's mind to the world, but it is said of the human mind only[33] through an illegitimate reduction to a natural or human position of the gracious or non-human identification of man with the *Deus Creator*. That which is other than the *mens secreta* is illusory or obscure or deceptive or hostile, and man is burdened or exhilarated by the creation of his own world. Consider Descartes' reduction of the world to a dream and his malignant demon, who has employed artifice to deceive him. Or the *Second Meditation*, in which, looking out a window onto a crowded street, he asks: "Yet what do I see but hats and cloaks that might cover artificial machines, whose motions might be determined by springs?"

Or the end of the second book of Hume's *Treatise on Human Nature:* "Methinks I am like a man, who having struck on many shoals, and having narrowly escap'd shipwreck in passing a small frith, has yet the temerity to put out to sea in the same leaky weather-beaten vessel. . . . My memory of past errors and perplexities, makes me diffident for the future. The wretched condition, weakness, and disorder of the faculties, reduces me almost to despair,

---

[32] In McKeon, *op. cit.*, I, 120, 118. Cf. Eckhardt, *Quaestio parisiensis: utrum in Deo sit idem esse et intelligere;* Nicolaus Cusanus, *De beryllo,* c. 6; Vico, *Scienza Nuova,* #331, #349.

[33] The pre-critical Kant: *De mundi sensibilis atque intelligibilis forma et principiis,* 2, 10: intuitus nempe mentis nostrae semper est passivus . . . divinus autem intuitus, qui objectorum est principium non principiatum, cum sit independens, est archetypus et propterea perfecte intellectualis. In the *Critique of Pure Reason* the thing-in-itself and the obscure material not yet formed by the categories are a check against an assimilation of the human mind to the *intellectus archetypus;* the *Opus Postumum* moves further in the direction of an interpretation of the human mind as autonomously constituting principle. The Plotinian parallel (5, 9, 5) has not yet been psychologized; see Husserl, "Phenomenology," *Encyclopedia Britannica,* 14th ed., 701a.

and makes me resolve to perish on the barren rock on which I am at present, rather than venture myself upon that boundless ocean, which runs out into immensity. . . . I am . . . affrighted and confounded with that forlorn solitude, in which I am plac'd in my philosophy, and fancy myself some strange uncouth monster, who not being able to mingle and unite in society, has been expell'd all human commerce, and left utterly abandon'd and disconsolate. Fain wou'd I run into the crowd for shelter and warmth; but cannot prevail with myself to mix with such deformity. I call upon others to join me, in order to make a company apart; but no one will hearken to me. Every one keeps at a distance, and dreads that storm, which beats upon me from every side. . . . All the world conspires to oppose and contradict me." World-alienation or loss of being-in-the-world is also loss of being-with-others.

In the world, then, we encounter with certainty only ourselves, because the relevant world has become that which is the product of human speculation and action. "Wherever we search for that which we are not, we encounter only the pattern of our own minds."[34] Philosophy becomes the science of the human mind—just as theology was the science of the divine mind. The remembering and rejection of the theological context effects a Copernican revolution in the relation of the self to the world: the world and the self itself are what has been constructed, imposed, created. Only that is sure.

Let us hear Kant "on the ground of the division of all objects into phenomena and noumena";[35] "We have now not only traversed the region of the pure understanding, and carefully surveyed every part of it, but we have also measured it, and assigned to everything therein its proper place. But this land is an island, and enclosed by nature herself within unchangeable limits. It is the land of truth (an attractive word), surrounded by a wide and stormy ocean, the region of illusion, where many a fog-bank, many an iceberg, seems to the mariner, on his voyage of discovery, a new country, and while constantly deluding him with vain hopes, engages him in dangerous adventures, from which he never can desist, and which he never can bring to a termination. But before venturing upon this sea, in order to explore it in its whole extent, and to arrive at a certainty whether anything is to be discovered there, it will not be without advantage

---

[34] Arendt, op. cit., 287.
[35] *Critique of Pure Reason*, "Transcendental Analytic," chap. III (Meiklejohn trans.).

if we cast our eyes upon the chart of the land that we are about to leave, and to ask ourselves, firstly, whether we cannot rest perfectly contented with what it contains, or whether we must not of necessity be contented with it, if we can find nowhere else a solid foundation to build upon; and, secondly, by what title we possess this land itself, and how we hold it secure against all hostile claims?"

The Kantian critique of the theoretical life denies to the human mind a God-like vision (*intuitus originarius*), but yet at the same time it puts the human mind in a constituting relation to the world. This manoeuvre is characteristic of modern philosophy, which oscillates between the presumption of rationalism and the despair of empiricism, and lives on the patrimony of a murdered father, operating out of theological presuppositions while rejecting the rules of the theological game.

When the theoretical life breaks down under the burdens of its theologization, one turns to Hume's game of backgammon or to the second or third Kantian critique, to Romanticism or Marxian revolution, but these positions are quite different from the Greek *bios politikos* and *bios praktikos*, which were the matrix of the *bios theoretikos*, not a refuge from it or a usurpation of it.

When Hegel speaks of "that voyage into the open, where nothing is below or above us, and we stand in solitude with ourselves alone,"[36] when he speaks of Fichte's "pure Ego above the ruins of this body and the shining stars"[37] (echoing Descartes' "I denied that I possessed a body . . . and was persuaded that there was absolutely nothing in the world, that there was no sky and no earth"), we hear the *mens secreta* of Augustine with a difference. Augustine had said "I entered into my *intima* and I saw above my mind the unchanging light" and "I entered into the seat of my soul, nor were you there, lord of my soul."[38] The self and the world were possessed out of the transcendent creator. In contrast is the structure of Descartes' *Meditations:* God and the world are possessed out of self-possessed mind: mind is isolated from the world and from God, which may be illusions and deceptive; mind using itself regains God; mind gains the world through the objectivity of ideas guaranteed by the divine truth, whose evidence is based on the mind's evidence to itself when separated from everything else.

---

[36] *Logic*, trans. Wallace (London: 1950), 66.
[37] "Fragment of a System," *Early Theological Writings* (New York: Harper and Sons, 1961; Torchbook), 318.
[38] *Conf.* 7, 10; 10, 25.

We have concerned ourselves with what the theologoumenon of creation becomes in modern philosophy. The modern philosophical appropriation and corruption of other theological truths could be shown: the union of divine and human nature in one Person is echoed in Hegel's concern to sublate all difference between finite and infinite; the *exinanitio Dei* in the Incarnation becomes for Hegel a necessity for the fall of the divine nature itself into finitude and negation ("the speculative Good Friday") and for an identification of *logos* and history; the *felix culpa* becomes the dialecticization of evil in German Romanticism; Hegel perverts the theology of the Trinity by introducing process into the divine nature; the self-divinization of man in modern atheism remembers the divinization of man through grace but refuses to receive it under the conditions of grace; Christian eschatology is the condition of the possibility of modern philosophies of history.

Nietzsche's attack on world-alienating other-worldliness—"Among Germans I am immediately understood when I say that philosophy has been corrupted by theologians' blood . . . German philosophy is at bottom an insidious theology"[39]—and the British empiricists' position that the view of the "economic observer"[40] is the human view of the world are attempts to escape a philosophical position determined by theologoumena, but they regain neither the Greek nor the medieval position and remain more reactions than genuine non-modern positions. Kierkegaard rejects Hegel's pseudo-theology in the name of a sound theology,[41] but we can ask, "What is philosophy for Kierkegaard?"

The bifurcation of the phenomenal and the noumenal, of man as a being-in-the-world and as transcendental ego, haunts modern philosophy; and this cleavage is not explainable by philosophical (human *qua* human) principles; the extra-philosophical principle

---

[39] *Antichrist* I, 10.
[40] G. R. G. Mure, *Retreat from Truth* (Oxford: Blackwell's, 1958), chaps. II-IV.
[41] ". . . the fact that the doctrine of the God-Man . . . is taken in vain, the qualitative distinction between God and man is pantheistically abolished—first speculatively with an air of superiority, then vulgarly in the streets and alleys. Never anywhere has any doctrine on earth brought God and man so near together as has Christianity. . . . Neither has any doctrine ever so carefully defended itself against the most shocking of all blasphemies, that after God had taken this step it then should be taken in vain, as though God and man coalesced into one and the same thing . . . ," *Sickness unto Death*, trans. W. Lowrie (Garden City, N.Y.: Doubleday and Co., 1954; Anchor Book), 248.
[42] Husserl, *Ideas*, 169.

at work is the theological condition of mind (theologoumena are known by faith, not because they are evident or manifest), of which the modern world-alienation of mind is a corruption. Since man is a being-in-the-world and not God, and since philosophy is the human way of seeing being, the form of philosophy which is concerned with or dominated by the implications of a non-worldly human view of being will end in the destruction of that human theoretical life which is philosophy. And indeed end-positions of modern thought like those of Nietzsche, Schopenhauer, Dilthey, and Marx can be characterized as rejections of the theoretical life.

What comes after the end? We might recall Aristotle's cyclic ontology and say: a return to the beginning. Both Husserl and Heidegger seek to re-ground and re-originate philosophy after its destruction, to lead philosophical activity back to its root or beginning. For Husserl this beginning as radical and originating must be without presuppositions, and since individual and human consciousness as part of nature or the world, which "is not absolute in a philosophical sense,"[42] have presuppositions, philosophy cannot take them as its foundation. The *epoché* enables philosophy to present itself as a strict science;[43] it is the instrument of the reduction by which First Philosophy is established on a principle (the region of pure consciousness) which is rigorous, without contingency and beyond a particular point of view. "As a man I should no longer be, and again I should have no neighbors." "We that are men existing in the world are appearances unto ourselves."[44] Radical reflection gains a non-worldly Archimedean point, transcendental subjectivity, "into which nothing can penetrate and from which nothing can escape."[45] The beginning philosopher seeks an absolute situation; but the givenness of worldly experience is inadequate; worldly experience is provisional and implies unfilled meanings, illusions, doubts, revisions; the contingency of the world cannot be transformed into necessity; therefore philosophy as contemplation of that which is first and necessary must be consituted through an act of world-annihilation (*Weltvernichtung*). This act is "reversion to that which is already presupposed *implicite* in all presupposing and in all questioning and answering."[46]

For Heidegger the first or philosophical question is "What is the

---

[43] Cf. Aristotle, 982a25-27.
[44] Husserl, *Ideas*, 167; "Phenomenology," *EB*[14].
[45] Husserl, *Ideas*, 153.
[46] *Ibid.*, 19.

meaning of to be?", to be in full differentiation from beings. But the meaning of to be is hidden; what available being then can we question regarding it?—man, the only phenomenality concerned with to be, the only manifest being constituted by the power to raise the question "What does to be mean?" To answer this question we must question ourselves, the questioners, concerning the condition of the possibility of our questioning: man as unthematic or forgotten understanding of the meaning of to be. The beginning or foundation for talking about the meaning of to be—Fundamental Ontology—is man himself understood as *Dasein*, the presence of to be in the world or that available being open to and concerned with to be in full differentiation from beings, open to and concerned with as forgetter and questioner. Man's being is always already in the world with others; man's being is thrown (*geworfen*), that is, he cannot master the presuppositions of his being. The condition of the possibility of ontology or of raising the question "What is being?" and more radically, of the question "What is the meaning of to be?" is *anamnesis*[47] or recollection of that which is both hidden and best known: man himself as *Dasein*, the epiphany or showing forth of to be itself in ordinariness and everydayness, to be passionately (*gestimmt*) in the world with others.

Heidegger seeks a re-petition and re-origination (*Wiederholung; Grundlegung*) of philosophy and this desire to recover and uncover the foundations of philosophy is the positive meaning of "the destruction of the history of ontology," which he calls a necessary condition for a return to origins. This return is found in the "fruitful *bathos*"[48] which recalls man to himself as finitude and temporality—ecstatic toward to be itself in full differentiation. Thrownness and Fundamental Ontology and being-in-the-world-with-others are both equivalents to and rejections of *epoché* and First Philosophy and pure consciousness. Man is the beginning of philosophy, although the ultimate philosophical theme is not "What is man?" but "What is the meaning of to be?" Heidegger's humanism is a *lucus a non lucendo*.[49] But in raising the first question or talking about the meaning of to be, man cannot step out of his own ontological locus, the place in which to be has meaning for him: himself in the world with others. In a marginal note on Husserl's

---

[47] Heidegger, *Kant*, 241-242; 250.
[48] Husserl, *Ideas*, 29; cf. W. Jaeger, *Aristoteles* (2d. ed.; Berlin: Wiedmannsche Buchhandlung, 1955), 359, last line: ". . . das fruchtbare Bathos. . .".
[49] Heidegger, *Brief ueber den Humanismus*, 94.

draft for the article on phenomenology in the Encyclopedia Britannica, Heidegger asks a question which touches the characteristically modern ambiguity at the center of Husserl's position: "What is the mode of being (*Seinsart*) of the absolute ego: in what sense is it the same as the factual I, in what sense is it not the same?"[50] Husserl's return to the beginning is a radicalization of the Cartesian beginning, that is, it is a return to the beginning of the end. For Heidegger philosophy or asking radical questions is inseparable from the worldliness, finitude and temporality of the questioner and from the veiledness of the questioned. "Ontology is an index of finitude; God has no ontology."[51]

"Are *terminus a quo* and *terminus ad quem* merely heuristic or do they belong to the essence of philosophy?"[52] That the ground or that which is first is questionable or that the *terminus a quo* (man as the phenomenal locus of to be, the caretaker of to be) and the *terminus ad quem* (the to be itself) are different is philosophy for Heidegger. For Husserl, on the other hand, philosophy is constituted there where the *terminus a quo* is as absolute and presuppositionless as that *terminus ad quem* characteristic of all philosophy.

The theme of philosophy for Husserl is transcendental subjectivity, the knower as such, differentiated from the factual, human knower. Its method is phenomenological, that is, every meaning is ordered toward the adequate self-givenness of the meant; every open intention is to be filled in intuition or primordial dator consciousness of the intended itself manifesting itself by means of itself (the repetition of "itself" expresses the unmediated character of the presence of the object).

Combining theme and method, we can say that the regulative idea of transcendental phenomenology is the grasp of the essence of the knower simply speaking, of world-constituting consciousness (not of consciousness as part of the system of nature) in the mode of original and adequate self-givenness, in absolute evidence. Because transcendental subjectivity contains *apriori* and immanently all possible acts of consciousness, and because every act of consciousness is necessarily ordered toward the adequate self-presentation of an object, the adequate *logos* of transcendental subjectivity is also the

---

[50] Tijdschrift voor Philosophie, XII (1950), 268.

[51] Davos Arbeitsgemeinschaft Cassirer-Heidegger, 1929 (Protocol) [Beilage IV, Guido Schneeberger, Ergaenzungen zu einer Heidegger-Bibliographie (Bern: *pro manuscripto*, 1960), 19].

[52] *Ibid.*, 23.

adequate *logos* of the plenitude of the knowable: being. Because all being is for consciousness (although not for factual, human consciousness), an adequate grasp and expression of the system of possibilities of consciousness[53] is also an adequate grasp and expression of being itself. The *eidos* of pure subjectivity, which is the condition of the possibility of all factual subjectivities and of all possible experiences, will include a typology of objectivities and of the correlative modes or styles of experiencing them. The absolute *ego cogitans* brings with it the *plenum cogitabilium* and of their correlative modes of givenness. Transcendental egology then is also universal ontology, *mathesis universalis*, the adequate science of being. This adequate science of being, reached as the adequate science of the fount of all possible acts of consciousness is "the infinite open country of the true philosophy, the 'promised land' . . . ."[54] Transcendental phenomenology is a map or geography of mind as the knower of the plenitude of being.

The theme of philosophy for Heidegger is man in the world with others open to yet forgetting the meaning of to be itself. Heidegger defines the method of philosophy through an analysis of the meaning of *phainomenon* and *logos*: the letting be seen of that which shows itself, letting it be seen precisely in the way in which the self-manifesting uses itself to show itself. Philosophy then for Heidegger is universal phenomenological ontology, taking as point of departure, which can never be left behind, the analysis of man as *Dasein*. The question of Aristotelian First Philosophy, namely, "What is being as being?" must be transcended toward the question "What is to be itself?" and an answer to this question presupposes an answer to the question "Whence can the meaning of to be itself be grasped?" The analysis of *Dasein* in *To Be and Time* answers the last question, but the work remains a torso. What follows it tends toward obscure aphorism and violation of language. And this must necessarily be so: the meaning of to be as it is in itself is veiled; we can only speak of it as it manifests itself through ourselves, the forgetters and questioners; to try to speak of it and make it manifest as it is in itself is to tend toward silence and darkness. "Holy words are lacking to us," says Heidegger, in the words of Hoelderlin.[55] Silence is the mode of manifesting the unspeakable. The second part of the work, whose first part appeared as *To Be and Time*, was to

[53] Cf. Aristotle, 432a2.
[54] Husserl, *Ideas*, 29.
[55] "Remembrance of the Poet," trans. Werner Brock, *Existence and Being* (Chicago: Regnery, 1949; Gateway Edition), 243-269; "Heimkunft", VI, 11: "Schweigen muessen wir oft; es fehlen heilige Namen."

reverse the perspective of the first part and take up the point of view of the to be itself; the fact that it never appeared witnesses that there is no adequate *phainomenon* and *logos*, no adequate manifestation of and speaking about, no adequate phenomenology of that which is first in itself: the to be itself.

In conclusion we might ask what light the principles of Aquinas' thought can cast on these two attempts to answer the question "What is philosophy?" We might say that for St. Thomas there is no knowledge without, on the one hand, the *reditio completa intellectus in se ipsum,* the radical reflection of the mind on its own nature and possibilities, which are infinite, and without, on the other hand, the *conversio ad phantasmata,* the incarnation of mind, the fact that the metaphysical is reached only in the *separatio* or negative judgment: the world does not exhaust the *ratio essendi,*[56] the plenitude of being is non-worldly but the human mind is worldly, knowing nevertheless its own worldliness. We might say further that for St. Thomas, on the one hand, *esse est primum et principium omnium, praehabens in se omnia,* the to be itself is the first, and that, on the other hand, philosophy must proceed *per ea quae sunt priora quoad nos et apud nos inveniuntur;* that by way of which we seek to understand the first is not the first itself, the fully differentiated or pure to be, but something other, that which is first for us, the twice-dirempted to be, creaturely and worldly.

Aquinas says that there are two ways toward understanding the first and divine things: *secundum quod per effectus manifestantur* and *secundum quod ipsae se ipsas manifestant.* The first is the way of philosophy, the second that of theology. The plenitude of being is not adequately manifest in the self-manifestation of worldly being, though worldly being is only as a similitude of the plenitude of being, and thus can be adequately known only when its exemplar and the constituting relation to that exemplar are adequately known. But only God Himself adequately knows Himself as He is in Himself and as He is imitated by creatures. Since human subjectivity is constituted as reflexive or self-possessed openness to the plenitude of being, man is never merely a being among other beings, yet as incarnated subjectivity he is only as in the world. He can grasp his infinite depth and possibility only in so far as he turns to the world and lives out finite possibilities. Since the plenitude of being is infinite and since man is as openness to it, an adequate *logos* of human subjectivity can be found only when the *logos* which flows

---

[56] *Husserliana* VIII, 166, 30-31: "Das Seinsall des Weltkindes ist nicht das Seinsall schlechthin."

from God's adequate self-possession and which is His adequate self-manifestation is found. But the Word which is adequate to God can be spoken only by God Himself. Philosophy seeks to speak of the plenitude of being by speaking of man in the world; but the world is neither absolute plenitude nor is man an absolute subject. Philosophy then cannot speak a divine Word; it must look to God Himself adequately speaking Himself to find that Word, that is, philosophy must look to theology, not for those words which philosophy itself can speak, but for that Word which by its very nature it can never speak.

What then can our position be in the crisis of self-understanding in which philosophy finds itself today? On the one hand we cannot ignore the theological context of our philosophical activity. Theology is a fact witnessed even by those who most ardently reject it or its relevance, and the fact of theology precludes a rejuvenation without difference of a Greek philosophical position, a position unaware of a divine Word. But on the other hand we wish to be released from the burden of handling theologoumena philosophically; we wish to experience the human mind in all its humanness. "What the thing is to God, we do not know; the absolute suchness of an absolute world would be relative to the perfect knowledge of a divine observer outside the world. It is an idle question beyond any faculty of man. I venture no answer. I have to do with man."[57]

Perhaps theology itself has something to say which would be of help in saving both these positions: the relevance of theology and the humanness of philosophy. Theology tells us that a participation in God's knowledge of Himself and his creatures is not a *debitum* of human nature and that neither loss of praeternatural gifts nor elevation by supernatural gifts destroy that nature. Philosophy as the human view of being has no right to a theology, but a sound theology requires of us a philosophical experience or an experience of being by the human mind in all its humanness. Theology itself requires us to listen to philosophy speaking in Socrates when he says: "If you ask me what kind of wisdom I possess, I reply, wisdom such as may perhaps be attained by man, for to that extent I am inclined to believe that I am wise; whereas the persons of whom I was speaking have a superhuman wisdom, which I may fail to describe because I have it not myself; and he who says that I have, speaks falsely, and is taking away my character."[58]

[57] Kurt Riezler, *Man: Mutable and Immutable* (Chicago: Regnery, 1950), 56; 69, 71.
[58] *Apology*, 20.

2

THE CONCEPT OF PERSONALITY IN GREEK AND CHRISTIAN THOUGHT*

by

C. J. DE VOGEL

I should like to raise the following precise question:
Is it true that the concept of personality was not known to the Greeks, but was framed within the sphere of Christian faith and for the first time formally defined by Boëthius, a Christian author of the first half of the 6th century, on the border-line of Antiquity and the Middle Ages?
Let me explain.

1. It has been observed[1] that the Ancients—Greeks, and Romans as well—had no word for what we call either *person* or *personality*, by which we mean: man as a moral character, free and responsible, individual and unique. The term *persona* or πρόσωπον, it is said, was not used by philosophers, nor reflected on. It was used in Roman law[2] and handled by jurists, to indicate man as a subject of rights and obligations, and in this function corresponds with the Greek word πρόσωπον, which is found in Greek papyri. In ordinary language both *persona* and πρόσωπον meant primarily *mask*, secondarily the rôle played in a drama. In the 4th and 5th centuries the term persona is used in the theological controversies on the three "persons" in the Trinity (here the Greeks used the term ὑπόστασις, which was a philosophical concept), but no philosophical definition is found before Boëthius.

---

* The greater part of this article was spoken in a somewhat abridged form in two lectures to The Catholic University of America, Washington, March 1962.
[1] E. Gilson, *L'esprit de la philosophie médiévale*, Paris² 1944, ch. X. The argument was renewed by R. Klibansky, in a plenary session of the first international congress of Medieval Philosophy, Louvain 1958. The text of this lecture is not found, however, in the volume of the Acts, entitled *L'homme et son destin,* Louvain 1960.
[2] Gaius, *Inst.* I 8-9, I 48.

2. According to Christian faith and doctrine, God's providence aims at the individual. Man has not been created as a species, but he was called into being individually. Hence, God bestows his providence on the individual man and leads him to his individual destination. Greek philosophical thought, however, was essentially directed to what is general. For Plato, there cannot be any true knowledge of the concrete things which are ever changing and in which no identity is found. Philosophy has to seek the eternal archetypes, of which sensible things are the images. Aristotle, certainly, made a considerable effort to come to a philosophy of concrete being, and *in a sense* he did come to it. But only in a sense. By assuming that things are what they are by their intelligible essence,[3] and that this essence is grasped by the human intellect,[4] he can strictly account for our knowledge of natural objects. Only—what we know of them is exactly not that which constitutes their individual being. For only as soon as the intelligible "form" is realized in "matter," does individuality come in.[5] And "matter" is the part, or rather the aspect, of man which is not intelligible. To put it exactly, matter is *infraintelligible*, and matter is said to be the principle of individuation.— Now, if such was the tendency of the most classical metaphysical thought of Antiquity, how could the Ancients have any right valuation of personality? How could they possibly have produced a *metaphysics of the person*, as Christianity has?

For in that great era of speculative thought which was the 13th century, we find St. Thomas Aquinas, though he accepted Aristotle's theory of form and matter, defining the soul of concrete man as "a form which possesses substantiality, and communicates this to the human composite." Thus, man's individuality, though it presupposes matter, appears to be qualified much more by the reasonable soul, which is its higher, spiritual aspect. And we find St. Thomas declaring that "person" signifies "that which is most perfect in nature as a whole".[6]

Towards the end of the same century Duns Scotus elaborated a true philosophy of individual being (*entitas individualis* or *singularis*), rejecting the Aristotelian-Thomistic principle of individuation (matter) and substituting it by the object's "thisness" (*haecceitas*), which is its ultimate reality.[7] While Aristotle, followed

[3] *Metaph.* Z 17, 1041a 26-32, b 4-9; cp. also Z 6.
[4] *Anal. po.* II 19, 100a 10ff.
[5] *Metaph.* Z 10, 1035b 30-31.
[6] *Summa theol.* I, 29, 3, Resp.
[7] *Opus Oxoniense* II 3, 6, nr. 15; cp. *De anima*, c. 22.

by St. Thomas, taught that scientific knowledge concerns universals, Scotus, though granting the exactness of this doctrine, observed that in the very act of intellectual knowledge a certain direct and intuitive recognition of the singular thing as existing is implied. Moreover, while Scotus recognized the fact that the human intellect does not understand the singular objects fully, he held that this fact is not due to unintelligibility of the singular thing in itself,[8] but to a certain imperfection of our intellect in its present state.[9] For individual things are the true goal of creation. They are certainly known by the divine and angelic intellects. They must be even known by us, in a sense at least, since we can love individual beings, and love presupposes knowledge.[10]

3. All that is said by Christian thinkers, from St. Ephrem of Nisibis (4th cent.) up to St. Thomas and Duns Scotus, is said in function of the analogy existing between God and man: human personality has its basis in the personality of God, after whose image and likeness man was created. We are persons because we were made by a Person, and participate in His Personality,—i.e. in His Rationality by our faculty of thinking, in His Providence by our power of using other things to some purpose, in His Will by our faculty of choice and self-determination. Christians could develop a philosophy of personality because they believed in a supremely personal God. For the Ancients, who did not know God as a Person, the very basis of a metaphysics of the personality was lacking.

This is essentially what was brought to the fore in defense of the above-cited thesis by such a great scholar of Medieval philosophy as was (and is) E. Gilson. The argument was renewed by R. Klibansky in the first international Congress of Medieval Philosophy, Louvain 1958. It might seem not quite easy to contradict these arguments and to advocate the opposite thesis. Yet, this is what I am going to do.

I might start by demonstrating that, first of all, a *word* for either "person" or "personality" is by no means lacking, neither in Greek nor in Latin. Next, I could prove that the first metaphysics of man as a moral person is found in Greek philosophy, and of man in his individuality as well. And finally I could argue that it is not well-founded to isolate the Christian concept of God completely from the Greek pre-Christian thought; that there are more links between

---

[8] *Op. Ox.* 113, 6, nr. 16.
[9] *Ibid.* II 3, 9, nr. 9.
[10] *De anima* 22.

Greek philosophy and Christian faith than were recognized by those who advocated the above-mentioned thesis. But let me rather begin by defining for what we are going to search in the Ancient world, and next try to outline what is found there that could contribute something to a better understanding of the problems of "person" and "personality" in Greek and Christian thought.

I

First, then, I would suggest to distinguish between "person" and "personality."

A. *Person* is *man as a rational being and moral subject,* free and self-determining in his actions, responsible for his deeds.

B. *Personality* is *man's individual character,* his *uniqueness.*

1. Every man as such is a person. He is so in virtue of his reason, by which he is superior both to things and animals. His quality of being a moral subject (self-determination and responsibility) depends on the faculty of reason. Very young children are not responsible. Mentally abnormal people are responsible only in so far as their reason is intact.

Now it is clear that, in this general sense, there is a great deal of reflection on the "person" in Greek philosophy. In fact, this reflection is as old as Pythagoras and Heraclitus. It becomes very explicit with Plato and Aristotle, and even most emphatical in the Stoa with its cult of inner freedom. The theory of free will (self-determination) as a proprium of man was elaborated in the acute criticism of Carneades (in the so-called New Academy), directed against the Stoic doctrine of Fate.

This developed theory of man as characterized by self-determination dates from the second century B.C. We find it again in a very reflected form in the last great Greek philosopher, who was Plotinus. He asserts that man as a spiritual being transcends nature, and this more radically as his soul is innerly detached from the body and connected with that transcendent order from which it draws its being.

From the 17th and 18th centuries onwards (Locke and Chr. Wolff[11]) philosophers begin to define the person by the element of self-reflection and self-consciousness. In this view they are anticipated by the Stoics, and by Plotinus as well: Epictetus, that small man with his fierce spiritualism and his total surrender to the divine Will, thanked God for many gifts—that we have hands to work with, that we can eat and drink, can grow without paying attention to it, and can recover by sleep—but in particular he thanked God for the capacity of being conscious of all these things,—i.e.: for self-consciousness.[12] And in Plotinus we find the self-reflection of the soul as the most appropriate way of ascent to God "the Father."[13] We even find repeatedly the reflection on self-reflection.[14]

All this, then, belongs to "man as a person" in the general sense of the term.

2. Every man is an *individual character*, and this is what is called *personality:* man in his uniqueness.

Sometimes it is said that, though it is true that every man is a person (in the general sense), certainly not every man is a personality (in the individual sense). By way of argument it is added, that "person"—which is a general quality of man—does not admit of degrees, whereas "personality" does. Further, granting that, surely, some Greeks were what "we" could call personalities, it is said that, on the whole, the Greeks did not have that particular interest in man as an individual character, which is so characteristic of the modern man. It could be even doubted whether the Greeks were aware of man's uniqueness at all.

As to the first of these assertions, if we keep to the definition that "personality" is man's individual character, it must be said that, up to a certain degree at least, every man *has* a personality, and the argument that "person" does not admit of degrees while "personal-

---

[11] John Locke, *An Essay Concerning Human Understanding* (first published in 1690), book II, ch. 27, sect. 9, defined "person" as: "a thinking, intelligent being, that has reason and reflection, and can consider itself as itself."

Christian Wolff emphasized the criteria of self-consciousness and remembrance of one's identity: "Meminit se esse idem illud ens quod ante in hoc vel isto fuit statu" (*Psychologia rationalis*, 1734, p. 660).

Later, this view occurs frequently with Neo-kantian philosophers, e.g. Windelband in his *Einleitung* (Engl. transl. 1921, p. 281): "individuality which has become objective to itself." Since men possess this capacity more or less, one can be a "personality" in a higher or a lower degree.

[12] *Diatr.* I 16, 17-18.
[13] *Enn.* V. 1, 2.
[14] *Enn.* I 4, 10; cp. IV 4, 2.

ity" does, proved to be erroneous. For "person" as explained above depends on man's rationality, and this is by no means proper to all men in the same degree. How far an individual man is actually self-determining and responsible, depends both on his intellectual gifts and on his will; moreover, on his education and *milieu*, on the degree of intellectual and—"personal" development he has reached; finally: on his individual character.

That is to say: how far an individual man will be actually a "person"—which of course he *is* always in principle—, is as much a matter of degrees as his intellectual level and his moral character. And all this taken together makes—his "personality"!

In other modern languages it is usual to speak of *"being* a personality," much more than of "having" something of the kind. And by this usage, in fact, one does not simply mean *any* kind of individual character, including such cases in which the individual is more or less underdeveloped as to his intellectual and moral qualities. It happens not unfrequently that the individual character—which, in principle, is always there—is rather negatively determined. These, then, are the cases in which one feels inclined to say that such persons "are no personalities." Evidently that may be said. Only, keeping to our definition it will be more accurate to say that every individual man as such has his personality—which, evidently, may be more or less developed, more or less "interesting," more or less valuable in our eyes.

The second remark raises an interesting problem. Were the Greeks interested in man as an individual character, as much as moderns are interested in it? Were they aware of man's uniqueness? By responding to these questions I shall touch on that prephilosophical life and thought which is always presupposed in philosophic reflection. And in fact, we must say a word of that before dealing more explicitly with philosophical theory. For how could there have been a philosophical reflection on personality if, practically speaking, man's personal character had neither been perceived nor appreciated by the Ancients? "If first things are abolished, second things are, too." That is a good Platonical (and Aristotelian) principle.

Let us then state two points.

First, the Ancient Greeks were often men of a highly developed individual character.

Second, they are frequently described as such in Greek literature, from Homer and the lyrics on to the Hellenistic "characters" and historical biography under the Roman Empire.

Thirdly, the authors of these works reveal themselves as very individual characters.

A few words to explain.

From the beginning of Greek literature a very "personal" world is placed before our eyes. A people is fighting ten years—in order to restore one particular woman to one particular man, who was her husband. We find a young commander-in-chief, angry in his offended pride, obstinately refusing to take part in the battle, because one particular girl had been taken from him, a girl he liked, and who had been allotted to him as his due part in the spoils. Later we find that same man weeping bitterly, when Patroclos, the friend who took his place, has been killed. Only then we see him returning into battle, to seek the man who killed his dearest friend and make him pay for that.[15]

Elsewhere, we find Odysseus' wife waiting twenty years for the return of one particularly beloved person. "For such a person I miss, always remembering him, a man whose fame is wide in Hellas and Argos, its centre."[16]

Wolfgang Schadewaldt mentions as one of the characteristics of the Homeric man: "the faculty of self-determination, which is even respected by the gods."[17] That is what we called *person,* as a general characteristic of man. I quite agree that the Homeric men were persons. Only, something more can be said, namely, that several of these persons—an Achilles, an Odysseus, Nausikaä, Penelope—appear to us as highly individual characters, such as we use to call "personalities." And the poet who created this strongly living world of men and women, acting and reacting passionately, could not possibly

---

[15] *Iliad* 18, 144 (Achilles speaks to his mother Thetis):

νῦν δ' εἶμ' ὄφρα φίλης κεφαλῆς ὀλέτηρα κιχείω
"Εκτορα

The word κεφαλή (head) for person, in particular *dear* person, is found in several verses of the *Iliad*. In b. XXIII, 94 Achilles addresses Patroclus who, after his death, appears to him in his dream: Τίπτε μοι, ἠθείη κεφαλή, δεῦρ' εἰλήλουθας; Cp. *Il.* VIII, 281: Τεῦκρε, φίλη κεφαλή.

[16] *Odyssea* I 343:

Τοίην γὰρ κεφαλὴν ποθέω, μεμνημένη αἰεί,
ἀνδρὸς τοῦ κλέος εὐρὺ καθ' 'Ελλάδα καὶ μέσον "Αργος.

Also the opening line of Sophocles' *Antigone*—'Ω κοινὸν αὐτάδελφον 'Ισμήνης κάρα—should be remembered in this context. To this line Jebb noted: " The periphrasis (as with κεφαλή) usually implies respect, affection, or both (cp. Horace's *tam cari capitis*)."

[17] Wolfgang Schadewaldt, *Hellas u. Hesperien,* Zürich u. Stuttgart 1960, p. 15.

have created that, unless he was strongly interested in the behavior and the motives of individual men.[17a]

Homer was only a beginning. Many others came after him. To mention a few names: does not Archilochus of Paros present himself to us as a person of a vigorously individual character? and Sappho, and her brother Charaxus, who went to Egypt for no other reason than to ransom one particular young woman from the house where she served?[18] And what about the women's portraits drawn by Semonides of Amorgos?[19] Are not they "personal," as much as the "characters" of Theopharastus are? True, these characters of women, compared to various animals, are "types." But the description presupposes an interest in and attentive observation of individual character. It might be noticed here that the type of "persons lacking personality" is not missing in Semonides; they are described as being made of earth by the Olympians: as knowing neither good nor evil (they are not even a normally developed moral subject!), while their unique achievement is: eating, "And even if God makes a bad winter, she does not draw her chair a bit nearer to the fire."[20]

Next, there are the three great tragic poets, representatives of the same genre, but differing greatly the one from the other by their individual characters. And the persons they created in their tragedies, are not they individual characters, too, sometimes of so marked an independence and full-grown self-determination that, according to our use of language, we might call them "strong personalities"—take an Antigone—, sometimes the more "common" kind of character, yet individual, which we find, for instance, in an Ismene, or in Electra's sister Chrysothemis?

Then, keeping to the fifth century, there is Herodotus. If anything is characteristic of his way of writing history, it would be: that, as the true "ground" of historical events, he sees human persons acting, according to their individual characters.

That in Plato's dialogues there is quite an amount of picturing of

---

[17a] This was clearly recognized by Prof. T. B. L. Webster, *Greek Art and Literature, 700-530 B. C.*, London 1959, pp. 24-45. "In the *Iliad* and *Odyssey* the great heroes stand out as individual figures, and Homer was particularly interested in them when they took difficult decisions or exhibited characteristics which were not contained in the traditional picture of the fighting man."
See also A. R. Burn, *The Lyric Age of Greece*, London 1960, pp. 157-185.

[18] Sappho fr. 25 Diehl. Cp. Sappho fr. 23 Diehl; restituted and translated into English by J. M. Edmonds, *Lyra Graeca* I (1922), fr. 35. Charaxus' journey to Egypt is mentioned by Herodotus II 135.

[19] Semonides fr. 7 Diehl.

[20] Fr. 7, 1. 21-26.

personalities, is a fact known to everybody and too obvious to be controversial. Let me just mention, as an instance, the discourse of Aristophanes in the *Symposium,* and the appearance of Alcibiades in that same work.

That Socrates was a "personality" can be hardly contested. Surely, Plato depicts him as an example of what a philosopher should be. But did not he depict him with strictly individual features, and such as could be easily either confirmed and recognized or rejected as untrue by any Athenian of those days? One may think, for instance, of the story of Socrates' behavior in the camp near Potidaea, told by Alcibiades in the *Symposium*,[21] of his protestation against the condemnation of the ten generals of the battle of the Arginusae, and of his behavior when he was ordered by the government of the so-called "Thirty" to go and bring Leon of Salamis up to the City.[22] In general, one may certainly think of the kind of discussions Socrates is holding with the citizens of Athens according to the *Apology* and many of the Platonic dialogues, of the peculiar "ironic" attitude we find him practising, always asking questions, bringing others into "aporia," and never formally teaching.[23] No doubt, these things were features of the "personality" that was Socrates.

But other Greek philosophers—Plato and Aristotle, the different representatives of their Schools, the different heads and members of the Stoa, of Epicurus' "Garden," and of the Sceptic School—were not they "personalities" as well? Some of them are described to us with very striking and highly individual features. Among the Pre-Socratics both Heraclitus and Empedocles appear to us as "personalities" in the emphatic sense.[24] The Cynic Diogenes was to the Greeks almost as much an example of the philosophical style of life as Socrates was; but does not Aristippus appear to us as a highly personal character as well?[25] In the early Peripatetic School it is a man like Lyco, that sportsman and *grand seigneur,* who strikes us most by the extravagance of his behavior.[26] If the fact that one goes against a rather generally accepted rule of life offers a criterion for being a personality, then surely Lyco was. But maybe a many-sided

---

[21] Plato, *Symposion* 215a-220d.
[22] Plato, *Apol.* 32b-e.
[23] In Plato, *Republic* I, the sophist Thrasymachus reacts violently against Socrates, reproaching him exactly for this method (337a, 340d, 341a-c).
[24] Heraclitus, see Diog. L. IX 1; Empedocles: fr. 112 Diels. Also the fragm. 111, 115, 117D.
[25] Diog. L. II 65-83.
[26] Athenaeus, *Deipnosoph.* XII 69, 547-548b (fr. 7 Wehrli); Diog. L. V. 65-68.

scholar like Theophrastus, or a scientist like Strato, or a Demetrius of Phaleron who combined the study of philosophy and history with the practice of a ruler and a politician, were personalities as much, though in a different sense. Certainly Pyrrho of Elis, the founder of the Sceptic School, was an outstanding personality.[27] But what about Arcesilaus? What about Cleanthes or Epictetus? What about a late Cynic like Demonax, whose character and behavior were described by Lucian? And lastly, does not Plotinus appear before our eyes under very personal features?[28]

Evidently, this is not all we could mention in the ancient world. There are the Letters of Cicero, of Pliny, and of Julian; there was an historian like Tacitus, who excelled in psychological analysis; there were the *Lives* of Plutarch, and the *Meditations* of the Emperor Marcus. We are really not in lack of evidence when holding that the ancient Greek, the Hellenistic and the Roman world abounded in very personal characters, and that the very fact that so many of them were described in various forms of literature proves the authors' and their readers' interest in that individual physiognomy which we call personality.

One thing only we can grant to our opponent, who thinks the Ancients were rather indifferent towards man's individuality: he is perfectly right when observing that they were not interested in it *in the same way* as moderns often are.—Or should I rather say: *were?* Antiquity produced numerous and striking descriptions of individual characters; but it never produced such a *genre* as modern psychological novel. The stream of self-analysis by which we were overflowed in a recent period of modern literature, was alien to the Ancients. But—should *that* kind of interest in man's individuality be normative? Is not our own generation witness of a retroflux? Do not we find ourselves that quite a part of modern self-analysis had something morbid in it,—and could not we conclude that perhaps the Ancients in their kind of interest in personal life and character were more sound than moderns often are?

---

[27] Diog. L. IX 61-68.
[28] Porphyrius, *Vita Plotini,* in *Plotini opera* ed. Henry-Schwyzer, t. I, Paris 1951.

II

Let us now turn to philosophy and see how far the Ancients gave a *theory* both of "person" and of "personality" in the sense defined above.

First, the distinction I made and the definitions I proposed are found exactly in this sense in Cicero's *De officiis* I 107:

"We must realize that we are invested by Nature by two characters (duabus *personis*), as it were: one of these is universal (*communis*), arising from the fact that we are all alike endowed with reason and with that superiority which lifts us above the brute. From this all morality is derived (*omne honestum decorumque*), and upon it depends the rational method of ascertaining our duty (*ratio inveniendi officii*). The other character is the one that is assigned to individuals in particular. For just as there are great differences in the matter of spiritual endowment—some, we see, excel in speed for the race, others in strength for wrestling; and, as to outward appearance, some have stateliness, others comeliness—so diversities of character are still greater." Follow a number of Roman instances, next, a few Greek ones.

In the same treatise (a few pages further on[29]) Cicero also speaks of *propria natura*, man's own, particular "nature," as opposed to the universal laws of human nature—*universa natura*—and says: "Everybody must resolutely hold fast to his own peculiar gifts, in so far as they are peculiar only and not vicious. We must follow the bent of our own particular nature.—For nothing is proper that 'goes against the grain,' as the saying is—that is, if it is in direct opposition to one's natural genius."

We know what was Cicero's source when he wrote the first books *De officiis*: it was Panaetius' work *On duties*. And it is almost sure that Panaetius used the Greek word *prosopon* where Cicero speaks of *persona*, while he used the word *physis* where Cicero speaks of *natura*. Both a word for, and a concept of, both "person" and "personality" are found, then, in Greek philosophy, shortly after the middle of the second century B.C., namely, in Panaetius of Rhodes, who was in those days the head of the Stoa, and lived for a number of years in Rome, where he belonged to the circle of Scipio Africanus and Laelius. Panaetius not only formally defined the concepts of person and personality; but, by considering them under the

[29] *De officiis* 110.

aspect of the universal and particular *nature* of man, he also integrated them into a universal system of metaphysics.

This system was old. It brings us back to the end of the sixth, or the beginning of the fifth century B.C., to the Ionian philosopher Heraclitus of Ephesus. He speaks of a *Logos*, which is common to all things and is the ruling principle of their coherence.[30] One might say: the Logos is the cosmic Law, which establishes a certain equilibrium or tension of the fundamental opposites that exist in the universe and are in eternal strife.[31] Therefore, man must listen to the Logos and follow it, if he will have any true understanding. But, since the Logos is a universal principle, this does not only regard the order of physical things; it comprehends the moral and social order, too. Hence, Heraclitus could say: "The citizens should fight for the Law as if for their city-wall" (fr. 44). "For all human laws are nourished by one, which is divine. For it governs as far as it wills, and is sufficient for all, and overcomes all" (fr. 114). Since, then, individual men have to submit their private views to this universal Law in order to attain to wisdom and to Truth, they also must act *"according to nature"*—that is: according to the divine Law, which is common to all things—listening to it (fr.112).

I do not wish to say that *self-reflection of man*—which, according to so many later philosophers, is the criterion of personality—originated with Heraclitus. I rather think it was already there with Pythagoras and his community at Croton, who tended to conform their individual and social life to the ruling law and principles of the cosmos. Nor was it lacking in Anaximenes, who recognized the analogy of man as a microcosmos with the macrocosmos which is the universe. But at least in Heraclitus we find a clear-cut instance of self-reflection. "I began to search for myself" (fr.101). "You can not find the boundaries of the soul, though travelling in any direction. So deep is its Logos" (fr.45). "The soul has a Logos within it, which increases itself" (fr.115).

In the last-cited fragment *logos* appears to be a principle of spiritual growth. To the question of: how does the individual man attain to wisdom? three replies are given by the ancient Ionian philosopher:

(1) Wisdom is reached by an interior development of some innate principle (fr.115).

---

[30] Heraclitus, frs. 1, 2, 50 Diels VS; see also fr. 30 and 31.
[31] Frs. 8, 51, 53, 10, 60; cp. Diog. L. IX 7-9; Heracl. fr. 67, 88, 62, 76.

(2) Wisdom is attained by deliberate choice: if man submits to universal law (fr.2).

A third reply is given in fr.118, where we read that "the dry soul is wisest and best." This explanation should be understood as a physical-cosmological statement. It should be remembered that for Heraclitus *fire* was the basic element, whence all things come and into which they once will all return.[32] Opposite elements pass the one into the other. Now fire is opposite to water, and "It is death to souls to become wet" (fr.77).[33] Why?—Because soul is the purest manifestation of the cosmic fire. According to its nature, it should be dry. Then, it is wise.

However primitive this might seem, Heraclitus' theory is the basis of the Stoic philosophy of nature, including man's nature taken universally, which is man as a rational being, and man's individual character, which is his personality. The Logos, which is the Law of the universe and immanent in it,[34] is a "creative fire," pervading the material world, yet a Divine Force, ruling it,[35] sometimes called "Noûs" or intellect, more frequently Pneuma,[36] identified with God, Providence and Fate (Heimarmene);[37] called Zeus and addressed in prayer as "Father," to whose will man should submit spontaneously and with a total surrender.[38] It is in this act of voluntary surrender to the Divine Will that human liberty consists.[39]

The three replies of Heraclitus to the question of: "how man attains to wisdom" are present in this theory. (1) There is an innate principle of rationality in man, called a "germ of logos."[40] This principle should develop just by natural growth. (2) A personal act of deliberate choice is required, to accept voluntarily the in-

---

[32] Diog. L. IX 7; Heracl. fr. 90.

[33] Heraclitus observed drunken people, as appears from his fr. 117: "When a man has got drunk, he is led stumbling by an immature boy, not knowing where he is going; having his soul wet."

[34] Diog. L. VII 134.

[35] Aetius, *Placita* I 7, 33; cf. Diog. L. VII 156. De Vogel, *Greek Phil.* III 902 a-c.

[36] Diog. L. VII 135 (νοῦς); Aëtius, *Plac.* I 7, 33 (πνεῦμα).

[37] "God": in the above cited passages; for Heimarmenè and Pronoia see *Gr. Phil.*, nrs. 918 a-d, and 927 a-b, 928-930.

[38] Thus Cleanthes in his Hymn to Zeus. *Gr. Phil.* 943.

[39] *Gr. Phil.* 944.

[40] "Seminal reasons" (σπερματικοὶ λόγοι) are mentioned e. g., in the above-cited passage of Aëtius (*Plac.* I 7, 33) where he speaks of the origin of the cosmos, cp. Diog. L. VII 136; Origenes, *Contra Celsum* IV 48. On soul as originating from the "seminal reason" or "seminal reasons," since she is *a part* of it and will return to it after death, see: Marcus Aur. IV 14; VI 24.

exorable Law of the universe, which is the divine Will. (3) As the Logos-God is a fiery breath (pneuma) which pervades the universe, so the soul itself is "fiery breath,"[41] since she originates from the seminal Logos and is a part of it.

It will be evident that in this philosophy man's rationality is solidly anchored in a metaphysical ground. Moreover, it will be clear that the Stoic theory of man's rationality comprehends both a universal and an individual aspect. For the rest, Panaetius, who represents the so-called Middle-Stoa, was said to be almost as much a disciple of Plato and Aristotle as of Zeno and Chrysippus; and we have good grounds for believing that, in particular in his interest in man's individual character, he owes quite a good deal both to Plato and to Aristotle. Let us then turn to these two great masters and see how they laid the basis for any further theory of man as a moral subject, of freedom and responsibility in general, and of a phenomenology of moral character in particular.

---

1. In the myth of Er (*Rep.* X 617de) Plato expressed the principle of free will and self-determination. Er, a native of Pamphylia, was a valiant man, killed in battle. Ten days later, his body was found undecayed, brought home and laid on a funeral pyre, to be burnt the third day. But after two days he came to life again and told what he had seen in the other world. He describes how he saw the souls of all those who journeyed with him being judged, and partly sent to a place of suffering and punishment for every deed of iniquity they had been found guilty of, partly admitted into a heavenly place to enjoy sights of inconceivable beauty. He met with many others, who came back from one of these places and told him of their experiences. After a period of thousand years, these souls were to be incarnated anew. A large number of lots of earthly lives would be put before them, and they had to make their choice. An announcer mounted on a platform and said:

"A proclamation of Lachesis, maiden daughter of Necessity. Souls of a day, here shall begin a new round of earthly life, to end in death. No guardian spirit (daimon) will cast lots for you, but you shall choose your own destiny. Let him to whom the first lot falls choose first a life to which he will be bound of necessity. But Virtue owns no master: as a man honours or dishonours her, so

---

[41] πνεῦμα ἔνθερμον, ap. Diog. L. VII 157; cp. Tertull., *De anima* 5. *Gr. Phil.* 903.

shall he have more of her or less. The fault is his who chooses; God has no fault."[42]

After these words the lots are scattered among the souls. Next, a large number of sample lives are laid before them. There are lives of all kinds of social conditions, high or low birth, wealth or poverty, lives of different physical or intellectual capacities. Only, there is not anything of moral character in any of these lives. For it is the soul itself which, after having made its choice, has to give to the life of its choice its personal and moral character.

Thus, it is said in *Laws* X that the fashioning of men's characters is left entirely to themselves, under this condition, however, that Gods and daimons are our helpers in the eternal conflict between good and evil.[43]

How strongly Plato believed in the value of education in view of the forming of man's character, appears in many pages of the *Republic* and the *Laws*. Both works, in fact, are full of this preoccupation; that is: of that "care of the soul" which, according to the *Apology*, Socrates felt as a duty imposed on him by the Delphic God.[44]

We know precisely what in Plato's eyes was a fully developed personality: a man in whom each part of the soul takes its due place and exercises its particular function; which means, that those parts which are of a lower nature are completely subordinated to that part which according to its nature is superior or supreme. A state of the soul in which this equilibrium is reached, is called by Plato: *justice*.[45] And "justice" is, he says, the specific "virtue of the soul."[46]

Now, how is this virtue realized? That is: how does man attain to this state of inner equilibrium, which would make him a personality in the full sense? We know what was Plato's reply to this question: that state of inner equilibrium in which man's lower soul is totally subdued to his reason, is safely attained only by those whose intellect contemplates the transcendent Reality of exemplary and perfect Being. These are: the philosophers.[47] The contemplation of transcendent Being is only attained by a purification of the inner man, by a detachment from sensible things and from the de-

---

[42] Plato, *Rep.* X 617d-e; trans. Cornford (slightly modified).
[43] Plato, *Laws* X 904a-906b. *Gr. Phil.* nrs. 392-393.
[44] Plato, *Apol.* 21a-24b; 28b-31c.
[45] Plato, *Rep.* IV 433d-e, 435b-c, 441e-442b.
[46] Plato, *Rep.* I 353c-d.
[47] Plato, *Rep.* V 476b-d, 479e-480a; VI 484b. Cp. *Laws* XII 965b-c.

sires of the body.⁴⁸ This kind of spiritual training then, described both in the *Phaedo* and in the *Republic,* is presupposed. But the vision itself of the archetypal World, and of its ultimate "Ground" which is "the Good," that remains always a matter of spiritual "intuition," not transferable by the master on his students just by teaching. It is, and will always remain, an extremely personal interior vision.⁴⁹ And on this vision depends that state of inner harmony, which Plato called "justice."⁵⁰

We may conclude. According to Plato, "virtue" in a more popular form does exist in men on a prephilosophical level; but the higher kind of virtue depends absolutely on philosophical insight. It is only on that level that the total subordination of man's lower soul to his higher soul will be a completed fact. And there only "personality"—in the sense of the achieved and mature individual character—will be found. I should like to emphasize that in this view of personality two elements are necessarily presupposed: first, the *objective existence* of a supra-personal order of transcendental Being; second, the *individuality* of the strictly personal act of "seeing" that suprasensible Reality.

Thus, for Plato personality is founded on a metaphysical and transcendent reality. It is at the same time conditioned by a most objective Truth and by a most individual contact with that Truth.

2. As to Aristotle, in the *E.N.,* b. III, ch. 1-5, he defined precisely the conditions of responsibility for actions. In these chapters we have what might be called a developed theory of man as a moral subject. All the rest of the *E.N.* is dedicated to the description of the particular virtues. It is evident that in this description quite an amount of observation of individual behavior and character is involved. That is then what might be called "Aristotle's interest in personality." Meanwhile, a few other problems must be raised.

When dealing with Plato we could say that it is clear to us *what* in the eyes of this philosopher would be "a personality" in the full sense of the word. Can we say so with regard to Aristotle, too? Let us try. And let us try to do so while using the same standard which we used in Plato's case. When is it that any individual man attains

---

⁴⁸ Plato, *Phaedo* 64a-67d; cp. *Rep.* VI 505d-511e; VII 514a-518d; 521cd; 540a-c.
⁴⁹ Plato, *Rep.* VI 609c; cp. *Epist.* VII 341cd.
⁵⁰ See the distinction made in *Phaedo* 82ab between "popular and social virtue" on the one hand and the higher virtue of the philosophers on the other (82c). Cp. the virtue that may be due to ὀρθὴ δόξα (right opinion) in *Meno* 97a-c, which must be "fastened" by reason, just as the statues of Daedalus (97c-98a).

to that level of personal achievement, where we can speak of a "personality" in the strong sense?—Speaking in Aristotle's terms and concepts we must say: in nature every individual being is then most perfect, when it realizes its own essence as perfectly as possible. The "form" or intelligible essence of the thing is at the same time its "end." E.g.: a circle is most perfect, when it realizes most perfectly that which is contained in its definition.[51] The "form," which is the essence, is "that for which" the object came into being. It is its "good," whose realization is called virtue.[52]

Now, what is the essence of man?—Man is defined by his most peculiar function, which is: thinking. Consequently, exercising this function well will be man's particular virtue.[53] Granting that there are more "virtues of the soul," Aristotle declares that "the Good for man" exists of "the activity of the soul according to that virtue, which is best and most perfect among them."[54] And that is: the activity of the intellect.

What else can we infer from this than that, if any individual man realizes a scholar's life to a high intellectual standing, this man, if any, should be said to have attained to the highest perfection possible to any of his kind? And does not this imply, since this individual man has reached the supreme virtue, that this man actually is the *best of men,* and as such a personality of the highest quality?

In front of this conception everyone of us will have his doubts. We all feel that the scholar's intellectual excellence is on no account a guarantee for his moral character; and we can hardly imagine that Aristotle would have thought differently of that—Aristotle, who made such a vigorous protest against that identification of theoretical and practical Reason which is expressed in the Socratic maxim that "nobody sins willingly."[54a] What could be well ascertained is: that the man who spends a life on intellectual work and does that well, is *usually* (but not always) a man of self-control and moderation, always a man of perseverance and tenacity. But—there is no guarantee at all that he will be a just man in social relations,[55]

[51] Aristotle, *Phys.* VII 3, 246a 13-17; II 2, 194a 27-36; II 3, 195a 23-25; II 7, 198a 25. Cp. also *Metaph.* Δ2, 1013a 26, and Z 17, 1041a 26-32, b 4-9.
[52] Aristotle, *Phys.* II 2 and 3, ll. cc.
[53] Aristotle, *EN.* I 7, 1097b 22-1098a 18.
[54] Ib., 1098b 16-18.
[54a] *E.N.* VII 2, 1145b 27-28: "This theory is manifestly at variance with plain facts."
[55] For Aristotle, "justice" means first of all: giving his due part to everybody, as is—and was—the usual meaning in ordinary language. Here I take the word simply in its traditional sense, not as Plato defined it.

a brave person in dangers, a good and faithful husband, an amiable and loyal friend. He may be a haughty and disagreeable person, a miser and a coward, a selfish and rather an unsocial character. And what is most curious: Aristotle knew that. For he did not hold, as Plato did, that virtue is essentially one, and that, therefore, the man who possesses one virtue, must possess all of them. But then we should observe that, in fact, the man who fulfills in his individual life that virtue which for Aristotle was supreme, is not as such the morally virtuous man. The fatal consequence will be that, at least in principle, for Aristotle the ideal of the human personality is almost separated from moral virtue, while being one-sidedly concentrated on the intellectual side of man.

In Plato this was not so. For him the higher, philosophically founded virtue always presupposed the lower ones and, so to say, fed them continually by its contact with eternal Truth. Hence it might be said that for Plato a more harmonious, though certainly spiritualistic, ideal of personality was prevailing, while for Aristotle the intellectual ideal tended to infringe upon the all-round human one, even upon its moral character.

For the rest, Aristotle was far from being indifferent to the moral character of living men in all their diversity. Moral virtues are to him true excellences. Only, the intellectual excellence supersedes them all. And what among moral virtues is the kind of character which clearly seems to have been most admired by Aristotle himself? No doubt it was the character of the *magnanimus*, called by him *greatness of soul*.[56] Now it is curious to say: nowhere we feel so alien to Greek virtue as when confronted with this portrait:—the portrait of a man who is continually aware of his own excellence and value; who by every action, by every movement, by every attitude of his body deliberately tends to emphasize the excellence and dignity of his own person, never spontaneous, neither simply good to others nor just by nature because he cannot be different from what he is. Aristotle's great-souled man is so great of soul that he by preference forgets the benefits conferred by others on his person, while he has a very good memory of benefits conferred on others by himself. . . .

We can hardly help ironizing a bit on this kind of greatness of

---

[56] Aristotle, *E.N.* IV 3, 1123a 34-1125a 16. Cp. on this portrait: W. D. Ross, *Aristotle*, London⁴ 1945, p. 208. "As a whole the picture is an unpleasing one. . . . The passage simply betrays somewhat nakedly the self-absorption which is the bad side of Aristotle's ethics."

soul. The matter is that our own ideal of personality is very different. But let us beware of saying that the ideal of Aristotle's great-souled man was "*the* Greek ideal." It was *Aristotle's*. With the Greeks we shall not find it again—and, sincerely speaking, we can only wonder that *this* ideal of human personality was adopted by Medieval Christian thinkers, who for the rest transformed it so that it might seem to be a Christian character.[57]

Meanwhile, the following remarks must be made. Apparently we have been wrong when inferring from Aristotle's theory of man's perfection that he who fulfills the supreme function of man would be for this philosopher the highest personality. If personality be defined as "moral character," the term cannot even be applied to that kind of men who, according to Aristotle's definition, realize the ideal of humanity.—On the other hand, the *magnanimus* was, in fact, in Aristotle's eyes the achieved human character. His virtue is said to be "the crown of virtues," and to presuppose or include all the others. For "greatness of soul"—which is defined as "claiming much while deserving much"—is a good man's virtue.

What we find in Aristotle, then, when considering his ideal of humanity, is a strange kind of disintegration, since by him the supreme and most peculiar perfection of man is detached from moral personality and, while seemingly transcending it, is actually made into a kind of amoral perfection of the intellect alone.[58]

In the Stoa a return of the Socratic conception of the unity of virtue can be observed. Moreover, in this school the interest is concentrated on the moral character of man. Here too a certain common ideal is found of what the human personality is called to. A common ideal—and we Christians, do not we have our common ideal of a Christ-like personality, as well?[59] But we may be sure that every realization of this ideal—in so far as an ideal can be realized at all—is extremely individual. As to the Stoic ideal, we find it depicted in Cicero's *De finibus,* at the end of the third book.[60] The chapter

[57] See on this curious development the highly interesting study of R. A. Gauthier O.P., *Magnanimité.* Paris 1951.

[58] Aristotle, *E.N.* IV 3, 1123b 27-1124a 5.

[59] The later Cardinal John Henry Newman described this ideal rather impressively in some of his Anglican sermons (*Parochial and Plain Sermons* VI 22, p. 319ff.; VII 8, p. 114, ed. Longmans). Cp. my work *Newman's gedachten over de rechtvaardiging,* Wageningen 1939, p. 334f., 496f., 518f.

[60] Cicero, *De fin.* III 75f. More texts on the Stoic ideal of the wise man are cited in my *Gr. Phil.* III, nrs. 1046-1050. Important is Cicero's criticism of Cato, *Pro Murena* 29. 60-31. 64 (*Gr. Phil.* 1050b).

begins by these words—which reveal to us that in those days the term *persona* was used in ordinary language, probably quite commonly, to denote what we call personality:

"How dignified, then, how lofty, how consistent is the character of the Wise Man (*persona sapientis*) as they depict it!"

To the Stoics the wise man is essentially qualified by his complete detachment from the outward things of life. Therefore, he alone is always happy and perfectly free. Being subject to nobody's authority, he alone is a King and Master. He is rightly unconquerable and invulnerable; beautiful by spiritual beauty, and rich because he knows how to use all things. Elsewhere, it is added to this picture that the wise man never fails, and consequently never changes his opinion. It is this doctrine of which Cicero said (in the *Pro Murena*, when criticizing the famous Cato) : "this is just a bit too hard to be either true or natural"![61]

Let us notice that both Aristotle's *magnanimous* (in so far as this character was concretely realized) and a rigid Stoic such as Cato was were doubtless what we call "personalities." We find them later in a mitigated style, and so to say "humanized." First, the *magnanimous* in Panaetius' version[62]—still "a great and lofty spirit, who despises human things," but not a selfish man, cultivating his own dignity; much more a sincere admirer of moral goodness and striving after that as after the only real good. Next, there is the wise man in the later Cynic style as we find him, for instance, in Demonax: a simple and gentle person, who calms the excited, comforts those who suffer and makes peace between those who quarrel; a truly amiable man, graceful and humorous, who conquered everybody and influenced all kinds of people in an admirable way.[63]

Very striking is the kind of personality which we find in the Emperor Marcus' *Meditations*. According to his social position this man might have been a *magnanimus* in Aristotle's sense. He was not. He was a humble one, penetrated on the one hand by the thought of the vanity of human life,—but at the same time always keenly alive to the fact that man has a great moral task.[64] He considers his own military exploits *sub specie aeternitatis*,[65] and chal-

[61] "paulo asperior et durior quam aut veritas aut natura patitur" (*Pro Murena* 29. 60).
[62] Cicero, *De off*. I 65-68.
[63] Lucianus, *Demonax* 3, 7-10, 21, 28, 63. *Luciani opera* ed. Jacobitz, vol. II p. 195. De Vogel, *Gr. Phil*. nrs. 1257-58.
[64] Marcus Aurelius II 17; V 33, 1-3. Cp. also IV 48, the end.
[65] Marcus Aur. X 10.

lenges himself to simplicity, goodness, and love of God and man.[66] The word *hileōs*, which means both *gracious* and *kindly*, is used repeatedly.[67]

Now these few instances of gentleness and loving-kindness in Greek philosophers of the second century A.D. are not isolated ones. One should remember Plutarch, whose moral attitude was first of all characterized by that virtue which he called himself "*philanthropia*," love of our fellow-men, and even in a larger sense, love of our fellow-creatures, including animals.[68] For Plutarch this virtue was so important, and so comprehensive, too, that Hirzel, who wrote an excellent chapter on this subject, could say that, whosoever by reading Plutarch's works casts a glance at this man's family or circle of friends, has the impression of looking into a sanctuary of loving-kindness.[69] We might say, in fact, that, exactly as for Aristotle the crown of virtue was that kind of pride which he called "greatness of soul," and for the Stoics that wisdom which consisted essentially of a complete detachment of outward things, thus for Plutarch the ideal of human character—say: personality—lay in that virtue which is so much closer to the modern mind that has been formed by the influence of Christianity: the love of our fellow-men.

Is that a new element in Greek ethics and reflection? If that might seem so, it is only due to the incompleteness of my exposition. In the fourth century B.C. the good Xenophon depicted Cyrus as an example of that same virtue: *philanthropia*.[70] Nor was he an exception in that age. The orator Isocrates speaks in exactly the same way of a king's character (he should be *philanthropos*: 2, 15; 9, 43); he says that the Athenians should behave in this way towards other peoples (4, 29), and that King Philip of Macedonia should display *philanthropia* and mildness towards the Greeks (5, 114 and 116). Other Attic orators—Aeschines and in particular Demos-

---

[66] Marcus Aur. VI 30; VII 31. For the love of our fellow-men found in Marcus, see in particular VII 13 (Gr. Phil. nr. 1272a).

[67] Marcus Aur. XII 36.

[68] A number of passages are cited in my *Gr. Phil.* III, nrs. 1322-24. See also R. Hirzel, *Plutarch*, the chapter on "philanthropia."

[69] Hirzel, *Plutarch*, p. 29.

[70] A few passages in Xenophon's *Cyropaedia*: I 2, 1 (Cyrus was $\psi\upsilon\chi\grave{\eta}\nu$ $\phi\iota\lambda\alpha\nu\theta\rho\omega\pi\acute{o}\tau\alpha\tau\sigma\varsigma$), I 4, 1; VIII 2, 1; VIII 4, 7 (towards his friends); VII 5, 73 (towards his enemies conquered in war). Also Xen., *Agesilaus* I 22; *Mem.* I 2, 60.

thenes—use the term in the same way.[71] From the end of the third century B.C. onward the word is found repeatedly in inscriptions (plebiscites),[72] frequently in the 1st-4th centuries A.D., where citizens are officially praised for this virtue. Thus, in an inscription of Magnesia on the Maeandros, the emperor Julian is called a most "philanthropos" king.[73] In papyri of the second, third and fourth centuries the term is even used as a fixed epitheton or title of *imperatores* and *praefecti regii*.[74] In the fifth and sixth century papyri the love of Christ is denoted by the word philanthropia.[75] The word is similarly used in several passages of the N.T. and in Christian authors.[76]

S. Tromp de Ruiter, who described the history of the word and concept of *philanthropos* and *philanthropia* in a paper in *Mnemosyne* 1931, concludes his interesting study by the statement that the word of the Gospel, as a *philanthropos nomos*, did not come into a world without love. That is true. What I wish to add to the results of that excellent study are the following few points.

First, it is still a hardly acknowledged fact that on the basis of trustworthy historical evidence we can know for sure that the explicit doctrine of love of our fellow-men as a divine principle and commandment originated in the early Pythagorean school. Pythagoras, when arriving at Croton, addressed the senate and different groups of people, and roused them to mutual love (philia), concord and harmony, and this in imitation of the laws and principles

---

[71] Aeschines I, 137; Demosthenes 20, 165 (one should oppose φιλανθρωπία to φθόνος); 18, 12 (" Listen, man of Athens, to the law of φιλανθρωπία "); 21, 148 (συγγνώμη κ. φιλανθρωπία καὶ χάρις); 21, 43 (αἴδεσις καὶ φ.); 25, 81 (ἔλεος, συγγνώμη καὶ φ.); 18, 268 (φιλάνθρωπος κ. κοινός); 24, 24 (φ. καὶ δημοτικός); 21, 128 (μέτριος, καὶ φ. opposed to ὠμὸς κ. βίαιος).

Also ps. Arist., *De republ. Ath.* 16, 8.

[72] E.g. Dittenberger, *Syll.* 548; 558. The history of the word is dealt with by S. Tromp de Ruiter in *Mnemosyne* 1931, p. 271-306; *De vocis quae est φιλανθρωπία significatione atque usu.*

[73] Dittenberger, *Syll.* 906 B.

[74] In papyri of the 2nd and 3rd cent. the imperator and praefectus regius are addressed as ἡ σὴ φιλανθρωπία. After the 4th cent. the formula is ἡ σοῦ φιλανθρωπία.

In pap. Oxyrrh. IV 705, 21 the emperors Septimius Severus and Caracalla are addressed: ὦ φιλανθρωπότατοι αὐτοκράτορες.

[75] ἡ φιλανθρωπία τοῦ Σωτῆρος: God and Christ are called ἐλεήμων κ. φιλάνθρωπος.

[76] *Acta apost.* 27, 3; 28, 2; *Epist. ad Titum* III 4. Origenes IV 83, 26; III 2, 11.

ruling the cosmos,[77] and symbolized by the unanimous company of the nine Muses.[78] Though our direct witnesses about all this are fairly late (Jamblichus, Porphyrius, Pompeius Trogus and Diodorus), it should be remembered that their testimony reaches back to the fourth century B.C. (Aristoxenus, Dicaearchus and Timaeus), and is supported by the fragments of Archytas, which bring us back to the beginning of the fourth century or the end of the fifth.

When in Plato's *Gorgias* Socrates, in defending justice against the attacks of Callicles, refers to "wise men" who teach that the universe is held together "by communion and friendship, by orderliness, temperance and justice," we may be sure that the reference is to the Pythagoreans, whose representative Archytas was well-known in those days and was greatly respected by Plato.[79] Later, in the *Timaeus*, when giving an explicit theory on the genesis of the cosmos, Plato starts from the basic idea that in this visible world things are well and beautifully arranged.[80] He concludes, therefore, that it must have been made by a good Creator who arranged it according to an eternal pattern. That is: the cosmic order is explained by Plato as having its archetype in a supra-sensible and perfect world of eternal Being, of which it is an image (*eikoon*), realized by a transcendent Cause, who himself cannot be anything but a thinking Mind or Noûs.[81] Thus, Plato goes his own way in metaphysics, separated from the older Pythagorean conception of the universe by his marked transcendentalism.

After Plato, the doctrine of his later years in which he traced all

[77] The address of Pythagoras to the senate of Croton is recorded in Jamblichus, *Life of Pyth.*, ch. 45-46. Cp. also the address to the young men of Croton, ib., ch. 40 l. 8-41, l. 4. These discourses are also mentioned in Justinus' *Epitome*, that is: Pompeius Trogus (first cent. B.C.), whose source was the Sicilian historian Timaeus (4*th* cent. B.C.). Further: Jamblichus, *Vita Pyth.* 33-34, and Porphyrius, V.P. 21 (from Nicomachus), whose ultimate source is Aristoxenus (fr. 17 Wehrli). Here Pythagoras is described as the bringer of peace and harmony in Southern Italy and Sicily.

And most of all Jambl., *V.P.* 229-230: on Pythagorean friendship. That the passage contains ancient Pythagorean thoughts, appears from parallels in Diodorus (X 8, 1f.), which go back to Aristoxenus, and Archytas fr. 3 Diels.

[78] The cult of the Muses appears in Pythagoras' discourse before the senate of Croton according to Jambl., *V.P.* 45. Though evidently we do not pretend that the form of these discourses goes back to the historical Pythagoras, I do think the argument of the cult of the Muses is probably authentic.

[79] The Pythagorean influence in this passage of the *Gorgias*, and in Plato's later ideal of the philosopher-statesman has been acknowledged and rightly emphasized by J. S. Morrison in *Class. Quart.* 1958, p. 198-218.

[80] Plato, *Timaeus* 29a.

[81] Plato, *Tim.* 29b-30c; 34a-b; 42e 5; 47e 4 (τὰ διὰ νοῦ δεδημιουργημένα) ff.

things existing back to two ultimate Principles, the One and the indefinite Dyad, is confounded with Pythagoreanism, which from the sixth century onward was a clearly dualistic theory, in which the principle of Limit was opposed to the Indefinite.[82] An amalgamation of the two theories is found in Alexander Polyhistor's report of what he called "Pythagorean doctrine," which in this form must go back to the second century B.C.[83] The most remarkable point is: that here the doctrine has a clearly monistic form. Apparently this is a post-Platonic development.[84] In this form the platonized Pythagoreanism is continued through the first centuries of our era. It was essentially a metaphysical theory in which number-speculations played an important rôle.[85] But it must have kept the ethos of ancient-Pythagorean *philia:* of friendship and harmony, not only between men, but between men and animals as well. Thus, Pythagorean "love" is known to Plutarch and mentioned by him explicitly.[86]—This then is one line of love of one's fellow-men as an ideal of personality in the Greek world.

Second. Another line, not dependent on the Pythagorean tradition, originates with Socrates. Socrates going about on the market and in the places of exercise of young people, talking with everybody who is willing to answer to his questions, interrogating them about "what is virtue,"—this Socrates is not just searching for intellectual clearness in behalf of himself; he "cares about the souls of his fellow-men," in particular of his fellow-citizens "because they

[82] Plato's theory of first principles is found in Aristotle, *Metaph.* A 6, 987b 18-27. Cp. in particular the pages on *peras* and *apeiron* in Plato's *Philebus*, 24a-25b. Very important is the text of Hermodorus ap. Simpl., *Phys.* 247, 30-248, 15, and its parallel in Sextus Emp., *Adv. Math.* X, 263-276. De Vogel, *Gr. Phil.* nr. 371.

The old-Pythagorean συστοιχία is mentioned in Aristotle, *Metaph.* A 5, 986a 15 ff. (*Gr.Phil.* nr. 42), and traced back to the days of Alcmaeon of Croton.

[83] Diog. Laert. VIII 25-35. *Greek Phil.* nr. 1279. References are given there.

[84] Besides *Gr.Phil.* l.c. I dealt with the matter anew in *La théorie de l'ἄπειρον chez Platon et dans la tradition platonicienne* (*Revue philosophique*, Paris 1959, p. 21-39). A. J. Festugière, who published an important study on the "*Mémoires Pythagoriques* cités par Alexandre Polyhistor" in *Revue des Etudes Grecques* 1945, deals again with the Pythagorean monism in the chapters II and III of his fourth volume of *La révélation d'Hermès Trismégiste*, entitled *Le Dieu inconnu et la Gnose*. See in particular the section on *La monade* ἀρρενόθηλυς, pp. 43-51. Here he concludes by dating the origin of the conception somewhere between Xenocrates and Diogenes of Babylonia, that is probably in the 3rd cent. B.C. I can agree with that.

[85] See the nr. 1285 in my *Gr. Phil.* III and the literature mentioned there. Also Festugière in the above-mentioned chapters of *Le Dieu inconnu et la Gnose*.

[86] Plutarchus, *De sollertia animalium* 959F. Cp. Jambl. V.P .229.

are nearer to him by birth."[87] And when in the *Gorgias* Plato, speaking through the person of Socrates, opposes philosophy to rhetoric, it is by this criterium: that rhetoric does not care about the souls of those it tries to persuade, while philosophy does.[88]

The line of Socrates is continued by Plato, for whom philosophy is not just personal insight into a transcendent truth kept to the philosopher himself; but, by the very light of this view of eternal Reality he feels driven back to his less endowed fellow-men and acknowledges the duty of leading them and their lives according to the standard known to him.[89] Here then we find a second line of love of one's fellow-men, clearly felt as a divine commandment.[90]

Third. Tromp de Ruiter, while concluding his above-cited study, suggested that the new ideal of humanity expressed in the term *philanthropia*, is not of philosophical origin, or at least was not particularly promoted by Antisthenes and the Cynics, but much more by such Attic orators as Isocrates and Demosthenes. In this context I should like to raise the following questions.

How is it that for Xenophon philanthropia came to be a moral ideal? Did he produce it from his own mind or heart? —And then the orators, who knew this ideal in almost the same period of time. Did Aeschines produce it, or was it Isocrates who created this ideal? But—both Xenophon and Aeschines were Socratics. And could it not be that the ideal of humanity and loving-kindness which we find so frequently in those fourth century authors, is a kind of echo of that care about his fellow-men which was so essential to Socrates, and may be a remote echo of the Pythagorean philia, too? I do think at Athens the influence of Socrates prevailed. Now Socrates' "philanthropia," let us say,[91] was certainly continued by Plato, be it in a strictly aristocratic form (this term being taken not in the traditional sense of birth, but in the sense of a personal and intellectual aristocracy). But is it true that among other Socratics no trace is found of an ideal of humanity?—Here Tromp de Ruiter failed to see how the ancient Cynics actually cultivated a kind of humanitarianism which, in fact, had its roots in Socrates' philanthropia. It is in this Socratic School that, from the beginning, the

---

[87] Plato, *Apol.* 29d-30a.
[88] Plato, *Gorgias* 502d-503a; 515a ff.
[89] Plato, *Rep.* VII 540a-c.
[90] Socrates feels his philosophic task as a kind of mission, imposed on him by the Delphic God: Plato, *Apol.* 29d-30a; 30d-31c. As to Plato: *Rep.* 540a-c; cp. 508c-509c.
[91] Xen., *Mem.* I 2, 60 calls Socrates φιλάνθρωπος.

stress was not laid on learning and scholarly research, but, on the contrary, on practical training.[92] "Virtue," said Antisthenes, "is a matter of deeds, not of many arguments or learning."[93] When in the third century Bion of Borysthenes starts his method of popular preaching on moral subjects, addressing himself to the larger circle, it must be granted that at least the conditions for such a method— which are in principle: recognizing man as a rational being, capable of being so addressed—were created a century before, by such disciples of Socrates as were Antisthenes and (indirectly) Diogenes of Sinope.[94]

The line of ancient Cynicism was continued in the Stoa: we know that Zeno was a disciple of the Cynic Crates.[95] And here, then, we have a fully developed theory of a natural community of all rational beings, and find its practical consequences in all kinds of human relations.[96] Here, then, we have a third line of love of one's fellow-men, clearly different both from the Pythagorean and from the Platonic tradition, but certainly going back to the fourth century B.C. or the end of the fifth.

Fourth. In the *Cyropaedia* IV 3, 10 Xenophon, reflecting on human behavior and personality, writes the following sentence: *"For nothing is so much our own as we are to ourselves."*

These words are a typical expression of the belief in what we might call: a culture of personality. It is also a typical expression of self-reflection of the individual man, which in this case is the more remarkable, as Xenophon is so far from being a philosopher. Yet, in this he proves to be a true Socratic. Both in the Cynic and in the Cyrenaic Schools, usually called by the name of Minor Socratics, the "culture of personality" is continued; the interest in the forming of the moral character is very much alive, about a century

[92] Diog. Laert. VI 2 (the example of Heracles), 70 (double askesis), 103 (no interest in theoretical problems).

[93] Diog. L. ib. 11.

[94] This was well recognized by H. Kesters, whose last work *Plaidoyer d'un Socratique contre le Phèdre de Platon*, Paris-Louvain 1959, was reviewed by me in *Forum der Letteren* 1961, p. 187-192.

[95] Diog. Laert. VII 2-3; De Vogel, *Gr. Phil.* III, 885 a-c.

[96] See my *Gr.Phil.* III, nrs. 999-1001 (on *oikeiosis*); 1069a, b (the doctrine of *societas hominum inter ipsos*). The basis of this doctrine is the κοινὸς νόμος (Cleanthes, in *Gr.Phil.* nr. 943; Cicero *De republ.* III 33, in *Gr.Phil.* nr. 1066c). See also 1205 (Antiochus of Ascalon ap. Cic., *De finibus* V).

Practical consequences: in marriage, see *Gr. Phil.* III, nrs. 1147 (Antipater) and 1230a (Musonius Rufus); in international relations, *Gr. Phil.* 1000b, 1070 a-c (Cicero); in social conditions, *Gr. Phil.* 1069a, 1071 a-c (the equality of all men; nobody is a slave by nature).

before the Hellenistic Schools are founded. The "working at oneself," as a specifically human task and a matter which falls first of all under our personal responsibility, is clearly recognized, not only in the Socratic Schools, but by a man like Xenophon as well.

III

We cannot close this, albeit a somewhat rapid study of personality in Greek philosophy, without saying a word of Plotinus, that last great and highly interesting thinker of pre-Christian Antiquity. The three most note-worthy characteristics of Plotinus' reflection on man and human personality are: 1. his marked spiritualism; 2. the note of self-reflection; 3. the philosopher's particular interest in man's individuality and its metaphysical grounds. Let us consider these three points.

1. In the first treatise of *Enn.* I, entitled *What is the living being, and what is Man?* Plotinus reflects on sense-perception.[97] It is clear that perception is realized through the body,—but somehow *we* are the subject of it. How? Obviously because we are not separate from "the animal," even though certainly other and nobler elements go to make up the entire many-sided nature of man. But the soul (which is of a higher, spiritual nature) cannot perceive the sensible objects directly. It does only indirectly, grasping the "impressions" made on "the animal" by sensation. And these impressions are already intelligible. The soul's perception, then, is in fact an active contemplation of "Forms."[98] And by means of these "forms" the soul alone acquires the lordship over "the animal": discursive thinking, opinions and intellection arise. And from this moment we are peculiarly *"We."* Before this there was only the "ours"; but at this stage stands the *"We,"* in higher regions presiding over the animal.[99]—"There is nothing against calling the entire composite being 'animal,' mingled in its lower parts; but above this region begins the veritable man. The inferior parts are what is akin to the lion, and of the order of the multiple brute. The veritable man, then, coincides essentially with the reasonable soul,

---

[97] Plotinus, *Enn.* I 1, 7, line 6 ff. I give an exact paraphrasis, sometimes adopting the wording of MacKenna's beautiful translation.
[98] εἰδῶν μόνον ἀπαθῶς εἶναι θεωρίαν.
[99] ἄνω ἐφεστηκότες τῷ ζώῳ.

and in this reasoning it is this *We* that reasons, in that the use of reason is the activity of the Soul."

This is what Plotinus repeated many times and in different contexts: the veritable man is the spiritual man, who possesses the spiritual virtues (I 1, 10); the higher, spiritual soul is our true self (II 1, 5, the end); it is that which dominates the passions (II 3, 9).[100] The individuality of the compound, which in a sense may be called man, begins on a lower level: feelings, desires and strivings have their own individuality—and Plotinus is interested in its grounds[101] —but "personality" can begin only on that level where the veritable man begins. In general, man living in a body is called *rational* (logikos) :[102] it is the level of discursive thinking, not yet that of the intuitive thinking of Noûs, which has its objects within itself. But this rationality of man not only always depends on Noûs, in so far as, ontologically speaking, Soul springs from Noûs. That is, so to say, an objective fact. But in its individual life the soul's degree of spirituality is very different, and depends on the actual contact this particular soul entertains with that Superior Reality which is called Noûs.[103]

Therefore, the ideal of personality lies for Plotinus in that spiritual state of the soul which is called by him by the name of virtue.[104] "Wisdom" is of that level: the level of Noûs.[105] This implies that the wise man is above outward things, and this he *must* be: otherwise he would be just a decent man, who is of a mixed life and character and not worthy of being called happy.[106] On the other hand, it does not imply that Plotinus' spiritualized man would be necessarily an eremite, living to himself and separated from community with others, at least from ordinary life. Plotinus' own life, as described by Porphyry, teaches a different lesson. Here that great contempla-

[100] By pathè is meant all those feelings, desires and strivings which as such belong to the inferior part of man.

[101] E.g. *Enn.* VI 4, 6.

[102] Thus, in I 1, 7 (the end) " man " is identified with λογικὴ ψυχή. But cp. VI 7, 5 and VI 7, 9, lines 5-10, where it is suggested that "yonder" man is no longer λογικός.

[103] On the various levels of soul see in particular *Enn.* IV 3, 4. lin. 21-37. Cp. also IV 8, 17, 1-14 (the soul's intermediate place between sensible things and Noûs) and VI 2, 22, lin. 28-35. An ἐπιστροφή to the spiritual world is needed: IV 8, 4.

[104] Virtue is a kind of "spirit" and "such a state as to make the soul being spiritualized" (*Enn.* VI 8, 5, lin. 34-37).

[105] *Enn.* I 4, 14.

[106] *Enn.* I 4, 15, lin. 1-8; I 4, 16, lin. 1-15.

tive of the world beyond appears to us as the centre of a fairly numerous household, which is a refuge for widows and for orphans. We find him personally occupied with the interests of the individual members of this community: supervising the schoolwork of a naughty boy, looking after the property of the children confided to his care (for "as long as they are no philosophers," he used to say, "their property and their income should be safe"), and acting as an arbiter in quarrels.[107] Far from being a rather absent-minded and egocentric character, he appears to us as always at the call of all those who had only the slightest acquaintance with him,[108] and as a man of a wonderful penetration into character. Of this Porphyry gives us a few remarkable instances.[109]

No doubt, the portait is for us somewhat surprising. But let us grant at least that in the practice of life—and this is perhaps the most severe test—Plotinus proves to be a genuine disciple of Plato who, instead of isolating his philosopher from practical life, sent him back into it and imposed on him the task of leading others. Plotinus not only *taught* that philosophical virtue presupposes and contains the social ones; he demonstrated and he practised it in his own personal life.

He was "gentle," says the biographer,[110] and what was called in those days *philanthropos*. Of his strong spiritualism we have no exact parallel in Plato. In Aristotle we have: both in the *Protrepticus* and in the *E.N.*[111] It is reproduced by Cicero, and found in Seneca as well.[112] Later a similar view of man is found in Epictetus and in Marcus Aurelius.[113] Plotinus used to refer to the *Alcibiades Maior* as to a Platonic text.[114] In fact the formula "man=the soul" which stands there might be rather a sign that this dialogue is not authentic. On the whole, Plotinus' spiritualism is a slightly exaggerated Platonism, and his ideal of personality, though essentially

[107] Porphyrius, *Vita Plotini* 9.
[108] *Ibid.*, lin. 19.
[109] Porphyrius, *Vita* ch. 11, mentions a few instances.
[110] πρᾶος ἦν: *Vita*, ch. 9 lin. 18.
[111] Aristotle, *Protr.* fr. 6 Ross (Fragm. Selecta p. 35, lin. 12-13); *E.N.* X 7, 1178a 2-3.
[112] Cicero, *De republ.* VI 26: Nec enim tu is es quem forma ista declarat, sed mens cuiusque is est quisque. Cp. Seneca, *Epist.* 65, 15; *Epist.* 102, 22; *Ad Marciam de consolatione* 25. Greek Phil. nrs. 959, 960.
[113] For Epictetus the σωμάτιον is one of the outward things, which are not essential to us. *Diatr.* I 29, 5-8; 9-12. Cp. II 6, 20-27. Marcus Aur. X 38; XII 3, 1-2. Gr. Phil. nrs. 1295, 1265.
[114] E.g. in *Enn.* V 1, 10, lin. 10: οἷον λέγει Πλάτων τὸν εἴσω ἄνθρωπον. Cp. [Pl.], *Alcib. Mai.* 130c.

faithful to Plato's spirit, bears unmistakably the stamp of a later period in the development of Greek thought.

2. *Self-reflection*, as we observed, in Greek philosophy was at least as old as Heraclitus. Socrates declared emphatically that a life without self-examination is not worth living for a man.[115] Both in Plato and in Aristotle there is quite an amount of self-reflection. For Plato it was an indispensable condition of that philosophical virtue which is superior to the popular kind.[116] The latter may be attained by "right opinion"—but as such it lacks the lasting and stable character of that virtue which is knowledge, and whose subject is able to give an account of himself.[117] In Aristotle, self-reflection is not so much focused on the individual self, unless in view of some general conclusion such as: the nature of man as such, his eudaemonia, the rôle of pleasure in it, etc. One could hardly deny self-reflection to Aristotle, but at least it is less explicit and of another kind than Socrates' or Plato's was.

The Stoics had a word for and a theory of self-consciousness: by Chrysippus it is literally called con-science (syneidesis);[118] others speak of the gift of "following oneself" in the sense of being aware of oneself and one's physical functions.[119] This elementary form of self-consciousness is proper to man from the moment of his birth and is, so to say, a gift belonging to his physical constitution. On the rational level the self-reflection of man extends to his being able to understand the divine administration of the world,[120] and of recognizing himself as not only a *part*, but an *organical* part, that is, a *member* of the whole.[121] Here the Stoic self-reflection reveals itself as of quite a metaphysical character. How personally this could be felt, may be seen, for instance, in Epictetus, *Diatr.* II 10, where we read (after the above-cited statement of man's capacity of understanding the divine administration of the world):

[115] Plato, *Apol.* 38a. That by the formula ὁ ἀνεξέταστος βίος Socrates meant not "a life without inquiry" or "investigation," in the sense of any research, but precisely "giving an account of oneself," of one's own words and notions, of one's style of life and moral character, too, is quite sure. Cp. e.g. *Laches* 187e; *Gr.Phil.* nr. 208a.

[116] *Phaedo* 82a-b.

[117] *Meno* 97a-98a. Above, n. 50.

[118] Chrysippus ap. Diog. Laert. VII 85: συνείδησις. Cp. Cicero, *De fin.* III 5, 16: sensum sui habere. *Gr.Phil.* nr. 999.

[119] Epictetus, *Diatr.* I 16, 15-18, praises God for many gifts, but particularly because he gave us τὴν δύναμιν τὴν παρακολουθητικὴν τούτοις. *Gr.Phil.* 929a.

[120] *Diatr.* II 10: Σκέψαι τίς εἶ. Man is παρακολουθητικὸς τῇ θείᾳ διοικήσει and can reason upon the consequences thereof (§ 3). *Gr.Phil.* 1242.

[121] Marcus Aur. VII 13: μέλος, —οὐ μέρος. *Gr.Phil.* 1272a.

"Next, bear in mind that you are a Son. What is the profession of this character?[122] To treat everything that is his own as belonging to his father, to be obedient to him in all things, never to speak ill of him to anyone else, nor to say or do anything that will harm him, to give way to him in everything and yield him precedence, helping him as far as is within his power.

"Next, know that you are also a Brother. Upon this character also there is incumbent deference: obedience, kindly speech, never to claim as against your brother any of the things that lie outside the realm of your free choice, but cheerfully to give them up, so that in the things that *do* lie within the realm of your free moral choice you may have the best of it. For see what it is, at the price of a head of lettuce, if it so chance, or of a seat, for you to acquire his goodwill—how greatly you get the best of it there!"[123]

Plotinus knows a similar kind of self-reflection—similar in so far as for him, too, man in his spiritual essence springs from a Divine Origin, and has to remember his Father, a thing which the soul can best realize by reflecting on itself and its own spiritual nature. That is what is done in the first chapters of the treatise on *the Three Fundamental Hypostases* (*Enn.* V 1).

Self-consciousness is often mentioned in the *Enneads*.[124] In the 7th treatise of *Enn.* VI, ch. 41 (on *How the multiplicity of ideal Forms came into Being, and on the Good*) we learn that the word "Know yourself" is a precept for those beings that have a multiplicity in themselves; not for that which is perfectly one. For this is the First, and exists in a way beyond the order of knowledge, thinking and being aware of oneself.

This is confirmed in a number of other passages.[125] Noûs, which

[122] πρόσωπον.
[123] Epictetus, *Diatr.* II 10, 7-9. Translation by W. A. Oldfather.
[124] παρακολουθεῖν ἑαυτῷ in *Enn.* I 4, 5, 1. 2; I 4, 9, 1. 1; II 9, 1, 1. 41-44; III 9, 9, 1. 12 ff., 1. 18-20; IV 4, 1. 10; V 3, 13, 1. 6 ff. παρακολούθησις in I 4, 10, 1. 28. συναίσθησις: III 4, 4, 1. 10; III 8, 4, 1. 15-22; IV 4, 2, 1. 31; IV 4, 8, 1. 20; IV 4, 24, 1. 22; V 4, 2, 1. 12-19; V 6, 5, 1. 1-5; V 8, 11, 1. 19-24; VI 7, 41, 1. 22-26.

Sometimes συναίσθησις is used to express the common sensitiveness of parts of a whole. Thus, *Enn.* IV 4, 45, 1. 8; VI 4, 9, 1. 36. In these passages συναίσθησις is a synonym of the stoic term συμπάθεια.

[125] V 6, 5, 1.1-5: That which is perfectly one does not need συνάισθησις. It is beyond self-perception and any intellection.—The same in III 9, 9, 1. 12-20.

In V 4, 2, 1. 12-19, the One is considered—exceptionally!—as νοητόν, and as a *perfect* intelligible Object opposed to Noûs, which is a multiplicity and is intelligible in the secondary sense. The First Νοητόν is not needing anything; it has no deficiencies. It has as it were συναίσθησις, and a kind of thinking different from that of Noûs! (Mind the οἷονεί in this passage! One could not say that Plotinus flatly contradicts himself).

contains already a principle of multiplicity, could not exist, and cannot even be conceived of, as not knowing itself (treatise *Against the Gnostics:* II 9, 1). Also the soul of the cosmos as a whole, though one should not attribute any perception to it, must have a consciousness of itself, exactly as we have it.[126]

Man living in a body is, normally speaking, a self-conscious being: he can "follow" his own sensitive and intellectual activities. But— it may happen to him to fall ill or to lose the normal use of his intellect, either by an accident or by old age: he will no more be able to "follow" his own functions. What about this state of man? —This is what Plotinus answers. What we call self-consciousness is so to say a reflection of the continuous activity of Noûs on the level of soul which, if it is in a state of harmony, forms a kind of smooth and shining mirror. The mirror may go into pieces. Then, man will no more be aware of himself. His intellect will seem to be disturbed. In fact, the activity of Noûs goes on. It is only the reflected image that fails. For Noûs is always active and, being of a higher level, does not depend on material conditions.[127]

Therefore, there is no reason to believe that the wise man's happiness will be disturbed or lost in such a case as was mentioned above. On the contrary, there are good grounds for holding that the higher activity of the intellect is operating better and purer, if not reflected in that mirror of the soul. For are not actually those moments of our life the best and most happy, in which we are so absorbed in some noble activity—say in reading, or in a courageous act—that we are no longer aware of ourselves?[128]

Plotinus knows a higher state of man than that of life in a body. We learned that "yonder" he will no longer be a "logikos"—that is: a subject of discursive reasoning—but will live the life of Noûs of which he will be a part, or rather a member.[129] And what will follow from that state as to the self-consciousness of man? On coming yonder, will the soul be still aware of being this or that individual,—of being Socrates or Callias? Plotinus deals with these questions in the opening chapters of *Enn.* IV 4. This is what he says. Yonder, the soul will be completely absorbed in the contemplation of its object, which is: intelligible Being as a whole. It has left behind itself the life in a body, and the state of discursive think-

---

[126] IV 4, 24, 1.22: no αἴσθησις, but a συναίσθησις αὐτοῦ.
[127] I 4, ch. 9-10.
[128] I 4, 10, 1.21-33.
[129] VI 7, 5; VI 7, 9.

ing which is going from one thing to the other. All those things have passed away. Now, the Soul is living in Eternity: in a continuous "Now," in which there is the totality of Being. In that totality there is diversity: there is a multiplicity of intelligible objects. The soul when living yonder sees them all at the same time (which is not any "time" at all), as a many forming a unity. And in that unity it will also see itself and know itself.[130]

Thus, Plotinus could say first: Yonder, there will not be any memory of oneself, that one was Socrates (in earthly life) or whosoever.[131] But next: there will be certainly a knowledge of oneself, because living in the intelligible World (which is a thinking Mind) it will think itself and know itself as being included in the Whole, and it will see the totality of things in seeing itself.[132]

It is often said that Plotinus' philosophy tends to an impersonal Unity, in which the human personality is to be dissolved. Immortal life of the individual person, as believed in by Christians and taught by Christian revelation, would be completely lacking in Plotinus. This might be an error. I mean this. I have met more than once with strictly orthodox and deeply believing Christians who said, when speaking of the life hereafter: "I suppose we shall be too much absorbed in the vision of God to have still any time either for ourselves or for one another."—This might seem somewhat naïve as to the form of expression. Yet, what the speakers meant, might be profoundly true. One thing, I think, should be added: namely that, in so far as we shall "see" ourselves and others, we shall see them, no doubt, *in His light;* that is: *in Him.* We should not forget that it has been said that "God will be everything in all," and that the same is said of Christ.[133] Moreover, it should be borne in mind that "we shall be changed."[134]

That is what Plotinus said. Modern translations, however excellent they may be, are sometimes a bit confusing, or even treacherous, if one does not possess a broader and very precise knowledge of the philosopher's whole way of thinking. For instance, MacKenna's translation—on the whole a highly admirable work—reads at the beginning of IV 4,2:

"We come now to the question of memory of the personality.

---

[130] IV 4, ch. 1-2.
[131] IV 4, 2, 1.1-3.
[132] Ib., 1.10-14, 30-32.
[133] I *Cor.* 15, 28; *Coloss.* 3, 11.
[134] I *Cor.* 15, 40-52.

"There will not even be memory of the personality; no thought that the contemplator is the self—Socrates, for example—or that it is the Intellect or Soul."

The word "personality" stands here for the Greek "himself" or "oneself": yonder, there will not even be memory of "oneself." That is to say: the soul, which is now living in Eternity, is no more concerned with *what it was* in earthly life. It has no memory of that state. But it *is* aware of itself as it is now. And—what is now, that is the *spiritual* man instead of the "logikos." In fact, we shall be changed.[135] But there is a continuity!

That this is so for Plotinus too, will appear in our next section.

3. Plotinus was keenly interested in the problem of the soul's individuality and its metaphysical ground. The problem of personal immortality is dealt with in one of the first treatises of the *Enneads*,[136] and also that other very Plotinian problem of: How is it possible that, while Soul is an indivisible substance, individual souls have their own particular feelings, perceptions and thoughts.[137] After these questions had been raised and had been answered more or less clearly in the earliest treatises, Plotinus discussed them anew and very penetratingly, in the three long treatises *Difficulties on the Soul* in the second series of his works.[138] They appear again in the first treatise *On the integral omnipresence of Being* (VI 4).[139]

Plotinus is very far from explaining the soul's individuality by its being bound in a body. On the contrary, if there are individual souls, that must be because yonder there are individual Spirits. For, since the nature of the soul is of an order superior to that of matter and the body, it cannot depend on that which is below, but must depend on that which is beyond it. Therefore, Plotinus had to ask the question: *Is there an Idea* (=archetypal Form) *of the individual being?*—It was in one of the early treatises that he asked this question.[140] And here is his reply:

If I and everybody go back to the Intelligible, then every individual being has its origin yonder.

---

[135] VI 7, 5; VI 7, 9.
[136] IV 7.
[137] IV 2, ch. 1-2; also IV 1, and IV 9, 1-2.
[138] IV 3-5, which have been called "a vast history of the individual soul, from its origin in universal soul up to its descent in a body" (E. Bréhier, IV p. 13).
[139] VI 4, 6: on the possibility of individual feelings and perception. VI 4, 14: Whence the difference between individual souls?
[140] V 7, 1.

But may not one archetype be reproduced by many concrete beings? And, therefore, might not one archetypal Man suffice for all?—It is very interesting to see what Plotinus answers to this question. He says: no, for different individuals one Reason-Principle cannot account. If men were different as to their "matter" only—say: as to the form of their body or the colour of their eyes—, one intelligible Form might suffice. But such is not the case. Human beings differ the one from the other by innumerable variations of the intelligible type: this is no question of various pictures or images reproducing the same original; the individual human beings differ so greatly as to demand distinct Reason-Principles.

I do not hesitate to say: here we have a full-grown metaphysics of the personality.

"But," it may be asked, "did not Plotinus say that the soul, on coming yonder, will not remember *who* it was, whether Socrates or whosoever? And what else is this but the loss of personality,—since personality implies: being aware of one's identity as an individual?"

Here is Plotinus' reply.[141] "Nothing of what *is* will be lost. For in the intelligible world the Spirits will not perish, because they are not divided according to the order of the body; but every one remains, possessing in its own distinct character the same identical being."

That is to say, viewed from below, soul when grown into Spirit will not lose its distinct character. On the other hand, viewed from above, there is a clear continuity: for souls, depending each on a Spirit, will be an *expression* each of their Spirit, and so to say a development of it.[142]

"But," somebody might say, "are not there several other passages in the *Enneads* in which Plotinus clearly abandoned that principle of assuming intelligible Forms (or Ideas) of individual Beings? Does not he contradict that early theory of his own in later, apparently more definitive treatises?"[143]

I do not think so. A careful reading of the related passages will reveal that in those cases the point of view was different, and that those passages do not annul the theory expounded in V 7: that indi-

---

[141] IV 3, 5, 3-8.

[142] ἐξειλιγμένοι μᾶλλον ἢ ἐκεῖνοι (IV 3, 5, 10). A modern reader might feel inclined to observe that, if soul is an "unfolding" of Noûs, in a sense at least soul will be "more" than the intelligible archetype. This is true, and Plotinus does not deny it. He does not mean, however, that the "additions" are any real gain.

[143] The passages referred to are: *Enn.* V 9, 12; VI 3, 9; VI 5, 8, 39 ff.

vidual men must have an individual archetype in the intelligible world. First, there is V 9, 12, where it is said that "Ideas are of universals, not of Socrates, but of Man." The author hesitates whether differences in the complexion of individual men should not be taken to differences in the Idea. He seems inclined to admit this, but adds that "Matter also has its effect in bringing about such-like features." The instances mentioned are: the snub-nosed and the aquiline type, and different colors of the skin, of hair and eyes, etc. Now these are exactly the matters which for Plotinus do not make the personality.—On the whole, we should observe that this chapter bears the character of short notes; the possibility of assuming Ideas of individual men is left open; it is found to be necessary as to man's rational aspects—in so far as he is a reasoning being and possesses arts and crafts[144]—but not with regard to accidental physical varieties. According to Porphyry's list, the treatise V 9 is of a very early date. V 7, though belonging also to the first group, is placed considerably later.

In VI 3, which belongs to the second group, ch. 9, Plotinus opposes Aristotle's doctrine of matter as the principle of individuation: he denies that Matter could contribute anything to that which the individual man really is. Man's essential being has its roots elsewhere: yonder. Against Aristotle Plotinus maintains strictly the supremacy of the intelligible archetype: it is not the particular which adds anything to the universal; on the contrary, it owes its very being to the universal, for it exists only by participation in that.— "We may be told that Man (the universal) is Form alone, Socrates Form and Matter. But on this very ground Socrates will be less fully Man than the universal; for the Reason-Principle will be less effectual in Matter."[145] The question of whether any "Forms" of individuals should be assumed, is not in discussion here. What is maintained is: that the intelligible archetype is always more perfect than the particular and has an ontological priority.

Neither does the last alinea of VI 5, 8 interfere with the principle that individual men should have their archetype "yonder." What is in discussion here is of a different nature. "It would be absurd to introduce a multitude of Ideas of Fire, each several fire being shaped by a particular idea. The Ideas of fire would be infinite!"[146]

We do not deny that there are some further problems behind

---

[144] Εἰ δὲ ἀνθρώπου ἐκεῖ, καὶ λογικοῦ ἐκεῖ καὶ τεχνικοῦ (V 9, 12, the beginning).
[145] Trans. MacKenna (VI 3, 9, 32-34).
[146] VI 5, 8, 39 ff.

these questions, nor should I like to assert that Plotinus solved them all definitively. Many a modern reader of Plotinus might feel unsatisfied and might ask whether it should not be admitted that by our concrete and individual existence *something actually new is created which never existed before,*—so that it must be granted that by this our concrete life *something is "added" to eternal Being.* I think Plotinus would have thought this rather a pretentious assumption. He was so profoundly penetrated by the thought of that mighty Reality of eternal Being, that our own imperfect world—even of that which we proudly call our own spiritual creation: our arts and sciences, our culture, moral order and technical achievements, our philosophy too,—seemed small to him and of a lower order, vanishing as a mist. And surely, let us grant, it *is* a high pretention to assume that something of our life might finally appear to be of some value for eternity. I think that, if a Christian may believe this, it is on a religious ground, much more than on the mere basis of philosophical reflection. These things are of an unfathomable depth.[147]

So far then for Plotinus on personality. From this one can easily understand, at least in principle, how he philosophized on the person: man as a moral subject, free in his choice, could be explained by Plotinus only within the framework of his metaphysics. Man is essentially a spiritual being, and the more he is living on the level of Noûs, the more will he be beyond the concatenation of natural events, which are determined by the laws of a lower order. Soul in its essence cannot depend on the body and on Matter. Soul turning itself to the Spirit fulfills its essential nature, and by this very act maintains its superiority to the laws of the physical order of the universe.

Centuries before, Carneades had criticized Chrysippus' doctrine which made of man a part of nature: since in nature everything is determined by preceding causes, and man is part of nature, there is no room for free will under this fatality. Against this Carneades introduced free will as an independent cause.[148] He simply argued from obvious psychological facts: "If everything happens by necessity, nothing will be in our power. But something *is* in our power. Therefore, not everything happens by fate." To this argument he

---

[147] Yet, *something of this was seen* both by Plato and by Plotinus (e.g. Plato: *Laws* X 904a-906b; Plotinus, *Enn.* III 2, 8-10).
[148] Cicero, *De fato* 14, 31-15, 35. *Greek Phil.* nr. 1124.

added the justified remark that not every fact or event which preceded is the cause of that which follows.—All this is very true. Only, *how* man who, as a physical being, is a part of nature, in his actions *can* be beyond the natural law, Carneades could not explain. Plotinus could. This is what he said:[149]

"Soul we must bring into the world of things as a separate principle, not merely the Soul of the Universe, but the soul of the individual with it. This, no mean Principle, is needed to be the bond of union in the total of things, not itself a thing sprung like the other things from life-seeds, but a first-hand Cause, bodiless and therefore supreme over itself, free, beyond the reach of cosmic Cause; though, brought into a body, it will not be unrestrictedly sovereign; it will hold rank in a series.

"Now the environment into which this independent principle enters, when it has come to the midpoint, will be largely led by secondary causes. The action of the soul will be in part guided by this environment, while in other matters it will be sovereign, leading the way where it will. The nobler soul will have the greater power; the poorer soul the lesser.—

"Given all the causes, all things must happen necessarily.—But when our Soul holds to its Reason-Principle, to the guide, pure and detached and native to itself, only then can we speak of personal operation, of voluntary act. Things so done may truly be described as *our* doing, for they have no other source; they are the issue of the unmingled Soul, a Principle that is a First, a leader, a sovereign, not subject to the errors of ignorance, not to be overthrown by the tyranny of the desires which, where they can break in, drive and drag, so as to allow of no act of ours, but mere answer to stimulus."

Let us summarize and conclude.

From Homer and the ancient lyric poets the Greek world appeared to us as a very personal world: the Homeric heroes appear to us as personalities, and some of the lyric poets as well. Their poems are full of personal elements. The classical Greek poets of tragedy no doubt were highly individual characters themselves, and created such characters in their works. From the fourth century onward we found a particular interest in the psychology of moral characters, a *genre* which was practised by Aristotle and his early School.

[149] *Enn.* III 1, 8, 4-15; 9, 2-3, 9-16. Trans. MacKenna. Cp. also III 1, 4 (*Greek Phil.* 1425a), and III 2, 8-10 (*Gr. Phil.* 1430-32).

Coming to the philosophers we found the word *persona*—a translation of the Greek *prosopon*—both in the sense of "person" and of "personality" in Cicero's *De officiis*, where the two concepts are explicitly defined. Both the term and the definitions go back to the Middle-Stoic philosopher Panaetius of Rhodes, who lived in Rome shortly after the middle of the second century B.C. The Stoic metaphysics of Nature, which is behind these definitions, recalled to us the ancient Ionian philosopher Heraclitus of Ephesus. There is the beginning of one line.

We found another starting-point in Pythagoras: he taught his disciples, and all the citizens of Croton who would listen to him, to conform their lives to the ruling principles of order and harmony in the cosmos. We found here a doctrine of *philia*, practised in the Pythagorean circle, and meaning nothing but: love of one's fellow-men, based on a certain (meta-)physical theory of the universe.

A third line started with Socrates: a line of self-reflection and searching for a rational foundation of our moral principles. Plato, while continuing this line, found such a basis by assuming a transcendent and unchangeable Reality which is the object of noetic thought. Here, human personality is achieved by contemplating that transcendent world. Man's "virtue" in the full sense, including social virtue, is attained in and through that contemplation. It is that state which, centuries later, was called by Plotinus: "being spiritualized."

In Aristotle we found a certain disintegration of the personality: on the one hand, man attains to "the end for which he was made" in a scholar's life of theoretical thinking; on the other hand, we found in Aristotle an ideal of man as a moral character in the type of the *megalopsychos*. The first ideal was deliberately placed above the level of moral virtue and not considered as including it, the second was said to contain all other moral virtues and be the crown of them. As a character, the latter seemed to us of a remarkable egocentricity and haughtiness, while the former does not grow into the shape of a personality at all.

In the Stoa great emphasis was laid on the liberty of man with regard to outward things, on the rationality of his nature, and the natural kinship between man and man. In the later Stoa in particular we found an ideal of humanity in which a certain kindness and love of one's fellow-men are as strikingly expressed as in some later either Platonic or Pythagorean authors, such as Plutarch and the Neopythagorean Iamblichus.

Last of all we spoke of Plotinus. We found his doctrine, both of person and of personality, particularly rich. The liberty of the moral subject and the individuality of man's personal character were founded on the spiritual nature of the soul, which springs from and is continually dependent on the transcendent reality of Noûs. Thus, Plotinus appeared to us to have given a true *metaphysics of the personality*. The soul's ground "yonder" is not conceived of as an impersonal ground, lacking individuality. What Plotinus rejected was Aristotle's doctrine that matter is the individualizing principle. He was convinced that the personality as such must have its ground in the transcendent order. Coming "yonder," it will keep its individual character even its self-consciousness—not, evidently, the awareness of itself as it was in its earthly state, but in its present state: in Noûs.

We conclude:

The assertion that in Greek philosophy no concept of "person" or "personality" was framed, that classical Antiquity had no word for such a concept, and that it was first defined by Boëthius who was a Christian, was proved to be an error. The earliest formal definition dates from some seven centuries before Boëthius. It was a Greek definition, and the word used in Greek and Latin for "person" and "personality" must have been quite a familiar word which, in the first centuries of our era, became almost a synonym of "man." Thus, we can understand that the jurist Gaius, when collecting the whole mass of unarranged material of jurisprudence into a textbook of civil law, started by making a broad division into three main parts: law concerning the person—law concerning things—and law concerning actions (*persona—res—actiones*).[150] *Persona* is here practically synonymous with "man" or "individual man." It has hardly any moral or say "philosophical" sense: something like "bearer of rights and duties." Nowhere in Gaius is such a definition found. And if we might think that implicitly this was what Gaius meant by his first section, we shall be disappointed. For, going on reading what he says on *ius* concerning "persons," we shall find that persons may be either *sui* or *alieni iuris,* and that the former category only were those who had "rights," while the latter—though called "persons" in the general sense of the term—lacked liberty and "rights" in a sense most shocking to our modern feeling. For instance, for Gaius slaves were "persons." But this did not imply, at least until

[150] Gaius, *Institutionum commentarius* I 8.

the middle of the second century A.D., that they had any rights. And when they first obtained a certain protection by law, under the Emperor Antoninus Pius, their "rights" were still very few, very elementary, and almost negative according to our standard.[151] —What interests us here is: that apparently in Gaius' day the word *persona* was generally used simply to indicate individual man, exactly as we use the word fairly frequently in our day.

When in the fourth century theological reflection needed a word for "person" in the sense of "own, particular character," they *did* use the term *persona* in Latin, but not the Greek *prosopon*. Why? Probably because in those discussions the more metaphysical-philosophical term of *hypostasis* appeared to be more dignified and more appropriate to indicate the divine Persons of the Trinity. After all, the word "prosopon" was taken from the theatre, while *hypostasis* was a scholarly term, limited to the most abstract regions of philosophy.

As to Boëthius' definition of *persona*,[152] it is essentially a Neoplatonic concept, expressed in corresponding Latin terms. There is nothing particularly Christian in it. If it is a "metaphysical" definition, since Boëthius called man not just a rational being, but an "individual *substance*,"—he could do so because Plotinus had led the way. And actually, the metaphysical meaning and real profoundness of the definition can be only understood by those who know the background of those words. And who could know that better than those who read and studied the *Enneads?*

Surely, medieval thinkers have been very interested in the problem of individual being and of individual man. Neither Bonaventura nor Duns Scotus was satisfied by Aristotle's theory of individuation by Matter. But they were not first in saying that Matter could not be the cause of individual character, only Form could. Plotinus led the way. And even St. Thomas, though adopting Aristotle's theory of the human compound, felt the need of going his own way by attributing substantiality to the soul which functions as the "form." Once more, he could only do so by following where Plotinus had gone first.

---

[151] Gaius, Ib. I 52-53.

[152] Boëthius' definition is found in the treatise *De duabus naturis et una persona Christi*, c. 3. It runs: *Persona est naturae rationalis individua substantia*.

3

PHILOSOPHY, EDUCATION, AND THE CONTROVERSY ON ST. AUGUSTINE'S CONVERSION

by

EUGENE KEVANE

The Catholic Church always has considered the conversion of St. Augustine one of the most significant events of her life across the centuries, and has accorded it a liturgical honor second only to the conversion of St. Paul.[1] An integral part of that vast movement of persons to Christ which constituted the conversion of classical antiquity as a whole, no other personal history in that movement is so well documented. In addition to Possidius' life of St. Augustine, written by a man who lived with the Bishop of Hippo for many years, there are the many references scattered through Augustine's own works and his invaluable personal review of his writings in the *Retractationes* composed toward the end of his life. In addition to these more ordinary although copious sources, however, St. Augustine has left to posterity a conscientious history of his conversion in the *Confessions*. The universal respect for his intellectual and spiritual qualities, especially for the role of truth and truthfulness in his thought and character, has caused men through the intervening centuries simply to accept the unique self-revelation as the straight-forward historical truth on his conversion, uttered for men and before men, but to God himself. A traditional view of his conversion has resulted, based on the *Confessions*, "which can be summarized in two affirmations: in 386, St. Augustine was converted to Christianity; his life at Cassiciacum immediately afterwards was

[1] Cf. *Martyrologium Romanum* (Taurini: Marietti, 1932), p. 129: "24 Aprilis: Mediolani conversio sancti Augustini Episcopi, Confessoris et Ecclesiae Doctoris; quem beatus Ambrosius Episcopus veritatem fidei catholicae docuit, et hac die baptizavit."

that of a fervent neophyte preparing for baptism by prayer and penance."[2]

In the face of this long acceptance, however, a controversy has arisen in recent times which obscures the nature of St. Augustine's life and work. "It may come as a surprise to many admirers of Augustine," writes Professor O'Meara, "to learn that for nearly three-quarters of a century a large number of important scholars have maintained that Augustine in 386 was converted not to Christianity but rather to Neo-Platonist philosophy."[3] Nor does the dispute show any sign of abating. Writing in 1960 in his introduction to the English translation of Portalié's survey of St. Augustine's doctrine, first published at the opening of the present century, Professor Vernon J. Bourke emphasizes the continuing difficulties in which the traditional view has become involved. "Concerning the personal life of Augustine," he writes, "one of the most significant controversies had started before Father Portalié wrote and has continued to the present day. This is the dispute about the details of his conversion . . . Father Charles Boyer strongly supported the historicity of the *Confessions* and maintains the sincerity of Augustine's religious conversion. More recent works have stressed the complexity of the problem."[4]

In view of the continuing life of the matter and the importance of the problem in itself, it may be worth while to review the controversy from the beginning in order, if possible, to clarify its various causes; this done, a solution will be proposed from the distinct, although closely related, viewpoints of Christian philosophy and the idea of Catholic education.

---

[2] Charles Boyer, *Christianisme et néo-platonisme dans la formation de Saint Augustin* (Rome: Officium Libri Catholici, 1953), p. 17.

[3] John J. O'Meara, *The Young Augustine: The Growth of St. Augustine's Mind Up to His Conversion* (London: Longmans, 1954), p. 131. For a brief summary of the controversy, see *ibid.*, pp. 131-133. A comprehensive survey of the matter is contained in O'Meara's "Introduction" to his *St. Augustine: Against the Academics*, (Westminster, Maryland: The Newman Press, 1950), pp. 18-32; the controversy, he states, "has received little notice in English" (*Ibid.*, p. 18). An earlier historical sketch is contained in Sister Mary Patricia Garvey, *Saint Augustine: Christian or Neo-Platonist? From his Retreat at Cassiciacum until his Ordination at Hippo* (Milwaukee: Marquette University Press, 1939), pp. 3-38; likewise antedating recent work, especially that of Courcelle and O'Meara, is Romano Guardini, *The Conversion of Augustine* (Westminster, Maryland: The Newman Press, 1960), a translation of a German original which appeared in 1935.

[4] Vernon J. Bourke, in Portalié-Bastian, *A Guide to the Thought of Saint Augustine* (Chicago: Regnery, 1960), "Introduction," p. xxiv.

The Modern Criticism of the *Confessions*

The controversy is ordinarily dated from 1888, when Gaston Boissier in France and Adolf Harnack in Germany published apparently independent monographs which laid down the thesis that St. Augustine's earliest works, the *Dialogues of Cassiciacum,* are incompatible with the traditional acceptance of the historicity of the *Confessions.*[5]

Boissier launched the idea with enduring force into modern Augustinian scholarship that the *Dialogues of Cassiciacum,* documents written in the weeks following Augustine's resignation from the chair of rhetoric at Milan, portray a state of mind and soul in direct conflict with the account he himself gave a dozen years later when he had become the Bishop of Hippo.[6] The historicity of the *Confessions,* therefore, cannot be simply accepted in the traditional way. The *Confessions* portray the conversion in one way, he maintains, and the "philosophical dialogues" in another: "Not that the facts are different, but the general coloration has been changed."[7]

It is not that St. Augustine voluntarily altered the true picture. "Everyone agrees, on the contrary, that his sincerity is his greatest merit . . . but one must not forget that the *Confessions* were written eleven years after his baptism." Augustine fell into the common human habit of "perceiving one's past life in the light of present opinions and impressions."[8] Boissier sees rightly that St. Augustine's occupation at Cassiciacum is the crucial point. What was the activity, he asks, at *la retraite de Cassiciacum?*[9] He supervised the villa, he wrote letters—"and the rest of his time was given to study. But here we meet a surprising fact," continues Boissier. "This study is not devoted exclusively to the Sacred Scriptures, the only pursuit, it seems, which would befit a penitent. In the picture Augustine traces of his activities at Cassiciacum, there is hardly question of anything but the profane sciences, especially grammar and rhetoric.

---

[5] For a review of the few scattered tendencies to distrust the *Confessions* prior to 1888, cf. U. Mannucci, "La conversione di S. Agostino e la critica recente," in *Miscellanea Agostiniana* (Rome: Tipografia Poliglotta Vaticana, 1931), Vol. II, p. 26.

[6] Cf. Gaston Boissier, *La fin du paganisme: Étude sur les luttes dernières religieuses en occident au quatrième siècle* (Paris: Hachette, 1891), tome I, "La conversion de saint Augustin," pp. 339-379; previously published in *Revue des deux mondes,* 85 (Jan. 1, 1888), 43-69.

[7] *Ibid.,* p. 340.

[8] *Ibid.,* pp. 340-341.

[9] Cf. *ibid.,* pp. 366-379, devoted to the discussion of this topic.

We note that the classical authors are analyzed at Cassiciacum with the greatest care. On one occasion an entire book of Vergil is explained in the period before dinner, and Augustine continues thus on the following days. (cf. *C. Acad.* I, 15; *De ord.* I, 26). It truly appears that Augustine is simply continuing his professional capacity as *rhetor* for a few selected students."[10] Boissier gives his interpretation of these facts with the remark that it is difficult to understand why Augustine devotes his first liberty to the school exercises for which he professes such disgust, and goes on to discuss the *Dialogues of Cassiciacum* as purely philosophical exercises, in the Platonic and Ciceronian literary genre.

Boissier arrives in this way at two Augustines, one of the *Confessions,* the other of the *Dialogues.* "Since these two personalities differ from each other," he asks, "can we know which is the true one, the philosopher or the penitent?"[11] The continuing discussion of these apparent alternatives, conceived as a dilemma, constitutes the controversy on St. Augustine's conversion.

Adolf Harnack states his intention to "get rid of a widespread prejudice" by viewing St. Augustine's conversion as "a course of development" quite natural for those times and indeed a commonplace process "such as not a few of Augustine's contemporaries passed through."[12] This prejudice, "for the existence of which, it is true, he is himself to some degree responsible," consists in understanding the *Confessions* as the report of "a wild wastrel or a heathen, who, after a life of vice, is suddenly overcome by the truth of the Christian religion. No view can be more mistaken."[13] Augustine as a matter of fact is simply a Christian boy who undergoes the normal effect of his immersion in the secularized state of society; he wins victory over himself at last, with the aid of the authority of the Catholic Church, "because in the message of this Church he has experienced the power of breaking with the world and devoting himself to God."[14]

"In his external life," continues Harnack, "this change presents itself as a breach with his past; and it is in this view that he has himself depicted it. To him there is here nothing but a contrast

---

[10] *Ibid.,* p. 368.
[11] *Ibid.,* p. 376.
[12] Adolph Harnack, *Augustin's Confessionen* (Giessen: J. Ricker'sche Buchhandlung, 1888); English translation, *Monasticism, Its Ideals and History; and The Confessions of St. Augustine* (London: Williams and Norgate, 1913), p. 138.
[13] *Ibid.,* p. 139.
[14] *Ibid.,* p. 140.

between the past and the present. But in his inner life, in spite of his own representations, everything appears to us a quite intelligible development. It is true—and we understand the reason—that he was unable to judge himself in any other way."[15] Harnack explains that no one, recounting his passage from sin and error over to God, can possibly call the earlier portion of his path the way of truth.

"But others, both contemporary and later, may judge differently; and in this case such a judgment is made specially easy. For the man who here speaks to us is, against his will, compelled to give evidence that, even before his conversion, he strove unceasingly after truth and moral force; and, on the other hand, the numerous writings he produced immediately after his 'break with the past,' prove that the break was by no means so complete as the *Confessions*—written twelve years afterwards—would have us believe. Much of what only came to maturity in him during those twelve years, he has unconsciously transferred to the moment of his conversion. At that time he was no ecclesiastical theologian. In spite of his resolve to submit himself to the Church, he was still living wholly in philosophical problems. The great break was limited entirely to worldly occupations and to his renunciation of the flesh; the interests that had hitherto occupied his mind it did not affect. Thus it is not hard to refute Augustine out of Augustine, and to show that he has in his *Confessions* antedated many a change of thought. Yet, at bottom, he was right. His life, essentially, had but two periods . . ."[16] Harnack arrives in this way, although somewhat hesitantly, at the same two distinct and contrasting Augustines, one of the *Dialogues of Cassiciacum*, the other of the *Confessions*.

It remained for others to undertake detailed study of this basic thesis of the two scholars; the thirty years following the publication of these monographs were to see several works, mostly doctoral dissertations tracing to the inspiration of Boissier and Harnack, which represent careful scientific efforts to gather the evidence for the new view of St. Augustine's conversion. Friedrich Loofs emphasized the role of Neoplatonism, a point which will receive increasing atten-

---

[15] *Ibid.*

[16] *Ibid.*, p. 141. Harnack's hesitancy and even self-contradiction are noteworthy. "As a whole," he writes on p. 127 of the same work, "in the presence of death itself, he makes it (*The Confessions*) as a witness of the truth. It was not to be a mingling of *Dichtung* and *Wahrheit;* but he meant, plainly and without reserve, to show in the book what he had been."

tion in the development of the new interpretation.[17] In 1908 the studies of Hans Becker and W. Thimme appeared, defending the new position with much critical apparatus, and deepening the contrast with the traditional view.[18]

Becker, dedicating his work to Harnack as his Major Professor to whom he owes his *Anregung*, gathers evidence to show that the *Confessions* represent the suddenness of Augustine's conversion, while the *Dialogues of Cassiciacum* enable the modern analyst to see the truth of the matter, namely, that "Augustine is a man who matured gradually," whose conversion was "a process."[19] Becker's procedure is to develop "a sharp opposition" between the *Confessions*, a construct designed to contrast "nature" and "grace," and the quite different psychology of the *Dialogues of Cassiciacum*.[20] These represent a positive attitude toward the culture of this world, in contrast with the penitential spirit of the *Confessions* and their tone of flight from the world. "Noteworthy is the fact that Augustine in the *Dialogues* holds philosophy up as the guide amid the errors and temptations of life."[21] From the *Confessions* one would expect Cassiciacum to reflect struggles like those of Luther in the cloister cell at Erfurt, but Augustine actually reports "a country idyll," where "his chief concern is to arouse enthusiasm for philosophy in the minds of two young students."[22] Becker identifies this phi-

[17] Cf. Friedrich Loofs, "Augustinus," in *Realencyclopädie für protestantische Theologie und Kirche* (Leipzig: J. C. Hinrichs'sche Buchhandlung, 1897, 3rd edition), Vol. II, pp. 257-285.

[18] Cf. Hans Becker, *Augustin: Studien zu seiner geistigen Entwicklung* (Leipzig: J. C. Hinrichs'sche Buchhandlung, 1908), and W. Thimme, *Augustins geistige Entwickelung in den ersten Jahren nach seiner "Bekehrung"* (Berlin: Trowitzsch, 1908).

[19] Hans Becker, *op. cit.*, p. 16: "allmählich herangereift," "einen Prozess." The account of the episode in the garden at Milan in the *Confessions* has given rise to the traditional view of the suddenness of the conversion; "Dem wirklichen Verlauf seiner inneren Entwicklung, wie er selbst in den Tagen seines jungen Christentums gezeichnet hat, entspricht eine derartige Auffassung allerdings nicht," p. 17.

[20] *Ibid.*, p. 12: "ein scharfer Abstand." The *Confessions* are written out of "a preconceived standpoint," according to a theological thesis which Augustine has in mind as a bishop: "Das Schema von Sünde und Gnade, nach dem er die Theologie und Kirche des Abendlandes bis in unsere Tage hinein orientiert hat, legt er mit aller Schärfe auch an sein eigenes Leben," p. 8.

[21] *Ibid.*, p. 10; cf. his entire *I Teil*, "Psychologische Momente in der Entwicklung Augustins," pp. 9-62.

[22] *Ibid.*, p. 13 and p. 15; "Immer und immer wieder weisst er auf die Philosophie hin als auf das Mittel, sich im Leben zurechtzufinden," p. 15. It is a peaceful, orderly and even a happy life, where Augustine takes the leading role in philosophical conversations; there is no sign of a penitential struggle, nor of a contrast with his earlier life. Cf. p. 14.

losophy: "In his first five writings, the *Weltanschauung* of Augustine is still completely conditioned by the Neoplatonic philosophy . . . Only three years later, in the *De moribus ecclesiae*, does the fixed faith of the Catholic Church appear for the first time."[23] "When Augustine went to Cassiciacum, therefore, his development toward Christianity was by no means accomplished . . . only in 387 or thereabouts can one say that he has found in Christianity that for which he had sought through his many years of search for truth."[24] "Augustine's development," Becker concludes, "followed a completely different path than he himself presents in his *Confessions*, and which has since become traditional. This is the result of the more recent research. . . ."[25]

In France, L. Gourdon had published a doctoral study eight years before the appearance of the works of Becker and Thimme, along similar lines, but with even more drastic conclusions. In the *Confessions* and the *Dialogues*, he writes, "we are in the presence of two conversions and two different men."[26] These works are in "flagrant contradiction" with each other.[27] "The conversion of St. Augustine, intimately linked with the general development of his thought and with his entire spiritual history, found its effective termination in the years just before 400 A.D. Although he himself tells us in the *Confessions* that his conversion was fully accomplished at one stroke in 386, we say that it took place slowly and gradually, that it took place little by little, and was only completed in the year 400."[28] "In 386, Augustine went through a crisis which converted him, first, to a good moral life, and secondly, to the Neoplatonist philosophy. Nothing else."[29]

These works received restatement and detailed elaboration in Prosper Alfaric's massive treatise which appeared in 1918 under the title, *The Intellectual Evolution of St. Augustine, Vol. I, From Manicheism to Neoplatonism*, the first of a projected three-volume study intended to be fully comprehensive and finally definitive.[30] In it he seeks to demonstrate with all the weight of critical scholar-

---

23 *Ibid.*, p. 56.
24 *Ibid.*, p. 59.
25 *Ibid.*, "Vorwort," p. iii.
26 Louis Gourdon, *Essai sur la conversion de St. Augustin: Thèse présentée à la faculté de Théologie Protestante de Paris* (Cahors: A. Coueslant, 1900), p. 46.
27 *Ibid.*, p. 51.
28 *Ibid.*, p. 87.
29 *Ibid.*, p. 45.
30 Cf. Prosper Alfaric, *L'Evolution intellectuelle de saint Augustin*. Vol. I, *Du manichéisme au néoplatonisme* (Paris: Emile Nourry, 1918).

ship the fact that the *Confessions* are historically unreliable, that Augustine was a Neoplatonist at Cassiciacum, and that the *Dialogues of Cassiciacum* are nothing else than the purely philosophical exercises of a disciple of Plotinus and Porphyry. The dissertation was conducted under the supervision of Salomon Reinach, L. Lévy-Bruhl, and C. Guignebert, names of a stature in critical scholarship on classical antiquity at the turn of the century sufficient in themselves to highlight the fundamental nature of this dispute. The sharpness of the controversy is evident from Alfaric's summary of his position: "When Augustine received baptism, he accorded so little importance to this rite, that in the writings of this period, in which he frequently speaks of himself and of everything which interests him, he never made even the most distant allusion to his baptism. Hence he was at the time hardly Catholic. Without doubt he had accepted Christian tradition, but he considered it simply a popular adaptation of Platonic wisdom."[31]

"Augustine adopted Platonism before adhering to Christianity," Alfaric writes "and only came to the latter because he judged it, after examination, to be in conformity with the former.... And even subsequently to this, he held for some time much more strongly to the doctrine of Plotinus than to Catholic dogma."[32] "Morally as well as intellectually," Alfaric concludes, "it was Neoplatonism to which Augustine was converted, rather than the Gospel."[33] His final conclusion, already cited, follows directly from these positions. "In Augustine," Alfaric writes, "the Christian disappears behind the disciple of Plotinus. Had he died after publishing the *Soliloquies* or the treatise *On the Greatness of the Soul,* he would be considered simply a convinced Neoplatonist, more or less tinctured with Christianity."[34] Augustine's teaching does indeed modify Plotinus in adapting Neoplatonism to Christianity, according to Alfaric; "but he transforms Catholicism still more in adjusting it to the Neoplatonist philosophy, and he looks upon Catholicism as a lower form of

---

[31] *Ibid.*, "Préface," p. viii; translated by John J. O'Meara, *St. Augustine: Against the Academics, op. cit.*, p. 20.

[32] *Ibid.*, pp. 380-381.

[33] *Ibid.*, p. 399. The sweeping character of Alfaric's study is conveyed strikingly by his lengthy discussion, pp. 415-513, of St. Augustine's works published prior to his ordination in A.D. 391. Alfaric states his general conclusion in positive terms: "The doctrine which has been summarized here is seen to be essentially Neoplatonic and is inspired primarily by Plotinus," p. 515.

[34] *Ibid.*, p. 527.

wisdom, good only for weaker intelligences or those still novices in the quest."³⁵

Such, then, is this fundamental change from the traditional understanding of St. Augustine's life and works in the period during and immediately after his conversion. The scholars whose work reaches a climax in Alfaric's volume share a common approach to the *Confessions* and a common denial of the historicity of Augustine's self-revelation; at the same time, it should be noted, the basic proof adduced rests upon the *Dialogues of Cassiciacum*. The entire problem turns about the manner in which these earliest writings are to be understood.³⁶

From the beginning, other representatives of Augustinian scholarship took up the defense of the historicity of the *Confessions*, a defense which culminates in the writings of Father Charles Boyer, S.J., of the Gregorian University in Rome, works which have been crowned by the French Academy. So strongly consistent and so well documented was Boyer's defense, published in 1920, that Alfaric, apparently in view of it, did not proceed with his study: his second and third volumes have never appeared. It seems, therefore, that the proper juncture has been reached for a short survey of the chief works which prepared for Boyer's research, and for a summary of his contribution to the study of the problem.

The Defense of the *Confessions*

Friedrich Wörter, writing in 1892, seems to have been the first to take exception to the position of Boissier and Harnack, devoting a few pages of his traditional exposition of St. Augustine's development to the new theory.³⁷ He rejects what he considers an ex-

---

³⁵ *Ibid.*, p. 515.

³⁶ Cf. U. Mannucci, *op. cit.*, p. 25: The proof adduced by "la nuova critica" is the fact that St. Augustine, "dopo la presunta conversione.... scrisse dei dialogi, i famosi opuscoli di Cassiciaco.... in cui—a tacere che serba un silenzio completo sull'evento di Milano non trasparisce affatto l'uomo convertito, quindi già cristiano, ma solo il filosofo, il *Neoplatonico* in fieri.... " [his emphasis].

³⁷ Cf. Friedrich Wörter, *Die Geistesentwickelung des hl. Aurelius Augustinus bis zu seiner Taufe* (Paderborn: Ferdinand Schöningh, 1892), p. 210; for the discussion of the new view, cf. Chapter X, "Kurze Charakteristik des Lebenslaufes Augustins. Die Faktoren seiner Bekehrung," pp. 62-66. Wörter's summary of the Boissier-Harnack thesis shows his awareness of the role of philosophical presuppositions in the matter: "Augustin sei nicht . . . plözlich (durch göttliche Gnade) von der Wahrheit der Christlichen Religion ergriffen worden. Vielmehr allmählich, auf dem Wege wissenschaftlichen Strebens und Forschens habe sich seine Bekehrung nach ihrer intellektuellen Seite vollzogen . . ." p. 63.

aggerated contrasting of the *Confessions* and the *Dialogues of Cassiciacum*, in view of the explicit evidence in the latter that they are the work of a Catholic man. "Augustine was happy over his liberation from school and from the disciplines he had been teaching, rhetoric and the rest, but not because of a liberation from philosophy, with which he continued to concern himself after his conversion."[38] Wörter concedes that there are certain stages by which Augustine came to the Catholic faith, but it does not follow that his conversion was a purely natural process. "Harnack's position regarding St. Augustine depends upon viewing Christian life in general as a merely natural development."[39]

Portalié's article, "Augustin (Saint)," in the *Dictionnaire de*

[38] *Ibid.*, p. 65.
[39] *Ibid.*, p. 64. Others have perceived the same factor at work in what Mannucci calls "the recent criticism," which views St. Augustine's conversion as "un procedimento del tutto naturale": cf. his "La conversione di S. Agostino e la critica recente" in *Miscellanea Agostiniana* (Roma: Tipografia Poliglotta Vaticana, 1931), Vol. II, p. 25. Cf. L. de Mondadon, "Les premières impressions catholiques de saint Augustin," *Études*, 119 (1909), 444: "Tendance extreme à minimiser le surnaturel." More recently, in his review of Courcelle's *Recherches sur les Confessions*, in *Doctor Communis 4* (1951), 110, Boyer calls attention to the same factor in connection with Courcelle's "pénible" twenty-page effort to minimize the episode in the garden at Milan: "On doit pourtant regretter qu'il ait trop cédé à cet esprit prétendu critique qui minimise ou meme supprime ce qui pourrait suggérer une intervention surnaturelle ou seulement providentielle." How can this be done, he asks, "sans accuser Augustin d'imposture?" The controversy, in addition to the theological and philosophical presuppositions, involves the personal honor and integrity of Augustine as a man and a Catholic bishop, and by implication the honor of the Catholic clergy, as well as the inference, drawn "piu audacemente" by Alfaric, to use Mannucci's words, that Augustine found a higher and stronger motive of intellectual and moral progress in Neoplatonism than in the Christianity of Ambrose and Monica. It is for these reasons that the controversy has divided Augustinian scholars in the way pointed out by Karl Holl in his lecture before the Prussian Academy in 1922: "Diese Auffassung [Harnack's] hat sich bei den protestantischen Forschern, man darf sagen, durchgesetzt. Loofs, Scheel, Thimme Becker, Alfaric, geben sie mit wenigen Abwandlungen wieder. Ich begnüge mich mit dem Satz von Thimme: 'Dass Augustin in Cassiciacum durchaus nicht als ein gewöhnlicher christlicher Pönitent, eigentlich nicht einmal als werdender Christ, sondern als werdender Platoniker zu beurteilen ist.' . . . Dagegen verhalten sich die katholischen Forscher Bardenhewer, v. Hertling, Mausbach ebenso entschieden ablehnend, ohne dass freilich von dieser Seite her ein ernsthafter Versuch unternommen worden wäre, die eigene Auffassung tiefer zu begrunden." K. Holl, *Augustins innere Entwicklung* (Berlin: Walter de Gruyter, 1923), pp. 8-9. We shall allow Holl's omission of Boissier and Boyer to pass without comment. In the present study, the primary interest is with the work of scholars who have defended the *Confessions* by the investigation of the historical evidence which illuminates the conversion of St. Augustine as a fact of history.

théologie catholique (Paris: Letouzey, 1902), touches the essentials of the defense, supporting Wörter, but again only briefly.[40] "The time he developed in his mind a blend of Platonic philosophy and revealed doctrine. The principle which governed the evolution of ten years from 386-396," he writes, "comprise a period when Augustine became acquainted with Christian dogma. During this his thought has been misunderstood recently and deserves a clear explanation . . . . Until modern times no one had doubted that Augustine was a Christian . . . . Today, however, some critics uncover a radical opposition between the philosophical dialogues . . . and the state of soul described in the *Confessions*."[41] After summarizing the statements of Harnack, Loofs, and especially Gourdon, Portalié makes the points which form the nucleus of the defense of the *Confessions,* and which were to be fully elaborated in the future work of Boyer. "Wörter," he writes, "has anticipated and treated these assertions as they deserve. The discussion is quickly resolved by means of these solidly-established facts: (1) Augustine was baptized, as all admit, at Easter, 387. Who will believe that this was a meaningless and empty ceremony? (2) The material facts of the *Confessions* (and not only the state of his soul) would have to have been falsified with unashamed brazenness: the scene in the garden, the example of the solitaries, the reading of St. Paul, the conversion of Victorinus, the ecstasy of Augustine when reading the Psalms with Monica—all that fabricated after the deed was done! (3) Finally, Augustine composed such apologetic works as *On the Morals of the Catholic Church* in 388, when he would not even have been a Christian! The reader is free, moreover, to consult the dialogues themselves. Undoubtedly there is all the difference between the *Confessions* and the philosophical dialogues that such diverse literary types and purposes demand. The dialogues are a purely philosophical work. . . . How could works of this nature tell of the victories of grace? Only incidentally do they reveal the state of soul of the solitary, but they tell enough of it to prove that their author is the converted Augustine of the *Confessions*. The first thing to

---

[40] Cf. Portalié-Bastian, *A Guide to the Thought of Saint Augustine* (Chicago: Regnery, 1960), pp. 10-19.
[41] *Ibid.,* pp. 14-15.

consider is the ruling purpose which directs these philosophical inquiries."[42]

The Abbé Jules Martin, in his contribution to the series *Les Grandes Philosophes,* follows a different approach: he ignores the controversy completely and simply allows a comprehensive and objective exposition of St. Augustine's philosophical thought, existing as a consistent entity throughout all his writings, to clarify the fact that it is the work of a Christian mind.[43] That this is his conscious intention is indicated by his statement in an earlier article: "The inspiration of the four dialogues is as Christian as that of the *Confessions.* This is so obvious that it would seem to be superfluous to point it out."[44] Due to Boissier's views, however, Martin proceeds to cite in great detail the passages of the *Dialogues of Cassiciacum* which demonstrate their Christian authorship and hence their basic harmony with the *Confessions.*[45]

In Germany Mausbach, writing on another topic after Becker and Thimme had published, adverted to the controversy in ten pages packed with facts in defense of the *Confessions.*[46] All in all, however, the defense thirty years after the launching of the controversy was still without a comprehensive and detailed *ex professo* statement of its case comparable to the weighty works of scholarship which the criticism of the *Confessions* had produced, and which apparently was culminating with the announcement of Alfaric's three-volume study.[47] It was the place and function of Charles

[42] *Ibid.,* pp. 15-16. This "quick resolution of the discussion," however, did not take place: Thimme and Becker proceeded with their comprehensive studies from the opposed standpoint and published them, it has been noted above, in 1908. Obvious as the "solidly established facts" appeared to the defense, it seemed nevertheless to labor, from the beginning, under some factor which has prevented it from winning a decision and conclusive victory in the dispute.

[43] Cf. Jules Martin, *Saint Augustin* (Paris: Félix Alcan, 1901).

[44] Jules Martin, "Saint Augustin à Cassiciacum: veille et lendemain de sa conversion," *Annales de philosophie chrétienne,* 39 (1898-1899), 307-308.

[45] *Ibid.,* 308-316 and 410-428.

[46] Cf. Joseph Mausbach, *Die Ethik des heiligen Augustinus* (Freiburg: Herder, 1909), Vol. I, pp. 5-16; reprinted without change in the new edition, 1929. "Trotz feiner Einzelbemerkungen Thimme's halte ich gegenüber seiner Auffassung das obengezeichnete [namely, from the *Confessions*] Entwicklungsbild aufrecht," p. 8, fn. 1. Mannucci (*op. cit.,* p. 28) considers that Mausbach's dense paragraphs "contengono in realtà tutti gli elementi atti à construire una solida dimostrazione della giusta tesi."

[47] Cf. Mannucci (*op. cit.,* p. 28): "... e non so se ciò provenga pel giusto disprezzo delle stravaganze di questa critica, o per la difficoltà del problema, che presuppone un lungo studio."

Boyer, who dedicated his work to Portalié, to provide this type of scholarly investigation of the evidence concerning the historicity of the *Confessions*.[48] His work is characterized by keen theological and philosophical perception, but he intends his method of approach to be that of the positive historian concerned to respect, without distortion or suppression, the evidence of the documents. "We have arrived," he writes, "at the center of our study. Under what influence did that change of life called the conversion of St. Augustine take place? Christianity? Or Neoplatonism? This question is decisive .... The results accumulated up to this point will give us powerful assistance in the research of the truth concerning this fact of history."[49]

To summarize Boyer's exposition and to place its chief points in a logical progression, he first disposes of Harnack's point of departure, the popular impression that St. Augustine's conversion resulted from some bolt out of the supernatural world which separated his life with miraculous suddenness into black and white. "The literary and oratorical preoccupations of St. Augustine's panegyrists," he writes, "frequently have led them to represent his conversion as a sudden, total transformation of his personality .... His life would be divided into two periods without rational connection. A miracle, without previous preparation, would have created a new Augustine at one stroke. It was felt that Augustine is to be understood in this way, by virtue of the mere fact that he attributed his conversion to the action of God and his Church. But the narrative of the *Confessions* presents an entirely different picture .... It is this which Harnack has not sufficiently noted ... [and] it is this which seems to have been the origin of the idea of narrating St. Augustine's personal history differently than he himself does, and of opposing the *Dialogues of*

---

[48] Cf. Charles Boyer, *Christianisme et Néo-platonisme dans la formation de saint Augustin* (Paris: Gabriel Beauchesne, 1920). For the purposes of the present study, the new edition, revised by the author (Rome: Officium Libri Catholici, 1953), was compared with the first edition; unless otherwise noted, citations will be made from the revised edition. There is, however, no substantial change of any kind in the new edition; it simply brings the references up to date. Cf. also his summary, "La dialectique de la conversion de saint Augustin" in *Essais sur la doctrine de saint Augustin* (Paris: Gabriel Beauchesne, 1932), pp. 1-40, and his study of St. Augustine's philosophy, *L'idée de vérité dans la philosophie de saint Augustin* (Paris: Gabriel Beauchesne, 1920).

[49] Charles Boyer, *La formation* ... (1953), p. 115.

Cassiciacum to the *Confessions*."[50] It becomes basic in Boyer's work, therefore, to show that St. Augustine himself describes his conversion as a process which entailed several stages, especially the distinction between the "conversion of his mind" and the "conversion of his heart."[51] There was indeed a "process" and a "development," but not the purely natural or even vitalistic "evolution" which has been so often the presupposition of the new theory.

Boyer, in the second place, demonstrates by a careful analysis of the documents that St. Augustine returned to the Catholic faith prior to his reading of the Platonists.[52] This crucial point is frequently missed; indeed, Boyer can say that "ordinarily it has been presumed that Augustine was prepared for the act of faith by his reading of the Neoplatonists."[53] This is the lasting accomplishment of Boyer, for it removes the theory that Augustine was converted to Neoplatonism from any foundation in the facts. Boyer concedes a role to Neoplatonism in the formation of St. Augustine's mind from this point forward, but not that he was converted initially to Neoplatonism as such.[54]

As an outgrowth of this demonstration Boyer in the third place gathers much valuable material on St. Augustine's own thought, how it is different from that of Plotinus, and in what way it depends on

[50] *Ibid.*, pp. 123-124. Cf. p. 127: "L'auteur [des *Confessions*] présente son histoire, non pas d'un point de vue rationaliste, certes, mais comme un développement rationnel. S'il entend bien que la suite de ses événements n'avait rien de nécessaire, et qu'elle a été créée par sa propre liberté et par l'action divine, il la croit néanmoins ordonnée et intelligible, et c'est pourquoi il estime, en la racontant, glorifier Dieu."

[51] *Ibid.*, chap. III, "La conversion de s. Augustin," pp. 115-134, *passim;* for an *ex professo* discussion of these stages, cf. "La dialectique de la conversion de saint Augustin," in *Essais . . . (op. cit.),* pp. 1-40. "Le retour d'Augustin à la foi ne constitue que l'une des étapes de ce que l'on appelle sa conversion . . . Bien avant de se donner pleinement à Dieu, à cette heure de grace qu'il vécut dans son jardin de Milan, le brillant rhéteur était revenu à la foi de son enfance. Avant la conversion du coeur avait eu lieu la conversion de l'esprit," pp. 3-4. It should be noted that Wörter, *op. cit.*, p. 65, had pointed out that there were stages in Augustine's return to the faith, and that Jules Martin distinguishes the formation of his "sens chrétienne et intelligence chrétienne," his "conviction chrétienne totalement formée," and the later "décision de vivre en parfait religieux" which took place in the garden. Cf. his *Saint Augustin* (Paris: Felix Alcan, 1901), p. 16.

[52] Cf. Boyer, *La formation . . .* (1953), pp. 47-74, for the *ex professo* demonstration of this point.

[53] Charles Boyer, *Essais . . .* (1932), p. 4.

[54] Cf. Boyer, *La formation* (1953), pp. 172-173, "Role considerable du néoplatonisme dans la formation de saint Augustin," but "Sa subordination au christianisme."

the Neoplatonist teacher. He does not, however, come to a decisive position regarding the nature of St. Augustine's philosophy—whether it is "Christian Neoplatonism," or "Christian philosophy."

Finally, Boyer discusses the kind of life that Augustine led at Cassiciacum in the weeks following his conversion, and the nature of the *Dialogues of Cassiciacum* which he composed during this time.[55] Solid evidence is presented from these philosophical works themselves that they exhibit the thought of a Catholic mind and reflect the life of a Catholic man. In this, Boyer amplifies the work of his predecessors. The opposed theory has been disposed to minimize or even to overlook this evidence; but when it is considered objectively, the supposed contrast between the *Dialogues of Cassiciacum* and the *Confessions* proves to be an artificial modern construct.[56] "The opposition," Boyer concludes, "which has been pretended between Augustine's Neoplatonism and his Christianity never was apparent to himself. In his mind, the elements of his philosophy existed with the articles of faith in an indivisible and ordered unity which took its form from the principle of authority."[57]

The defense of the historicity of the *Confessions,* conducted along these four lines, seemed to win an overwhelming victory; not only did Alfaric fail to publish his remaining volumes, but non-Catholic scholars, such as Nörregaard[58] and Holl,[59] subscribed in their works to the basic positions established by Boyer. Pierre de Labriolle, five years after Boyer's work appeared, states that "a reaction is begin-

---

[55] *Ibid.,* Chap. IV, "Cassiciacum," pp. 135-167.

[56] Becker *(op. cit.,* pp. 10-11) admits eight texts of the *Dialogues* which bear witness to their harmony with the *Confessions,* but judges that they are too few. "Mais saint Augustin n'eut-il révélé qu'une seul fois," asks Boyer, "dans les *Dialogues,* la réalité de son christianisme, ne devrait-on pas l'en croire? *La formation* . . . (1953), p. 150.

[57] Boyer, *La formation* . . . (1953), pp. 193-194.

[58] Cf. D. Jens Nörregaard, *Augustins Bekehrung* (Tübingen: Verlag von J. C. B. Mohr, 1923). This work, which was first conceived in Harnack's seminar at Berlin in 1911, ended as a refutation of Alfaric independent of Boyer and arriving at substantially the same conclusion: "Der Neuplatonismus war in Wirklichkeit nur eine ganz kurze Zeit das Primäre für Augustin, in dem er vor der Bekanntschaft mit ihm in einer solch ständigem Berührung mit christlichen Gedanken gewesen war . . . und schon so stark zum Christentum hineingezogen worden war, dass die neue Philosophie für ihn ein Mittel wurde, sich das Christentum aneignen zu können," p. 242.

[59] Cf. Karl Holl, *op. cit.*

ning to set in, favorable to the historicity of the *Confessions*."⁶⁰ Father Boyer himself was conscious of his success. "The historical validity of the *Confessions* of St. Augustine," he writes in 1932, "while disputed in these recent times with more ardor and assurance than even that of the poems of Homer, has emerged from the controversy more strongly confirmed and more clearly manifest than ever."⁶¹ It seemed this time that the discussion was indeed resolved, as Portalié had put it thirty years before, by means of the solidly established facts.

Such, however, was once more not to be the case. "More recent works," to cite Professor Bourke again, "have stressed the complexity of the problem," and he refers to the studies of P. Courcelle and J. J. O'Meara.⁶² Father Boyer himself has noted the new turn in the matter. "M. Pierre Courcelle," he writes in his review, "has taken up once more the examination of the historical value of the *Confessions* of St. Augustine. This discussion, which was quite lively thirty years ago, seemed to have concluded in favor of the incomparable autobiography. Very recently, however, the doubts have begun to be affirmed anew...."⁶³ As a matter of fact, the controversy has returned vigorously to life, and indeed one must say that increasing concession is being made by Catholic scholars to the view which Boyer thought to have refuted, the view that St. Augustine

---

⁶⁰ Pierre de Labriolle (Trans.) *Saint Augustin: Confessions* (Paris: Société d'Edition "Les Belles Lettres," 1925), "Introduction," p. xxii: "It is imprudent," he adds, "to substitute for St. Augustine's testimony *des conjectures infiniment plus incertaines.*"

⁶¹ Charles Boyer, *Essais* . . . (1932), p. 1.

⁶² Vernon J. Bourke, in Portalié-Bastian, *op. cit.*, "Introduction," p. xxiv.

⁶³ Charles Boyer, review of Courcelle's *Recherches*, in *Doctor Communis*, 4 (1951), 109. The new delicacy of the question is reflected in Father Boyer's carefully-worded "Préface de la nouvelle édition" of *La formation* . . . (1953): ". . . il nous semblait . . . très opportun de maintenir à l'usage des hommes d'études une interprétation des *Confessions* qui a pour elle l'autorité des textes et l'appui d'une longue tradition . . . Là ou les innovations nous semblaient contraires à la vérité, nous l'avons dit sans détour, comme sans passion. Notre désir de ne mécontenter personne ne pouvait nous enlever le souci de conserver entière à nos contemporains la lumière qui rayonne de la formation d'Augustin, telle qu'il l'a lui-meme décrite sous le regard de Dieu." As noted already, the fact is that Father Boyer's new edition is actually not new; it is a verbatim reprint of his original work, with the addition of some footnote references to the more recent literature. The only significant addition to the text is his "Examen d'un position récente," pp. 107-113, a sharply critical analysis of Courcelle's failure to remain faithful to the documents. "Chose étrange, plus d'une fois, M. Courcelle, si attentif à des détails minimes, ne voit pas les faits principaux; absorbé par l'étude d'un grain de sable, la montagne lui échappe," p. 112. In

was converted initially to Neoplatonism, and that the *Dialogues of Cassiciacum* do indeed reflect a largely philosophical state of soul, and therefore tend to refute the other Augustine of the *Confessions*.[64]

In his detailed study of St. Augustine's self-revelation Courcelle, in fact, has attempted to find an entirely new approach.[65] "The purpose of this study," he states, "is not to advance a solution to the controversy now half a century old, but to take the problem out of the beaten path."[66] This is to distinguish the theological from the biographical components, as he terms them, then to set literary history to work upon the resulting text. What the success has been in Boyer's view, is evident from his comments already cited. One thing, however, is clear: the defense of the historicity of the *Confessions* seems to labor anew under some hidden factor which has prevented it from winning a decisive and conclusive victory in this dispute.

What might this factor be? "The first thing to consider," Portalié wrote, long ago, "is the ruling purpose which directs these philosophical inquiries," the *Dialogues of Cassiciacum*.[67] The powerful resurrection of the opposed theory, but now in works far removed from the Harnack-Becker-Alfaric group of earlier years, can be appreciated best, perhaps, by studying its apparent effect upon the

---

his review in *Doctor Communis*, loc. cit., p. 111, Boyer is quite specific: it is his careful demonstration that St. Augustine returned to the Catholic faith *before* he read the Neoplatonist books which is being overlooked. "M. Courcelle n'admet pas qu'Augustin soit revenu à la foi chrétienne avant de lire Plotin. Mais pourquoi ne discute-t-il pas les textes ou s. Augustin l'affirme?" Boyer mentions Conf. VI, 5 (7); VII, 5 (1); VII (11); one should add *La formation* . . . (1953), pp. 47-74, the *ex professo* demonstration.

[64] Cf., for example, Karl Adam, *Saint Augustine: The Odyssey of His Soul* (New York: Macmillan, 1932), for an early instance of the spirit of concession on this point, apparently motivated by the desire to have Augustine appear in marked contrast to St. Thomas. Cf. pp. 7-8. Boyer's demonstration that Augustine returned to the faith prior to his reading of the Platonist books is missed entirely. Cf. pp. 16-18. ". . . He was redeemed by a second great experience, the reading of Neoplatonist writings. . . . That was the knowledge which freed him and banished all doubt," p. 18. "But he saw Catholicism at that time in a Neoplatonic light. Or rather, he then identified Christianity in essentials with Neoplatonism . . .," p. 21. *Conf.* VII, 17 represents a "Neoplatonist ecstatic contemplation," p. 22. It is all as if Boyer's works, and those of his forerunners in this defense, had never been written.

[65] Cf. Pierre Courcelle, *Recherches sur les Confessions de saint Augustin* (Paris: E. de Boccard, 1950).

[66] *Ibid.*, p. 12.

[67] Portalié-Bastian, *op. cit.*, p. 16.

most recent and fundamental study of St. Augustine's conversion in the English language, that by Professor O'Meara.[68] His basic approach, in quite obvious contrast to the work of Boyer, appears in the topics of his Chapter IX, "Neo-Platonism for the Few: The Ascent of the Soul"; and Chapter X, "Neo-Platonism for the Many: The Universal Way." It was a "conversion to philosophy," in A.D. Nock's sense, to be followed later by the submission of intellect and will to the Catholic faith.[69] What, then, will be Professor O'Meara's view of Augustine's ruling purpose at Cassiciacum and in the *Dialogues?*

"During those leisurely days of the autumn and early winter of 386," he writes, "Augustine with his mother, brother, son, some cousins, Alypius, Evodius, and two young men who were entrusted to him for instruction, spent their days attending to the chores in the house and in the fields, sitting under a tree by the meadow or, when it was wet, in the baths discussing philosophy and reading Cicero and Vergil. Augustine prayed and wrote when he was not otherwise engaged."[70] Out of this activity the *Dialogues* came forth. "Other writings were projected," continues O'Meara, "for he proposed to write a series of works treating of the disciplines introductory to philosophy and some (such as *On the True Religion*) may have been begun. It would seem that for the moment, at any rate, he proposed to devote himself to philosophy, philosophical or semi-philosophical writing, and the sweet companionship of his friends—while at the same time integrating all of this to his new life as a Christian. There is no hint of any further plan."[71]

It is indeed possible that Augustine had no plan at Cassiciacum beyond this "country idyll" and some general intention to "devote himself to philosophy." The question is whether such is the actual Augustine, the real Augustine of history as known by means of the documents which are available.

---

[68] Cf. John J. O'Meara, *The Young Augustine: The Growth of St. Augustine's Mind up to his Conversion* (New York: Longmans, 1954). On the other hand, witness the recent strong affirmation of Boyer's position by M. F. Sciacca, *St. Augustin et le Néoplatonisme: la possibilité d'une philosophie chrétienne* (Louvain: Publ. Univ. de Louvain, 1956), p. 2: "A l'église il est venu *(Conf. VII, 9)* . . . *avant et indépendamment* de la lecture des livres des platoniciens" (his emphasis).

[69] *Ibid.*, p. 142; cf. pp. 131-155, *passim.*

[70] *Ibid.*, p. 192.

[71] *Ibid.*

St. Augustine's Purpose in the *Dialogues of Cassiciacum*

St. Augustine himself provides the point of departure. It is a striking passage in the dialogue on *The Happy Life* where he states that he has set up the discussion and arranged for the stenographic record of the teaching process which he is conducting, because the resulting published dialogue has some relationship to "the difficult matter I was undertaking".[72] In other words, St. Augustine is not on a leisurely retreat in the countryside, nor is he simply preparing for baptism, but in the intense and consistent manner which his character and personality lead one to expect, he is pursuing a project of some kind, and indeed not an easy one. What is this "difficult matter" which Augustine was undertaking at Cassiciacum? Will he still be pursuing it at Thagaste? To answer this question, the evidence must be sifted in detailed fashion, to determine as precisely as possible the nature of the *Dialogues of Cassiciacum*.

The Happy Life is St. Augustine's first extant work: it stands at the head of the vast body of his *opera omnia*. This significant dialogue, furthermore, is commonly acknowledged to establish his point of departure in philosophy. St. Augustine builds his philosophical thought upon an absolute foundation of personal certitude, which is furnished by human consciousness of selfhood and of existence: "At least you know you are alive."[73] In other ways as well, this treatise from those weeks at Cassiciacum provides the fundamentals of St. Augustine's philosophy, its personal concern, its preoccupation with the life and happiness of each human soul, and with the fundamental relationship of the quest and the possession of truth to this human happiness. All of this is certainly true. The fundamentals of Christian philosophy as a distinctive body and heritage of thought on the human scene can be found in this short dialogue. It seems, however, that full justice is not done to this dialogue when it is viewed as nothing else than a purely philosophical exercise. This is the crux of the matter, and must be analyzed in detail.

The very arrangements made for the dialogue reflect definite purpose, some larger intention. St. Augustine assembles his small group with complete authority, exactly as a full-fledged professional teacher at work, and arranges for the stenographer with a certain air of

---

[72] St. Augustine, *De beata vita*, 1, 6: Ludwig Schopp (Trans.), "The Happy Life," in *Writings of St. Augustine* (New York: Cima Publishing Co., 1948), I, p. 50.

[73] *De beata vita*, 2, 7; *op. cit.*, p. 51.

solemnity which rings through the words of the dialogue itself. Augustine names the members of the group, and takes pains to explain why the two younger boys, not yet finished with their training in grammar, are included in the discussion. "I believed their common sense was needed for the difficult matter I was undertaking."[74] St. Augustine is animated by some project or plan. This remains an enigma unless the fact is kept in mind that the entire proceeding reflects a teaching process. It is this educational activity which reveals the nature of his "difficult undertaking" and which permits one to understand why he arranged for the stenographic record of these discussions and their publication which launched him on his literary career.

Taking his philosophical point of departure, then, from the absolutely certain biological fact that each person is a body and has life, St. Augustine leads his youthful students to the conclusion that "life belongs only to the soul."[75]

Immediately Augustine leads the group from a discussion of the growth of the body through food to wonder whether the soul has a way of growing. "What about the soul?" I asked, "Is there no food proper to the soul? Or do you think that knowledge is its nutrition?" 'Obviously,' said our mother. 'I believe that the soul is not nourished except by the understanding and knowledge of things.' "[76]

St. Monica, an active participant in the discussion, representing, one might well believe, the voice of the Catholic Church in St. Augustine's artistry, places the entire purpose of the group and of the dialogue on *The Happy Life* squarely in the field of education. The body indeed grows; but the "growth" of the soul is not a mere biological development, not a growth in the biological sense. There is an analogous growth of the soul, to which definite attention must be paid and for which careful provision must be made: this is nothing else than the function of the field of education. This dialogue stands revealed in this way as a truly striking treatise on educational philosophy, which must be read to be appreciated. Excerpts cannot do it justice.

Augustine goes on to guide the discussion toward the understanding that there is a hunger of the soul, analogous to bodily hunger. This undernourished condition can become so serious that illnesses of the spirit betray it, just as malnutrition of the body eventually

---

[74] *Ibid.*, 1, 6; *op. cit.*, p. 50.
[75] *Ibid.*, 2, 7; *op. cit.*, p. 52.
[76] *Ibid.*, 2, 8; *op. cit.*, p. 53.

makes itself manifest in the appearance of the body. There will be ills of the spirit and of the mind which reveal the presence of educational impoverishment. When this unhappy condition of the educational establishment prevails, Augustine teaches, souls are left "hungry and famished."[77] Indeed, he leaves no possible doubt that he is discussing the field of education in one of the most fundamental aspects, in the very content of its curriculum. "Then we state correctly," he concludes for his group, "that the souls of people not scientifically trained and unfamiliar with the liberal arts are, as it were, hungry and famished."[78]

Continuing in the same chapter, Augustine leads the analysis towards an insight into qualitative excellence in educational fare. Here further understanding presents itself of the "difficult matter" upon which St. Augustine has embarked. It is a project which envisages the renovation and restitution of the heritage of *paideia,* full in the spirit of Plato and of Cicero in the *Hortensius;* there is revealed here a consistent continuation of Augustine's thinking and career, made now suddenly efficacious through his conversion to Christ in the garden at Milan. He is still engaged professionally in education, and indeed in a more fundamental way than ever before.

"The quality of this meal," Augustine continues, "I will reveal, if you are hungry."[79] This seems to be his statement of the intention which he has in mind when composing the works of this period of his life. He is concerned with the quality of the fare of the soul to be provided by a properly organized and implemented educational system. As the skilled educator knows, there must be a desire

[77] *Ibid.,* 2, 8; *op. cit.,* p. 54.
[78] *Ibid.* The relevance of St. Augustine's educational doctrine in our time is plain to see, for the two contemporary centuries just ending have witnessed the rise of philosophies which belittle the concept of the liberal arts and which have undermined their use in popular education. The consequences are visible over wide areas of contemporary social life. Hence Pope Leo XIII was careful to point out the educational necessity for the restoration of sound philosophy. When philosophy was fundamentally sound, he writes, "the liberal arts flourished as never before or since; but, neglected and almost blotted out, they lay prone since philosophy began to lean to error and join hands with folly," *Aeterni Patris* (August 4, 1879); cf. *The Great Encyclical Letters of Pope Leo XIII* (New York: Benziger, 1903), p. 55. Cardinal Newman was keenly aware of this process which leaves souls "hungry and famished"; "the result on ordinary minds," he writes, "and on the common run of students, is less satisfactory still; they leave their place of education simply dissipated and relaxed by the multiplicity of subjects, which they have never really mastered, and so shallow as not even to know their shallowness," *The Idea of a University* (New York: Longmans, 1947), p. 132.
[79] St. Augustine, *De beata vita,* 2, 9; *op. cit.,* p. 55.

for learning and some perception of its purpose before learning can take place. "Although this may be too obscure for your understanding at present," St. Augustine tells his students, "you will certainly concede, when the souls of the uneducated are filled, that there are likewise, as for body, two kinds of food for souls: one healthful and beneficial; the other unhealthful and harmful."[80] This is the point of departure of the *Dialogues of Cassiciacum;* it stands at the very beginning of the dialogue which by common consent launches the philosophical career of St. Augustine. Indeed, it can be called rightfully the birthplace of Christian philosophy as such. It is not a birth distinct and separate from the field of education, but an integral part of it, exactly as the philosophy of Plato himself was developed as a renewal and a deepening of the ideals of Greek culture.[81]

It is impossible, furthermore, to ponder upon this passage without reflecting upon St. Augustine's career in the rhetorical schools of classical antiquity. From the time that he became interested in the love of wisdom, the pursuit of philosophy, at his reading of the *Hortensius* when he was nineteen years of age, and from his change of profession from law to teaching, Augustine has been in search of wisdom within the field of education. What else can his reference to the two kinds of food for souls, one healthful and beneficial, the other unhealthful and harmful, signify, except that he has in mind a philosophy of education which is able to provide the spirit of man with a criterion for understanding and judging this difference? If these luminous and measured passages are analyzed from the viewpoint of the field of education, it seems that Augustine himself states explicitly the true nature of the *Dialogues of Cassiciacum*. It is his word, and not our interpretation, that he is far from a leisurely spiritual retreat, that he is involved in a "difficult undertaking"; it is he who specifies for us exactly what it is. It is the elaboration of an educational food and fare for souls which will be helpful and beneficial, as contrasted with that torrent of human custom bearing souls down to the ocean of immorality and unhappiness, which he

---

[80] *Ibid.,* 2, 8; *op. cit.,* p. 55.

[81] Cf. Werner Jaeger, *Paideia: The Ideals of Greek Culture* (New York: Oxford University Press, 1939-1945), esp. Vol. II, *passim;* e.g., "Reform of the Old Paideia," pp. 208-211. Jaeger speaks of "the fundamental paideutic tendency of his (Plato's) philosophy" ("Preface," p. xiv); it appears that St. Augustine, often called the "Christian Plato," built his Christian philosophy with the same "paideutic tendency." This seems to be the precise point of the *Dialogues of Cassiciacum*.

experienced so deeply in his personal life.[82] Instead of a contrast between the *Confessions* and the *Dialogues of Cassiciacum*, a strikingly complete harmony and fundamental unity and truly Augustinian consistency are readily visible, if this educational plan, involving a definite purpose and intention, is kept in mind.

It is worthwhile to pursue this fundamental point further. "The quality of this meal, I will reveal," Augustine assures his students, "if you are hungry. For in case I tried to feed you against your will and taste, my undertaking would be in vain and prayers should be said that you would be more desirous for those meals than for the ones of the body. This will be the case if your souls are healthy, for sick souls, as can be seen in a diseased body, refuse their food and spit it out."[83] A certain disposition of soul is necessary in students, if this healthful and solid and substantial education which Augustine is planning is to be found tasteful. Indeed, Augustine, Christian soul that he already is, sees that those responsible for young people must pray for them, that these intellectual and spiritual dispositions prerequisite for sound education be found in their souls. More and more clearly it emerges into view that the man at Cassiciacum is not a Neoplatonist but a Catholic thinker, devoting his thought to the Christian education of youth.

"By the expression of their features," the dialogue continues, "and by their words of approval, all said they were ready to accept and eat whatever I had prepared."[84] "Then I spoke again: 'We wish to be happy, do we not?' No sooner had I said this, then they agreed, with one voice."[85] Augustine comes in this way to the theme of this particular dialogue, after his general statement of the purpose underlying the fundamental undertaking upon which he had embarked. He did so, one can well believe, in a general way when he read the *Hortensius* at the age of nineteen, but again in a particular and unbelievably concentrated way since his conversion to Christ in

---

[82] Cf. St. Augustine, *Conf.* I, 16 (25-26; *The Confessions of St. Augustine*, translated with an introduction and notes by John K. Ryan (New York: Image Books, 1960), Chap. 16, "The Influence of Immoral Literature," pp. 58-59. This eloquent passage describes and characterizes the corrupt condition of *paideia*, the educational system of classical antiquity; St. Augustine's works contain a program which, far from discarding the heritage, saves and renews it by applying to *paideia* two healing founts, Christian philosophy and *Doctrina christiana*. Just how he did this is a worthy and practical object of study, for it touches the roots of our contemporary heritage of Western and Christian culture.

[83] St. Augustine, *De beata vita*, 2, 9; *op. cit.*, p. 55.
[84] *Ibid.*
[85] *Ibid.*, 2, 10; *op. cit.*, p. 55.

the garden at Milan. In a sense, there has been no change in his life nor any departure from the field of education, but rather a more intensive search and grasp and possession of wisdom, still in this same teaching profession.

His thesis is clear: happiness is the health of the soul and this health of the soul depends upon the fare which the soul is given. The structure arranged in human affairs to feed the souls of men is the educational establishment. There is the closest relationship between the happy life for men, therefore, and the kind of education which is planned for them in their formative years. Augustine's dialogue is designed to make this point explicit. Happiness depends on knowing what to desire, and this in turn depends upon education. How else can young people gain this indispensable knowledge which illumines what they should desire?[86] Still leaving nothing to inference on the part of his modern readers, St. Augustine explicitly brings Cicero's *Hortensius* into the discussion and holds it up to his students as the basis upon which his school, *schola nostra*, is founded. This is the nature of the school at the villa at Cassiciacum. The classical philosophical heritage of mankind is directly related to this educational fare of the soul. Indeed, St. Augustine calls the insight which the *Hortensius* represents "the very stronghold of philosophy," and congratulates his Catholic mother for her mastery of its essential point. As he explains elsewhere in the *Dialogues*, she possesses this mastery by virtue of her faith. Thus the harmony between the philosophical heritage of man and the cultural work of the Catholic Church is laid down at the very outset of this treatise which marks the birthplace of Christian philosophy.

"Behold, not the philosophers," Augustine writes, "but only people who like to argue, state that all are happy who live according to their own will. This, of course, is not true, for, to wish what is not fitting is the worst of wretchedness. But it is not so deplorable to fail of attaining what we desire as it is to wish what is not proper. For, greater evil is brought about through one's wicked will than happiness through fortune."[87] Here the flashing mind of Augustine moves rapidly from his first positions and point of departure to the very center of educational philosophy—the role of the will, namely,

---

[86] Cf. *Ibid.*, 2, 10; *op. cit.*, p. 56.
[87] *Ibid.*

and the question of value theory and value judgment.[88] It should be mentioned also that he states the educational truth in the face of the Rousseauist current of the last two hundred years, which defines educational truth and educational value in terms of personal license rather than this quest for truth and wisdom which provides the youthful soul with the principles it needs for living not according to its own will, but for willing to attain what is proper. This is the universe of Catholic educational thought leading to the Christian formation of youth and to Christian living: it is removed by a profound philosophical abyss from the current of educational thinking which derives from Rousseau to Dewey and the contemporary permissivists.

"Then Licentius spoke up: 'You must tell us what a person has to wish in order to be happy, and what kind of things he must desire.' "[89] Augustine intends this to indicate what young people naturally desire from their teachers and from the educational system. For it is the educational establishment which is called upon to provide young people with this knowledge on what a person has to wish in order to be happy, and what kind of things he must desire. We have here a basic premise of Christian humanism in education, elaborated as one thing with Christian philosophy. As the dialogue continues, Augustine formally accepts the request of the youthful Licentius, himself about nineteen years of age, that very age when Augustine, as he recalls so well, discovered the love of wisdom by reading Cicero's *Hortensius*. " 'But what preparation should a man make to gain happiness,' I asked," says St. Augustine, continuing from Licentius' question.[90] Augustine stresses constantly the concept of preparation, which is simply the process of education. This preparation of the mind for happiness includes the preparation of the mind for seeing truth, for grasping intelligible, non-material reality, for coming to a real conviction or assent that God exists and for appreciating what it is to be a human soul. This is the recurrent theme of all of the *Dialogues of Cassiciacum;* seen from the vantage point of education, they portray in a philosophical manner the work of the teaching profession. It is the work of the teacher to organize the "order of learning" in such a way that the

---

[88] The treatises *De moribus ecclesiae* and *De libero arbitrio*, composed at Rome later in this period of his life, fall readily and naturally into this perspective.
[89] St. Augustine, *De beata vita*, 2, 10; *op. cit.*, p. 56.
[90] *Ibid.*, 2, 11; p. 57.

souls of young people gradually are prepared precisely for this happiness, which is itself nothing else than the possession of God, the truth on divine things and on the greatness of the soul.

In paragraphs which must be read in their context to be appreciated, Augustine leads his small group of youthful students logically past the position of the secularists and materialists of his time directly to God himself. The God whom Augustine teaches in this educational program is the God "eternal and ever-remaining."[91] "This, of course, is so certain," replied Licentius, "that the question is unnecessary." With pious devotion all the others agreed. " 'Therefore,' I concluded," St. Augustine states, " 'whoever possesses God is happy.' " St. Augustine makes it clear in this fashion that the group of students at Cassiciacum sees the reality of almighty God exactly as Augustine himself had come to see that reality through his study of the heritage of classical philosophy and through the gradual dawn of intellectual clarity regarding the spiritual nature of God in the course of his mental development at Milan. There is a fundamental and central consistency here between the chapters of the *Confessions* and these pages of the *Dialogues*.[92] This is a Catholic group and the project is one of Catholic education, involving the knowledge and the love of God, the God of Christianity. This is the happy life, the possession of God. This is the end of the quest for wisdom. This is what Augustine has found in his conversion. This is why he is at the villa, under the general supervision of St. Ambrose, preparing for baptism. At the same time, however, his active and penetrating mind is already at work, projecting a "difficult undertaking," a continuation of his profession of teaching in a new program which will lead youthful spirits to God and the soul, and which will make the work of the educator in the fullest sense a service of God.

The very beginning of St. Augustine's literary apostolate is a philosophical exercise, it is true, but not in the genre imagined by the new "critical theory" of his conversion. The dialogue on *The*

---

[91] *Ibid.*, 2, 11; p. 58.

[92] Cf. in particular *Conf.*, Book VII; John K. Ryan, *op. cit.*, pp. 157-180. This entire book is a striking description of the manner in which St. Augustine's mind penetrated to the characteristic themes of Christian philosophy, which contrast with Neoplatonism, but which the natural soundness of Plato's philosophical tradition as a whole foreshadows and prepares. Cf. in particular Chapters 10-12 (16-18), *op. cit.*, p. 170-172 for the ascent to *ipsum esse subsistens*, to *creatio ex nihilo*, and to the *ordo providentiae:* the birth of Christian philosophy in St. Augustine's mind.

Happy Life is rather a philosophical analysis of Christian humanism in education. Philosophy is portrayed as the specifically human activity; St. Augustine presents it as a formative influence on youth, as a method of learning and teaching, and as a discipline with a content in its own right. This is the genuine humanism of the tradition of the Christian education of youth, where humanism is not mere philology, but the philosophical study of all the arts and disciplines of human culture, crowned by "the science of wisdom and virtue" itself.[93] From St. Augustine's early work in these treatises on educational philosophy this fundamental concept of Christian humanism in education will enter into the monastery and cathedral schools to become the common intellectual and humanistic patrimony of our civilization.

In this same second chapter of *The Happy Life*, Augustine exemplifies philosophical method in teaching. Teaching done in such a way that the youthful mind actually grasps this solid and substantial health-giving fare must be accomplished according to a certain definite method. This teaching is to be a gradual process, Augustine explains, keeping to his figure of speech: "For the mind also in its feasts," he tells us, "may go to excess if it indulges too greedily in the meal—in this way it digests poorly, and the conse-

[93] *De magistro* 14 (45). Joseph M. Colleran (trans.), *St. Augustine: The Greatness of the Soul, The Teacher* (Westminster, Md.: The Newman Press, 1950), p. 185: "The science of virtue and wisdom" is included among the subjects taught. That St. Augustine held this view consistently to the end of his life as a bishop is clear from the *Liber retractationum;* cf. I, 6, *De libris disciplinarum*. Cf. *De ordine* II, Chapter 5, *passim*. For a penetrating analysis of the decline of the concept of humanism in education from the philosophical level of the Quattrocento to the merely literary and philological approach of more recent times, see Ernesto Grassi und Thure von Uexküll, *Von Ursprung und Grenzen der Geisteswissenschaften und Naturwissenschaften* (München: Leo Lehnen Verlag, 1950); the authors lament that "wir heute unter humanistische Studien nur noch philologische und literarische Untersuchungen, aber nicht mehr die Erörterung philosophischer Probleme verstehen," and they speak of our contemporary need "den Begriff 'humanistische Studien' aus den Fesseln und Einschränkungen (zu) befreien, in denen sein eigentliches Wesen vergessen oder verdeckt wurde," and "den Reichtum und die ursprüngliche Weite zuruckzugewinnen, die er im Zeitalter des Humanismus besass," (p. 9). This illuminates the precise role of philosophical content and philosophical method in the educational program exemplified in the *Dialogues of Cassiciacum*. To state the full truth of the matter, this relevance of philosophy to humanism in education is a Catholic heritage descending not from the Renaissance but from St. Augustine and the Patristic Age, and is witnessed strikingly in our own day in the recent work published under the patronage of Cardinal Pizzardo, *Filosofia e formazione ecclesiastica*, (Città del Vaticano: Tipografia Poliglotta Vaticana, 1960).

quent discomfort is no less harmful to the health of the mind than is hunger itself. Therefore, if you do not object, we will take up this question tomorrow, when we are hungry again."[94] Here, then, is another important insight into Augustine's purpose in the *Dialogues of Cassiciacum*. They exemplify sound methodology of teaching. They demonstrate how teaching ought to be done, if this philosophical approach which gives a substantial content and a health-giving character to the fare of the mind is to be achieved by the teaching profession.[95] If this fundamental principle is

[94] St. Augustine, *De beata vita* 2 (13); Ludwig Schopp, op. cit., p. 60.

[95] Both Eggersdorfer and Marrou have noticed this fact about the *Dialogues of Cassiciacum*, but St. Augustine's biographers and students of the controversy on his conversion for the most part have paid it little or no attention, perhaps because the point has not been seen in the larger context of St. Augustine's plan and program for education as the unifying theme of his life from his conversion to his ordination and indeed to the end of his life. Be that as it may, the testimony of the two scholars on the true nature of the *Dialogues* is unequivocal. "Es sind Niederschriften wirklich gehaltener Gespräche," states Eggersdorfer, "die er mit seinen Schülern geführt hat zu keinem andern Zwecke, als um sie in der bezeichneten Weise zu erziehen." Cf. *Der heilige Augustinus als Pädagoge* (Freiburg: Herdersche Verlagshandlung, 1907), p. 74. "Es scheint ihm von vornherein klar gewesen zu sein, dass der Unterricht einer gewissen Einheit und Konzentration nicht entbehren dürfe. So rückt er die philosophischen Disputationen in den Mittelpunkt und macht ihnen die Lektüre dienstbar," *(Ibid.,* p. 79). Also cf. *ibid.,* p. 81, where Eggersdorfer discusses St. Augustine's view *(Contra Academicos* I, 4) that philosophy is relevant to all levels of education, calling it his *Haupterziehungsgrundsatz,* and linking it with the quest for truth and wisdom which for each young person ought to be the substance of education. Eggersdorfer even anticipates the contemporary ado concerning critical thinking, showing that St. Augustine had in mind what is actually the only sound approach to this currently popular goal in teaching, (Cf. *ibid.,* pp. 85-87).

Marrou understands the *Dialogues of Cassiciacum* in relation to the rivalry between literary and philosophical culture visible throughout the century-long history of *paideia*. Cf. *Saint Augustin et la fin de la culture antique* (Paris: Editions E. de Boccard, 1958), p. 169 ff.; 173 ff. Cf. esp. his Chapter VI, "Reductio artium ad philosophiam: Exercitatio animi," pp. 299-327, in which Marrou demonstrates clearly that the *Dialogues of Cassiciacum* exemplify St. Augustine's method of teaching, a method which recurs, as Marrou shows (pp. 315-327), in the later *De Trinitate*. Noteworthy also is Marrou's comprehensive grasp of the relationship of this *exercitatio animi* in educational method to the entire larger Patristic concept and program of moral reform, the catharsis and *purgatio animae,* a relationship which is essential to a proper understanding of St. Augustine's educational apostolate. "Tout cela est encore exercise, gymnastique intellectuelle. Ce n'est pas de ma part une simple hypothèse. Augustin s'est expliqué de la façon la plus claire. . . . Cf. *De magistro* 8 (21) . . . ce role pédagogique, pour cet assouplissement de l'esprit," *(Ibid.,* p. 308). Marrou even sees a definite plan of composition in the *Dialogues,* reflecting what we might call Augustine's "lesson plan" in approaching the elucidation of a topic with a group of youthful students, (Cf. *Ibid.,* p. 310).

borne in mind, the nature, plan, and purpose of all four *Dialogues* become clear. In fact, in several places Augustine explains why he is using a circuitous route to a truth rather than a direct and brief one. Always it is this same intention of manifesting how the mind, granted our human condition, must move gradually and laboriously toward insight and understanding in these philosophical fundamentals which he is introducing into the content, process, and method of education.

While this symposium on *The Happy Life* is taking place, Augustine in his teaching procedure and methodology at Cassiciacum also has launched a series of discussions, with careful attention to stenographic reporting, which later will be published as the dialogues *Against the Academics*. He explicitly links the two *Dialogues,* showing that they both form part of this "difficult undertaking" which inspires the general intention in his mind.[96] Without truth, he says, there can be no happiness. The Academics bar the pathway to truth, hence they fail to attain to wisdom and therefore they lack the secret of the happy life. The total educational situation, in other words, must be based upon a sound philosophical foundation which perceives the ability of the human mind to attain truth since it was made for that purpose. Thus the central thesis of the discussions in the *Against the Academics* is directly related to this educational project and undertaking which Augustine unveils so clearly in *The Happy Life*.

Analyzed in this way from the point of view of the field of education, which to be sure is St. Augustine's own field since his decision upon a calling in life when he read the *Hortensius* as a student, it becomes apparent that his very works contain the correct answer to the question at hand. He does indeed have a further plan, beyond his need of a physical rest, beyond his interest in philosophy, indeed beyond his baptism itself, which he saw as a beginning. This further plan is a "difficult undertaking" in the field of Catholic education, a plan for qualitative excellence in education which has been maturing in his professional life and experience since he read Cicero's *Hortensius*. It is this paideutic tendency and character of his philosophical ideal which makes him in a fully legit-

---

[96] St. Augustine, *De beata vita* 2 (13); Ludwig Schopp, *op. cit.*, p. 60: " 'Do you think,' I asked, 'that the business we undertook with the Academics is completely finished?' " St. Augustine goes on to show that happiness depends upon wisdom, and wisdom is one thing with the knowledge of the truth, which in turn is the realm and function of education.

imate sense the Christian Plato; it is this, furthermore, which makes his baptism his personal fulfillment and his conversion in the garden at Milan truly the conversion of *Augustinus rhetor*—as such.[97]

Christian Philosophy and a Paideia of God

With this insight into the purpose of the philosophical dialogues, it is possible to return to the controversy of St. Augustine's conversion with the orientation needed for solving the protracted controversy and for identifying the factor which seems to have hindered the defense of the *Confessions* from winning a finally conclusive victory in the dispute. This approach is simply to follow the admonition of Father Portalié himself.[98] These considerations are offered simply as a complement to the work of Father Boyer; they are intended on the one hand to round out certain aspects of his research, and on the other hand to call renewed attention to the abiding validity of the fundamental demonstrations which he accomplished.[99]

---

[97] Seen in this perspective, the *Dialogues of Cassiciacum* are something of a misnomer, for St. Augustine wrote several other works up to his ordination which, as it frequently has been noted, bear an obviously similar stamp. Indeed, many of his works up to his ordination and even beyond to the *De doctrina christiana*, which climaxes his "difficult undertaking," form part of this plan for the renovation of the heritage of paideia, to make of it a *tuta via* for Catholic youth. The key to the understanding of his philosophical works is this paideutic character, and the fact that he was working simultaneously on school textbooks designed to animate and illuminate the liberal arts with this new clear-eyed Christian philosophy of God and the soul. Does this not define in the concrete framework of his life-long professional interest, his intense quest for wisdom in the very structure and process of education? Cf. St. Augustine's own statement at the end of his life as a bishop, *Retr.* I, 5 (6). To pursue this analysis of his further philosophical and educational works would extend the present sketch of the controversy on St. Augustine's conversion beyond its limit; I hope, however, to publish shortly a more detailed study of the life and work of the Bishop of Hippo in relation to the field of education.

[98] Cf. Portalié-Bastian, *A Guide to the Thought of St. Augustine* (Chicago: Regnery, 1960), p. 16: "The first thing to consider is the ruling purpose which directs these philosophical inquiries." In pointing out that Boyer's study of St. Augustine's life and work in the months at Cassiciacum does not penetrate to a full perspective on this plan and purpose, it should be noted that the same has been true in general of both the exponents of the "new criticism" and the defenders of the historicity of the *Confessions*, including also Portalié: "There (at Cassiciacum) he devoted himself to true philosophy. . . ." (*Ibid.*, p. 13); "The dialogues are a purely philosophical work. . . . (P. 16). It is the paideutic character of the philosophizing and the ruling purpose of elaborating a Christian paideia which is omitted from the picture (pp. 11-19).

[99] Cf., for example, the omission of Boyer's works from the "Select Bibliography" given by O'Meara, *op. cit.*, pp. 210-211, which includes in a total of thirty-one titles, thirteen in French.

The controversy on St. Augustine's conversion has turned about two points, both having to do with Cassiciacum. The first is the question of the type of activity which Augustine carried on at the villa. The second concerns the kind of philosophy which occupied his mind. When the activity is seen as a purely philosophical exercise and the philosophy is thought to be Neoplatonism as the result of a standard conversion to philosophy, then indeed it will become possible to wonder why the *Dialogues of Cassiciacum* are animated as they are with a spirit so apparently unlike the *Confessions*. Then the modern reader will indeed begin to graft onto Augustine his modern misconception of the purpose which Augustine actually had in mind in the two types of works. In this way the modern reader can come to the interpretation of the new criticism, which wants to hold that the philosophical works written at Cassiciacum represents not Christian philosophy but Neoplatonism.[100]

It is possible, however, and apparently it is also a fact supported by the relevant documents, that the *Dialogues of Cassiciacum* are philosophical in nature not because St. Augustine has not yet been fully converted to the Catholic faith, or because his state of soul is quite unlike his report in the *Confessions,* but because he has a practical reason, a ruling purpose, which involves philosophy in a very definite and specific way. When this practical purpose is seen to be educational in nature, always within his conversion to the Catholic Church and indeed within his decision to embrace a religious life, a helpful vantage point is gained for analyzing accurately the kind of philosophy which is occupying his mind. It is the educational perspective which reveals the dialogues clearly as works of Christian philosophy and not of Neoplatonism; not, however, as

[100] Or perhaps some philosophical entity, which probably has its real existence more in modern writings than in ancient minds, called Christian Neoplatonism. It is clear that the controversy on St. Augustine's conversion touches at several points the recent entirely distinct controversy on the existence and the nature of Christian philosophy. Those who hold that Christian philosophy is simply the philosophical thought held by the world in general at a given time, adopted and adapted because it seems timely to do so in the interests of communication, will not want to see Christian philosophy in St. Augustine, but rather "Christian Neoplatonism." It is beyond the scope of the present study to pursue this particular question further. Cf. Luigi Bogliolo, *Il problema della filosofia cristiana* (Brescia: Morcelliana, 1959), and Etienne Gilson in his "revue critique" of Alfaric's volume *(Revue philosophique,* 88 (1919), 503: "Le seul fait qu'Augustin ait admis dès le début la création et l'égalité des personnes divines suffirait à établir qu'il fut immédiatement catholique et non plotinien."

pure philosophy, but rather as applied philosophy, the seminal works of St. Augustine's Christian philosophy of education. It follows immediately that the concern for Vergil and the liberal studies in general, the love for philosophy, the continuing academic interests, and all the other points adduced in alleged conflict with the *Confessions* have their natural and rightful place in the life at the villa and in the *Dialogues of Cassiciacum*. There is no conflict with the *Confessions*. There are not two Augustines, nor does the later Augustine report inaccurately the man whom St. Ambrose was preparing for baptism. He was *Augustinus rhetor,* the man who always has been admired for his truthfulness, his love of truth, and his greatness of mind and soul: a greatness fully capable of having in mind so large a ruling purpose as the regeneration and renewal of the educational profession which was a part of his person and which all his life had constituted his concrete way in the quest for wisdom.

The perspective from the field of education serves also to illuminate certain points in the defense of the historicity of the *Confessions* which seem to be the factor which has hindered thus far its full and lasting victory over the recent theory of the two conversions and the two Augustines. A discussion of these points may serve to clarify the paideutic character of St. Augustine's early works, which has been advanced as a positive solution to the persistent attempt to portray a conflict between the *Confessions* and the philosophical dialogues.

The first point is the fact that the *Dialogues of Cassiciacum* have seldom been seen as emerging directly from the act of teaching and in relationship to the field of education. In the reflections which opened the controversy on St. Augustine's conversion, Boissier adverts explicitly to the academic character of the months at Cassiciacum. "It truly appears," he writes, "that Augustine is simply continuing his professional capacity as *rhetor* for a few selected students."[101] Boissier thus verges upon the solution to the controversy in the very act of launching it. But he veers away with the remark that it is difficult to understand why Augustine devotes his first liberty from the school exercises, for which he professes such disgust, to a program which seems to include those same school exercises: and he proceeds to discuss the *Dialogues of Cassiciacum* as purely philosophical exercises. Later writers, on both sides of the controversy, tend to follow Boissier in viewing the philosophical

---

[101] Boissier, *op. cit.,* p. 368; cf. the passages already cited.

dialogues largely out of relationship with this continuing professional work in the field of education; in fact, sometimes the field of education simply drops out of sight.

Like Boissier, Boyer approaches more closely to the educational relationship than his successors in the defense, but again like Boissier he ends by missing the mark. Boyer notes the fact that Augustine was continuing his teaching profession at Cassiciacum, directing the academic work of students, and even continuing the use of profane authors. "But these young people are Christians," he writes, "and their teacher is concerned with their total formation. . . . Everything which takes place now has a new value, and the studies on the lower level prepare for the highest ones. If Christianity always has counted so many teaching religious, we should not be surprised to see a convert continue as an apostolate what he had abandoned as an empty and a dangerous profession. Forming these young sons of his own friends must have appeared as a noble task to Augustine . . ., and at the same time an opportunity to oblige the benefactors who doubtless were continuing to assure his material needs."[102]

This actually contains, *materialiter,* the key to the nature of the *Dialogues of Cassiciacum* and to the full refutation of the opposed theory. Augustine was continuing his professional work in the field of education, but now as an apostolate; Cassiciacum was a genuine school, indeed a Catholic school, the actual fountainhead of the educational institution of the coming Christian culture of the Western world. But in Boyer's account education is viewed as something incidental to Augustine's life at the villa, a mere private favor to his benefactors, or perhaps an unwanted task which he was obliged still to fulfill. Speaking *formaliter,* the entire larger reality of the situation is missed, the plan, the project, the "difficult matter he was undertaking" which engrossed Augustine's mind and formed the concrete setting and purpose of his philosophizing.[103] "More even than to rhetoric," notes Boyer, "a place of honor was given in the *Dialogues* to philosophy."[104] This is true, of course, but not sufficiently strong: it merely juxtaposes rhetoric and philosophy, and seems to miss the full importance of the use of Cicero's *Hortensius* at the villa. This was no school of rhetoric, in the sense of the classical past; it was *nostra schola,* a new departure in educa-

[102] Charles Boyer, *La formation,* etc. (1953), p. 141.
[103] *De beata vita,* 1 (6), already cited.
[104] Charles Boyer, *ibid.,* pp. 141-142.

tion in which philosophy is restored to its rightful place and full function. "The solitaries of Cassiciacum," continues Boyer, "devoted long hours to philosophical conversations,"[105] on topics which renew the "profane dialogues" of Cicero.[106] This seems not to convey the real point of the *Dialogues,* as exemplifying pedagogical method on the one hand, and as illustrating on the other hand the manner in which the most fundamental themes of Christian philosophy relate to purposes in the Christian education of youth. Noting how certain characteristic words, such as philosophy, science, wisdom, and discipline, recur throughout the *Dialogues,* Boyer asks, "Is it not evident that Cassiciacum, in that year's end of 386, was nothing else than an oasis of independent philosophy?"[107] Boyer states that Boissier, Loofs, Gourdon, and Alfaric concluded in this manner, but were deceived in so doing: "There is nothing in this view but an appearance."[108]

He proceeds to prove, with points fully valid as far as they go, that the reality was not the Neo-platonist philosophical group which these authors suppose, but actually the practice of Christian perfection, one of the meanings commonly given to the term philosophy in the early Church.[109] The fact is, however, that these four words are school words, the stock-in-trade of the teaching profession, especially when imbued with the ideals of the *Hortensius.* When the defense omits the ruling purpose of the philosophical dialogues in this way, it can never really defeat the theory of the two Augus-

---

[105] *Ibid.,* p. 142.

[106] *Ibid.*

[107] *Ibid.*

[108] *Ibid.* "Mais il n'y a là qu'une apparence." This amounts to a concession of the basic position asserted by his adversaries; his attempt to circumvent it is somewhat off the mark; hence the continuation of the controversy.

[109] Cf. Boyer, *ibid.,* pp. 142-147. Boyer's third argument notes that "the subjects discussed in the *Dialogues* constitute the foundations of the religious life" (*ibid.,* p. 146). This is indeed true, for they are the basic themes of Christian philosophy. They are also, *ipso facto,* the themes in terms of which the Catholic philosophy of education conceives the ends of education. Speaking of the *De ordine,* Boyer terms its subject "Providence and evil," problems which engaged Augustine all his life, (*ibid.,* p. 147). The fact is that *De ordine* is a treatise on the order of studies necessary for preparing youthful minds to perceive the order of Providence in general. The same complete omission of the educational character, relevance, and content of the *Dialogues* characterizes the second appendix of Boyer's work, "Analyse des *Dialogues* à Cassiciacum," pp. 181-202.

tines.[110] The position of the opponents continues to seem plausible, and indeed to rest upon plain evidence needing no arduous effort to clarify. When, on the other hand, the *Dialogues* are viewed as the exemplified application of Christian philosophy to the renewal and reform of education, the defense meets the new theory upon its own ground, the historicity of the *Dialogues,* in a decisive rebuttal.

The second point is a certain lack of definiteness on this crucial question of the historicity of the *Dialogues of Cassiciacum.* From the beginning of the controversy, the theory of the two Augustines has planted its case squarely upon the historicity of the philosoph-

[110] The proponents of the new theory, it goes without saying, do not describe the paideutic character of the philosophical dialogues, for their entire position rests upon interpreting them as exercises in pure philosophy, in fact, as a Neoplatonism of some kind. The defenders of the historicity of the *Confessions* seem usually to portray the life at Cassiciacum in almost the same terms as their opponents, as noted already in the instance of Portalié. Wörter, *op. cit.,* p. 65, explicitly excludes the field of education from Cassiciacum: "Augustin freute sich, nicht die Philosophie, mit der er sich nach seiner Konversion gleichwohl beschäftigte sondern die Schule und die von ihm gelehrten Disziplinen, wie Rhetorik und dergleichen, aufgeben zu können." Thus the interpretation of "pure philosophy" is fostered; it is then but a short step to viewing Augustine's inner self as "purely philosophical," and at variance with the state of soul described in the *Confessions.* Mausbach, *op. cit.,* p. 12: "Die Gesselschaft, in der er auf dem Landsitze sich befand, bestand zum teil aus studierenden Jünglingen...." No other reference is made, and the educational purpose thus is omitted entirely. Mannucci, *op. cit.,* p. 40, likewise misses the educational character of Cassiciacum, calling it simply a time for "lo studio delle questioni filosofiche"; this "aveva nulla di innaturale nelle condizioni d'animo in cui egli si trovava; al contrario, quello studio gli era *allora* assolutamente necessario," (his emphasis). This is an excellent example of excessive concession to the opposed theory; it should be noted, furthermore, that it does not take into consideration Boyer's careful demonstration that St. Augustine was not philosophizing at Cassiciacum because of personal need. He had already won his way to the basic positions of Christian philosophy. Cf. finally H. Gros, "La valeur documentaire des Confessions," *La vie spirituelle* (1927), p. 173: "Les Dialogues représentent-ils le christianisme intégral? Ils ne visent pas à ce but . . . Augustin s'y exprime en catéchumène lettré. C'est un néophyte du christianisme, mais un néophyte remarquablement averti." In this way, the *Dialogues* are misconceived exactly as the new criticism misconceives them; it is difficult as a result to prevent them from being used, plausibly, against the historicity of the *Confessions.* The insights of Eggerdorfer and Marrou have been noted, but those scholars seem not to have applied their perception of the nature of the *Dialogues* to this controversy or to the larger question of the relationship of Augustine's entire life and work to the field of education. The same is true of F. E. Tourscher in his articles in *The Ecclesiastical Review,* 83 (1930), 113-124, and 89 (1933), 113-125.

ical dialogues.[111] This has opened the way to a tendency on the part of the defense to support the historicity of the *Confessions* by derogating from that of the *Dialogues of Cassiciacum*.

On the one hand, Boyer feels a strong compulsion to admit their historicity. "To begin with," he writes, "these writings are 'dialogues.' They belong to a literary genre which has its customs, its liberties, its manner of speaking. A fictitious component is admissible in it. Without doubt, these works of Augustine are more real than the dialogues of Plato or Cicero. They were actually held."[112] Boyer cites several references to Augustine's use of the stenographer, then makes his strongest statement in a footnote: "For our part, especially because of the manner in which the *Retractationes* report the composition of the *De beata vita* (*Retr.* I, 11, P.L. 32, 588), we think that the *Dialogues of Cassiciacum* were in fact written according to the way they were held"; and he refers to Ohlmann and van Haeringen, the classic defenders of their historicity.[113]

On the other hand, however, Boyer immediately opens the door to the conclusion, seemingly illogical in the face of his reference to Ohlmann, that the *Dialogues* are not historical because Augustine edited the stenographer's copy—which of course he did.[114] "It would seem to us," he concludes rather hesitantly, "not quite prudent to oblige oneself always to take the *Dialogues* according to the rigor of the letter. The *Confessions*, on the contrary, pertain to a

---

[111] Cf. Gourdon, *op. cit.*, pp. 50-52, in his rebuttal of Wörter, whom he accuses of taking the *Confessions* as a historical source against the *Dialogues of Cassiciacum*. ". . . C'est employer, selon nous, une fausse méthode, car c'est méconnaître le *point de vue historique*," p. 51 (his emphasis). Gourdon lists the advantages of the dialogues as documents relating to Augustine's mind in the weeks of his conversion, and asks: "Pour toutes ces raisons, les *Dialogues* n'ont-ils pas une valeur historique supérieure à celle des *Confessions?*" P. 52. Thus the new theory seems to possess the calm security of an objectively sound position, and to enjoy the feeling of superiority given by its monopoly of the sound critical method. It seems to itself to represent the scientific approach.

[112] Charles Boyer, *La formation* . . . etc., (1953), p. 24.

[113] *Ibid.*, p. 25, n. 1: ". . . nous pensons que les *Dialogues de Cassiciacum* ont été de fait écrits à mesure qu'ils étaient tenus; cf. D. Ohlmann . . . et van Haeringen. . . ." Cf. Desiderius Ohlmann, *De S. Augustini Dialogis in Cassiciaco scriptis* (Argentorati: Ex officina typografica "Der Elsässer," 1897), the solid demonstration that Augustine was reporting real discussions, not inventing a literary production, not producing a fiction. Ohlmann's work has abiding value.

[114] "Toutefois, il les retouchait . . .," Boyer, *ibid.*, citing *Contra Academicos* I 1 (4).

genre which is more incompatible with fiction."[115] In addition, Boyer continues, Augustine's purpose in the *Dialogues* is not to narrate his personal history; the passage of some time, furthermore, has its advantages, giving perspective when one recounts personal history. "One must expect," he concludes somewhat tortuously, "that the *Dialogues*, despite their authority as an intimate journal, describe St. Augustine to us with more confusion, with a lesser sense of proportion, and by that very fact, with less truth than the *Confessions*."[116] In other words, Boyer, even while citing Ohlmann, is making a large concession to the position that one must choose between the two works of Augustine on this point of historical veracity, as if one Augustine does indeed, as Harnack puts it, refute the other.

The third point is a further development of the second, the fact that some defenders of the *Confessions*, since Boyer's works, have tended to weaken still more, giving up altogether the concept of the historicity of the *Dialogues of Cassiciacum*. The pressure which the new criticism has placed upon Augustinian scholarship is readily visible, for example, in Professor O'Meara's efforts to deny this historicity. "But in the main," he writes, "although there may be much solid fact enshrined in them, the *Dialogues of Cassiciacum* are works of fiction and must be treated with appropriate reserve."[117] "It was often customary in such dialogues," Professor O'Meara continues, "to pretend that the discussions actually took place and consequently a number of conventions were employed to lend verisimilitude to the claim. Among these conventions was the supposed even verbal accuracy of the report of an actual discussion. Augustine conforms very closely to the conventional practice in all these

[115] Boyer, *ibid:* ". . . Les *Confessions* appartiennent au genre qui répugne davantage à la fiction."

[116] *Ibid.*, p. 26; "On doit s'attendre à ce que les *Dialogues*, malgré leur autorité de journal intime, nous racontent saint Augustin avec plus de confusion, avec un moindre sentiment des proportions, et par là même avec moins de vérité que les *Confessions*." This sentence seems to carry a contradiction within itself; furthermore, it seeks the solution to the challenge of the opposed theory once more by assuming some defect in St. Augustine's works. If ever there has been a writer whose works cannot be categorized according to degrees of truth, it is St. Augustine. In general, it seems a vain hope to solve this question, as some try to do, by assuming an inability in St. Augustine to think, to remember or even to write well, apart from his personal integrity. The difficulty actually may not be in St. Augustine at all, but in that of grasping the true nature of his works on our part so many centuries later.

[117] J. J. O'Meara, *The Young Augustine*, p. 193.

matters, and the historicity of the discussions between him and his circle must inevitably be suspect."[118]

Professor O'Meara, in other words, adopts the position that the *Dialogues of Cassiciacum* are simply a literary genre in the philosophical tradition of Plato and Cicero. He grants, however, that it is "not unlikely . . . that Augustine attempted to hold the discussions, and either recorded them for editing afterwards, or wrote up discussions that had just taken place."[119] "Moreover," he concedes, "the prefaces to the works give without any doubt many historical facts, and there are other detailed points favoring the historicity of certain episodes."[120]

Here again there is the failure to meet the new theory on its own ground, a failure which gives the controversy its continuing life and has made it seem at last insoluble.[121] Professor O'Meara's defense seems to writhe under the torturing impact of the opposed theory, which rests, as we saw, precisely upon the historicity of the *Dialogues,* and the apparent foundation which this historicity would give to the charge that they reflect the work of a convert to Neoplatonism, not Christianity, and that they therefore render the *Confessions* historically unreliable.

Our purpose here has been to advance the view that the *Dialogues* emerge into a different position when they are seen from the field of education. When the years from the garden in Milan through his baptism up to his ordination are seen as one consistent intellectual period, in which Augustine turns to authorship because he now has a mission in the field of education, then the literary works of this period fall into a certain definite and natural perspective and into a natural, not an artificial, grouping. It is somewhat of a misnomer, it has been noted, to call the first four published works of St. Augustine the *Dialogues of Cassiciacum*. This introduces the danger of setting them off artificially from the

---

[118] *Ibid.*

[119] *Ibid.*

[120] *Ibid.*, p. 193; cf. the same author's *St. Augustine: Against the Academics, op. cit.*, pp. 24-32. The indications of historicity, "being fictional, are worthless" (p. 25); ". . . their untrustworthiness as guaranteeing facts," (p. 29). Cf. also his "The Historicity of the Early Dialogues of Saint Augustine," *Vigiliae Christianae,* 5 (1951), 150-178.

[121] Cf., for example, H. I. Marrou, who relegates the controversy to a footnote with the remark, ". . . quand la critique s'exerce trop longtemps sur la même question elle arrive bientôt à un point mort: les arguments s'échangent et s'accumulent, sans grand profit . . ."; *Saint Augustin et la fin de la culture antique* (Paris: E. de Boccard 1958), "Introduction," p. xiii, n. 1.

other works of this period when he is a layman working toward a suitable philosophy and program of education for Christian youth, which he intends to organize and to pursue within the framework of the new institution of monasticism.

Reflecting upon St. Augustine's own numerous statements, we cannot avoid the conclusion that he is describing a factual situation in the *Dialogues of Cassiciacum;* he is not indulging a rhetorical device or a literary genre, not writing works of fiction. The *Dialogues* have an authentic ring of historical validity to them which has provided the new theory with its enduring position in this controversy. This historicity of the *Dialogues* has seemed self-evident to Tillemont, to Ohlmann, to E. K. Rand, as well as to Marrou in our own day.[122]

It is of course possible that St. Augustine invented all of this and that the *Dialogues of Cassiciacum* are works of fiction. It seems to be a possibility, however, which is not supported by the evidence. Nor is it necessary, furthermore, to interpret the *Dialogues* in this fashion in order to defend the historicity of the *Confessions* and the integrity of St. Augustine as a bishop.

On the basis of the evidence adduced so far, it seems safe to say that the descriptions of Augustine's mind and activity at Cassiciacum which omit the field of education are not in accord with the facts. Augustine himself, as we have seen, tells us that he has a definite plan in mind, which he calls his "difficult undertaking." We stand here at the crux of the entire controversy, which seems ultimately to turn upon this view of Cassiciacum which omits its contact with the field of education. This point could be studied

[122] Cf. Le Nain de Tillemont, *Mémoire pour servir à l'histoire ecclésiastique* (Paris: 1702), Vol. XIII, p. 87: "Jusqu'au moindre mot"; cf. Ohlmann, *op. cit.;* cf. Edward Kennard Rand, *Founders of the Middle Ages* (New York: Dover Publications, 1957), first edition, Harvard University Press, 1928), p. 256: ". . . he wrote certain dialogues, the record of actual conversations, taken down by a stenographer, doubtless somewhat embellished in their published form, that recall the day of Tusculum and prophesy the academies of the Renaissance, and the schools of Guarino and Vittorino." We could only add to this that they prophesy even better the *Questiones* of the twelfth century and the *Questiones Disputatae* of St. Thomas Aquinas, for they contain the vast edifice of education in Christendom, one cannot avoid the thought, almost as a *ratio seminalis.* Cf. finally H. I. Marrou, *op. cit.*, p. 309, n. 1: "L'historicité de ces dialogues parait incontestable, bien qu'il se soit trouvé des érudits pour la contester . . . Mais cf. *contra* Ohlmann . . . Augustin fait plusieurs fois allusion au sténographe qui recueillait les échangées. . . ." In general, even Marrou's great work seems somewhat to reflect the distorting pressure of the opposed theory: "Le pas est fait," he writes, "Augustin n'est plus un rhéteur, mais un penseur, un philosophe . . ." (pp. 166-167).

further in Augustine's letters to Nebridius, as well as in the content and significance of his treatises on the liberal arts and disciplines of human culture. All of these are in his mind at this time, an integral part of his "difficult undertaking." The central point about the acitivity at Cassiciacum is the fact that Augustine is conducting a school. O'Meara, we have seen, omits this more completely than either Boissier or Boyer. In connection with his activity along these lines St. Augustine is actively engaged in planning a new theory and practice of education, the reflection of the new Christian philosophy which he has found, introducing into education his philosophical insight into the spiritual reality of God, into creation from nothingness, and into the intellectual discernment of the providential order in the universe.

The view that Augustine "for the moment, at any rate," as Professor O'Meara says, intends to devote himself simply to "philosophy and philosophical writing and the sweet companionship of his friends," is not realistic.[123] Augustine is a teacher. The formation of youth is his very life: it has been so for years. He has never been a writer, nor has he ever manifested interest in philosophy purely and simply for its own sake. He has made contact with monasticism under St. Ambrose at Milan: the idea of the "service of God" has definitely entered his thought. The central question is the manner in which Augustine conceives this service of God. The evidence in the *Dialogues of Cassiciacum* appears to place this definitely in the field of education. He looks upon his service of God as a continuing contact with the field of education. He intends to develop a Christian *paideia,* realizing under the mighty power of Christ that aspiration of classical antiquity which was embodied in Plato and Cicero.

Seen from the field of education, there is a striking consistency and unity in Augustine's thought, as well as in his outward activity, from his reading of the *Hortensius* as a youth of nineteen and the forsaking of the field of law for a career in education, through his conversion at Milan and his writing of the *Dialogues of Cassiciacum,*

---

[123] Cf. J. J. O'Meara, *op. cit.,* p. 192. Note the striking similarity of Gourdon's picture of the country idyll, *op. cit.,* pp. 44-45: "Dominé par des souvenirs classiques, il profite de ses loisirs, et de la société de quelques disciples et amis, pour imiter, en leur genre de vie, quelques illustres maitres de l'antiquité .... Il ne rompt pas avec sa vie passé; il se nourrit encore de littérature, de poésie et de philosophie, Il conserve les mêmes gouts et les même besoins profanes." For Professor O'Meara, of course, Augustine is a Christian at Cassiciacum, while for Gourdon, he is not.

to the "school of perfection" at Thagaste and the entire body of his published works up to his ordination as a Catholic priest. When the *Dialogues of Cassiciacum* are understood as treatises in Christian philosophy at work in the field of education, intended to exemplify the kind of teaching, content, and method which Augustine wished "our school" to possess in contrast with "those other schools," the schools of rhetoric of imperial Rome from which he had just resigned, then the controversy on his conversion no longer has an object. Everything falls into its place exactly as Augustine states the case; nothing is wrong with any of his works, nor with his sincerity in composing them. His *Confessions* describe the actual mind which he had during his conversion and baptism. They form one piece with the educational thought and practice at Cassiciacum. The *Dialogues of Cassiciacum* are fully historical, edited, of course, for publication. They contain clear evidence that they are the work of a Christian thinker or philosopher, a Catholic man who makes unequivocal references to his faith, as Boyer successfully points out. Neoplatonism is not concerned in any intrinsic or substantial way. Seen in the light of Augustine's "difficult undertaking," an educational program organized and implemented to constitute a safe way for Christian youth, the *Dialogues of Cassiciacum* are not in contrast or opposition with the *Confessions,* but in full harmony and accord with them.[124] It seems possible that the entire controversy on the conversion of Augustine has arisen because insufficient attention has been paid to the massive contact of the life and work of St. Augustine with the field of education.

St. Augustine and the Conversion of the Classical Civilization

A great fact stands written across the face of universal history. It is the fact that the Christian era has followed upon the pagan times of antiquity. The classical civilization declined and fell. After it there developed in the Western world a new kind of social order called Christendom, or Western civilization. In such a gigantic succession in human social life, education could not but be involved, for it is the life-process, the dynamic factor, in both cultural

---

[124] Cf. *Confessions,* I, 15 (24); P.L. 32, 672: "in rebus non vanis discere . . .: et ea via tuta est in qua pueri ambularent"; John K. Ryan, *op. cit.,* p. 58: "I learned many useful words in such studies, but they could have been learned from things that were not vain. This last is the safe way in which children should walk." Elaborating this way was the educational concern of the Fathers of the Church generally. St. Augustine, by virtue of his place among the Fathers, occupies a unique position in this historic Christian education of youth.

continuity and cultural change. The decline and fall of the Roman Empire, the political and social embodiment of the classical culture, was one thing with the snuffing out of the schools of antiquity. When the light of history brightens again, in the times of Charlemagne, Alcuin, and the rest, schools are returning to life and activity everywhere, and a new Athens, as Alcuin puts it, is coming into existence in the Western world. But, wonder of wonders, these new academic institutions are not the old classical schools simply restored; they are all monastery and cathedral schools, multiplying everywhere in the West even beyond the boundaries of that other, earlier, Rome. Their guiding light, furthermore, is the new paideia of God elaborated by St. Augustine. His works are everywhere the guide to the educational practices of *doctrina christiana,* and his philosophical thinking forms the educational theory of this new academic institution which transmits the essential values of this new Western world. It is a distinct civilization, therefore, indeed a new creation, as Toynbee says, but at the same time one which is affiliated to the classical civilization of the past.[125]

There always has been among Western men some perception of St. Augustine's world-historical position and greatness, and of the importance of his conversion for universal history as an unfolding social process. It has been viewed also outside the Catholic Church as something more than another personal event taking place in the stream of world history.[126]

This is fully appreciated when his conversion is viewed from the standpoint of the field of education, for then it is seen to entail the conversion and the reform, the regeneration and the renewal, of the educational institution of the Western world and, potentially, of all mankind. The conversion of St. Augustine, the *rhetor* who em-

---

[125] Cf. Arnold J. Toynbee, *A Study of History* (London: Oxford University Press, 1935), Vol. I, pp. 51-63; cf. Vol. VII, "Universal States," pp. 1-379, *passim,* for a wide variety of instances illustrating the fact that "the Catholic Church became . . . a beneficiary of the Roman Empire. . . ." (p. 376).

[126] Wilhelm Dilthey, *Einleitung in den Geisteswissenschaften* (Leipzig: 1883) Vol. I, p. 334, terms "die Nachwirkung seiner Schriften als eine welgeschichtliche." Cf. J. Mausbach, *op. cit.,* Vol. I, p. 3: " . . . nur weltgeschichtliche Massstäbe zu seiner Würdigung ausreichen." For a good study and appreciation of this stature of Augustine in relationship to the civilization which preceded his conversion and to that which was to come after it, cf. E. R. von Kienitz, *Augustinus: Genius des Abendlandes* (Wuppertal: Abendland Verlag, 1947); e.g., p. 8: ". . . eine der universalen Gestalten der Menschheit," p. 12: "Augustin, der so machtvoll Hand anlegte bei der Grundlegung unserer abendländischen Kultur, scheint uns vor anderen berufen, Fährmann über die Würbel der Zeitenwende zum neuen Ufer eines neuen Weltentags zu sein."

bodied so fully and so magnificently the cultural and educational heritage of mankind, was perhaps the most important single factor and personal event in that process of affiliation, in Toynbee's sense, which links the heritage of the classical past with the Western and Christian civilization which has come to dominate the history of the Christian era. Seen in this fashion, the conversion of St. Augustine involves both the fundamentals of Christian philosophy and the "philosophy of history" or meaning of the Christian era.[127] The controversy on St. Augustine's conversion turns ultimately on the question whether it was good that mankind of classical antiquity turned to God in the Catholic Church, and whether it can be good for Western civilization, now becoming the world civilization, to turn away.

[127] Gaston Boissier sees St. Augustine's importance to the Christian era in the simple fact that his philosophical dialogues contributed somewhat to the survival of profane letters and secular culture. "Violà ce qui donne de l'intérêt aux *Dialogues philosophiques* . . . c'est par là que cette retraite de Cassiciacum, qui semble d'abord n'être qu'une crise passagère dans l'existence d'un homme, prend une certaine importance dans l'histoire même de l'humanité et mérite l'étude que nous venons de lui consacrer." "La conversion de s. Augustin," *Revue des deux mondes*, 85 (1888), 69. For Harnack, Augustine's personal conversion is an interesting study, one which can be solved by the theory of the two Augustines, but the social significance of his conversion, its meaning in the Christian Era, is a problem in quite another dimension. "Even if we keep in mind the state of the times," he writes, "how strange is it nevertheless that this rich and untiring spirit, striving after personal Christian piety, should only attain it by submitting to the authority of the Church! . . . The solution of this problem I shall not here attempt. . . ." *op. cit.*, pp. 168-169. A wholly different concept of the conversion of St. Augustine, in which it is seen to launch a vast philosophical and theological development in the schools of Christendom, growing homogeneously across the Christian era under the guiding light of the magisterium of the Church, and placing the work of St. Thomas Aquinas in organic relationship to St. Augustine's program of *doctrina christiana*, is implied by the foundation at Rome in 1960 of the *Institutum Patristico-Mediaevale "Johannes XXIII."* Here the meaning of the conversion of St. Augustine for the Christian era as a whole receives its full academic appreciation and elucidation in the present day. Seen in this light, the work of the Church in the Christian era is the fundamental regeneration and renewal of man and his works; St. Augustine's conversion occupies a place of unique importance in this historic mission and accomplishment.

4

ST. THOMAS AQUINAS AND THE DOCTRINE OF ESSENCE

by

GILBERT B. ARBUCKLE

In philosophy, as in every field of learning, we progress by building upon the work of those who precede us. Scholastic writers have in general been especially mindful of this principle. However, it has sometimes happened that in certain areas they have widely neglected to make use of important contributions of nonscholastic writers. Valid modern doctrines have been rejected upon the mistaken supposition that they were incompatible with the basic teachings of the scholastics and especially St. Thomas. Other modern doctrines have been rejected because they contradicted teachings that were mistakenly regarded as a fundamental and unalterable part of the system of St. Thomas. This has been the case with the doctrine of essence.

According to St. Thomas the essence is "what is expressed by the definition."[1] This is repeated in passages where he refers to a definition as the statement of the essence of a thing.[2] The declaration of the essence, or definition, he teaches, sets forth the genus and difference of a thing and constitutes the answer to the question *Quid*

---

[1] St. Thomas Aquinas, *Summa theologiae*, ed. P. Caramello (Romae: Marietti, 1952), I, q. 29, art. 2, ad 3. ". . . essentia proprie est id quod significatur per definitionem."

[2] St. Thomas Aquinas, *In metaphysicorum Aristotelis expositio*, ed. M. R. Cathala (Romae: Marietti, 1950), VII, lec. 4, par. 1537, p. 372. "Definitio enim ratio est significans quod quid est. . . ." Cf. *In Aristotelis librum de anima*, ed. A. M. Pirotta (Romae: Marietti, 1948), I, lec. 1, par. 10, p. 4. "Definitio enim notificat essentiam rei. . . ."

est? or What is the thing? Hence the essence is known also as the *quidditas* or whatness of the thing.[3]

St. Thomas's doctrine of genus and difference is closely connected with his teaching concerning the constitution of material being. A body subject to substantial change must be composed of prime matter and substantial form. Prime matter is pure potency, or the capacity to receive substantial form; it is that which is in potency to the form which is acquired or lost in substantial change. Prime matter, he teaches, is not merely the privation of form but a reality that must be recognized as the subject of the substantial mutations of bodies. Substantial form is the actuality of prime matter and is related to it as act to potency. Unlike the composite, it can be neither produced nor destroyed, just as animal, unlike this or that animal, can be neither produced nor destroyed.[4] While the distinction between matter and form is real and not merely logical, neither can exist apart from the other. For it is only through the form that the composite of matter and form receives existence.

These two constituent principles of material being, St. Thomas teaches, belong to the essence of a substance and are each signified by its definition. The genus is taken from matter, and the difference from form, and together they constitute the definition which signifies the composite of matter and form defined.[5]

However, while the definition represents the substance, the parts of the definition are not related to the parts of the substance in the same way that the whole definition is related to the whole substance. For each of the parts of a definition can be predicated of the substance defined but, since no integral part can be predicated of the whole, the parts of a substance cannot be predicated of the substance.[6] Thus we can say that man is an animal and that man is rational, but not that man is soul or that man is matter. This is

[3] St. Thomas Aquinas, *Opuscula philosophica, de ente et essentia*, ed. R. M. Spiazzi (Romae: Marietti, 1954), cap. I, par. 3, p. 5. "Et quia illud per quod res constituitur in proprio genere vel specie, est hoc quod significatur per definitionem indicandem quid est res, inde est quod nomen essentiae a philosophis in nomen quidditatis mutatur; et hoc est quod Philosophus frequenter nominat quod quid erat esse, idest hoc per quod aliquid habet esse quid."

[4] St. Thomas Aquinas, *In met.*, VII, lec. 8, par. 1458, p. 355.

[5] *Ibid.*, VII, lec. 9, par. 1463, p. 358. "Et inde est quod genus sumitur a materia, differentia a forma, species autem a forma et materia simul."

[6] *Ibid.*, VII, lec. 9, par. 1462, p. 358. "Nam partes definitionis praedicantur de definito, sicut de homine, animal et rationale; nulla autem pars integralis praedicatur de toto."

because the genus and difference do not represent what they signify in the same way that the definition represents the whole substance. The substance of man is signified by the definition of man, but the animality of the substance is not signified by the genus of man, nor is the rationality of the substance signified by the difference of man. Rather, animality is the originative source from which the genus is taken and rationality is the originative source from which the difference is taken. Thus St. Thomas writes:

> . . . the parts of a definition signify the parts of the thing, insofar as the parts of the definition are taken from the parts of the thing; not in that the parts of the definition are the parts of the thing.[7]

Thus animal is taken from one part of man, his sensitive nature, and rational is taken from another, his rational nature. Together they constitute the concept, or definition, that signifies the whole man.

The genus expresses the whole essence of the species, St. Thomas teaches, but it does so in an indeterminate way. It expresses a form without specifying the way in which the form may be realized. The determinate way in which this is realized is expressed by the difference, which is related to the genus as act to potency or as the determining to the determinable. Hence, while the genus expresses the whole essence of the species, its unity does not prevent it from comprehending species that are essentially different. Thus he writes:

> Although the genus signifies the whole essence of the species, it is not necessary that different species in the same genus have one essence. For the unity of the genus comes from its very indetermination or indifference . . .[8]

If the genus expressed something numerically one in the species that fell under it, it would be impossible for the species to be essentially different. However, since the unity of the genus comes from its indetermination, it is not actualized by the difference in the same way that matter which is numerically one is determined by form. When the difference is added to the genus the indetermination is

---

[7] *Ibid.*, VII, lec. 9, par. 1463, p. 358. "Partes definitionis significant partes rei, inquantum a partibus rei sumuntur partes definitionis; non ita quod partes definitionis sint partes rei."

[8] St. Thomas Aquinas, *De ente et essentia*, cap. 2, par. 13, p. 9. "Quamvis autem genus significet totam essentiam speciei, non tamen oportet ut diversarum specierum, quarum est idem genus, sit una essentia; quia unitas generis ex ipsa indeterminatione vel indifferentia procedit. . . ."

removed and with it the cause of the unity of the genus.⁹ Hence, considered in respect to the form by which the essence of a species is determined in nature, the genus is not one. For while the unity of the species represented by the definition is physical as well as logical, the unity of the genus is only logical.¹⁰

The characteristics set forth in the statement of genus and difference are referred to by scholastic writers as the essential notes of a thing. They are distinguished from properties by the fact that properties, although always present in the thing and found in nothing else, do not constitute the thing. They belong to, or inhere in, but are not themselves identical with, the thing. The essence is described as the ground and cause from which the properties flow. Thus rationality is said to be an essential note of man and risibility a property because rationality is the cause of, or the reason for, man's risibility.

However, it is important to understand that ontologically all essential notes are accidents. Even rationality in the definition of man, St. Thomas teaches, signifies something that is ontologically an accident. Rationality signifies the power of reason and hence a power that inheres in, or belongs to, the substance in which it is operative. Thus he writes: ". . . as the power of the soul is not its essence, it must be an accident; and it belongs to the second species of accident, that of quality."¹¹ This will be true of a power whether it be subjected in the soul, as are the intellect and will of man, or subjected in the composite, as are the sensible powers of man. All are powers of a subject to which they are related as accidents.

What then is the difference between accidents that are called essential notes and those that are not? One of the clearest statements of St. Thomas's position on this point is found in a passage of his *De veritate*. In treating of the intellect as a faculty of the soul, St. Thomas considers the objection that reason makes man essentially distinct from the brute. Since "an accident cannot be

⁹ *Ibid.*, cap. 2, par. 13, p. 9. "Unde patet quod, per additionem differentiae, remota illa indeterminatione, quae erat causa unitatis generis, remanent species per essentiam diversae."

¹⁰ St. Thomas Aquinas, *In physicorum Aristotelis expositio*, ed. P. M. Maggiolo (Romae: Marietti, 1954), VII, lec. 8, par. 947, p. 847. "Sic igitur species est unum quid a forma una in rerum natura existente: genus autem non est unum; quia secundum diversas formas in rerum natura existentes, diversae species generis praedicationem suscipiunt. Et sic genus est unum logice, sed non physice."

¹¹ St. Thomas Aquinas, *Summa theol.*, I, q. 77, art. 1, ad 5. "Et hoc modo, cum potentia animae non sit euis essentia, oportet quod sit accidens: et est in secunda specie Qualitatis."

the principle of an essential distinction,"[12] it would seem impossible for the intellect to be a faculty, and hence an accident, of the soul. In answer he writes:

> ... because essential differences are unknown to us, sometimes we define by using accidents in place of them, as these designate or make known the essence, as proper effects make known a cause; whence sensile, as it is a constitutive difference of animal, is not taken as it names a power, but as it names the essence itself of the soul, from which such a power flows; and it is the same with reason, or with that having reason.[13]

Thus St. Thomas does not deny that sensile in the definition of animal and rational in the definition of man signify properties, and hence accidents. They are properties from which other properties flow; they are ontological accidents that make known the essence as an effect makes known its cause. According to St. Thomas, the essence that they make known, sometimes called the transcendental essence, is identical with the substance of the thing.[14] This is never immediately expressed by the definition, for it is that which has whatever is set forth in the definition.

It may be observed that in the passage above St. Thomas says that "sometimes" we define by using accidents in place of essential differences. This might seem to support the position that sometimes we state the essence itself and that at other times we state only properies that proceed from the essence. However, the implication is misleading. So far as the transcendental essence, or substance, is concerned, it is impossible to state it directly either in a definition or in any other way. Whatever the characteristics we dis-

---

[12] St. Thomas Aquinas, *Quaestiones disputatae, de veritate*, ed. R. Spiazzi (Romae: Marietti, 1953), q. 10, art. 1, ob. 6. "Accidens non potest esse principium substantialis distinctionis."

[13] *Ibid.*, q. 10, art. 1, ad 6. ". . . quia substantiales rerum differentiae sunt nobis ignotae, loco earum interdum definientes accidentalibus utuntur, secundum quod ipsa designant vel notificant essentiam, ut proprii effectus notificant causam: unde sensibile, secundum quod est differentia constitutive animalis, non sumitur a sensu prout nominat potentiam, sed prout nominat ipsam animae essentiam, a qua talis potentia fluit. Et similiter est de ratione, vel de eo quod est habens mentem." Cf. *Summa theol.*, I, q. 29, art. 1, ad 3. ". . . quia substantiales differentiae non sunt nobis notae, vel etiam nominatae non sunt, oportet interdum uti differentiis accidentalibus loco substantialium . . . accidentia enim propria sunt effectus formarum substantialium, et manifestant eas." *Ibid.*, I, q. 77, art. 1, ad 7. *Ibid.*, I-II, q. 49, art. 2, ad 3. *In de anima*, I, lec. 1. *Quaestiones disputatae, de potentia*, ed. P. M. Pession (Romae: Marietti, 1953), q. 9, art. 2, ad 5.

[14] St. Thomas Aquinas, *In met.*, VII, lec. 17, par. 1648, pp. 394, 395. ". . . substantia, quae est quod quid erat esse, se habet ut principium et causa. . . ."

cover in a substance, they remain characteristics that are present in the substance. The substance itself, or transcendental essence, can be known only as the ground or support of the characteristics attributed to it. Moreover, in the passage above St. Thomas is dealing with the definitions of man and animal. These definitions are among the few where scholastic writers have reached any agreement as to our possessing an essential knowledge of a thing. Hence if we do not immediately state the essence in such cases, it would be impossible for them to maintain that we ever do.[15]

We must distinguish here another sense in which it is said that sometimes we state the essence and sometimes accidents that flow from it. There are passages in which St. Thomas speaks of our using accidental differences in place of essential differences where the essential differences, if known, really could be set forth in a definition. For example, in treating of division as it is used in obtaining definitions he writes:

> ... sometimes, in dividing ... one divides by accidental differences because he is not able to discover proper and per se differences. For sometimes necessity requires that we use, in place of per se differences, accidental differences, insofar as they are signs of certain essential differences unknown to us.[16]

Here the essential differences of which St. Thomas speaks are differences which, while ontologically accidents, are manifestations of the transcendental essence. Hence by accidental differences that are signs of essential differences, he means here accidents that are signs of other more fundamental but unknown accidents by which the substances differ. Differences that are accidental in this sense are, as it were, perceived signs of unperceived signs of the essence.

What meaning are we to give the term *essence* in interpreting the principle that the essence is the proper object of the human

[15] In other passages St. Thomas writes in terms implying that essential differences are always unknown to us. Cf. *De ente et essentia*, cap. 6. "In rebus enim sensibilibus etiam ipsae differentiae essentiales nobis ignotae sunt, unde significantur per differentias accidentales, quae ex essentialibus oriuntur, sicut causa significatur per suum effectum."

[16] St. Thomas Aquinas, *In met.*, VII, lec. 12, par. 1552, p. 374. "... quandoque aliquis dividens ... dividat per ea quae sunt secundum accidens, propter hoc quod non potest invenire proprias et per se differentias. Aliquando enim necessitas cogit ut utamur, loco per se differentiarum, differentiis per accidens, in quantum sunt signa quaedam differentiarum essentialium nobis ignotarum." Cf. *Scriptum super sententiis*, ed. M. F. Moos (Parisiis: P. Lethielleux, 1956), II, dist. 35, q. 1, art. 2, ad 3. "Sicut aliquando utimur non veris differentiis loco verarum, propter earum occultationem, ... ita etiam loco veri generis potest poni aliquid per quod genus magis innotescat."

intellect? St. Thomas's position on this point is acutely treated by Geyser, who also distinguishes between the essence as the complex of essential notes and the transcendental essence from which they flow. This distinction, he suggests, answers to that represented by the terms *essentia rei materialis* and *essentia rei spiritualis*.[17] Then, referring to the doctrine of St. Thomas, he asks:

> Can it now be validly maintained of this second kind of "essentia" that it constitutes the "obiectum proprium intellectus humani"? This must, it seems to me, be denied, for the simple reason that since we cannot at all know the in-itself of this essence, we must determine the latter rather *indirectly:* namely as that something, not in itself given to us, which constitutes the inner ground and subject of such and such accidents and relations which manifest it.[18]

This is an accurate interpretation of the doctrine of St. Thomas. According to him, the proper object of the human intellect is the essence or quiddity, which constitutes the answer to the question: What is it? This is not the transcendental essence itself, or substance, but the set of characteristics that the definer must attribute to the thing in order to identify it. The proper object of the human intellect is that quiddity, the knowledge of which enables us to distinguish an object from all that is not the object. This cannot be the supposit itself, because we can recognize a thing as distinct from all others only by perceiving that it has such and such characteristics that other beings do not have.

Since St. Thomas defines the essence as what is expressed by the definition, it will repay us in examining his doctrine to consider certain examples of progress in the development of definitions. Let us consider the development of the definition of an acid. When the researches of Sir Humphrey Davy, J. L. Gay-Lussac, and L. J. Thenard established the presence of hydrogen in muriatic acid, now known as hydrochloric acid, it was conjectured that hydrogen was one of the essential constituents of an acid. Subsequent discoveries of its presence in nitric, sulphuric, and other acids where it was not

---

[17] Joseph Geyser, *Auf dem Kampffelde der Logik* (Freiburg: Herder, 1926), p. 195.

[18] *Ibid.*, p. 195. "Lässt sich nun wohl von dieser zweiten Art der 'essentia' behaupten, sie bilden das 'obiectum propsium intellectus human'? Dies muss, scheint mir, verneint werden, und zwar aus dem einfachen Grunde, weil wir das Ansich dieser Wesenheiten überhaupt nicht kennen, wir die letzteren vielmehr indirekt bestimmen müssen: nämlich als dasjenige uns in sich selbst ungegebene Etwas, das den innern Grund und Träger der und der es kennzeichnende Akzidentien und Relationen bildet."

previously known to exist confirmed many in the opinion that hydrogen was one of the essential characteristics of acid and should be placed in its definition. When S. A. Aubemis established the fact of ionization in aqueous solution acids he proposed a new definition: an acid is a substance that ionizes in water to yield hydroxide ions. This represented a marked advance in the explanations of many of the properties that had been observed in acids. In 1923 J. N. Bronstead and P. N. Lowry independently introduced the following definition: an acid is any compound that can transfer a proton to any other compound, the compound that accepts the proton being a base. Still further investigation led to Lewis's definition of an acid as a substance with the capacity to become attached to an unshared pair of electrons during a chemical reaction.

Every step in this development of the definition of acid was the result of the discovery of something more fundamental as the ground and cause of the properties observed in the individual substances known as acids. Eventually it became clear that no one set of characteristics was the ground and cause of all the others in every way or even in one way that could be considered more important than any other. Furthermore, some definitions formed by joining the characteristics that had been discovered to be the ground and cause of others included substances never regarded as acids. Other definitions based upon equally fundamental explanations of the properties of individual acids excluded some substances that had long been considered prime examples of acid.

Today it is recognized that either one of several definitions may be adopted and each will comprehend individuals having very radical affinities. At the same time, no matter which definition we adopt, some of the individuals comprehended by our definition will have very basic affinities with substances excluded by the definition but included by another definition. Which definition we adopt depends on which set of characteristics we take as a basis of classifying individual substances. Hence in the vast literature that has been devoted to the subject of acids, and their correlatives, bases, we find that the definition of acid has become a question of advantages and disadvantages, of good system and bad. The definition of Bronstead and Lowry has the advantage of applying to non-aqueous solutions and of codifying and simplifying acid-base reactions. The Lewis definition, which embodying a highly satisfactory explanation of many of the properties of individual acids, has the disadvantage of excluding certain conventional acids and compounds like boron triflouride and zinc chloride. Today the definition of an acid is regarded a matter of nomenclature and, since 1946, most chemists have identified the substance they have in mind as a Lewis acid, an electrophilic reagent, or a cationoid reagent.

Many other successful researches in the physical sciences have shown that material substances may be so constructed that there is no one set of characteristics that stands out as the ground and cause of all others. The characteristics present in them may be related to each other as are those of a triangle. One may ask whether it is an essential note of a triangle to have three angles and a property to have three sides, or whether it is an essential note to have three sides and a property to have three angles. An essential note is distinguished from a property by its being the ground or cause from which the property flows. Yet from each of the above characteristics of the triangle the other may be deduced; from each the other flows and, in different ways, each is the ground of the other. Where the characteristics of a material substance are related like this, and where the essentiality of characteristics is based upon their being the ground and cause of others, which set we take as essential depends upon the viewpoint from which we judge of grounds and causes. For this reason different things may be found essential in an object when it is studied in different sciences. Thus Schiller writes:

> In actual use the essence is not one but many, not objective but subjective, . . . not fixed but variable, not absolute but relative. Nor is it ever the whole of the thing; it is whatever aspect of it is most important for the purpose in hand. . . .[19]

Even this extreme statement is not so radically opposed to the doctrine of St. Thomas as it first might seem. For the essence thus described as relative is not the transcendental essence that St. Thomas identifies with the substance, but the complex of accidents which proceeds from the substance. The essence to which Schiller refers consists of the complex of essential notes contained in the definition to which individuals are subordinated. According to St. Thomas these notes are always accidents. He stresses that the transcendental essence is made known by certain accidents, or properties, that flow from it. However, it does not follow from this that in every substance there must be one set of accidents that are the ground and cause of all the others in every respect or even in one

---

[19] F. C. S. Schiller, *Logic for Use* (London: G. Bell & Sons, 1929), p. 21.

major respect. Neither does it follow that one set of characteristics must stand out above all others as manifestive of the transcendental essence. If in the case of man there is such a set, it cannot be assumed that such a set must be found in all other substances.

This unfounded assumption underlies much that is written about kinds of definition and the kinds of essential knowledge corresponding to them. According to Maritain, quidditative definitions, such as "Man is a rational animal," give us a dianoetic knowledge of substances, that is, a knowledge through "accidents (properties) which manifest them, at least in their most universal notes."[20] A descriptive definition, on the other hand, such as the definition of a chemical element in terms of its color, specific gravity, or other properties, gives us only a perinoetic knowledge of substance, that is, a knowledge through signs "which are known *in place of* the natures themselves."[21] By means of the characteristics set forth in such definitions, writes Maritain, "it is impossible . . . to attain in any degree whatever the substantial nature in itself or in its formal constitutive."[22]

The properties set forth in quidditative definitions are distinguished by their "explicative fecundity," for many other properties can be deduced from them. Thus from the fact that man is rational we can deduce that he is risible, social, and free. In such definitions one characteristic is said to appear as the reason for all the others. On the other hand, the properties set forth in descriptive definitions are said to be "sterile," in the sense that we can deduce no others from them. We know that such properties belong to the substance but not why they belong to it.[23] Upon this basis is founded

[20] Jacques Maritain, *The Degrees of Knowledge*, trans. under the supervision of Gerald B. Phelan (4th ed.; London: Geoffrey Bles, 1959), p. 206.
[21] *Ibid.*, p. 206.
[22] *Ibid.*, p. 206.
[23] *Ibid.*, p. 206. Garrigou-Lagrange illustrates the difference between the two kinds of definition in this way: "We know . . . that mercury is a corporeal substance, a liquid metal, but we do not know its specific difference. . . . We have only an empirical descriptive definition, which does not succeed in rendering *intelligible* the properties of this body. We are content to say: mercury is at ordinary temperature a liquid metal, silvery in colour, which solidifies at —40 degrees, boils at 360 degrees, is very heavy; its salts are very active antiseptics, but also very toxic. We observe the facts but cannot know the *why*. . . . If it is a question of man, on the contrary, then among all the notes common to all men: rationality, liberty, morality, sociability, speech, religion, etc., one of them, rationality, appears as the *raison d'etre* of all the others." *Le sens commun, la philosophie de l'être et les formules dogmatiques.* (3me éd.; Paris: Beauchesne, 1922), pp. 104-105.

the distinction between the dianoetic and perinoetic knowledge of essences.

However, it must be pointed out that we can often state the reason for the properties set forth in descriptive definitions. It is a part of the work of the scientist to discover such reasons. The real difference between the so-called quidditative and descriptive definitions is more often that in the latter, while we know the reasons for the properties, there is not one reason for all the properties. We know the substance in the way that we do because that is the way in which it manifests itself. Moreover, it is doubtful that any property is sterile in the sense that no other property can be deduced from it. Even from such things as the color, specific gravity, and boiling point of a substance the scientist can infer a great deal. Hence the fact that from one property we are able to deduce others involves a matter of degree and cannot serve as an adequate explanation of the radical distinction that is based upon it.

This teaching concerning the dianoetic and perinoetic knowledge of essence arose out of the assumption that in every substance there must be one set of characteristics, known or unknown, that are the ground and cause of all others. When we reject this assumption the doctrine appears in a different light. Our inability to find a set of characteristics that stand out as the ground and cause of others may be due not to the limitation of our knowledge but to the structure of the thing. If characteristics flow from a substance, not through the medium of a select few, but on coordinate levels, then the properties set forth in its so-called descriptive definition cannot be called "exterior signs and masks of the veritable (ontological) properties."[24] In such cases there are no other properties. Neither can they be called "empiriological properties, substitutes for properties properly so called,"[25] since there are no other properties for which they substitute. They are themselves ontological properties in the same sense that St. Thomas calls rationality a property of man: they proceed from the substance and make it known in the manner that an effect makes known its cause. To deny the name of property to a characteristic because it is not the ground and cause from which all other characteristics of the substance flow is to create the possibility of a substance without properties.

---

[24] Jacques Maritain, *The Degrees of Knowledge*, p. 207.
[25] *Ibid.*, p. 207.

This doctrine concerning the dianoetic and perinoetic knowledge of essence as presented above is not a necessary corollary to St. Thomas's principle that a substance is made known by its properties. It is based upon an assumption concerning the relation of characteristics in a substance that cannot be deduced from any metaphysical principles. However, it must be noted that this assumption appears to be found in St. Thomas too. It is reflected in several of the passages cited above as well as in all the texts usually cited to explain the notion of perinoetic knowledge.[26] It is virtually explicit in St. Thomas's statement that "we are ignorant of the several properties of things, and we are unable to find the perfect notion in the many properties that we grasp by sense."[27] However, this assumption is no more a necessary part of St. Thomas's fundamental metaphysical doctrine concerning essence than his teaching regarding the four elements. It is not necessary to explain the unity of a substance; it pertains more to the natural sciences than to philosophy. Its retention by later writers and the effort which they have made to elaborate new metaphysical doctrines upon it has been only the source of needless conflict between science and philosophy.

St. Thomas defines a definition as the statement of the essence of a thing. If a substance may manifest itself by many properties, connected in a great number and variety of ways, what principles are to be followed in framing definitions? Let us consider some of the successful work that has been done in establishing definitions in the natural sciences. Here it often happens that characteristics once considered essential are later regarded accidental and that others, once unnoticed or considered accidental, are later judged essential. Thus, for example, it was determined that for zoological purposes the characteristics men originally joined in their definition of a fish should not be retained and that a whale should not be considered a fish. Hence the concept, or definition, signified by the word was altered and, as in the case of acid, a slightly different set of individuals was comprehended by the new definition. Rickert describes the activity in this way:

---

[26] Cf. St. Thomas Aquinas, *In met.*, VII, lec. 12, par. 1552, p. 374. *In sent.*, II, dist. 35, q. 1, art. 2, ad 3.

[27] St. Thomas Aquinas, *Summa contra gentiles* (Romae: Apud Sedem Commissionis Leoninae, 1934), I, c. 3. "Rerum sensibilium plurimas proprietates ignoramus, earumque proprietatum, quas sensu apprehendimus, rationem perfecte in pluribus invenire non possumus."

But scientific investigation must also subject to an examination the reason for directing attention to certain characteristics in an especially higher degree, and then it often sees the activity whereby characteristics are taken as essential other than those which were formerly taken and which attracted the attention of men before scientific inquiry, and thus of bringing under the general concept things other than those to which men have given the same name, for example, to exclude the whale from the fish class.[28]

The idea of any object is always the idea of something with such and such characteristics. In every object there are countless characteristics and any concept representing that object can express only a selected group of these characteristics. For the definer the question always is which characteristics these shall be. The ideas by which men first represent individual objects are usually composed of characteristics that are relatively external but for some reason, ordinarily a combination of psychological factors and practical circumstances, have attracted attention to themselves above all others.

These are the characteristics to which Rickert refers when he says that scientific inquiry must question why attention has been given to certain characteristics "in an especially higher degree." They form the concept by which the individuals signified by the definiendum are represented at the beginning of the inquiry. The transition to what is called an essential concept is made when investigation shows that there is reason for selecting a different set of characteristics to form the concept expressing what it is of which the individual shall be considered an instance. Thus the marine characteristics that constituted the first concept of a fish were found of far less significance than the characteristic of suckling the young. Hence arose the concept of fish based upon oviparosity, a concept which was a member of a more systematic set of concepts that placed trout and salmon in one class under the name of fish and the viviparous whale in another under the name of mammal.

[28] Heinrich Rickert, *Zur Lehre von der Definition* (3te Aufl.; Tübingen: J. C. B. Mohr, 1929), p. 30. "Aber die wissenschaftliche Betrachtung muss auch den Grund, der die Aufmerksamkeit auf gewisse Merkmale in besonders hohem Grade gelenkt hat, einer Prüfung unterziehen, und da ist es denn Tatsache, dass sie sich oft veranlasst sieht, andere Merkmale der Objekte für wesentlich zu halten als diejenigen, welche die Aufmerksamkeit des vorwissenschaftlichen Menschen erregt haben, also andere Dinge unter einen gemeinsamen Begriff zu bringen, als das vorwissenschaftliche Denken mit demselben Namen benannt hat, z. B. den Walfisch nicht zu den Fischen zu zählen."

What are the reasons for taking certain characteristics as essential and declaring others to be accidental? The common explanation is that the essential characteristics are those which are the ground and cause of others, or those from which others can be deduced. We have already seen that this provides no absolute guide. Different characteristics may be the cause of others in different ways and a substance may be so constituted that no set of characteristics stands out as the cause of others in any pre-eminent way. In many fields of investigation essentiality is based upon the importance, significance, permanence, or fundamental nature of characteristics, or upon the way in which their selection results in a systematic classification of many objects. Yet experience has shown that these criteria too fail to provide any absolute standard of essentiality. Pressed far enough, all show themselves to involve either a matter of degree or relation to viewpoint or both.

It is because essentiality involves a relation to a viewpoint that characteristics which are regarded as essential in a thing as it is the object of one science may be accidental to it as it is the object of another. Sometimes it is even possible to construct different systems of concepts within the same science and then the scientist is obliged to adopt arbitrarily some viewpoint in respect to which he will distinguish the essential from the unessential.[29] This was the state of affairs in the early period of botanical science when some chose the number of stamens and pistils, others the shape and parts of the corolla, and others a still different set of characteristics as the basis of plant classification. Rickert suggests that Darwin's thought owed some of its rapid success to the fact that it furnished botanists and zoologists with a viewpoint for separating the essential from the accidental.[30] All prior classifications based upon the morphological likeness of organisms gave way to a classification based upon their evolution. This relation to a viewpoint, Ricket declares, underlies the notion of the essential in all other sciences.

> A closer investigation of the construction of concepts in the special branches of the natural sciences could not make clearer the train of thought here in question. It would always be a matter of presenting the guiding viewpoint in a special field

[29] *Ibid.*, p. 39.
[30] *Ibid.*, p. 39.

of investigation and then of seeing in the concepts of the science which studies the objects, what is essential in relation to this guiding viewpoint. *Without a principle of selection the separation of the essential from the inessential loses its meaning,* and without this separation there is no science.[31]

To a mind that could grasp all things, Rickert suggests, there would be no distinction of essential and accidental. But since man cannot grasp all reality at once and cannot devise any universal method, his striving for knowledge must proceed upon this distinction.[32]

Since the formation of the definition depends upon viewpoint, there is some freedom in constructing the definition to which we subordinate a given individual. There is more than one concept expressing what it is of which the individual is an instance. Reluctance to accept this is due for the most part to the conviction that freedom in definition is incompatible with the necessary and absolute character of truth. However, truth is found in the judgment, not the concept. The definer may sometimes adopt either one of several definitions, but once he adopts a certain definition M, he is immediately committed to one set of judgments concerning M and the denial of all others. The chemist may adopt the Lewis definition of an acid or the definition of Aubemis. If he chooses the first, then one set of individuals falls under the concept of acid, and if he chooses the second, another set of individuals falls under the concept of acid, or, what is the same, is what acid signifies. Thus the definer has some choice as to the way in which he represents the truth, or as to the aspect of truth he represents, but none as to the truth which is there to be represented.

From this explanation of essence nothing can be drawn to support the teachings of nominalism. While the same individual may sometimes be subordinated to different universals, or placed in different classes, the members of the class represented by the defini-

---

[31] *Ibid.*, p. 40. "Ein näheres Eingehen auf die Begriffsbildung in den einzelnen Zweigen der Naturwissenschaft könnte den Gedankengang, auf den es hier ankommt, nicht klarer stellen. Es würde sich immer darum handeln, den leitenden Gesichtspunkt in einem besonderen Forschungsgebiet aufzuzeigen und dann zu sehen, wie in die Begriffe der betreffenden Wissenschaft das an den Objekten aufgenommen wird, was in bezug auf diesen leitenden Gesichtspunkt wesentlich ist. *Ohne ein Prinzip der Auswahl verliert die Trennung des Wesentlichen vom Unwesentlichen ihren Sinn,* und ohne diese Trennung gibt es keine Wissenschaft."

[32] *Ibid.*, p. 40. From this it does not follow that to a mind that could grasp all there would be no distinction of substance and accident.

tion never fall in that class merely because they are signified by the same name. The definition remains universal in the sense that it represents what is common to many individuals, not in the sense that it is a symbol that stands for many individuals.

The foregoing doctrine is also incompatible with the teachings of conceptualism. It is sometimes possible for the definer to select either one of different sets of characteristics in forming the definition to which individual objects shall be subordinated. Nevertheless, he can select only characteristics that are in fact present in the objects to be comprehended by the definition. Therefore, the definition is not merely a mental construct that has no objective counterpart in reality. It expresses what is present in and common to all of the objects that are comprehended by it. It represents what was present in them before the definer undertook to define them and what will continue to be present in them when he ceases to think of them.

The foregoing explanation of essence is also incompatible with the teachings of exaggerated realism. According to the extreme realists, universals subsist apart from the mind and apart from the individual objects of experience. To each individual object there corresponds one universal and no other; the individual is a participation in that universal and no other. Obviously this teaching is inconsistent with the position that the same individual can be subordinated to more than one universal.

The analysis of essence given above is consistent with the doctrine of moderate realism. According to this doctrine, universality comes from the mind but it has a real foundation in things. We have had occasion to consider cases in which there is in things the foundation for more than one universal. We have shown that the same individual may be subordinated to different concepts, or universals, each of which represents a different aspect of the individual and none of which is more authoritative or more correct than any other. This too is in harmony with moderate realism's teaching that the universal never conveys a perfect or complete knowledge of the object it represents.

There is another sense in which the term essence is used which must be considered in studying the doctrine of St. Thomas. The essence may refer to a complex of characteristics that are essential in an individual or a concept in virtue of a relation to another concept. Thus Sigwart writes: "The distinction of essential and unessential is always found when we compare an idea with a previously given concept in which it is contained, and try to find in it the realization of the concept."[33]

This element of relation may be illustrated in the field of law. The statutes describe criminal acts and stipulate their punishment. In applying the law to a particular case, the court must determine whether or not there is present in the act of the accused all that is contained in the legal concept of the crime in question. All that is contained in the concept is essential; all that is omitted is inessential, or accidental. If one is charged with murder it is essential to establish that a man was killed and that his death was caused with malice aforethought by an act of the accused. It is inessential whether the weapon was a knife or a gun or whether the act was performed by day or at night because these are characteristics not contained in the concept of murder. They are among the many characteristics that an act may or may not have and still fall under the concept of murder, or, what is the same, still be what that concept represents. The same principle will apply in determining the essence of what is signified by other terms of speech. Thus characteristics may be called essential in individual substances and accidents, not only in respect to a viewpoint, but in respect to concepts constructed from that viewpoint.

If this principle concerning the relativity of the essence expressed by a definition led to relativism or skepticism, it would be impossible to admit it even in the definition of accidents. Relativism is no less objectionable in the study of such accidents as law, grace, faith, and the vices than it is in the study of substances. Therefore, we may obviate certain objections to this principle by showing that it is found in St. Thomas's teachings concerning the vices. In a passage treating of the distinction of sins, he writes:

> We find certain acts different from one another in the material specific difference which are nevertheless formally in the same species of sin, because they are directed to one and the same end: thus strangling, stoning, and stabbing belong to the same species of murder, although the actions themselves differ specifically according to the natural species.[34]

---

[33] Christoph Sigwart, *Logic*, trans. Helen Dendy (2nd ed. rev.; London: Swan Sonnenschein & Co., 1895), I, 275.

[34] St. Thomas Aquinas, *Summa theol.*, I-II, q. 72, art. 6, c. "Unde inveniuntur aliqui actus materialiter specie differentes, qui tamen formaliter sunt in eadem specie peccati, quia ad idem ordinantur; sicut ad eandem speciem homicidii pertinent iuglatio, lapidatio et perforatio, quamvis actus sint specie differentes secundum speciem naturae."

To be in the same species is to be of the same essence; to differ specifically is to differ in essence. Now how can strangling, stoning, and stabbing be of the same essence, murder, at one time, and be essentially different another? They can be so only because essentiality arises out of the relation to something else and in each case the acts are considered in relation to different concepts. In one case they are considered in respect to the concept murder, which we will assume to comprise the characteristics killing another, voluntary, and unjust. These are the characteristics that it is essential for an act to have if it is to be an act of murder. Whether the act is performed with a knife or a stone is accidental to murder because, not being set forth in the concept of murder, they are among the countless characteristics that an act may or may not have and still be what is expressed by the concept. On the other hand, when we introduce a set of concepts distinguished from each other by characteristics representing the ways in which a killing may be executed, then these characteristics become essential. If the question is whether an act is one of stabbing or one of stoning, then whether the weapon is a pointed instrument or a stone is essential because the first characteristic is one of those joined to form the concept of stabbing and the second is one of those joined to form the concept of stoning.

St. Thomas states that certain acts are "formally in the same species, because they are directed to the same end."[35] However, this is not because there is a special ontological connection between essence and the moral end of an act. It is because the system of concepts devised by the theologian to classify human acts is one grounded upon a distinction in the end of the act. Evil acts that are directed to the same moral end fall in the same species of sin because when they are referred to the system of concepts constructed by the theologian they all fall under the same concept, namely, the concept of an act having such an end. If they were referred to a series of concepts constructed upon a different principle, then the moral end would be accidental. Thus St. Thomas writes:

> Now moral ends are accidental to a natural thing, and conversely the relation to a natural end is accidental to morality. Consequently there is no reason why acts which are the same

[35] *Ibid.*, I-II, q. 72, art. 6, c. ". . . inveniunter aliqui actus materialiter specie differentes, qui tamen formaliter sunt in eadem specie peccati, quia ad idem ordinantur. . . ."

considered in their natural species, should not be diverse, considered in their moral species, and conversely.[36]

Acts considered in their moral species are acts considered in the classes in which they fall when acts are classified according to their moral ends. The natural species of an act is the class in which it falls when acts are classified according to their natural ends. What St. Thomas calls the natural species of acts are not to be regarded as classes of acts represented by concepts formed upon some especially authoritative basis. They are the classes represented by the ideas men form of acts when not constrained by the demands of a special science. One could speak with as much right of the psychological or sociological species of acts as of their natural or moral species.

This principle concerning the relativity of essence is illustrated by another passage in which St. Thomas treats of the distinction of sins. In this passage St. Thomas raises the question whether the difference between mortal and venial sin is specific, that is, essential, or accidental. He declares that it is accidental for these reasons:

> The difference between venial and mortal sin, or any other difference in respect of the debt of punishment, cannot be a difference constituting specific diversity. For what is accidental never constitutes a species; and what is outside the agent's intention is accidental. Now it is evident that punishment is outside the intention of the sinner.[37]

Obviously the difference between mortal and venial sin is enormous; the difference in punishments for them is infinite. All things considered, the difference between them is greater than that between any two venial or any two mortal sins. Why then does St. Thomas say that they differ accidentally? The assertion, "what is accidental never constitutes a species," by itself, amounts only to saying that what is not essential never constitutes the essence. The pivotal statement is that what is outside the intention of the agent is accidental. Why is what is outside the intention of the agent

---

[36] *Ibid.*, I-II, q. 1, art. 3, ad 3. "Fines autem morales accidunt rei naturali; et e converso ratio naturalis finis accidit morali. Et ideo nihil prohibet actus qui sunt iidem secundum speciem naturae, esse diversos secundum speciem moris, et e converso."

[37] *Ibid.*, I-II, q. 72, art. 5. c. ". . . differentia venialis et mortalis peccati, vel quaecumque aliis differentis quae sumitur penes reatum, non potest esse differentia constituens diversitatem speciei. Nunquam enim id quod est per accidens constituit speciem. Id autem quod est praeter intentionem agentis, est per accidens. . . . Manifestum est autem quod poena est praeter intentionem peccantis."

accidental? It is accidental only because the intention of the agent is tacitly understood as one of the things in respect to which essentiality is judged. Thus whether the difference is essential or accidental depends not upon how extensive or important the difference is but simply upon that in respect to which it is considered. The same principle explains St. Thomas's denial of any specific difference between sins of commission and omission[38] or between sins distinguished in reference to their causes.[39] It is not a matter of identifying what is essential in itself but, as Rickert says, of "presenting the guiding viewpoint in a special field of investigation and then of seeing . . . what is essential in relation to this guiding viewpoint."[40]

St. Thomas defines the essence as what is expressed by the definition. Some of the foregoing conclusions may be confirmed by an analysis of the methods he presents for establishing definitions. One method is that commonly known as the inductive method of definition. Scholastic writers sometimes refer to it by the title given the lectio of St. Thomas's commentary on the *Posterior analytics* of Aristotle in which it is discussed: "The method of investigating definitions through things similar and dissimilar."[41] St. Thomas begins his explanation of the method in this way:

> . . . if someone seeks the definition of a thing, it is necessary that he attend to those things that are similar to it . . . regarding the similar things it is necessary to consider what is found the same in all. . . .[42]

By things similar to the definiendum St. Thomas means instances of the object to be defined. The definer is to find what is the same in all of these, that is, he is to find what characteristic or set of characteristics they all have in common. For example, if man is the definiendum, individual men will be the instances of similar things and all will have rationality in common.[43]

---

[38] *Ibid.*, I-II, q. 72, art. 6.
[39] *Ibid.*, I-II, q. 72, art. 3.
[40] Heinrich Rickert, *Zur Lehre von der Definition*, p. 40. "Es würde sich immer darum handeln, den leitenden Gesichtspunkt in einem besonderen Forschungsgebiet aufzuzeigen und dann zu sehen, . . . was in bezug auf diesen leitenden Gesichtspunkt wesentlich ist."
[41] St. Thomas Aquinas, *In post analyt.*, II, lec. 16, "De modo investigandi definitiones per similia et dissimilia."
[42] *Ibid.*, II, lec. 16, par. 553, p. 386. ". . . si aliquis inquirit definitionem alicuius rei, oportet quod attendat ad ea quae sunt similia illi . . . oportet circa similia considerare quid idem in omnibus inveniatur. . . ."
[43] *Ibid.*, II, lec. 16, par. 553, p. 386.

The next step, St. Thomas writes, is to consider things that differ in species from the definiendum but are of the same species themselves and fall under the same genus as the definiendum. Continuing with the same example, horse will be of a species different from man and will fall under the same genus, animal. This new group of instances must then be examined to determine what they have in common. All horses, for example, have in common the ability to neigh.[44] Finally, the characteristic common to the first set of instances must be compared with that common to the second set. What is found common to both of these will be the definition of the thing.[45] If nothing can be found common to the two characteristics, then no definition can be given that comprehends both. The definer will know that what he seeks to define is not "one according to essence, but several."[46] St. Thomas concludes his exposition of the method with an illustration:

> . . . if we ask what is magnanimity, we ought to attend to certain instances of magnanimity, in order that we may know what one thing they have in them insofar as they are magnanimous. Just as Alcibiades is called magnanimous, and also Achilles, and also Ajax; all of whom had in common the one thing, which is that they could not endure injuries.[47]

The question, "What is magnanimity?" is a request for the definition, or essence, of magnanimity. The magnanimity of Alcibiades, that of Achilles, and that of Ajax constitute the collection of things similar to the definiendum. Inability to bear insult is the element common to this first set of instances. St. Thomas continues:

[44] *Ibid.*, II, lec. 16, par. 553, p. 386. "*Postea* considerandum est iterum in aliis, quae conveniunt cum prima in eodem genere, et sunt sibi invicem idem specie, sunt autem altera specie ab illis, quae primo accipiebantur, sicut equi ab hominibus; oportet etiam accipere quid sit idem in his, scilicet equis, puta hinnibile."

[45] *Ibid.*, II, lec. 16, par. 553, p. 386. "Cum ergo accipiatur quid sit idem in omnibus his, scilicet hominibus, quia rationale; et quid sit idem similiter in omnibus aliis, scilicet equis, quia hinnibile; iterum considerandum est si aliquid est idem in istis duobus acceptis, scilicet in rationali et hinnibili. Et ita est considerandum quousque perveniatur ad aliquam unam rationem communem. Haec enim erit definitio rei."

[46] *Ibid.*, II, lec. 16, par. 553, p. 386. ". . . illud cuius definitio quaeritur, non erit unum secundum essentiam, set plura: et ita non poterit habere unam definitionem."

[47] *Ibid.*, II, lec. 16, par. 554, p. 386. ". . . si quaeramus quid est magnanimitas, debemus attendere ad quosdam magnanimos, ut sciamus quid unum habent in seipsis, inquantum magnanimi sunt. Sicut Alcibiades dictus est magnanimus, et etiam Achilles, et etiam Ajax; qui omnes habent unum quid commune, quod est non sustinere iniurias."

Again we ought to consider others who are called magnanimous, such as Lysander or Socrates. For they have this in common, that they were not moved by good or ill fortune but kept themselves indifferent to both.[48]

By "others who are called magnanimous" St. Thomas refers to the *dissimilia* or second group of instances of a different species but the same genus as the first. The characteristic he finds common to them is their indifference to good and ill fortune.

There are now two sets of cases of magnanimity, the first having in common intolerance of insult and the second having in common indifference to good and ill fortune. The next step is to compare these two characteristics and determine whether or not they too have something in common. If they do, this final common element is the essence of magnanimity. If they do not, then there are two different species of magnanimity and it will be impossible to give a definition comprehending both.[49]

It is important to keep in mind the following principle. Wherever the inductive method of definition is used the set of characteristics that emerges as the common element is determined by the selection of instances of the definiendum. If objects possessing the characteristics abcx, abcy, and abxy are examined then ab will be the element common to all. If an object with the characteristics acxy is included, then b must be accounted accidental and excluded from the definition. Since the definition is determined by the cases selected, the validity of the method depends upon the criterion it provides for the selection of instances of the definiendum.

What criterion does St. Thomas offer for collecting the *similia*? He writes that in selecting instances one must be able to see plainly to what class they belong. The definer must choose only those that he distinctly recognizes as instances of the definiendum. This is the knowledge one must have before beginning the process of defining.[50] He illustrates, taking *simile* as the definiendum:

> ... if someone wishes to declare what *like* is, he will not consider everything that can be called like, but certain instances of

[48] *Ibid.*, II, lec. 16, par. 554, p. 386. "Iterum debemus considerare in aliis qui dicuntur magnanimi, sicut in Lysandro aut Socrate. Habent enim hoc commune, quod non mutabantur propter prosperitatem fortunae et per infortunia sed indifferenter se habebant in utrisque."

[49] *Ibid.*, II, lec. 16, par. 554, p. 386.

[50] *Ibid.*, II, lec. 16, par. 558, p. 387. "Hoc autem contingit, ut scilicet praeexistat aliquid evidens, si sit, id est contingat, separatim, id est distinctim, definiri per ea quae singulariter dicuntur, id est quae proprie conveniunt et distincte huic vel illi. ..."

like things; for example, what is called like in the matter of colors, and what is called like in the matter of figures. For something is called like in the matter of colors from unity of color; but something is called like in the matter of figures because the angles are equal and the sides proportional.[51]

Thus St. Thomas requires the definer to exclude from consideration any instance to which the name of the definiendum is applied equivocally or analogically. If the name has several meanings the definer must confine himself to one and then begin to collect his cases. Thus the criterion St. Thomas presents is briefly this: If the name of the definiendum can be univocally predicated of an object and the definiendum, that object is to be accepted as an instance of the definiendum.[52]

A word is said to be predicated univocally of two objects when it is predicated of each in exactly the same sense. In each predication the logical content of the concept signified by the word must be the same. Consequently, when the univocal application of a word is made the criterion of selecting instances, the group of instances placed before the definer must be distinguished from all others by the fact that each of them possesses, or is, what is expressed by the concept. The instances will yield as their common element, therefore, precisely what is contained in the concept by which the definer was guided in selecting them.

This will become clearer if we consider how the question, "What is x?" is inextricably bound up with the question, "Is y an x?" It is a common experience that the question, "Is y an x?" often leads to the question, "What is x?" Thus the question, "Is Scotus Erigena a scholastic?" leads to the question, "What is a scholastic?" The question, "Is this painting a work of art?" leads to the question, "What is art?" In all such cases it is recognized that before we can decide with certainty whether or not a thing is x, we must know what x is. Since what a thing is, or the answer to the question *Quid est,* is what is expressed by the definition, we must obtain a definition of x and see whether or not there are present in the disputed case all the elements set forth in the definition. However, when the definer undertakes to establish the definition by the in-

[51] *Ibid.,* II, lec. 16, par. 558, p. 387. ". . . si sliquis velit notificare quid est *simile,* non considerabit ad omne id quod potest simile dici, sed de quibusdam similibus; puta quomodo dicatur simile in coloribus, et quomodo dicatur simile in figuris. Dicitur enim simile in coloribus ex unitate coloris; dicitur autem simile in figuris ex eo quod anguli sunt aequales, et latera proportionalia."

[52] *Ibid.,* II, lec. 16, par. 558, p. 387.

ductive method, the question will arise whether y, or equally dubious and decisive cases, should be included among the instances of x. If the definer is confronted with instances the acceptance or rejection of which will materially alter the definition, he cannot ignore them on the grounds that it is not clear what they are and yet expect to establish a definition that enables him to decide upon them. The content of the definition is determined by the selection of cases and it is impossible to get out of the definition more than goes into the selection of cases. Consequently, the inductive method of definition is circular and invalid. It is "to look for the spectacles we are wearing by the aid of the spectacles themselves."[53]

The circularity of the method becomes the more apparent when we consider how incapable it is of obtaining the results that have been achieved in the development of definitions in every science. In prescribing that we are to be guided by the univocal application of the word, the inductive method of definition anchors us to the concept composed of the characteristics to which men first attended in forming their ideas of things. We cannot proceed by this method to the discovery and adoption of a more significant point of community as the basis of the definition because this is usually not the element common to the objects signified by the name at the beginning of the inquiry. It is the element common to a set of individuals that have not yet been brought together. It is a set of characteristics that are represented by a concept, or definition, not yet constructed.

[53] Christoph Sigwart, *Logic*, trans. Helen Dendy (2d ed. rev.; London: Swan Sonnenschein & Co., 1895), I, p. 249. Concerning the selection of instances Sigwart writes: "If we are guided by any motive, and not by mere caprice, it must be found ultimately in the fact that the objects are from the first recognised as similar, because containing certain elements common to all; that is, a general idea is already there, by means of which these objects are selected from amongst all others," *Ibid.*, p. 248. The general idea that is already there is the idea signified by the word. Hence to know that the name of x is predicated univocally of all the individual x's is really to know that they all fall under the definition of x, or all are what the word x signifies. For, as St. Thomas writes in his *Summa theologiae*, ". . . the idea signified by the name is the definition." *Summa theol.*, I, q. 13, a. 2, c. ". . . ratio enim quam significat nomen, est definitio." The case is not altered by anything that can be said relating to the distinction between what is commonly referred to as nominal and real definition. Cf. Heinrich Rickert, *Zur Lehre von der Definition*, pp. 70-76. We may observe that it is doubtful whether, in presenting the inductive method of definition, St. Thomas is doing any more than explaining the thought of Aristotle. He does not mention the method outside of his commentaries on Aristotle and he does not use it in framing any of his own definitions, not even his definition of magnanimity. Cf. *Summa theol.*, II-II, q. 129, art. 2, c.

It is possible that the definer, in using the method, may come to a set of characteristics that are the foundation of the relatively external ones on the basis of which he first collected instances. The new definition also may comprehend the same set of individuals represented by the definiendum at the beginning of the inquiry. Yet even here the definition cannot be called the product of the inductive method. It is the result of an analysis of the relationship between characteristics. In such cases the examination of a single instance would suffice to show that the characteristics placed in the definition are the foundation of those contained in the concept previously signified by the word.

St. Thomas presents a second method for distinguishing the essential from the accidental in his commentary on the *Metaphysics* of Aristotle. The definer is directed to consider the characteristic, the essentiality of which is in question, as the predicate of a proposition of which the definiendum is subject. If the characteristic is predicated absolutely, that is, if it expresses something that is identical with the subject, then it is essential. If it is predicated of the definiendum accidentally, that is, if it signifies something that belongs to or inheres in the subject but is not itself the subject, then it is not essential.[54] The difference is illustrated by two propositions, "Man is an animal" and "Man is white." In the first, the predicate expresses something that is the subject, not of the subject; therefore, it is essential. In the second, the predicate, white, expresses something that is not identical with man, but inheres in him; therefore it is accidental. St. Thomas explains the criterion in this way:

> ... the essence ... must be predicated absolutely. For those things that are predicated of something accidentally, do not pertain to the essence of that thing. For we understand this by the essence of something, that it can be suitably given in answer to the question what it is ... we cannot give as a suitable answer those things that are in it accidentally; just as when it is asked what is man, it cannot be answered that he is white or sitting or musical. And therefore none of the things, that are predicated accidentally of something, pertain to the essence of that thing; for to be musical is not to be you.[55]

[54] St. Thomas Aquinas, *In met.*, VII, lec. 3, par. 1310, p. 327.

[55] *Ibid.*, VII, lec. 3, par. 1309, p. 327. "... sciendum est de eo quod quid erat esse, quod oportet quod praedicatur secundum se. Illa enim quae praedicantur de aliquo per accidens, non pertinent ad quod quid erat esse illius. Hoc enim intelligimus per quod quid erat esse alicuius, quod convenienter responderi potest ad quaestionem de eo factam per quid est ... non possumus

This method is subject to the same defects as the inductive method of definition. If we take the subject of a proposition as the individual, then strictly speaking all the characteristics predicated of it are of it or in it. Even rationality, we have seen, is ontologically an accident that inheres in man. When it is said that the subject of a proposition is identical with a characteristic that is predicated of it absolutely, it is really meant that the subject is identical with something having that characteristic. A predicate is said to be predicated of a subject absolutely when it signifies one of the characteristics joined to form the subject concept. Now individuals can be represented by many concepts. Which characteristics should form the subject concept, or essential concept? The method of absolute and accidental predication gives no answer. It has the appearance of validity, as in the case of man, only where the concept signified by the name is already determined on some other grounds.

A third method proposed to obtain the essence of a thing is the method of division. In following this method the definer takes the highest genus by which the definiendum is comprehended and divides it by differences that exhaust the whole genus. Then he takes the inferior genus formed by the addition of that difference which is present in the definiendum and divides this in the same way.[56] By continuing this process he will eventually arrive at the last difference which forms the species of the definiendum. He will not proceed any further, for the definition or species of the definiendum is identical with the concept formed by the union of all the differences by which the concept is reached.[57] Thus the definition of man is identical with the concept of a rational, sensile, living, material substance.

This method too is inadequate as a means of discovering the

---

convenienter respondere ea quae insunt ei per accidens; sicut cum quaeritur quid est homo, non potest responderi, quod sit albus vel sedens vel musicus. Et ideo nihil eorum, quae praedicantur per accidens de aliquo, pertinent ad quod quid erat esse illius rei: non enim musicum esse, est tibi esse."

[56] St. Thomas Aquinas, *In post analyt.*, II, lec. 15, par. 550, p. 384. ". . . dividendo aliquod genus accipimus primas eius differentias, sub quibus divisum universaliter continetur; sicut quod omne animal est hoc vel illud, puta rationale vel irrationale, et accipimus quod illud quod intendimus definire, est hoc, puta rationale. Et iterum accipiemus hoc totum, scilicet animal rationale, et dividemus ipsum per differentias proprias. . . ."

[57] *Ibid.*, II, lec. 15, par. 550, p. 384. ". . . sed quando iam devenerimus ad ultimam differentiam, iam non erit dividere per alias differentias specificas; sed statim ultima differentia addita, hoc, cuius definitio quaeritur, in nullo differet specie a *simul toto*, idest a ratione congregata ab omnibus partibus acceptis. . . ."

essential. For success depends upon the observance of three rules, the first of which requires the definer to choose as differences only characteristics that pertain to the essence of the thing.[58] But which characteristics pertain to the essence? The method of division gives no answer.

The inductive method of definition and the method based upon absolute and accidental predication appear to be valid means of establishing what is essential because of their efficacy in determining what has already been taken in some way as essential. The essence at which they arrive is the set of characteristics that are essential in individuals insofar as these individuals are referred to a given concept.

We may see how the characteristics that emerge as the common element in the inductive method always turn out to be essential in this sense. If the definer collects instances of perjury they will all have lying and being under oath in common because these are the characteristics that were joined to form the concept of perjury in the first place. They constitute what it is of which he is collecting instances. These characteristics are essential because the essential characteristics are those contained in the concept to which a substance or accident is referred and this is always the concept expressing what it is of which the objects collected are taken as instances.

If, upon another occasion, some of these objects are considered as instances of something else, then the concept representing that something else becomes the new criterion of selection, the new concept to which the objects are referred, and the idea representing what is common to the objects. Thus if the definer, after determining the definition of perjury by the inductive method, employs the same method to obtain the essence of calumny, he will find that some of the same instances that were included in the class of perjurious acts must also be admitted to the class of calumnious acts. A different set of characteristics, lying and injuring the reputation of another, turns out to be the common element. At the same time these characteristics turn out to be essential in the acts of which he has collected instances because they are the characteristics contained in the new concept, calumny, to which the instances are now referred.

[58] *Ibid.*, II, lec. 15, par. 547, p. 384. ". . . oportet considerare . . . ut ea quae accipiuntur, praedicentur in eo quod quid est. . . ." The other rules are that the differences must be taken in the proper order and that no intermediate steps may be omitted.

The method of definition based upon absolute and accidental predication leads to characteristics that are essential in the same way. It declares that a characteristic is essential if, when predicated of the object, it represents something the object is; it is accidental if it represents something that belongs to or is of the object. When one applies this method in defining a substance or an accident it is true that the characteristics which are predicated of the object absolutely, or are the object, always turn out to be essential. However, this is because the characteristics that are the object are those contained in the concept expressing what the object is, or what it is of which the object is considered an instance. This is the concept to which the object is referred because it is the concept expressing what it is of which the individual is considered an instance. Perjury must be lying because that is one of the things joined together to form the concept of perjury in the first place. If we consider the same individual act as an instance of some other act, then a different set of characteristics will be the definiendum.

Similarly, a characteristic which, when predicated of an object, represents something that is of or in the object always turns out to be accidental because it is not contained in the concept to which the object is referred. Since it is not contained in the concept it does not constitute what that concept represents. Thus the method leads always to the concept expressing what it is of which the substance or accident is now considered an instance. It will do nothing towards constructing a concept, or definition, representing a class that is based upon the ontological significance of the characteristics of the individuals comprehended by it.[59]

[59] The same vicious circle is present in the widely accepted explanations of essence as "that by which a thing is what it is," "that without which a thing cannot be what it is," and "that which makes a thing to be of the class that it is." It is the complex of essential notes contained in the definition that answers to each of these descriptions. Thus it is by rational animality that an individual is a man. But why certain characteristics should be taken as essential notes and not others remains an unanswered question. When the essential is understood in any of these senses, then Rickert is correct in saying: "If we wish to know wherein the task of definition really consists, and how it must construct the concept, we cannot be satisfied with the provisional meaningless answer that it must declare the essential characteristics of objects. We must investigate rather what characteristics a scientific concept should have, and how they should be *found* essential, without thought having the meaning of speech as a guide or presupposing as already at hand the concept that it should first construct." *Zur Lehre von der Definition*, pp. 30, 31.

The method of division, we have seen, leaves unsolved the problem as to which characteristics should be selected in making the division. It may be objected that the guiding rule is that we take only the genus and difference and that a criterion for determining these is found in St. Thomas. According to St. Thomas, the genus is taken from the matter and the difference from the form of a thing. What pertains to the matter, he writes, is never ascribed *secundum se* to the species; what pertains to the form is found in every member of the species insofar as it belongs to that species.[60] However, this too provides no adequate criterion. There are always many characteristics that are not ascribed *secundum se* to the species and the question remains as to which of these shall be taken as the genus. Furthermore, if we do not yet know what is essential, we cannot know what individuals constitute the species. Not knowing this, it will be impossible to say which characteristics belong to the members of the species *qua* members of the species. Again this criterion appears valid, as in the case of man, only to the extent that it is already determined upon some other grounds, that certain characteristics are to be taken as essential.

The doctrine concerning genus and difference is usually given an exaggerated role in explaining definition and essence. Hugon writes that the rule prescribing that a definition give the genus and difference "expresses the essence itself of definition."[61] If the rule is not described in the same terms by other writers, it is usually regarded at least as prescribing the model for which the definer should always strive. Such a view is incompatible not only with the doctrine of many modern thinkers but with much that is found in St. Thomas.

The largest part of what St. Thomas writes concerning essence is found in his commentary on the second book of Aristotle's *Posterior analytics*. Here St. Thomas teaches that a definition should

---

[60] St. Thomas Aquinas, *In met.*, VII, lec. 9, par. 1473, p. 359. "Et ut sciatur quid est species, et quid est materia, dicendum est illud ad speciem pertinere, quod convenit unicuique inquantum speciem habet. . . . Sed id quod est materiale ad speciem, nunquam dicendum est secundum se de specie." Here the word *species* is used in the sense of *forma*. For in the preceding paragraph St. Thomas writes: ". . . non autem est pars statuae secundum quod statua accipitur solum pro specie, idest pro forma." *Ibid.*, VII, lec. 9, par. 1472, p. 359.

[61] E. Hugon, *Logica* (Paris: P. Lethielleux, 1902), p. 110. Hugon cites with approval the following statement of Janet: "One sees in what the rule prescribing that we define by genus and difference consists: it is not only a rule, a precept, it is the essence itself of definition: it is the universal law of all definition." *Ibid.*, pp. 110, 111.

contain the extrinsic causes of the definiendum and be set forth after the manner of a syllogism.[62] It is in the course of presenting this doctrine that he advances the arguments for the necessity of making a distinction between the definition of a thing and the definition of a name.[63] This distinction is urged for the purpose of showing that the definition of the *quod quid est* is more than a statement of the meaning of a name. It is the same *quod quid est* that St. Thomas goes on to describe as the essence that is expressed by a causal definition and that is set forth after the manner of a syllogism.[64] Moreover, it is in explaining this teaching concerning causal definition that St. Thomas presents the doctrine that either an accidental knowledge or a partial essential knowledge of a thing precedes the full essential knowledge that is expressed by its definition. The process of passing from partial essential knowledge to full essential knowledge is illustrated by the definitions of an eclipse and thunder, the same definitions used to exemplify the causal definition.[65]

Obviously this doctrine is not consistent with the position that a statement of the essence always consists of genus and difference. For genus and difference, it is taught, are taken from the intrinsic causes of the definiendum and here St. Thomas requires a statement of all its causes. However, it must be observed, that St. Thomas himself often writes as if essence were to be explained solely in terms of genus and difference. This impression, which is given especially in his *De ente et essentia*, is misleading. It is incompatible not only with what he writes in his commentary on the *Posterior analytics* but with his statement that "the perfect essential notion of a thing is gathered from all its causes."[66]

It must also be pointed out that St. Thomas does not equate essential unity with substantial unity. He acknowledges that the doctrine concerning causal definition cannot be applied in all cases.[67] Yet he states that where it does apply we are dealing with a definition that possesses the high degree of unity proper to essential definitions. He calls attention to the lesser degree of unity

---

[62] St. Thomas Aquinas, *In post. analyt.*, II, lec. 1.
[63] *Ibid.*, II, lec. 6, par. 465, p. 345.
[64] *Ibid.*, II, lec. 7, pp. 349-52.
[65] *Ibid.*, II, lec. 7, par. 475, pp. 350-51.
[66] St. Thomas Aquinas, *Summa theol.*, I-II, q. 55, art. 4, c. "Perfecta enim ratio uniuscuisque rei colligitur ex omnibus causis eius."
[67] *Ibid.*, II, lec. 8, par. 479, p. 354. ". . . in quibusdam per demonstrationem accipitur quod quid est . . . hoc non est possibile in omnibus."

characteristic of concepts representing things that are one accidentally, or one by conjunction, and contrasts this with the unity of concepts expressing the *quid est*.[68] The *quid est* to which he refers is the explanation of a thing in its causes and it is the causal definition of thunder that he gives to illustrate it.[69] He compares the statement, "It thunders because fire is extinguished in the clouds," with the statement "Thunder is the sound of fire extinguished in the clouds." Each of these propositions, he writes, signifies the same thing in different ways.[70] In the first, the definiendum is signified after the manner of a continuous demonstration; in the second it is signified after the manner of a definition. However, both signify the same *ratio* and it is the unity of this *ratio* that St. Thomas contrasts with the unity of accidental aggregations. Hence it is evident that St. Thomas ascribes to the concept signified by the definiens of the causal definition the same high degree of unity by which he distinguishes essential concepts from accidental concepts.

The distinction between the essential and accidental here in question is also explained in terms of the principle concerning the relativity of the essence. While the definienda of which St. Thomas demands causal definitions are not substances, they are not merely aggregations of accidents. For what is expressed by the causal definition is not an unrelated series of events but a complex of phenomena bound together by the causal law that explains it. Here something is judged essential or inessential on the basis of its relation to a series of causally connected events. The meaning of the essential in this sense is lucidly described in the following passage of Schuppe:

[68] *Ibid.*, II, lec. 8, par. 484, p. 355. "Ad distinguendum autem rationem significantem *quid est* ab aliis, subiungit quod dupliciter aliqua ratio potest dici una. Quaedam enim est una, sola coniunctione: per quem modum etiam habet unitatem Ilias. . . . Et per hunc etiam modum dicitur esse *una ratio*, quae est expositiva nominis, vel manifestativa ipsius rei nominatae per aliqua accidentia. . . . Alia vero ratio est una inquantum simpliciter significat unum de re una, cuius est ratio, et hoc non secundum accidens. Et talis ratio est definitio significans *quid est*."

[69] *Ibid.*, II, lec. 8, par. 487, p. 356. "Ille autem dicit *quid est* tonitrum, qui dicit quod est sonus ignis extincti in nubibus."

[70] *Ibid.*, II, lec. 8, par. 487, p. 356. "Utrumque autem horum significat eamdem rationem, sed per alium modum." Obviously, the fact that this explanation of thunder is erroneous has no bearing upon the point here in question.

Something is inessential, therefore, always only in relation to something or for something, never in an absolute sense; it is a question only of causal connection. For the purpose that one pursues in a given case, something is inessential because it is not suited to further that end; for a complex of appearances connected by a physical law, something is inessential because it is not bound up with this law.[71]

Taken as describing the essence immediately expressed by a definition, there is nothing in this that contradicts the basic teachings of St. Thomas. It should not be thought strange that in the writings of thinkers whose basic principles are in some ways radically opposed to those of St. Thomas there should be much that is capable of being incorporated into the system of St. Thomas. Truth is always perfectly coherent, but there are large areas where considerable agreement may be reached by thinkers with widely differing basic principles.

It may be asked whether or not the essence of a thing as considered from one viewpoint is any more valid than the essence as considered from some other viewpoint. Is there a viewpoint from which it can be judged with more authority than from any other what is truly essential? So far as concerns the essentiality ascribed to characteristics in virtue of their relation to something else, the very search for such a viewpoint would rest upon a misunderstanding. It would proceed from the same notions that prompted the search for what has been called a universal method, or a method of grasping the world in its totality. To human intellects, no such method is possible. According to Rickert, "every science has . . . its own method which it creates itself, and which must be suited to its own ends and purposes."[72] To one who had obtained some universal method everything would be essential because nothing would be accidental.

[71] Wilhelm Schuppe, *Grundriss der Erkenntnistheorie und Logik* (Berlin: R. Gaertner, 1894), pp. 134-35. "Unwesentlich ist also etwas immer nur in Relation auf etwas oder für etwas, niemals in einem absoluten Sinne; es kommt nur auf die Kausalverkettungen an. Für den Zweck, den man gegebenen Falls gerade verfolgt, ist etwas unwesentlich, weil es ihn nicht zu fordern geeignet ist, für einen naturgesetzlichen Komplex von Erscheinungen ist etwas unwesentlich, weil es nicht von diesem Gesetze gefordert wird."

[72] Heinrich Rickert, *Zur Lehre von der Definition*, p. 31. "Jede Wissenschaft hat . . . ihre eigene Methode, die sie sich selbst schafft, und die ihren Zielen und Absichten angemessen sein muss."

It is when we confine ourselves to one part, or one aspect, of reality, as we do in pursuing the ends of a special science, that the distinction of essential and accidental becomes meaningful in the present sense. We may observe that in this there is nothing that is incompatible with the basic teachings of St. Thomas. In speaking of the moral and natural species of acts St. Thomas never implies that the species, or essence, of an act as considered from one viewpoint is any more valid or authoritative than the essence as considered from any other viewpoint. It is simply a matter of representing reality by a system of concepts and judgments that are appropriate to the ends of a particular science.[73]

If by essence we understand the transcendental essence that is identified with the supposit, then we need not be concerned with the question of an absolute viewpoint because then essence is not relative in any of the ways explained above. The individual substance simply exists; that it is the substance it is does not depend upon the way in which it is conceived or the viewpoint from which it is considered. Here the question of relativeness, and hence of viewpoint, is irrelevant.

---

[73] For a thorough treatment of the questions relating to an absolute viewpoint and a detailed explanation of the reasons why many viewpoints are necessary in perfecting our knowledge of the universe, cf. Heinrich Rickert, *Die Grenzen der naturwissenschaftlichen Begriffsbildung* (4te Aufl.; Tübingen: J. C. B. Mohr, 1921).

5

THE QUESTION OF THE VALIDITY OF THE *TERTIA VIA*

by

Thomas G. Pater

I. INTRODUCTION

In recent years the third argument for the existence of God presented by St. Thomas Aquinas in his *Summa theologica* has been called into question not only by nonscholastic philosophers but by prominent scholastic authors as well.[1] There have been replies in defense of the *tertia via*, with the defenders somewhat outnumbering the antagonists.[2] Among the more significant articles on the subject, the last four, published from 1953 to 1957, each by a different author, have all been in favor of the third argument.[3] From such indications one might judge that the ayes had had the last word, not only literally but also logically. It is our contention, however, that the validity of the *tertia via* remains doubtful.

It should be emphasized that what is in question is the third argument for the existence of God in the *Summa theologica*. In

---

[1] For a chronological survey of the controversy see Thomas Connolly, "The Basis of the Third Proof for the Existence of God," *The Thomist*, XVII (1954) 285-299. Among those questioning the *tertia via* have been Paul Gény, Pedro Descoqs, and Fernand Van Steenberghen.

[2] The main writings in defense of the *tertia via* can also be found listed in Connolly's article, *ibid*.

[3] The four articles are: Dermot O'Donoghue, "An Analysis of the *Tertia Via* of St. Thomas," *Irish Theological Quarterly*, XX (1953) 129-151; Umberto Degl'Innocenti, "La validità della 'Terza Via,'" *Doctor Communis*, VII (1954) 41-70; Thomas Kevin Connolly, "The Basis of the Third Proof for the Existence of God," *The Thomist*, XVII (1954) 281-349; A. Pattin, "La Structure de la 'tertia via' dans la 'Somme théologique de saint Thomas d'Aquin,'" *Revue de l'Université d'Ottawa*, XXVII (1957) 26*-35*.

The only more recent article that has come to our attention is one by Manuel Gonzalez Pola, "El Problema de las Fuentes de la 'Tercera Via' de San Tomas de Aquino," *Studium*, I-II (1961-62) 137-206, which adds nothing new to the defense of the *tertia via*.

the *Contra gentes* St. Thomas presents an argument for God's necessity that is equivalent to a demonstration of God's existence and bears considerable resemblance to the third argument in the *Summa theologica*. But there are important differences. And no matter how unassailable the argument in the *Contra gentes* may be, the one in question here is the third argument in the *Summa theologica*.

Authors professing to present the arguments for the existence of God given in the *Summa theologica* have often restated the *tertia via* in such a way as to substitute an essentially different argument, either the one in the *Contra gentes* or still another formulation. Whatever is presented as a statement or explanation or defense of the *tertia via* should remain within the wording of the *tertia via*. This wording may allow of some difference of interpretation. But any acceptable interpretation must stay within the limits permitted by sound rules of criticism, with due attention to the content and related passages, and to the author's usual line of thought and usage of terms. An acceptable interpretation must avoid doing violence to the words of the text in an effort to twist them into a valid argument at any cost.

Of the articles in defense of the *tertia via*, we will consider mainly the one by Thomas Connolly,[4] with special attention also to the views of Umberto Degl'Innocenti.[5] Connolly's article is one of the most thorough treatments of the *tertia via* and also seems to come closest to St. Thomas' thought. Two other authors among the latest to write on the subject, Dermot O'Donoghue[6] and A. Pattin,[7] express much the same ideas as Connolly, but more briefly, and there is no reason to comment separately on their statements except incidentally. Degl'Innocenti's views, though also adhering closely to St. Thomas' words, differ in important respects from those of Connolly and merit some separate consideration. The opinions of the other defenders of the *tertia via* are substantially included in those of Connolly and Degl'Innocenti, or else have been more or less obviously at variance with the text of the *tertia via* and have already been refuted by Connolly and Degl'Innocenti as well as by others.

Before taking up Connolly's and Degl'Innocenti's arguments, it seems advisable to present a general survey of the *tertia via* and its

[4] *Loc. cit.*
[5] *Loc. cit.*
[6] *Loc. cit.*
[7] *Loc. cit.*

problems, and some remarks on the interpretation of particular points.

II. GENERAL SURVEY OF THE THIRD PROOF AND ITS PROBLEMS

The third proof can be arranged schematically, and the parts designated numerically for convenience in reference, as follows: "Tertia via est sumpta ex possibili et necessario, quae talis est.

1. Invenimus enim in rebus quaedam quae sunt possibilia esse et non esse;
   cum quaedam inveniantur generari et corrumpi,
   et per consequens possibilia esse et non esse.
2.a. Impossibile est autem omnia quae sunt talia esse:
   quia
   b. quod possibile est non esse, quandoque non est.
   c. Si igitur omnia sunt possibilia non esse, aliquando nihil fuit in rebus.
   d. Sed si hoc est verum, etiam nunc nihil esset:
   quia
   quod non est, non incipit esse nisi per aliquid quod est. Si ergo nihil fuit ens, impossibile fuit quod aliquid inciperet esse: et sic modo nihil esset;
   e. quod patet esse falsum.
3. Non ergo omnia entia sunt possibilia, sed oportet aliquid esse necessarium in rebus.
4.a. Omne autem necessarium vel habet causam suae necessitatis aliunde, vel non habet.
   b. Non est autem possibile quod procedatur in infinitum in necessariis quae habent causam suae necessitatis, sicut nec in causis efficientibus, ut probatum est.
5. Ergo necesse est ponere aliquid quod sit per se necessarium, non habens causam necessitatis aliunde, sed quod est causa necessitatis aliis."[8]

---

[8] *Summa theol.*, I, q. 2, a. 3. The text is given as in the Leonine edition, except that in statement 2b, where the Leonine has "Impossible est autem omnia quae sunt talia, semper esse," we have omitted the "semper," as in many of the manuscripts. This is the more intelligible reading and the one adopted by practically all authors. The Leonine reading would increase rather than diminish the difficulties.

There are two main steps in the argument: the first, from the existence of contingent beings, "possibilia esse et non esse," to the existence of some necessary being, and the second, from the existence of necessary being in general to the existence of a *per se* necessary being. There is no special difficulty about the latter part of the argument. The problems lie in the first part, specifically in 2b and 2c.

In the first part, St. Thomas begins by establishing the existence of beings that can be or not be through an appeal to the fact, attested by experience, that beings do come into existence by generation and go out of existence by corruption. He goes on to say that it is impossible that all things be of this kind, contingent. And it should be emphasized that the argument given by St. Thomas for this particular premise is the one in the following words introduced by the conjunction "quia." It is amazing how many authors, purporting to present or defend St. Thomas' *tertia via*, demonstrate the impossibility of a completely contingent universe by some argument other than the one given here by St. Thomas.

St. Thomas' argument begins with statement 2b, "Quod possibile est non esse quandoque non est." This immediately raises an objection. How does it follow, from the datum that a thing *can* not-be, that at some time it *must* not-be, or *will* not-be, or "is not"? This would seem to involve the absurdity of confusing possibility and necessity. Moreover, since St. Thomas himself admits that there is no contradiction, from the standpoint of reason, in the notion of a creature existing eternally (not only *in aeternum* but *ab aeterno*), he would seem to be inconsistent in holding here that anything that can not-be must *eo ipso* at some time not be.

St. Thomas continues (2c), "Si igitur omnia sunt possibilia non esse, aliquando nihil fuit in rebus." This statement evokes more than one objection. It will be sufficient for the moment to mention the most obvious. Even supposing that a contingent being must at some time not be, it does not seem to follow inevitably that, if all things were contingent, "at some time there was nothing." What is there, in these premises alone, to keep us from accounting for the existence of things by the hypothesis of one contingent being arising from another in a series without beginning or end?

It is perfectly true that if, *per impossibile*, all things were contingent, there would be no beings at all. But does this follow from statement 2b? That it must follow from that statement, if the *tertia via* is to be accepted as sound, should be plain from the word "igitur." To demonstrate the truth of 2c in some other way than as a consequence of 2b is to depart from the *tertia via*.

III. INTERPRETATION OF PARTICULAR POINTS, ESPECIALLY IN STATEMENT 2b

A. *The temporal element in the third proof.*

1. In general.

Many authors have evaded the difficulties of the *tertia via* by restating or explaining it in such a way as to eliminate all notion of time, either from the entire argument or at least from statement 2b.[9] In general these authors substitute for the *tertia via* an argument like the one in the *Contra gentes*.[10] The argument in the *Contra gentes* includes no reference to time. It argues simply that a contingent being, since it is of itself indifferent to being, must have a cause to account for its existence (and that, since an infinite series of causes is impossible, there must be a necessary being, and ultimately a *per se* necessary being). In thus substituting another argument for the one in the *Summa theologica,* some authors omit all mention of the temporal terms in the wording of the argument in the *Summa theologica*. Others attempt to account for those terms by interpreting them, especially the "quandoque," as referring, not to time, but only to a sequence or priority of nature. They point out that a contingent being of itself does not have existence but is, of itself, only in potency to existence, and that when it does exist, it is composed of the potency to exist and the

[9] This kind of interpretation, espoused by John of St. Thomas and Billuart, has also been adopted by most modern Thomists, according to Connolly, who himself rejects it. *Loc. cit.,* pp. 284-85. Henri Holstein, for example, says that the "quandoque" in statement 2b "a un sens purement métaphysique, nullement temporel." "Origines de la tertia via," *Revue philosophique de Louvain,* XLVIII (1950), 367.

[10] *Contra gentes,* I, c. 15: "Videmus in mundo quaedam quae sunt possibilia esse et non esse, scilicet generabilia et corruptibilia. Omne autem quod est possibile esse, causam habet; quia cum de se aequaliter se habeat ad duo, scilicet esse et non esse, oportet, si ei approprietur esse, quod hoc sit ex aliqua causa. Sed in causis non est procedere in infinitum, ut supra probatum est per rationem Aristotelis. Ergo oportet ponere aliquid quod sit necesse esse. Omne autem necessarium vel habet causam suae necessitatis aliunde; vel non, sed est per seipsum necessarium. Non est autem procedere in infinitum in necessariis quae habent causam suae necessitatis aliunde. Ergo oportet ponere aliquod primum necessarium, quod est per seipsum necessarium. Et hoc Deus est: cum sit causa prima, ut ostensum est." All quotations from St. Thomas in this article are given as in the Leonine edition unless otherwise indicated.

act of existence. Since in any being composed of potency and act, the potency precedes the act at least by a priority of nature, so in a contingent being the potency to exist precedes the act of existing, which is equivalent to saying nonexistence precedes existence. In this sense, they say, a contingent being "at some time," i.e. by a priority of nature, "is not."

It is difficult to see how it can be reasonably maintained that St. Thomas does not intend the *tertia via,* and specifically statement 2b, in a temporal sense. He uses several expressions that have either a predominantly or an exclusively temporal meaning: "quandoque non est . . . aliquando nihil fuit . . . etiam nunc nihil esset . . . non incipit esse . . .," etc. If St. Thomas does not mean to speak in a temporal sense, he could hardly speak more misleadingly. If he means to be understood in some sense other than temporal, is it not likely that he would speak differently, that he would at least use some clarifying expression, such as "saltem in ordine naturae"? Why indeed would he use temporal expressions at all? It would be much simpler and clearer to say "Quod possibile est non esse, de se non est" or "a seipso non esset" or something similar. Why complicate matters by saying it would not exist "at some time"? If the argument in the *Summa theologica* is meant to be basically the same as the similar argument in the *Contra gentes,* why does not St. Thomas use a formulation more like that in the *Contra gentes,* since, as admitted on all sides, the argument as stated in the *Contra gentes* is much less confusing?

If, on the other hand, St. Thomas does wish to be understood in a temporal sense, he could hardly speak more clearly. The term "quandoque" means "at some *time.*" "Quando" means "when" and is the term used by St. Thomas for the category of time. Deferrari's *Index to the Summa Theologica* gives forty-five instances of the use of the word "quandoque." In not one of these instances is the word used in a sense that would lend support to the nontemporal interpretation of 2b. Nor, to our knowledge, has anybody adduced an example of such usage anywhere else in St. Thomas' writings.

What can be found in St. Thomas' other writings is that he propounds what clearly seems to be the same opinion as that contained in 2b of the *tertia via* and in a strictly temporal sense. This may be seen especially in Book I, lessons 22-29, of his commentary on Aristotle's *De caelo et mundo.* Aristotle discusses the question of whether the world is generated or ungenerated, corruptible or incorruptible. He defends the view that it is ungenerated and incorruptible. In the course of his discussion a point that he develops at length is that a corruptible being cannot be eternal but must at some time corrupt and thereby cease to exist. St. Thomas develops this point further. That Aristotle and St. Thomas are speaking in a strictly temporal sense is obvious. Prescinding for the moment from whether St. Thomas agrees with Aristotle's opinion that a corruptible being must at some time corrupt, he does throughout these pages use in a strictly temporal sense expressions so much like statement 2b of the *tertia via* that it would be difficult to believe he means the latter statement in a different, nontemporal sense. To take just one striking example, he says, "Sic igitur patet quod omne corruptibile quandoque corrumpetur."[11] Moreover, while there is some problem in seeing how St. Thomas could agree with this particular opinion of Aristotle's, the fact is that he gives every impression of agreeing with it. He does remark, in the last paragraph in this same lesson, that Aristotle's views in this regard have to be interpreted in the light of Catholic faith, yet he concludes that "rationes praedictae [of Aristotle] in nullo impugnant sententiam catholicae fidei."[12]

It is in view of such evidence that the temporal interpretation of the *tertia via*, including statement 2b, has been more widely adopted by Thomists in recent years than it was formerly. And lest it be thought that this represents a complete innovation, it might be mentioned that the "Prince of Thomists," Capreolus, plainly interprets the *tertia via* in the fully temporal sense and gives no indication of having any doubt about it.[13] Of those authors who, in spite of all indications to the contrary, insist on interpreting the *tertia via* in a nontemporal sense, it is not amiss to repeat the words of Descoqs, "Avec de tels principes d'exégèse ne fera-t-on pas dire à un auteur n'importe quoi?"[14]
temporal element in a loose and unsatisfactory way. According to

2. The strict temporal sense of statement 2b.

Some authors acknowledge the temporal import of the *tertia via* as a whole and of statement 2b in particular, but introduce the

---

[11] *De caelo et mundo*, I, lect. 29, 8.
[12] *Ibid.*, 12.
[13] *Defensiones theologiae Divi Thomae Aquinatis* (Tours: A. Cattier, 1900-1908) I, dist. 3, q. 1.
[14] *Praelectiones theologiae naturalis* (Paris: Beauchesne, 1932-35) I, 253, note.

these authors, the meaning of 2b is something like this: a contingent being has nonexistence before existence, at least by priority of nature, and of itself is only in potency to existence; therefore of itself it would not come into existence but would remain nonexistent; therefore of itself it would "at some time" not exist.

While such an interpretation may at first glance appear neat and satisfying, it does not do justice to what St. Thomas, from all indications, seems to mean by "quandoque non est." It does not preserve the strict meaning of "quandoque," which is apparently the meaning St. Thomas intends. What St. Thomas seems to have in mind is a being that at some time does exist and only at some time, "quandoque," does not exist. The interpretation in question, on the other hand, makes the subject of 2b a being that would never exist. A contingent being considered precisely as a being that does not have existence of itself, as a being that of itself is only in potency to existence, and the like, is a being that would not exist at any time, not just at some time.

The point at issue is to a certain extent a question of the reason behind the "quandoque non est." St. Thomas clearly seems to have in mind not the kind of reason that would make a contingent being simply and eternally nonexistent, but the kind of reason that, while allowing the existence of the being for a time, would nevertheless demand its nonexistence at some time. The interpretation under consideration proposes the kind of reason that would make a contingent being simply and always nonexistent. In a sense it proves too much. While acknowledging the time element in 2b, it goes to the opposite extreme by making the time altogether unlimited instead of the limited time denoted by the term "quandoque."

Most of the argumentation already presented to show that St. Thomas is speaking in a temporal sense in 2b could be adduced also to show that he is speaking in a strictly temporal sense, that by "quandoque" he means exactly and only "at *some* time." That is the more obvious meaning of the statement, considered both in itself and in its context. It is the natural conclusion from the fact that St. Thomas begins his argument by speaking of beings that do exist. If St. Thomas meant the argument in the sense envisioned by the authors under consideration, it might again be asked why he would confuse the argument by introducing terms of such limited temporal significance as "quandoque" and "aliquando." If he meant the argument in that way, it would be much plainer to say that a contingent being by itself would not exist, or would not even begin to exist, or would never exist. But perhaps the most compelling reason for holding that St. Thomas means statement 2b in the strictly limited temporal sense is the fact that in the section of the *De caelo* to which we have already referred he makes assertions practically identical with statement 2b and unmistakably intends these assertions in the strictly limited temporal sense. He gives, in support of these assertions, reasons of the kind that would (assuming their validity) demand a temporal limitation of a being's existence, its nonexistence at *some* time, not its eternal nonexistence.

From all such indications, it seems at best highly unlikely that St. Thomas could mean statement 2b in a merely loose temporal sense.

B. *The supposition of a condition in 2b.*

The reader will have observed that some of the non-strictly-temporal interpretations of the *tertia via* assume an implied condition in 2b, by taking this statement to mean that a contingent being *of itself* would at some time not exist, or would not exist *unless* there is some other being, or in some comparable sense. Is this acceptable?

Considering its unqualified character, with no hint of a condition, considering also the tenor of the context, the statement gives every impression of having been meant as an absolute statement. There is also, as we will see later, strong external evidence, i.e. from what St. Thomas says elsewhere, in favor of understanding statement 2b as unconditional. But the evidence, whether internal or external, is not such as to exclude completely the possibility of an implied condition and due allowance will be made in this discussion for such an interpretation.

There is, however, one form of conditional interpretation of 2b that must unquestionably be rejected. It is an interpretation so superficial as hardly to merit attention, except that it is frequently encountered in presentations of the third proof. According to this interpretation, in statement 2b St. Thomas means to say that a contingent being would at some time not exist unless God exists. The authors who posit this kind of condition usually introduce it as an answer to the objection that, on St. Thomas' own admission, there is no apparent argument from reason alone against the eternal existence of a contingent being. These authors retort that St. Thomas admits the possibility of a contingent being existing eternally only on the condition of the existence of God, and that therefore it is irrelevant to appeal in this way to St. Thomas' admission of the possibility of eternal creation.

The simplest way to deal with this line of reasoning is to point out that it makes the rest of St. Thomas' argument foolish. If St. Thomas' meaning in 2b is that a contingent being must at some time not exist unless God exists, then his immediate conclusion in 3 should be, Therefore God exists. There would be no use in concluding only to necessary being in general and bothering with further steps in the argument before concluding to the existence of God.

The appeal, by those who question the soundness of the *tertia via*, to St. Thomas' own admission of the theoretical possibility of the eternal existence of contingent beings is in no way invalidated by the fact that St. Thomas admits this only on the condition of God's existence. The point of the appeal is simply that, on St. Thomas' own admission, there is no evident contradiction in the hypothesis of a contingent being existing eternally, and that consequently it does not seem to follow with strict necessity that "quod possibile est non esse quandoque non est."

C. *Precise meaning of "quod possibile est non esse."*

The expression "quod possibile est non esse" could, in itself, be understood as meaning any being that does not exist by its own essence, any being whose existence is distinct from its essence. This is the meaning that has often been attributed to the expression in some of the looser interpretations of the *tertia via*. But that St. Thomas does not mean the expression in this sense is apparent from the rest of the argument. "Possibile non esse" in this sense would be distinguished directly and adequately from being that is *per se* necessary. If St. Thomas meant "possible non esse" in this sense, he would not posit a third kind of being, that which is *necessarium per aliud*, or, as he says, "habet causam suae necessitatis." He must mean "possibile non esse" in a more limited sense, as distinct from both *necessarium per se* and *necessarium per aliud*.

Many authors hold that what St. Thomas means by "possibile non esse" in the *tertia via* is corruptible being, i.e. material being that is in potency to another form than the one it has. This interpretation does agree, in many respects, with what St. Thomas says both here and elsewhere. One of the main relevant passages is in the *Quaestiones disputatae de potentia*, q. 5, a. 3. Here St. Thomas, discussing the problem whether God could annihilate a creature, states that a thing can be said to be possible with reference to a creature in two ways: first, insofar as it is within the power of the agent, in this case God, to do this thing; second, insofar as there is within the creature itself a potency to this thing. With regard to the latter kind of possibility, he holds that not all creatures, but only corruptible material beings, can be properly said to have a potency for nonbeing.

> Potentia enim ad esse et non esse non convenit alicui nisi ratione materiae, quae est pura potentia. Materia etiam, cum non possit esse sine forma, non potest esse in potentia ad non esse nisi quatenus existens sub una forma, est in potentia ad aliam formam.[15]

St. Thomas says, in effect, that no being has within itself a potency to nonbeing precisely as nonbeing, and that the only way in which a being can be said to have within itself a potency to nonbeing is insofar as it has a potency to become something substantially different and thus to cease being what it was. And this is true only of corruptible material being, which is capable of exchanging one substantial form for another through corruption and generation. A created spiritual being, although contingent or *possibile non esse* in the sense that existence does not belong to it by its essence, is nevertheless a necessary being in the sense that it does not have within itself any such potency to *non esse* as is found in a material being. A created spiritual being or subsistent substantial form is, in this sense, in potency only to being. Adopting common scholastic terminology, we would say that a created spiritual being is "objectively" contingent—i.e. inasmuch as its nonexistence involves no contradiction—but "subjectively" necessary—i.e. inasmuch as it has within itself no real positive potency to nonexistence. A corruptible material being, in the same terminology, is not only objectively but also subjectively contingent.

Actually, according to St. Thomas, not even all material beings are subjectively contingent. Following Aristotle, St. Thomas thought that some material beings, the celestial bodies, are incorruptible because they possess "total forms," forms that completely satisfy the potentiality of their matter.[16] Whether or not the existence of such beings needs to be entirely rejected, as it now commonly is, it can be ignored for our purpose, and we can equate subjec-

---

[15] Ed. P. M. Pession (Turin: Marietti, 1949). St. Thomas says much the same thing in some of his other works, for example in the *Contra gentes*, II, 30.
[16] *De caelo*, I, lect. 6, 6.

tively contingent being, or corruptible being, with material being indiscriminately.

It would, therefore, be well in accord with what St. Thomas says in his other writings to hold that in the *tertia via* by the words "quod possibile est non esse" he means any corruptible, or material, being. This would also be well in accord with the first statement of the *tertia via* in which he says, "Quaedam inveniantur generari et corrumpi, et per consequens possibilia esse et non esse." We are not, however, arguing or agreeing that this is certainly what St. Thomas means. We agree that it may be what he means, and that there are good reasons for thinking so. There are nevertheless also good reasons for suspecting that he may mean something different. It will be better to postpone consideration of this other possibility for a moment.

IV. EVALUATION OF CONNOLLY'S AND DEGL'INNOCENTI'S ARGUMENTS

A. *Introductory remarks.*

Both Connolly and Degl'Innocenti agree with the temporal interpretation of the *tertia via,* including the strictly temporal meaning of 2b.

As to the meaning of "quod possibile est non esse," Connolly holds that by these words St. Thomas means a being with a subjective potency to nonexistence, a material, corruptible being. Degl'Innocenti is not as explicit about identifying *possibile non esse* with material being. In fact he suggests more than one possible interpretation of the term, as we will see. He does, however, speak mainly of *possibile non esse* as "corruptible" being, and, from most of what he says, he seems to mean "corruptible" being in the proper sense, material being.

The main difference between Connolly and Degl'Innocenti has to do with the more exact meaning of "quandoque" in 2b. Degl'-Innocenti holds that "quandoque non est" refers simply to nonexistence *after* existence. Connolly argues that a contingent being must have nonexistence both before and after existence, and that it is the nonexistence *before* existence that is principally intended in 2b.

We will consider first the arguments offered in defense of 2b, then those in defense of 2c. Among those in defense of 2b, we will

THE QUESTION OF THE VALIDITY OF THE *Tertia Via* 149

treat first the ones presented by Connolly, then those given by Degl'Innocenti.

B. *Arguments in defense of statement 2b.*

1. The natural desire argument.

a. The argument.

In his interpretation of the *tertia via,* Connolly appeals especially to the section of the *De caelo et mundo* to which we have already referred. In this section St. Thomas gives what can be considered, and are considered by Connolly, as two proofs of the statement, "Quod possibile est non esse, quandoque non est." St. Thomas speaks of the one proof as "per rationem metaphysicam," the other as "per rationem propriam scientiae naturalis."[17] The metaphysical argument he discusses at considerable length, the other very briefly.

The metaphysical argument can be summed up as follows: Whatever exists eternally, exists necessarily; therefore whatever exists non-necessarily, exists noneternally, which is the same as saying that whatever can not-be, at some time is not.

The conclusion obviously depends on the premise, "Whatever exists eternally, exists necessarily." On careful consideration of all that St. Thomas says in this section of the *De caelo,* it can be seen that this premise, and ultimately the entire metaphysical argument, is made to depend on the principle, "Omnia appetunt esse." All things seek being, all things have a natural desire for, a natural orientation to, existence, and therefore each thing has a natural tendency to exist as long as it can. If eternal existence is possible to a given being, that being will by this natural desire or tendency necessarily exist eternally. And if it necessarily exists eternally, then, since there is no time (outside of or beyond eternity) in which the being could also not-exist, it cannot be a contingent being, or a *possibile-non-esse.* Accordingly no eternal being can be a contingent being, and conversely no contingent being can be an eternal being; therefore a contingent being must at some time not be.

This line of thought may sound strange even to those who are fairly familiar with St. Thomas' philosophy—or perhaps especially to these. Anyone who wishes to be fully satisfied that it is St. Thomas' line of thought should read this section of the *De caelo.* We can, however, cite the following three particularly significant passages:

[17] *Ibid.,* lect. 29, 11.

> Illud quod semper est, scilicet per infinitum tempus, habet potentiam ut sit in infinito tempore: potentia autem existendi non est ad utrumque respectu temporis in quo quis potest esse; omnia enim appetunt esse, et unumquodque tantum est quantum potest esse. Et hoc praecipue patet in his quae sunt a natura, quia natura est determinata ad unum. Et sic quidquid semper est, non contingenter semper est, sed ex necessitate.[18]
>
> Id autem quod naturaliter est per tempus infinitum, necesse est esse: quia necesse est quod unumquodque tantum sit quantum natura rerum habet; non enim aliquid deficit esse nisi quando iam non potest esse, eo quod omnia appetunt esse.[19]
>
> Dicit [Aristoteles] manifestum esse quod impossibile est id quod est corruptibile, quandoque non corrumpi. Quia si quandoque non corrumpetur, potest non corrumpi, et ita erit incorruptibile: et tamen ponitur sempiterno tempore corruptibile existens: semper igitur, idest infinito tempore, erit simul actu corruptibile et incorruptibile. Sed quod corrumpitur non semper est, quod autem est incorruptibile, semper est: ergo erit aliquid simul possibile et semper esse et non semper esse, quod est impossibile, ut patet ex his quae supra dicta sunt; quia quod potest semper esse, ex necessitate semper est, unde non potest non semper esse. Sic igitur patet quod omne corruptibile quandoque corrumpetur.[20]

The dependence of the whole argument on the principle, "Omnia appetunt esse," is apparent in these passages. Connolly, O'Donoghue, and Pattin all acknowledge the importance of this principle in the argument.[21]

It may help to observe that, according to this line of thought, the proposition that a contingent being must at some time cease to exist is deduced not so much directly from any inherent tendency to nonexistence on the part of the contingent being as, indirectly or negatively, from a tendency to existence on the part of every being. Since all things seek being, everything exists as long as it can ("unumquodque tantum est, quantum potest esse") and a being does not cease to exist except when it cannot longer exist ("non enim aliquid deficit esse nisi quando iam non potest esse, eo quod omnia appetunt esse"). Accordingly, whatever *can* exist eter-

---

[18] *Ibid.*, lect. 26, 6.
[19] *Ibid.*, lect. 29, 5.
[20] *Ibid.*, 8.
[21] O'Donoghue, for example, says, "St. Thomas bases his reasoning on the principle: omnia appetunt esse" (*loc. cit.*, p. 142; cf. also p. 147). In Connolly's article *(loc. cit.)* see p. 320 and especially 330-333; in Pattin's *(loc. cit.)* p. 33.

nally, necessarily exists eternally ("quod potest semper esse, ex necessitate semper est") and whatever *does* exist eternally, necessarily exists eternally ("quidquid semper est, non contingenter semper est, sed ex necessitate"). Therefore what *can cease* to exist, *must* at some time cease to exist ("impossibile est id quod est corruptibile, quandoque non corrumpi"). More concisely, whatever exists eternally, exists necessarily; therefore whatever exists non-necessarily exists noneternally, or, in other words, whatever can not-be, at some time is not.

Such, in brief, seems to be St. Thomas' "metaphysical" argument.

b. First difficulty.

This argument raises at least two difficulties: (1) it does not seem to be true that every being necessarily seeks to exist as long as it can; (2) it does not seem that this argument can be correlated exactly with the notions of contingent and necessary being adopted by Connolly.

It does not seem true that every being necessarily seeks to continue in existence as long as it can. What about a being that *could* exist longer and yet freely chooses to allow or cause the cessation of its own existence? To be concrete, what about a man who freely commits suicide? It may be answered that free choice supposes a spiritual component which survives the cessation of the composite. The fact remains that in any such case the original being, the material composite, has ceased to exist, and has done so even though it could have continued to exist.

To make the objection more directly applicable to the discussion of the *tertia via*, we might advert to the case of a man living near the end of the world and included among those who (according to revelation) will not die, and yet who could presumably, at some previous point in time, freely choose to bring about his own death. Would not such a man qualify as a being that could cease to exist and yet never will? Would he not therefore negate St. Thomas' contention that, if a being does not cease to exist, its unending existence is a matter of necessity, of inevitable desire, and, conversely, the contention that what can not-exist must at some time not exist? Granted that the actual fact that some material beings will escape death is known only from revelation, this does not prevent its being validly introduced as an argument against St. Thomas' contention that all beings necessarily seek to exist as long as they can. The theoretical possibility of such exceptions would not depend on revelation and would still present the same objection to St. Thomas' argument.

However, the defenders of St. Thomas' thought in this respect might reply that the objection is based on elicited desire, a desire for, or choice of, either continued existence or cessation of existence emanating from the will, whereas St. Thomas' argument has to do entirely with natural desire, a desire on the part of the very essence or substance, a desire which *is* a necessary one, in itself not changeable by free choice.[22] They might insist that in this sense a being always exists necessarily as long as it exists, i.e. in the sense that there is in the essence a necessary ordination to, or clinging to, existence and that in this sense even the man who could commit suicide but does not, continues in existence "necessarily" if we consider only the necessary tendency of the essence to exist as long as existence is possible to it.

While this may be stretching the argument rather far, it seems to us that it has to be stretched this far if the argument, i.e. the argument based on the desire for existence, is to hold up at all. Understood in this sense the argument seems in some degree plausible, at any rate not clearly invalid. We therefore raise no main objection on this score, but suppose the validity of the *tertia via*, understood in this sense, up to this point. To recapitulate, from the viewpoint that any being that exists eternally does so necessarily—i.e. by a natural and necessary desire, as distinct from an elicited free desire, for existence—conversely a nonnecessary being, or *possibile-non-esse,* is a being that at some time does not exist.

c. Second difficulty.

Before pursuing the discussion further along the same line, it will be best to consider the second problem mentioned previously, the difficulty of correlating this argument based on natural desire with the notions of contingent and necessary being adopted by Connolly. If statement 2b is valid on the basis of St. Thomas' argument from natural desire as in the foregoing remarks, it would seem to be valid unconditionally and universally, independently of whether the being in question is or is not composed of matter and form. If eternal being is equated with necessary being on the basis of the natural desire of existence, then *eo ipso* without excep-

---

[22] Cf. Pattin, *ibid.* "Il s'agit évidemment d'un désir inné. Ce désir n'est pas un acte, mais un appétit ontologique, c'est-à-dire une tendance, une ordination transcendantale."

tion any nonnecessary being, or *possibile-non-esse*, is a noneternal being, one that at some time does not exist. From this viewpoint even a spiritual being that ceased to exist would be a *possibile-non-esse*, whereas a material being existing eternally would be a necessary being. It is the latter possibility that concerns us here. For if we admit that possibility, we cannot equate *possibile-non-esse* in statement 2b with material being and still hold that the statement is valid unconditionally.

It seems fairly clear that Connolly would agree that the statement was not intended by St. Thomas as unconditional. I think he would insist that *possibile-non-esse* means any being composed of matter and partial form, that such a being is by nature corruptible, and that it will necessarily corrupt *unless* some other being intervenes to prevent the corruption.

There are really two questions here: (1) Whether St. Thomas intends statement 2b in that sense; (2) Whether the statement can be sustained in that sense.

(1) St. Thomas' meaning.

Supposing, as Connolly holds, that in the *tertia via* St. Thomas is speaking in the same vein as in the *De caelo*, the answer to the first question, as to what St. Thomas means by "possibile non esse" in the *tertia via*, depends on what he means by "potest" in the statements already quoted from the *De caelo*, e.g.: "Non aliquid deficit esse nisi quando jam non potest esse" and "Quod potest semper esse, ex necessitate semper est."

At this point it becomes necessary to introduce a further division in the various kinds of possibility. Besides mere objective possibility and subjective possibility as such, there is what can be called concrete possibility. Something is possible *in concreto*, or all-things-considered, when all factors and conditions required for its realization are *de facto* present or actually available.[23] The realization of a thing may be possible objectively, since it involves no contradiction, and also subjectively, inasmuch as there is an actually existing capacity for this thing, and yet not possible concretely, or all-things-considered, since it depends on some external factor which actually is not and will not be provided. For example, that this bottle be filled with wine is objectively and subjectively possible

[23] In many respects a handier term than "concretely possible" would be "*simpliciter* possible" or "absolutely possible." But we have avoided using these terms in this connection since St. Thomas uses them in a different sense. Cf. e.g. *Contra gentes*, II, c. 30, and *De potentia*, q. 5, a. 3.

but not possible *in concreto* if the wine is de facto not available. That this dog will exist next year is objectively and subjectively possible, but not concretely possible if the dog is not provided with the food it needs to continue in existence. Contrariwise, it is not only objectively and subjectively but also concretely possible for a material being to exist eternally if all the factors required for its eternal existence are forthcoming. Moreover, if this material being had no choice or control regarding its own existence, it would be a being to which nonexistence is subjectively possible (since, as a material being, it is in potency to corruption) and yet a being to which nonexistence is *not* possible concretely or all-things-considered.

We can apply the same distinction to such terms as "contingent" or "corruptible," and speak of beings as subjectively contingent, subjectively corruptible, or concretely contingent, concretely corruptible, etc.

It also seems necessary at this point to introduce an additional term to designate a particular kind of necessity. We saw above that St. Thomas argues in the *De caelo* that every eternal being is a necessary being on the ground that "all things seek being." We also saw that to make this line of reasoning applicable we would have to limit the desire in question to natural desire as distinct from elicited desire. In lieu of any better term to designate a being that is necessary in this sense, we will call it an "appetitively necessary" being, understanding by this any being that exists eternally and therefore, at least by natural desire, can be said to have eternal existence necessarily. Conversely, from this point of view a noneternal being would be an "appetitively contingent" being. These may not be ideal terms, but they seem the best available.

With these distinctions in mind, we can return to the question of the interpretation of statement 2b and the correlation of this statement with St. Thomas' doctrine in the *De caelo*. The question at this point is what exactly St. Thomas means by "possibile non esse." Does he intend this to signify precisely a subjectively contingent being, a being with a real potency to nonexistence, therefore every material being and only material being? Or does he mean "appetitively contingent" being? In this second interpretation, both "possibile-non-esse" and "necessary being" abstract from whether the being in question is material or immaterial; in this interpretation even a material being, if *de facto* eternal, would be a necessary being rather than a contingent being (and conversely an immaterial being could conceivably be a *possibile-non-esse*).

We have already observed that if "possibile non esse" is taken in the second sense, as precisely the alternative to "appetitively necessary," this would provide for interpreting 2b as unconditional. We admit that this is a somewhat elusive interpretation, one that may seem rather far fetched. And as far as we can see none of the authors defending the *tertia via* seems to have understood it exactly in this sense. But it is an interpretation that appears to follow from much of what St. Thomas says in the *De caelo*. For example, he says, "Quidquid semper est, non contingenter semper est, sed ex necessitate."[24] He says "quidquid," without restriction, and apparently without regard to whether the being is material or immaterial. His basic reason, "Omnia appetunt esse," applies not only to immaterial beings but also to material. In lesson 29, when he states the principle, "Omne corruptibile quandoque corrumpetur," he states it as though he meant it as absolute. After mentioning that some, including Plato, would hold that the principle allows of exceptions, he nevertheless seems to agree with Aristotle in holding that the principle should be taken as unconditional.[25]

At any rate the interpretation of 2b in this sense—i.e. the interpretation of "possibile non esse" as "appetitively contingent" and the interpretation of 2b as unconditional—seems at least a possibly correct interpretation of what St. Thomas intends. It also seems an interpretation that would give statement 2b some validity, although a rather tenuous validity, as already explained. Accordingly, even if it is not what any of the defenders of the *tertia via* have meant it should be given due consideration. We will return to it later in connection with statement 2c, which depends on 2b. There it will be seen that, even accepting the validity of 2b in accordance with the foregoing interpretation, the argument as a whole breaks down at 2c.

(2) Inconclusiveness of the argument from natural desire if applied strictly to material being.

Let us see how statement 2b holds up on the basis of the argument from natural desire if we suppose that in this statement St. Thomas is speaking strictly of material being as such. This is apparently the understanding of Connolly, as also of O'Donoghue and Pattin. Connolly would hold that when St. Thomas says, in the *De caelo*, "unumquodque tantum est quantum potest esse," by

[24] *De caelo*, I, lect. 26, 6.
[25] *Ibid.*, lect. 29, 8.

"potest esse" St. Thomas means precisely subjective potency, and that only immaterial beings have no subjective potency to nonbeing whereas material beings have a subjective potency both to being and to nonbeing, that consequently an immaterial being, by the natural desire for existence, exists necessarily and always, whereas a material being not only can, but at some time must, not exist.

This, we acknowledge, is an extremely brief synopsis of Connolly's argument. But we cannot see in anything that he says, nor in anything that the other authors say, any conclusive reason for holding that a material being must at some time not exist simply and strictly as a consequence of the considerations of subjective potency and natural desire. Since from the standpoint of subjective potency a material being is in potency to be *or* not-be, why could it not, just from that standpoint, actually *be* forever? There seems to be no reason to place any inevitable time limitation on a being just because it has a subjective potency to not-be. However long a material thing exists, whether for a limited time or for eternity, it retains the subjective potency to nonbeing; the subjective potency to nonbeing, therefore, is not incompatible with either limited or eternal existence.

If indeed, as St. Thomas says, "*unumquodque* tantum est quantum potest esse" and "*omnia* appetunt esse," why would not even a material being, considered just with respect to subjective potency and the natural desire for existence, tend to exist eternally? Why would it not actually exist eternally unless some *other* consideration demanded a limitation of its existence? If, as St. Thomas says, because of the natural desire of existence "nothing ceases to be except when it *cannot* longer exist,"[26] and since from the standpoint of subjective potency alone an existing material being is just as capable of continuing in existence as of ceasing to exist, would it not follow that if a material being must at some time not be, the reason would have to be found in some ground other than subjective potency and natural desire?

Perhaps it will be suggested that the point of the argument is that, since the matter in a material being is in potency to other forms than the one it has and since everything, including *materia prima*, has a natural desire or tendency to be whatever it can, the material being would naturally tend to acquire other possible forms, to be something else. But—keeping in mind that we are consider-

[26] *Ibid.*, 5.

ing material being simply as such and abstracting from characteristics of this or that particular kind of material being—why should the "desire" or tendency to acquire another form be any stronger than the tendency to keep the form it has? Why not rather the contrary, since the form it has is the one in possession? And if—as Connolly holds, following St. Thomas—the loss of a substantial form by an existing material being means that the being ceases to exist, why, on the basis of natural desire of existence, would not the existing material being tend rather to continue indefinitely to be what it is, rather than to become something else and thereby itself cease to be?

Furthermore, even if material composition, considered just in itself, did necessarily entail a predominant tendency toward change, why could not this tendency be outweighed by other factors within the over-all composition of the concrete material being, i.e. by particular qualities and powers contributory to self-preservation?

To sum up, there seems to be no conclusive reason, based simply on considerations of subjective potency and natural desire, for holding that every material being must at some time not be.

2. The "natural science" argument.

As mentioned previously, Connolly uses in defense of statement 2b two arguments from the *De caelo*, the metaphysical argument that we have just considered and the "argument from natural science." The latter argument is stated by St. Thomas as follows:

> Et dicit [Aristoteles] quod etiam per rationem naturalem . . . potest considerari quod impossibile est id quod semper fuit postea corrumpi, vel id quod prius non fuit postea esse sempiternum. [Aristotle, opposing the view of those who held that the world is generated but incorruptible and defending his own view that the world is eternal, argues that whatever is ungenerated is incorruptible and vice versa, and that whatever is generated will corrupt.] Et hoc probat quia omnia corruptibilia et generabilia sunt alterabilia; generatio autem et corruptio est terminus alterationis; alteratio autem fit de contrario in contrarium. Et sic patet quod ex illis contrariis ex quibus aliqua fiunt cum prius non essent, ab illis etiam postea corrumpuntur, et in eadem reducuntur per corruptionem; sicut si aliquid ex calido factum sit frigidum, potest iterum a calido calefieri. Et sic patet quod illud quod est generatum, potest iterum corrumpi; et illud quod est corruptum, fuit quandoque generatum.[27]

[27] *Ibid.*, 11.

The exact meaning of the argument is not altogether clear. And Connolly does little more than state the argument, with no particular comment. The crux of the argument seems to be that, just as anything generated is generated from something contrary (as from a *terminus a quo*), so it can and will be corrupted by that same contrary (as by an efficient cause, we suppose).

The argument presents a whole array of difficulties. If the conclusion were limited to the claim that what is generated *can* be corrupted—which is all that St. Thomas himself says in the first half of his conclusion—there would be no quarrel with this, at least if understood in the general sense that whatever is generated is by nature the kind of thing that can be corrupted. But the argument must prove more than this if it is to be used in support of the *tertia via,* and it is intended to prove more than this in the *De caelo.*

Does the argument prove that a corruptible being must at some time corrupt? Even supposing for the sake of argument that the being in question *was* generated from something contrary, before we can conclude that this same being will in turn certainly be corrupted by that contrary, we would have to make at least three assumptions: (1) that this contrary is still in existence; (2) that circumstances will be such that it can affect the being in question; (3) that this contrary will be powerful enough to enforce the corruption. None of these assumptions are necessarily implied in the data of statement 2b of the *tertia via.* Nor is there any assumption or implication, in that statement, that the being in question *was* generated, as we have granted here for the sake of argument; statement 2b starts simply with an existent contingent being.

If it is difficult to see how this argument from the *De caelo* proves that a corruptible being must at some time corrupt, it is even harder to see how the argument proves, as it is supposed to prove, that a corruptible being must at some time have been generated. There is no need to enlarge on the difficulty in this respect.

Although St. Thomas speaks of the argument as taken from "natural science," we have considered the argument as essentially a philosophical one rather than an argument from natural science in the more usual modern sense of experimental science. St. Thomas himself seems to have made little if any distinction between "natural science" and "natural philosophy." And judging from the way he states it, the argument under consideration appears to be essentially a deductive one from the general nature and principles of substantial change. Could it be that St. Thomas intends the argument in a more inductive sense, i.e. as an appeal to an empirically established fact or law of nature that all corruptible beings do eventually corrupt and that all corruptible beings come into existence through generation? We rather doubt that St. Thomas means the argument in this more empirical sense. It seems advisable nevertheless to say a word about this possible interpretation.

The main weakness in such an argument is that experience, or empirical science, can tell us only about those kinds of corruptible beings that have been the actual object of the experience or the science. We suppose here again that what statement 2b means by a being that "can not-be" is a material being. If the *tertia via* is to be accepted as valid, statement 2b must be universal. It must be demonstrated that all material beings without exception tend inevitably to corruption. How could human experience, limited as it is, possibly demonstrate this? It might be highly questionable whether empirical science shows even that all those material things that have come under its observation necessarily tend toward corruption. But, letting that aside, the fact remains that empirical science, or experience, cannot say that there might not be other kinds of material beings than those that have come under its observation; it cannot exclude the possibility of material beings which, precisely because material, are corruptible, i.e. capable of corruption, and which nevertheless would not, by reason of anything either in their own make-up or in their environment, necessarily tend to corruption.

It might be suggested that in statement 2b St. Thomas is speaking only about corruptible beings as we know them, the corruptible beings of our experience. Even if this be granted, and even assuming—merely assuming—that all corruptible beings as we know them do tend inevitably to corruption, this will not help to validate the *tertia via*. There will then be a gap in the argument in statement 3. From the premise that all beings cannot be of the kind that not only are corruptible but necessarily tend to corruption, it will not be valid to pass immediately to the conclusion that there must be a necessary being, since this would be to ignore the alternative possibility of beings that are corruptible and yet do not necessarily tend to corruption.

3. Degl'Innocenti's arguments.

In his defense of statement 2b, Degl'Innocenti cites the following objection, "Why must that which is corruptible necessarily in fact corrupt?" The first part of his answer is as follows:

> Precisely because it is corruptible, we reply. The corruptible is, in fact, called such because it carries in itself the seeds of corruption. Now it is inconceivable that the seeds would never come to maturity and would not finally bear their fruit. Hence, just as that which is by nature immortal never dies because its nature compels it to live forever, and, contrariwise, that which is mortal must at some time die because it does not have within itself sufficient powers to resist death indefinitely, so that which is by nature incorruptible must always remain incorrupt, and on the other hand that which is by nature corruptible must one day corrupt, otherwise it would be no longer corruptible but incorruptible. In short, a corruptible being that did not corrupt would be a contradiction, like a mortal being that did not die.[28]

It is not easy to be sure of Degl'Innocenti's meaning, especially when he uses such figurative language as "seeds of corruption." But, in any event, he appears to be guilty of ambiguity in his use of the term "corruptible." He seems to introduce into the term more than is justified by either his own previous definitions or the data of the *tertia via*. He defines "corruptible" (which he considers the equivalent of "possibile non esse") as simply that which *can* cease by corruption.[29] And the premises of the *tertia via* speak merely of "*possibilia* esse et non esse" and "quod *possibile* est non esse." In the present passage, however, Degl'Innocenti seems to have in mind a being that not only can corrupt but that, in addition, has something about it that makes it *tend* necessarily toward corruption. Judging from the metaphors he uses, he seems to visualize not just material being in general, but a particular kind of

---

[28] *Loc. cit.* (supra n. 3) p. 56: "Appunto perchè corruttibile, rispondiamo. Il corruttibile infatti si dice tale perchè porta in se stesso i germi della corruzione. Ora non si concepisce che i germi non vengano mai a maturazione e non diano finalmente il loro frutto. Quindi, come ciò che è per natura immortale non muore mai perchè la sua natura lo obbliga a vivere sempre; e ciò che invece è mortale deve una volta morire perchè non ha in se stesso forze sufficienti per resistere indefinitamente alla morte; così ciò che è per natura incorruttibile deve sempre rimanere incorrotto, e ciò che all'opposto è per natura corruttibile deve un giorno corrompersi, altrimenti non sarebbe più corruttibile ma incorruttibile. Insomma un corruttibile che non si corrompe, sarebbe una contraddizione, come un mortale che non muore."

[29] "Il 'possibile non esse' non è soltanto ciò che può perire o 'perissable', ma ciò che può perire per corruzione; e ciò è reso molto bene dalla parola corruttibile e non da altre" (*ibid.*, p. 52). "Si noti la definizione del corruttibile: quod potest desinere esse per corruptionem" (*ibid.*, p. 54).

material being, living material being, and even more restrictively, the kind of living material being known to man, the kind that by natural development always tends toward corruption. We realize that Degl'Innocenti would not mean actually to restrict "corruptible being" to living beings. But he does seem to attribute to corruptible beings in general some positive tendency to corruption, similar to that found in living beings as we know them. And the supposition of such a tendency does seem to add something, arbitrarily, to the basic notion of corruptible as simply that which *can* corrupt.

Degl'Innocenti compares the corruptible to the "mortal." Is there not the same ambiguity here? If "mortal" is taken to mean simply "capable of dying," then it is indeed essentially the same as "corruptible" in the simple proper sense of that which *can* corrupt. But Degl'Innocenti is obviously taking mortal to mean, as it more commonly does mean, not just that which *can* die, but that which by nature *tends* toward death. And the corruptible is equivalent to the mortal in this sense only if the notion of such a tendency is added to the basic notion of corruptible as simply that which can corrupt.

Degl'Innocenti also seems to maintain, in the part of his argument already quoted, that statement 2b is unconditional, allowing of no exception whatsoever. He says, "It is inconceivable that the seeds would never come to maturity," and "A corruptible being that did not corrupt would be a contradiction." He goes on, however, to make clear that he does not mean these statements quite so absolutely as they sound. After mentioning the objection of Descoqs, that "it is not repugnant that a *de jure* corruptible being in fact never corrupt, just as it is not repugnant that a mortal being actually live forever," Degl'Innocenti replies:

> Here we are already outside the hypothesis contemplated. In reality that which *de jure* is corruptible can *de facto* not corrupt *only* if there is an incorruptible being which impedes in the corruptible being itself the natural effect of corruptibility, i.e. the actual corruption, and outside of the corruptible being suspends the action of the causes which concur in the corruption. In other words, a corruptible being which does not corrupt is a signal exception to the laws of nature. But who can introduce such an exception into a universe that supposedly consists entirely and only of corruptible things? Just as there is no means of immortality where all is mortal, so there is no source of incorruptibility where all is corruptible.

In the material universe, accordingly, there prevails an iron determinism and everything is so connected and interlinked that nothing can be isolated or withdrawn from the influence of the actions and reactions of natural forces. Moreover the law of the continuity of matter prevents the existence of vacuums or stagnant compartments; and just as everything is subject to motion, so it is subject to time, to before and after, to beginning and end. Therefore corruptible things left to themselves corrupt. Only by chance could a corruptible thing not corrupt. But that could not happen constantly; a corruptible thing cannot by chance remain always incorrupt, because that which happens by chance is verified only seldom and irregularly.[30]

From these further remarks, it can be seen that Degl'Innocenti supposes an implied condition in statement 2b, the condition that all things are corruptible. It merits repetition that the allowance of such a condition is a considerable concession, in view of the fact that statement 2b sounds very much like an altogether unconditional statement, and the fact that an unconditional interpretation seems to be confirmed by what St. Thomas says in the *De caelo*. We have, however, already granted that such an implied condition is not entirely excluded and we will continue to make allowance for it here.

The question is, even granting the condition posited by Degl'Innocenti, the condition that all things are corruptible, does it necessarily follow that a corruptible being must corrupt? The conclusion, and the justification of it in this particular section of Degl'In-

---

[30] *Ibid.*, p. 57: "Qui siamo già fuori dell'ipotesi contemplata. Infatti ciò che de iure è corruttibile può di fatto non corrompersi *solo* se esista un'ente incorruttibile che nel corruttibile stesso impedisca l'effetto naturale della corruttibilità, cioè l'effettiva corruzione; e fuori del corruttibile sospenda l'azione delle cause che concorrono alla corruzione. In altri termini: un corruttibile che non si corrompe è un'insigne eccezione alle leggi di natura. Ma chi può introdurre una simile eccezione in un universo che si suppone composto tutto di soli corruttibili? Come non c'è un farmaco d'immortalità dove tutto è mortale, così non c'è un fattore d'incorruttibilità dove tutto è corruttibile. Nell'universo materiale, poi, vige un ferreo determinismo, e tutto è talmente connesso e concatenato che niente può isolarsi o sottrarsi al gioco delle azioni e reazioni delle forze naturali. Inoltre la legge della continuità della materia impedisce che ci siano dei vuoti o compartimenti stagni; e tutto, com'è soggetto al moto, così è soggetto al tempo, al prima e al poi, all'inizio e alla fine. Perciò i corruttibili, lasciati a se stessi, si corrompeno. Un corruttibile potrebbe non corrompers siolo per caso. Ma ciò non potrebbe accadere costantemente: un corruttibile non può, per caso, restare *sempre* incorrotto, perchè ciò che avviene per caso si verifica molto di rado e saltuariamente.

nocenti's argument, might be debated from a number of angles, but we will limit ourselves to the most significant.

Degl'Innocenti admits that there could be an exception by chance, but maintains that this could be only for a while, not forever. Even supposing that an exception could occur only "by chance," is it so certain that this could be only temporary? What would be required in order to have an exception by chance would not necessarily be a continued realization of some complex set of factors. There would not necessarily be required anything more than the failure of some single condition to be realized, i.e. some one condition necessary for the corruption of the being in question. And what if the being in question were of such a kind that it could corrupt only upon the fulfillment of an extremely complicated and unlikely set of circumstances? Is it inconceivable that such a set of circumstances might never occur? Is it not in fact all the more conceivable that such a set of circumstances might never occur if we suppose the rigidly determined universe that Degl'Innocenti depicts?

It might be replied that if in a completely material universe a particular set of circumstances would never occur even in infinite time, this would mean that the occurrence of such a set of circumstances was impossible, and therefore a being that could not corrupt except under those circumstances would in effect be incorruptible. Degl'Innocenti in fact goes on to say something of this kind. "Granting merely for the sake of argument that there were a corruptible being that *de facto* never corrupted, such a corruptible being would be practically equivalent to a being incorruptible by nature, and it would be all the more true to say that not all things can be corruptible, which is what Aquinas has mainly in view."[31] We are not at all sure that Degl'Innocenti means this precisely in the sense of the point we have just suggested as a possible contention from his side. But regardless of what Degl'Innocenti himself intends here, the contention that we have suggested will not suffice to validate the *tertia via*. Granting that a being that could corrupt only under circumstances actually never realized in a completely determined universe would be in some sense an incorruptible being, it would not fit the notion of necessary being that St. Thomas has

---

[31] *Ibid.*, p. 57: "Dato e non concesso che ci sia un corruttibile che di fatto non si corrompa mai, tale corruttibile equivarrebbe, praticamente, a un incorruttibile per natura, e sarebbe ancora più vera l'affermazione che non *omnia possunt esse corruptibilia*, che è ciò a cui l'Aquinate mira principalmente."

in mind in the *tertia via*. By a necessary being St. Thomas plainly means a being that is necessary in a positive sense, a being that has some actual positive reason for its necessity, since he speaks of necessary beings as divided adequately into two kinds, those that have a cause of their existence in some other being and those that are *per se* necessary. The incorruptible being of our present hypothesis would be incorruptible in a merely negative way, i.e. merely for want of the circumstances or influences required for its corruption. Any argument that would conclude, however validly, from the existence of corruptible beings only to the existence of some such negatively incorruptible being would not justify concluding from the existence of corruptible beings to the existence of a positively necessary being.

Let us return to Degl'Innocenti's statement that a corruptible being which *de facto* did not corrupt would be practically equivalent to an incorruptible being. If, as seems likely, Degl'Innocenti means this not in exactly the particular sense that we have just discussed, but only in a more general sense, just at its face value, then it is even less acceptable in defense of the *tertia via,* and for much the same reason as we have already given. A corruptible being that happened not to corrupt would undeniably be in some respect, i.e. in actual duration, equivalent to an incorruptible being, but it would certainly not just *eo ipso* be what St. Thomas means by a necessary being. A being that never corrupts is not, simply as such, the same as a being that *cannot* corrupt, and proving the existence of the former is not proving the existence of the latter.

Continuing his defense of statement 2b, Degl'Innocenti gives further consideration to the "*de facto* incorruptible," and in such a way as to offer what amount to an alternative interpretation of this statement essentially different from the one he started with. He says:

> But perhaps the exclusion of the *de facto* incorruptible is already contemplated in the text, since St. Thomas deduces *de facto* corruptibility from actual corruption. He writes in fact, as we have seen: 'Invenimus enim in rebus quaedam quae sunt possibilia esse et non esse, cum quaedam inveniantur *(de facto)* generari et corrumpi, et *per consequens* possibilia esse et non esse. Impossibile est autem omnia quae sunt, talia esse.' Now these last words *(talia esse)* can also, without straining, be rendered thus: talia scilicet quae generantur et corrumpantur de facto, et ideo sint possibilia esse et non esse. And the same may be said of those that follow: 'quod possibile est non esse

(ex eo quod de facto corrumpitur) aliquando non est.' In other words the text permits also the following sense: some things *de facto* corrupt and therefore are said to be corruptible. But it is impossible that all things *de facto* corrupt and therefore are corruptible, because that which is said to be corruptible by reason of the fact that it really corrupts, at a given moment no longer exists. If therefore all things (omnia quae sunt) are corruptible because *de facto* they corrupt, 'aliquando nihil fuit in rebus.' In such a way the hypothesis of Aquinas would not regard precisely the *corruptible* that *can* corrupt (but can also, accidentally, not corrupt) but, on the other hand, would regard directly that which *de facto corrupts* and therefore *can* corrupt, or is corruptible. Thus the objection based on the *de iure* corruptible and the *de facto* incorruptible would no longer have any justification.[32]

In spite of Degl'Innocenti's claim that this interpretation can be placed on the *tertia via* "without straining," it seems to us a good example of distorting St. Thomas' words, and even making St. Thomas himself sound rather foolish, in an exaggerated effort to validate St. Thomas' argument. Is it plausible that St. Thomas would express himself as he does—in what would amount to such a roundabout and misleading way—if he really meant what Degl'Innocenti suggests? Could it be any clearer that what he is talking about formally and directly in the first part of the *tertia via* is the kind of being that *can* be or not be, "*possibilia esse et non esse,*" and that he adduces the actual corruption and generation of some beings only as evidence of the existence of "possibilia esse et non

[32] *Ibid.*, p. 57-58: "Fores però la esclusione dell'incorruttibile di fatto è già contemplata nel testo, perchè S. Tommaso deduce la corruttibilità dal fatto della corruzione effettiva. Scrive infatti, come abbiamo visto: 'Invenimus enim in rebus quaedam quae sunt possibilia esse et non esse, cum quaedam inveniantur *(de facto)* generari et corrumpi, et *per consequens* possibilia esse et non esse. Impossibile est autem omnia quae sunt, talia esse.' Ora queste ultime parole *(talia esse)* possono anche, senza stiracchiature, rendersi cosi: talia scilicet quae generantur et corrumpantur de facto, et ideo sint possibilia esse et non esse. E lo stesso si dica di quelle che seguono: 'quod possibile est non esse (ex eo quod de facto corrumpitur) aliquando non est.' In altre parole il testo permette anche il senso seguente: alcune cose di fatto si corrompono e perciò son dette corruttibili. Ma è impossibile che tutte le cose si corrompano di fatto e perciò siano corruttibili, perchè ciò che vien detto corruttibile per il fatto che realmente si corrompe, a un dato momento non è più. Se pertanto tutte le cose (omnia quae sunt) sono corruttibili perchè di fatto si corrompono, 'aliquando nihil fuit in rebus.' In tal modo l'ipotesi dell'Aquinate non cadrebbe precisamente sul *corruttibile* che *può* corrompersi (ma può anche, *accidentalmente,* non corrompersi); ma, all'opposto, cadrebbe direttamente su ciò che *si corrompe di fatto* e quindi *può* corrompersi, ossia è corruttibile. Cosi l'obbiezione basata sul corruttibile *de iure* e incorruttibile *di fatto* non avrebbe più ragione di essere."

esse," not as an element in the notion of such beings. The point could be demonstrated at length by a detailed review of St. Thomas' words, but this seems hardly necessary. Even if it were granted that by "possibile non esse" St. Thomas means formally a being that *de facto* corrupts, and therefore can corrupt, there would still be a flaw in the argument as a whole. It would still not be possible to conclude from the fact that not all beings can be of the kind that actually corrupt to the fact that there must be some incorruptible being, for this would be to ignore the alternative possibility of beings that are not incorruptible and yet *de facto* do not corrupt.

4. Summary of evaluation of arguments in defense of 2b.

If our criticism up to this point has been correct, among all the arguments in favor of statement 2b that we have considered we are left with only one that appears to have some validity. That is the argument that incorporates the elements of natural desire of existence and "appetitive necessity." It may help to recall that this is the argument that says that if a being is "appetitively contingent," then that being must at some time not exist, since this is simply the corollary to the consideration that any being that exists eternally thereby is a necessary being at least from the standpoint of natural desire of existence. We have already acknowledged that the merits of this line of argument may be very limited, and we are far from insisting that it is definitely the correct interpretation of statement 2b or that it is in its own right a genuinely meaningful and effective line of argument. We say merely that of the various interpretations of 2b, this seems the only one that qualifies as both a possibly correct interpretation and at the same time an argument of some discernible validity. It is this argument then that should be kept mainly in mind in the following discussion of statement 2c.

C. *Arguments in defense of statement 2c.*

After declaring that "what can not-be, at some time is not," St. Thomas continues, "Si igitur omnia sunt possibilia non esse, aliquando nihil fuit in rebus." We have already mentioned the obvious initial objection to this proposition, the objection based on the possibility of an endless series. Even granting that a contingent being must at some time not be, it does not seem to follow, from this alone, that at some time there would have been nothing, since this conclusion could be obviated by supposing that one contingent being derived from another in a series without a beginning.

To this objection the defenders of the *tertia via* usually reply that when St. Thomas says, "Si omnia sunt possibilia non esse," he means to include in the "omnia" not only individual complete substances but also such things as a series of beings, i.e. the series itself considered as a "being," and also the *materia prima* underlying a series of corrupted and generated beings.[33] This reply could be attacked, first of all, on the ground that it seems a rather implausible interpretation of St. Thomas' words. When he speaks of beings that are generated and corrupted and *therefore* can be or not be, and goes on to say, "Impossibile est omnia quae sunt talia esse," it is a little difficult to believe that St. Thomas is speaking of any kind of beings other than individual substances. We concede, however, that the interpretation advanced by the defenders of the *tertia via* is not definitely out of the question, and in criticizing statement 2c we will assume that when St. Thomas says, "Si omnia sunt possibilia non esse," he means to include in the "omnia" not only the individual beings in a series but the series itself as a being.

Even on this assumption, statement 2c can be criticized as inconclusive from at least two standpoints. St. Thomas says, "Si omnia sunt possibilia non esse, aliquando nihil fuit in rebus." Even granting the condition, "Si omnia" etc., in the wide sense advanced by the defendants, it can be asked, first, whether this would necessarily lead to "nihil" in the strict sense. And even granting that it would, it can be asked, secondly, whether this result (a state of nothingness) would necessarily have come about already ("fuisset") or might still be only in the future. The first criticism is particularly applicable to any defense of the *tertia via* maintaining that by "quod possibile est non esse" St. Thomas means formally a corruptible being, a material being. The second criticism is especially pertinent in relation to the argument involving the natural desire of existence and "appetitive necessity."

1. Why "nihil"?

We have seen that Connolly and other defenders of the *tertia via* maintain that in statement 2b St. Thomas is speaking of corruptible being in the strict sense. The nonexistence of which he speaks in that statement is the nonexistence that comes about through corruption in the strict sense, a change in which a material being loses the substantial form it had up to the time of the change and in that sense ceases to be, i.e. ceases to be what it was.[34] If this is the meaning of 2b, then it is difficult to see how any such change, or any suc-

[33] Cf. Connolly, *loc. cit.*, p. 342 and 344, and Degl'Innocenti, *loc. cit.*, pp. 59-61.
[34] Connolly, *loc. cit.*, pp. 299-308.

cession of such changes, could ever result in strict nothingness, since after the corruption there remains the underlying *materia prima*.

The defenders of the *tertia via* reply that this objection is contrary to the condition in 2c, "Si omnia sunt possibilia non esse," since the objection supposes the existence of something which is not corruptible, the *materia prima*. If everything were corruptible, they say, then even the *materia* underlying the change or changes would be corruptible, and thus it too would inevitably cease to exist, and with it everything.

We agree that the existence of *materia prima* itself is contrary to the supposition, "Si omnia" etc., if the "omnia" is understood to include not only individual substances but even such "partial beings" or principles of being as matter and form. The supposition, "Si omnia . . .," becomes in that light an impossible supposition, since *materia prima* itself cannot be, properly speaking, corruptible. But, even understood in that light (i.e. including *materia prima* in the "omnia") the supposition is not ours. It is the supposition made by some defenders of the *tertia via*. They make the supposition in that impossible sense just for the sake of argument, of course. We accept the supposition in the same vein, for the sake of argument, but we say that even granting the impossible supposition in their sense (and also granting for the sake of argument their contention that a material being must at some time corrupt) the supposition does not lead to their conclusion. It leads only to the cessation of existing things by change into something else. To put it another way, if *materia prima* itself were, *per impossibile*, subject to inevitable corruption, it would be composed of matter and form and this supposedly composite *materia prima* would itself at some time cease to be by reduction to its own constituent matter and the reception of a new form; it would not, on the premises adduced, cease to be by annihilation. It might even be argued that the supposition in question would lead to an infinite series of such fantastic divisions of *materia prima* itself into matter and form. A philosophically horrid prospect, no doubt. But the point remains that it is to some such result that the impossible supposition leads, rather than to total nothingness.[35]

[35] In answer to this objection Degl'Innocenti contends *(loc. cit.*, p. 58) that in the *tertia via* St. Thomas is speaking of total corruption, one that would leave not even *materia prima* ("corruzione totale" . . . "tale cioè che non abbia lasciato niente d'incorrotto, neppure la materia prima").

One difficulty in this solution is that it seems contrary to Degl'Innocenti's own definition of "corruptible." When he defines the corruptible as that which

2. Why nothingness in the past rather than in the future?

This objection is directed principally against any defense of the *tertia via* that would justify statement 2b by means of the combined considerations of natural desire of existence and "appetitive contingency." According to this interpretation of 2b, every eternal being would be an "appetitively necessary" being, and as a consequence any being that was "appetitively contingent" would be one that must at some time not exist. But, even granting this much, why could not the "some time" be still in the future? If it were still in the future, whether for an individual contingent being or for the whole series of beings, then the intended *reductio ad absurdum* in 2d, "etiam nunc nihil esset," would fail and with it the entire *tertia via*.

With reference to this objection it will be best, once again, to consider mainly what Connolly has to say. We do not mean to imply necessarily that Connolly fully espouses the interpretation of 2b based on what we have called "appetitive necessity" and "appetitive contingency." But his remarks in connection with the present question—why *nihil* in the past rather than in the future? —constitute the most significant efforts in this regard and include, directly or indirectly, what others have said.

Connolly acknowledges that the objection would be hard to answer if it were supposed that in statement 2b St. Thomas is speaking only of nonexistence after existence, rather than before, and if it were supposed that some contingent being, or series of contingent beings, has existed *ab aeterno*. On these grounds, he

---

"can perish by corruption" or "can cease by corruption" (cf. *supra* n. 29) he seems to indicate that he means corruption in the strict sense, and corruption in the strict sense implies that the *materia prima* remains after the corruption. It is true that St. Thomas himself says *(De caelo,* I, lect. 24, 8-9) that the term "corruptible" can be used in a wide sense, i.e. of something that can in any way cease to be, whether by corruption in the proper sense or in some other way. But he says that "corruptible" in the strict sense means able to "cease *by corruption,*" and here he obviously understands by the term "corruption" a process that would leave the *materia prima* in existence. Degl'Innocenti quotes some of these very passages and seems clearly to accept, as his definition of "corruptible," what St. Thomas calls the strict sense. It is difficult to see then how he can say that what St. Thomas means in the *tertia via* is a "total corruption" that would leave not even the *materia prima*.

The supposition of "total corruption" seems contrary, not only to Degl'Innocenti's definition of the corruptible, but also to his own main line of argument, which gives every indication of being based on a tendency to corruption in material things, corruption in the usual and proper sense, corruption that leaves in existence the subject of the corruption.

agrees, it would be difficult to give a reason why the total nothingness would necessarily have already come to pass.[36] He therefore argues that a contingent being, or *possibile non esse,* is a being that must have nonexistence not only after existence but also before, and that it is the nonexistence before existence that is essential to the argument of the *tertia via.* If it were true, as Connolly here contends, that every contingent being must have nonexistence before existence—and if it be granted that the "omnia" in 2c should be understood as referring not only to individual corruptible substances but even to such things as a series of corruptible beings, or the matter underlying the series—the rest of the *tertia via* would follow without difficulty.

Against Connolly's contention that when St. Thomas says, "Quod possibile est non esse quandoque non est," he means by the "non est" a nonexistence preceding existence, it has been objected by other authors that this seems contrary both to the natural import of the words and to what St. Thomas says elsewhere, e.g. "Nulla potentia respicit quod factum est in praeterito, sed id quod est in praesenti vel quod futurum est."[37] However, Connolly's interpretation is not necessarily excluded by any of these considerations. He might well admit that the *non-esse* in the first half of 2b, "possibile non esse," refers to the future, in accordance with St. Thomas' principle that potency regards only the present or the future, and yet argue that this is compatible with interpreting the "non est" of the second half of the statement as referring to nonexistence before existence, if it can be shown that every being that is in actual potency to nonexistence (in the future) is by that very fact a being which must actually have nonexistence not only after but also before existence.

The question then is whether it *can* be shown that a contingent being must have nonexistence both before and after existence. To prove this, Connolly again refers largely to the *De caelo.* We believe his reasoning consists essentially of two basic arguments, and we will consider these two arguments in turn.

a. First argument: The possible existence of a contingent being must be limited to a determined time.

Connolly argues that a contingent being must have nonexistence both before and after existence on the ground that the possibility

---

[36] *Loc. cit.,* p. 345.
[37] *De caelo,* I, lect. 29, 10.

of existence of a contingent thing must be limited to a determined time. Appealing to the *De caelo,* he lays down the basis of the argument as follows:

> Possible to be or not be must be said according to a determined time. . . . For if it is not so held, then impossibilities will ensue. Thus we have a contingent thing which is possible to be and not to be. Now if the existence of this contingent thing is not limited to a determined time, then there will be always more time in which it can exist. The logical consequence of this is that the possible thing can then exist in infinite time. So therefore we are led to the conclusion that this thing is possible to be in infinite time and yet it is possible not to be in infinite time. The absurdity is patent.[38]

Probably the first reaction of most readers of this paragraph would be to question the statement that "the absurdity is patent." It is indeed patently absurd that a thing exist "in one infinite time" and not exist in "*another* different time." But it is not patently absurd that a thing exist in infinite time and yet be *disjunctively capable* of not existing in that *same* time. Connolly, following St. Thomas, acknowledges this objection. He states the objection as follows:

> It is true, no doubt, that no potency is directed in act to two opposites at the same time. But there is nothing prohibiting a potency from being directed to two opposites in respect to the same time but under a disjunction. Although one cannot stand and sit at the same time, yet one can stand for a certain length of time and yet in that very same time he has the potency to sit. In terms of existence, we can posit an eternally existing being that is contingent or possible not to be and is not therefore a necessary being. So this contingent being could indeed not-be in respect to some part of the infinite time in which it is posited as always existing.[39]

In reply, Connolly says:

> St. Thomas refutes this objection by pointing out the lack of parity between the two cases inasmuch as one is concerned with contingency which we cannot apply to eternal being. In terms of existence, if a thing always exists, then it has the potency of being in eternal time. But since all things seek being, each thing is only as much as it can be.[40] This is espe-

---

[38] *Loc. cit.,* pp. 317-318.
[39] *Ibid.,* p. 319.
[40] Connolly thus translates the words, "Unumquodque tantum est quantum potest esse." It would be both more favorable to his own argument and more exactly expressive of St. Thomas' thought to omit the "only." St. Thomas' point in this particular statement is not so much to limit the existence of a thing to only what it can be as to insist rather on the positive aspect that a thing necessarily is as much as it can be.

cially clear in things that are from nature which is determined to one. Therefore it cannot be that an eternally existing thing is at the same time possible not to be or corruptible, because whatever exists eternally, does so not from contingency but from necessity.[41]

This brings us back to the argument from natural desire. That argument, from what we can see, amounts to saying that every eternal being is *eo ipso* a necessary being, in the sense that its eternal existence is necessary at least by natural desire, and *e converso* any being that is, from the same standpoint, contingent cannot be an eternal being but must at some time not exist. Accepting this argument and viewpoint for what it is worth, it must be admitted that the possible existence of a contingent being has to be limited to a determined time, in the sense that there must be some time in which it actually does not exist. But this, in turn, brings us back to the original objection: Why must this "some time" be both before and after the existence of the contingent being? Why could it not be only after its existence? Why would this not satisfy the condition that a contingent being cannot be eternal but must at some time not exist? Granting that, in the sense of this argument, the possible existence of a contingent being must be "limited" to a "determined" time, why would it not be sufficient, as far as this argument goes, that the possible existence be limited only posteriorly (or anteriorly) rather than both anteriorly and posteriorly?

Connolly cites a passage in the *De caelo* in which St. Thomas does, apparently, intend to dispose of this very difficulty. In this passage, speaking first of beings in general (rather than just contingent beings) St. Thomas says that potency can be attributed to a being either according to strictly finite time (having both a beginning and an end) or according to "strictly infinite time" ("tempus simpliciter infinitum," i.e. with neither beginning nor end). He says that the latter, like the former, satisfies the general principle that potency must be attributed to a being according to a "determined time," because even infinite time is "aliqualiter determinatum," in the sense that it is "that than which there can be no greater." But he goes on to say:

> Illud autem tempus quod est infinitum *quo,* idest secundum aliquid, scilicet secundum principium vel secundum finem, neque est infinitum simpliciter, quia potest eo aliquid esse plus, neque simpliciter determinatum, quia non habet aliquam

[41] *Ibid.,* p. 320.

certam quantitatem. Et ideo, secundum praedictam suppositionem, non potest esse quod aliquid habeat virtutem faciendi vel patiendi, sive essendi vel non essendi, aliquo tempore quod sit finitum ex una parte et infinitum ex alia. Quicumque autem ponit quod aliquid est ingenitum et corruptibile, vel genitum et incorruptibile, ponit quod aliquid habeat potentiam essendi vel non essendi tempore secundum quid infinito et secundum quid finito: ergo destruit praedictum principium suppositum [i.e. the principle that potency must be attributed to a being according to a determined time.][42]

It will be observed that, in order to prove that there cannot be a being that had no beginning and yet is in potency to cease existing, St. Thomas here simply falls back on the principle that potency must be said of a determined time and interprets that principle as not allowing for a time that is "determined" in the sense that it is infinite in one direction and finite in the other. But if even a simply infinite time can be considered "determined" on the ground that it is that than which there can be no greater, why could not a time that is anteriorly infinite and posteriorly finite also be properly considered determined, in the sense that anteriorly there can be no greater and posteriorly there is a very definite limitation? Why would not such a time be sufficiently "determined" to satisfy the argument in hand, since it does provide for "some time" in which a contingent being does not exist, and in that way obviates the contradiction of having a being that is an eternal and therefore necessary being and yet, in the same respect, a contingent being?

Is there any inherent contradiction in the notion of a being that is eternal anteriorly and yet could at some time cease to exist? We do not see why anyone would hold that there is, if it is admitted, with St. Thomas, that there is no discernible repugnance in the idea of finite beings, even material beings, existing *ab aeterno*. And no further argument is given, by St. Thomas or by Connolly, for holding that potency must be attributed to a being according to either "strictly infinite time" or "strictly finite time"—no argument other than the one that will be treated in the next section.

b. Second argument: No reason for cessation of existence unless there is a beginning of existence.

The main part of this argument is stated by St. Thomas as follows:

[42] *De caelo*, I, lect. 29, 3.

> Si ponamus quod aliquid ingenitum prius semper fuit, et postea corrumpatur in aliquo signo temporis, idest in aliquo instanti, nulla ratio potest assignari quare magis possit corrumpi in isto instanti quam in aliquo infinitorum praecedentium. . . . Posset autem ratio assignari si tempus praecedens poneretur finitum, quia posset dici quod haberet virtutem ad esse vel non esse in tanto tempore, et non in pluri: sed ex quo ponitur fuisse vel non fuisse tempore infinito, praedicta ratio cessat.[43]

On this basis St. Thomas concludes, "Et ideo necesse est ponere quod ingenitum potuerit non esse in quolibet instantium praecedentis temporis." If it is supposed that a being can cease to exist at a given instant and if it is true that there is no more reason why it can cease to exist at that instant than at any previous instant, then it must be admitted that it could have ceased to exist at any preceding instant. This however, St. Thomas continues, is impossible, because anything that has existed *ab aeterno*, has existed *necessarily ab aeterno* and could not have not existed during that time. "Id quod naturaliter est per tempus infinitum, necesse ets esse: . . . non enim aliquid deficit esse nisi quando jam non potest esse, eo quod omnia appetunt esse."[44]

We have already granted repeatedly that, in a certain sense, i.e. from the standpoint of natural desire, everything exists necessarily during whatever time it exists, and, from that standpoint, is not capable during that same period of ceasing to exist. But we cannot see that this is sufficient to justify the intended *reductio ad absurdum* in St. Thomas' argument or to prove that there could not be a corruptible or contingent being that had no beginning.

First of all, to admit that a thing exists necessarily from the standpoint of the natural desire of existence, is not to admit that it exists necessarily in every respect; or, to use the terms we have used previously, to say that a thing is necessary "appetitively" is not to say that it is necessary concretely or all-things-considered. There is therefore no contradiction in holding that existence is "appetitively necessary" to a being during whatever time it actually exists and holding that the same being is actually capable, all things considered, of ceasing to exist at one or more points during that same time as well as at the end of that time.

St. Thomas says there is no reason why a being without a beginning would be more capable of ceasing to exist at one instant than

---

[43] *Ibid.*, 4.
[44] *Ibid.*, 5.

at another ("quare magis possit corrumpi"). But is it necessary, in order that a thing cease to exist, that it be more capable of ceasing to exist at one instant than at another? A particular event can be equally possible at any number of different instants and yet happen at one or some of those instants and not at others. It may be equally possible on a number of different occasions for a man to perform some specific action and yet happen that he actually performs it on just one or some of those occasions. What is required is that there be a reason why the thing *actually happens* at the time or times it does and not at others (rather than a reason why it is more *capable* of happening when it does).

It may be contended that this is what St. Thomas means, that there could be no reason why a being would actually cease to exist at one time rather than another if that being had no beginning of existence. Connolly in fact translates St. Thomas' statement in this sense.[45] Is the argument any more effective in this sense? In other words, must it be admitted that there could be no reason for a thing to cease existing at one instant rather than another if that thing had existed *ab aeterno*? We do not see that this is so.

The argument may be debatable on more than one score, but we will mention only the main one. The main objection is that the argument seems to assume that the only way in which a cessation of existence can come about is as the end result of a strictly deterministic sequence of events, a sequence which must therefore have a definite beginning. The argument seems to ignore the possibility of existence or nonexistence coming about as a result of free choice. In other words, the argument seems to consider necessity and possibility only from the standpoint of natural desire and to disregard the possible role of elicited desire. Why could not the fact that a given being ceases to exist at a certain instant be due, either in whole or in part, to some cause or condition freely posited, either by that being itself or by some other being? Is this not what does happen in countless cases? And since it depends on a free choice, could it not happen at any point in time, even in time without a beginning and to a being that had no beginning?

Some defenders of the *tertia via* may protest that the introduction of free will is contrary to the condition understood in statement 2b, since this statement supposes that all things are corruptible and therefore material, whereas free will implies the existence of a spirit-

[45] *Loc. cit.*, pp. 329 and 345.

ual substance. But let it be recalled that our argument in this section is principally against the interpretation of the *tertia via* based on "appetitive necessity." According to this interpretation the *possibile non esse* of statement 2b is not necessarily identical with material being, and even a pure spirit could be a *possibile non esse*. *A fortiori* a being composed of matter and spirit could be a *possibile non esse*. Accordingly, even granting the supposed condition in 2b that all things are *possibilia non esse,* this would not exclude the existence and influence of free will, which could provide a sufficient reason for the termination of existence of a given being at any point in time, even after that being had existed *ab aeterno*.

If our observations are correct, neither of the two arguments adduced to show that a contingent being must have nonexistence before existence is conclusive. Accordingly, even if we grant that a contingent being must at some time not exist, there seems to be no reason why that time could not be still in the future. There seems to be no necessity of accepting the conclusion of statement 2c, "aliquando nihil fuisset."

V. SUMMARY

The foregoing considerations can be summed up in two points: (1) it seems extremely unlikely that the *tertia via* is intended by St. Thomas in any other than a strictly temporal sense; (2) when understood in a strictly temporal sense the argument seems inconclusive.

In the strictly temporal interpretation of the *tertia via,* it is understood that when St. Thomas says, "Quod possibile est non esse quandoque non est," by "quandoque" he means exactly "at *some time,*" that he is speaking of a sequence of time, not merely of a sequence of nature, and that he is speaking of a being that *does* exist at some time and only at *some* time does not exist, not of a being that would never exist at all. That St. Thomas means statement 2b in this sense seems clear not only from the text and context but also from his other writings, especially from very similar statements in the *De caelo et mundo*.

When statement 2b is understood in the strictly temporal sense, there seems to be only one line of argument that gives this statement any validity, and even that is a quite tenuous validity. This is the line of argument based on the notion of "appetitive necessity," according to which every being has a necessary natural desire to exist as long as it can. In this sense any being that exists eternally does so necessarily, and could from that standpoint be considered a necessary being. Conversely any nonnecessary or contingent being would have to be one that at some time does not exist. We have seen that the main weakness in this argument is that it ignores the function of elicited desire, according to which even a being that exists eternally could be one that does so freely rather than of necessity; and therefore, conversely, a being that is actually capable, by elicited desire, of not existing—a being that is, concretely or all-things-considered, contingent—might nevertheless exist eternally. The defense of 2b based on "appetitive necessity" takes only a partial view of reality. However, from this partial viewpoint it can be granted that in some sense, i.e. considering natural desire alone, every eternal being is a necessary being, and as a consequence that any contingent being is one that must at some time not exist.

But even conceding this much validity to statement 2b, there still seems to be a failure in the argument as a whole when we come to statement 2c, "Si igitur omnia sunt possibilia non esse, aliquando nihil fuit in rebus." For even granting that, in the narrow sense just allowed, a contingent being must at some time not be—and granting also the somewhat questionable contention that St. Thomas means the "omnia" in statement 2c to include such things as a series of beings and *materia prima*—there is no apparent reason why the nonexistence required by 2b would have to come about in the past and might not be still in the future. In this connection, too, the arguments advanced in defense of the *tertia via* seem to overlook the possible role of free will in determining when the nonexistence takes place.[46]

On the basis of all that has been said in its favor up to the present, the validity of the *tertia via* seems still open to question. If the *tertia via* can be shown to be valid, the task remains to be done.

[46] The apparent failure of some defenders of the *tertia via* to give due attention to the role of free will suggests the possibility that behind some of the arguments there may lie an excessively Banezian outlook.

6

THE METAPHYSICAL CRISIS IN PHYSICAL THEORY

by

Leo A. Foley

Reason may be employed in two ways to establish a point: firstly for the purpose of furnishing sufficient proof of some principle, as in natural science, where sufficient proof can be brought to show that the movement of the heavens is always of uniform velocity. Reason is employed in another way, not as furnishing a sufficient proof of a principle, but as confirming an already established principle, by showing the congruity of its results, as in astrology the theory of eccentrics and epicycles is considered as established because thereby the sensible appearances of the heavenly movements can be explained; not, however, as if this proof were sufficient forasmuch as some other theory might explain them.[1]

For some time, physical theory has been approaching a crisis, and the above citation from St. Thomas Aquinas enunciates the precise nature of the crisis: the role of reason in the establishing and verification of a point, whether this is a point in theology, philosophy, or the physical sciences. Moreover, St. Thomas illustrates with the characteristics of the sources of intellectual difficulty: observation, inference, conclusion, congruity with already established positions, and appeal to reality. All of these points are at issue in intellectual difficulties that are becoming of such importance that epistemology is as much an issue in science as discovery and achievement.

In brief, before going into this problem at greater length, we may say that the epistemological problems facing physical theory deal with the origin of concepts on the observational level, the value of these concepts on the same level, the further development of theory on the conceptual level, and the congruity of concepts on this level. This was a problem in St. Thomas's day, in which scientific theory was largely a matter of the fundamental principles of mechanics

---

[1] *Summa theologica*, I. 32, 1, ad 1. Translation of the Fathers of the English Dominican Province. (New York: Benziger, 1947). Other works of St. Thomas are quoted from the Marietti edition.

drawn from direct observation. It is much more a significant problem today when we are dealing with entities whose existence we infer and whose nature we must express symbolically rather than literally.

In St. Thomas's day, the application of the scientific method as advanced by Aristotle in the *Posterior Analytics* and *Topics* was a comparatively simple task. Today, the whole scientific method is the center of a great controversy in which established points are considered contexts rather than principles, intellectual directions rather than premises. Thus, for example, if there is one principle that seems to be established beyond all doubt, it is the law of gravity. However, in classical mechanics it has one significance. In relativity physics it has another. Since in such contexts, which sometimes conflict with, sometimes complement each other, the falling of bodies at a constant rate "verifies" either context, the only verification is that of a limited congruity of concepts in a given conceptual context. Physical theory thus has a tendency to get far from reality. And insofar as reality can verify any and all intellectual positions, theory can easily go in one direction while applied science can easily go in another.

One of the difficulties facing a scholastic philosopher, acquainted as he may be with the sciences, is the danger of making Aristotle and St. Thomas say too much. For example, because in the citation given we discover that St. Thomas could entertain the notion that the Aristotelico-Ptolemaic theory of the geocentric universe had only theoretical value, this does not mean that St. Thomas was in anticipation of Copernicus, Kepler, and Galileo. It shows the true depth of St. Thomas in another light, namely, that his intimate knowledge of the value and limitations of reasoning was such as to state the principles allowing for frequent variations in the conclusions of physical theory.

How did he do this? The answer to this question hinges upon two Thomistic positions: (1) acceptance in full of Aristotle's conclusions about abstraction, demonstration, and dialectic, and (2) development of the degrees of abstraction.

The Aristotelian doctrine of abstraction[2] is an outstanding

---

[2] Aristotle, *On the Soul*, 416b 33 ff. and 424b 20 ff. The Loeb Classical Library edition of the works of Aristotle has been used for the Greek text of all his works quoted here; *The Works of Aristotle*, ed. J. A. Smith and W. D. Ross, 12 vols. (Oxford, At the Clarendon Press, 1908-1952), has been used for the English translations.

achievement in the history of thought. It is the perfect reconciliation of the difficulties facing pre-Platonic and Platonic thought, the problem of the transcendence or immanence of the explanation of material reality.

Plato had given a profound and masterful answer to the problem in the *Timaeus,* wherein he has the plan of the universe in the divine thinking. In the *Meno* he had argued that the unlearned slave's intuitive recognition of the demonstration of the theorem of the square of the hypotenuse indicates a previous, pre-natal knowledge of such truths. In the *Sophist,* by his distinction between being and the one, he gave the answer to Parmenides' difficulties about divisible universal forms and ideals of ideals. Plato had defended the existence of ideals and forms, a problem that had plagued Greek philosophy, by placing them in the divine thinking. The significance of this answer is seen in St. Gregory of Nyssa's plan of creation,[3] and in St. Augustine's emphasis on the exemplars, which is given its most precise expression in the *rationes seminales.*[4] Nevertheless, despite his great vision of God the creator, Plato did not reduce the pattern of creation from the ideal world into the material world. His temporalizing and localizing of ideals into matter through time and space[5] did not really explain the material world. As Aristotle states,[6] Plato did not get beyond formal and material causes, thereby implying that he lacked a sufficient explanation of efficiency and finality.

We do not know whether Aristotle was really opposed to the philosophy of forms and ideals,[7] or whether he was merely dubious about them. If he were opposed to them, then his task was to reconstruct philosophy on a material basis. If he were merely dubious about them, then it was his task to see in what manner they existed. Since the manner of their existence was the point at issue, he could presume nothing therein and he must reconstruct them on the basis

---

[3] St. Gregory of Nyssa, *Explicatio apologetica in Hexaemeron* (περὶ τῆς ἑξαεμέρου) and *De hominis opificio* (περὶ κατασκευῆς ἀνθρώπου), Migne, *Patrologia Graeca,* 44.

[4] Cf. St. Augustine, *De Trinitate,* III, 8, P.L., 42, and *De Genesi ad litteram,* VI, 10, P.L., 34.

[5] Cf. *Timaeus, passim* in *Platonis opera,* ed. John Burnet (Oxonii: e typographico Clarendoniano, 1945) IV.

[6] Aristotle, *Metaphysics,* 988a 8 ff.

[7] Note that even though Aristotle frequently argues against a philosophy of forms and ideas he nevertheless returns to it as though he himself is unsettled in his argumentation. Cfr. *Metaphysics* 1069a 18 ff; 1076a 8 ff.

of sense knowledge to see if knowledge of the forms could, after all, be abstracted from sense knowledge.

The above is the background of the significance of Aristotelian abstraction. It is also the basis of his emphasis on the strength and weaknesses of demonstration.[8] Granted certitude, we can demonstrate. If we have only opinion,[9] then we must assume a conclusion according to the evidence, develop it logically to see to what we are committed, and seek verification in evidence from reality.

The distinction between demonstration and dialectic shows the different roles of logic in schematic thinking. In demonstration, it is the formal expression of certitude and properly deductive in applying the force of the conclusion to the members of the class. In dialectic it is also deductive, in form at least, but with the purpose of directing thought to evidence not yet attained in the form of "if . . . then. . . ." We may point out here that the distinction between the sciences as inductive and philosophy as deductive is too trite and too simple a classification. The sciences are far more deductive than philosophy. Deduction is a logical tool. Induction is in learning, not in logic. It is analysis in the process of abstraction. Since the sciences use deduction in directing the process of learning they are almost exclusively deductive. It is called the "application of an established principle," which established principle is a "conceptual context."

The use of deduction in scientific learning is its greatest danger. It could be its strength, insofar as it restricts reasoning to a unified attempt in a unified system of concepts which have some truth value. Nevertheless, since we pass from the known to the unknown, dialectic in scientific method offers the danger of an unconscious bias in favor of the familiar, especially in interpretation, and the unconscious selection of evidence favorable to the assumed thesis. The latter danger is especially present on the observational and experimental levels. The former danger is present on both levels. For example, the preoccupation with the familiar, in this case the radioactivity of uranium, kept the Curies seeking a strange isotope of uranium rather than a separate element. Even though their discovery of radium was an outstanding achievement, nevertheless, it was almost with reluctance that they abandoned the familiar in the quest for the new. On the conceptual level, the scientific method is offering more and more epistemological problems, especially in

---

[8] Aristotle, *Posterior Analytics*, 74b 5 ff.
[9] Aristotle, *Topics*, 104a 3 ff.

view of the several contexts. For example, in classical mechanics, wave mechanics, and relativity, such problems haunt contemporary physical theory.

The degrees of abstraction hinted at by Aristotle have their basis in his division of the theoretical sciences into physical, mathematical, and theological or metaphysical.[10] St. Thomas has two expressions of the degrees of abstraction, one in his commentary on Boetius' *De Trinitate*[11] and the other in his commentary on Aristotle's *Physics*.[12] As we know, he speaks of three levels of philosophizing determined by the subject matter considered and by our intention in philosophizing. The first deals with the ultimate principles of actual material. The second deals with the ultimate principles of the concept of quantity, "intelligible matter," as St. Thomas calls it, or "'conceptual space," as it is termed by mathematicians. This is the mathematical degree. The third, or metaphysical degree, deals with being as being. That is, whatever we think about can be said to exist, but in what manner? Only in the mind? In reality? This is the degree of possibles in relation to existence, or more properly, possible essences in relation to existence.

We can seriously question the adequacy of the three degrees if we look upon them as all-inclusive categories of thinking within a given level and with a given intention. Certainly, for example, cosmology becomes metaphysical at times, and at times metaphysics deals with matter and form.

However, the degrees of abstraction are an excellent starting point if we look to them as bases for the accurate delineation of problems. Actually, within the definition of the three degrees of abstraction, as considered by St. Thomas, a great deal can be obtained. By cosmological thinking and cosmological thinking alone we can obtain not only such fundamental philosophical principles as matter and form, motion, substance and accidents, and potency and act, but also such fundamental physical principles as mass, energy, force, velocity, and other such secondary effects of quantity and motion. The fact that we can obtain these notions by philosophizing may indicate why Aristotle discovered them and used them to establish the basic statements of mechanics.

In the second degree of abstraction we deal with the essence of mathematical theory, very properly quantity as understood and

---

[10] *Metaphysics*, 1064b 1; cf. *On the Soul*, 403b 10 ff.
[11] *In Boetii de Trinitate commentarium*, V, 1.
[12] *In libros Physicorum Aristotelis commentarium*, I., 1.

developed intellectually. In doing so we are faced with two possible developments: the notion of the continuum, which is at the heart of each and every geometrical system; and the notion of plurality, which is the basis for every arithmetic, every algebra, and every calculus ever devised. Furthermore, because the matter considered is intelligible or conceptual, freedom is given the intellect to develop such notions as the infinite, infinite space, infinite series of number, and infinitesimals.

The third degree of abstraction might be described as the problem arising out of the relations of possibles to actuals. It is exactly here that physical theory finds itself in epistemological difficulties.

Physical theory has three epistemological points of difficulty: (1) the phenomenon of discovery; (2) the hypotheses of observational and experimental data; and (3) the development of theory in the conceptual and contextual level.

The phenomenon of discovery is not as easy an experience as one may think. Scientific discovery is not a mere finding after the manner of Père Dallion's first sight of Niagara Falls. Scientific discovery has a background. The discoverer is searching. The problem, then, is the extent of the determination of the discovery by the context of the search.

One of the academic jokes that is supposed to show that science is grand fun is the statement that ". . . hypothesis is a rather long and high-sounding Greek word that really, you know, means only 'an educated guess.'" That is precisely the point. Is the scientific discovery really a guess? a hunch? an insight? Or is it really a logical process whose terms have been set by the conceptual context? A guess is always against a certain amount of data and is a tentative conclusion. An insight is not merely a brilliant flash out of nothing. It, too, has a context and may be an intuitive conclusion. There may be some unconscious ratiocination involved whose conclusion suddenly appears in the forefront of our attention. Authorities can be cited for every position, but it is interesting to note that Aristotle seems to lean towards the ratiocinative position. In his criticism of Platonic classification he states that there is the danger of assuming what is to be proved.[13] Later on he seems to take the position that since there are so many discoveries that are correct there must be a habit of right thinking involved. The proper order of premises, middle term, and conclusion must have

[13] *Prior Analytics*, 46a 32 ff.

been involved,[14] even though such is not in conscious intention.[15]

This may seem a minor point in logic. Nevertheless, it is a major point in epistemology. First principles are intuitive and the inferences therefrom are simple and direct. However, in dialectic, where the thesis is usually involved because of the lack of sufficiently convincing data and evidence, the thesis does seem to contribute to the discovery. A scientific discovery is always in view of or in connection with an already determined theoretical direction. Even if the discovery is recognized as being in opposition to the fundamental supposition, its significance and value are interpreted in terms and context determined by the fundamental assumption. This raises the rather uncomfortable question: Is there any truth in science that is not already determined, or at least tinged, by a theory predisposed to a given conclusion? This raises the further philosophical question: Are our scientific conclusions and concepts faithful to reality, or are they only possible answers to theoretical problems? This is in the realm of the relationship of possibles to actuality. It is properly a metaphysical problem, no matter how much we may attempt to limit the physical sciences to the first degree of abstraction.

Furthermore, it raises the question as to whether in the sciences the thought is the principle of the object. As moderate realists, we are steeped in the tradition that the object is the principle of the thought. This means that the sciences seem to involve inverted thinking. This, undoubtedly, is behind the popularity of Plato among theoretical physicists and philosophers of science. In Plato, at least in the Plato of the *Meno, Parmenides, Thaetetus, Republic,* and *Timaeus,* the thought is certainly the principle of the entity. However, such a comparison does injustice to the greatness of Plato. Further it does not sufficiently credit Aristotle in his moderate realism for showing how the thought can be the principle of the discovery, that is, how in dialectic, the thought can antecede the discovery of the object considered.

---

[14] *Ibid.,* 69a 25 ff.

[15] The outstanding champion of a logic of discovery is Charles Sanders Peirce, scientist and philosopher. Apt references to his reasoning and conclusions are: "Kinds of Induction" in *Collected Papers of Charles Sanders Peirce,* 8 vols., ed. Charles Hartshorne, Paul Weiss, and Arthur W. Burks (Cambridge, Mass.: Harvard University Press, 1931-1958) VII, 67 ff. "The Fixation of a Belief" in *Values in a Universe of Chance, Selected Writings of Charles S. Peirce,* ed. Philip P. Wiener (Stanford, Calif.: Stanford University Press, 1958) pp. 92 ff. and "Questions concerning Certain Faculties," *ibid.,* pp. 19 ff.

The second realm of difficulty in physical theory is on the observational and experimental levels. Actually, this is an extension of the previously considered point. Yet it has its own problems. The problem, briefly, is this: in the sciences we frequently must postulate the existence of entities or forces to answer the hitherto unsolved problems of real phenomena and events. We attribute properties to these postulated entities. Now, do these entities really exist, and if so, do they correspond to our concepts? A rather crude example of this is in the atomism of Leucippus in his attempt to save both the being of Parmenides and the obvious reality of change and difference. He took over the infinitesimals of Zeno and materialized them. Thus, he considered all bodies to consist of extremely minute indivisibles. The joining and separating of these tiny masses were, respectively, generation and corruption. Furthermore, he attributed definite geometrical shapes to the atoms, pyramidal, cubical, and spherical to explain, respectively, the gravitational, solid, and fluid properties of bodies. This is a good working theory, and as such, exists in the mind. Are there atoms in reality? If so, do they have the characteristics attributed to them by Leucippus? We must notice that this is at the heart of the problem of truth, and is, properly, a metaphysical problem. The answer, of course, will depend upon evidence, but already we are predisposed, simply because we cannot and probably never will be able to perceive atoms. We can perceive certain phenomena and events, and we must fashion an answer before we know that it is true.

Moreover, we must erect a systematic answer. It is not enough to state that atoms must exist to explain given phenomena. If matter consists of atoms, then atomism must explain every problem concerning the nature of matter. The same is true for modern atomic and nuclear theory. If matter consists of atoms, then atomic and nuclear theory must explain all material phenomena.

However, the problem becomes more complicated and the theory becomes more elaborate. We can trace the development of modern atomic theory through Rumford, to explain certain thermodynamical aspects of all matter, through Franklin, Faraday, and Maxwell, to explain electrodynamical characteristics, through Dalton, to explain the proportion of elements, and we can look to Brown's observations of particles in suspension for verification. Still, the electromagnetic properties of the accepted atom give rise to conceptual difficulties that have brought the theoretical developments of Thompson, Rutherford, and Bohr. Since energy is considered a normal state of matter, their postulates at once introduce the laws of moving bodies, especially the principles of angular momentum, and introduce analogies to planetary and orbital systems.

We have now gotten into analogical reasoning, which adds difficulties simply because the likeness in analogy supposes difference in reality. In order to account for the differences, and in order to reconcile them with what is accepted, theory has to be enlarged. Yet, if theory is the answer to real problems, it must be put to the test. It is no longer a question of observation. It is now a problem of experiment. Yet, how are we to devise the experiment save in terms of the acceptance of the theory? Here, we are already in a hypothesis of observation and a theory of experiment as such. It is more than the simple question: Is there, in reality, an entity called an electron that corresponds to the concept of a *beta* particle? The problem now is the amazing and bewildering prospect of experiment to be conducted by devices erected with a view to the theory to be established. It is here that St. Thomas might point out that this is the perfect example of the second type of reasoning he mentions: reasoning to verify an established position whose alternative might be true. This leads us to the third source of difficulty, that on the conceptual level.

This difficulty had its actual beginnings in the seventeenth century when Newton considered light as the emission of particles, whereas Huyghens considered it as waves. This was the origin of several conceptual systems that did not need further development until the early twentieth century. The theory of light as waves needed a medium, and thus was postulated the all-pervading ether whose existence was an extreme conceptual difficulty leading into the Michelson-Morley experiment suggesting that ether obeys none of the laws of physical entities and hence cannot be said to show any evidence of its existence. This gave rise to quantum mechanics interpreting light in terms of bundles of particles. However, light, in fact any radiant energy, still stubbornly maintains wave properties. In fact, the more we try to establish it as a particle, the more it seems to manifest wave properties. Similarly, the more we try to establish it as a wave, the more it seems to show particle properties. Yet, if radiant energy is as normal as matter in the ground state, and if both are matter under different forms, we must try to reconcile these difficulties. We must seek further and more inclusive concepts to take into account all kinds of matter and all material phenomena.

We suddenly discover that we are no longer dealing with reality. We are dealing with concepts, and our concepts oftentimes exclude each other. For example, Heisenberg astounded the scientific world with his principle of uncertainty. On the experimental level this simply means that we cannot measure the position and velocity of a particle simultaneously. This has its importance in theory, but it is not now of major significance. In fact, it is something that should have been discovered by a physics major many years before. Its difficulty is in the conceptual order, and briefly it is this: simultaneous or not, the concept of velocity has no significance whatsoever in relation to the concept of position, and vice versa.

Furthermore, since actual observation seems to show that the entire universe is made out of the same material in differing physical and chemical states, the laws of nature, whether on the macroscopic or on the subatomic level, should hold throughout the entire universe. Yet, we do not know enough about the behavior of particles or waves under extreme conditions. In fact, we do not know what is normal or what is extreme. Hence, there are different interpretations of identical phenomena and concepts in terms of other theories. For example, gravity is. Yet, in classical mechanics it is considered a rectilinear attraction. It is not that, but it is most convenient to consider it such, and in the problems of classical mechanics it is an adequate concept. In field theory and in relativity it is considered a relationship not between bodies but between positions. Each shows its "congruity of its results," and in the light of different problems each is considered valid. The same different conceptual contexts, each with its congruity of results, exist for almost every physical problem considered.

These difficulties on the conceptual level have given rise to different considerations of the nature of truth. We look upon truth as the conformity between the object and its concept. However, since in the physical problems mentioned the nature of the entity is assumed for dialectical and theoretical purposes, there is little relation to the extra-mental object. Thus arises the concept of truth as that of congruence. That is, a concept is considered true if it is congruent to an established conceptual system. This was a position resisted by Einstein, who seems to have taken the position that if reality is one there can be only one congruence or congruity. He attempted to unite the various systems into one unified system in his general relativity and unified field theories. How successful he was is another question. Nevertheless, his work was sufficiently commanding to be an incentive to Werner Heisenberg in pursuing the same quest.

A third concept of truth has arisen from the difficulties of the congruence notion. This is the intuitive notion, namely, that for some reason or other the thinker will take a stand in the midst of, away from, or even despite evidence. For some reason or other he is convinced of this position and takes it.

We can take one of several positions in relation to the difficulties considered above. We can brush them aside as purely conjectural and highly hypothetical. In this we will be as correct as anyone else. On the other hand we can imitate Bergson and Whitehead and maintain that although the sciences are great cultural achievements, their very method stands in the way of a full understanding of nature. We must, then, turn to reality, not to theory, for the data that it itself offers as the key to its own nature. This is a far healthier position, especially if we grant and respect the validity of the sciences as theories about the problems of nature. This is within the tradition begun by Aristotle's dialectic and respected by St. Thomas.

There is one thing we must do. We must grant metaphysical value to physical theory. Physical theory is not limited to the first degree of abstraction. It is formally mathematical, and hence flows into the second degree. Nevertheless, whether it is an attempt to explain nature or an attempt to explain the problems of nature, it does have metaphysical value because in its non-contradictory concepts it represents a system of possibles. The fundamental metaphysical problem of them all is existence, and physical theory represents the problem of existence precisely insofar as it consists of concepts having a possible if not actual relationship to reality.

However, even though the problems of physical theory transcend any single degree of abstraction, their three levels of problematic inquiry: the logic of discovery, the hypothesis of observation and experiment, and the congruence of concepts would generally elude our reasoning about them if we did not have the three degrees of abstraction on which to base ourselves. In other words, what at first sight seems to be the weakness of the degrees of abstraction is really their strength in application to theory accounted for but undoubtedly beyond the vision of St. Thomas when he first enunciated them.

7

PRIVATE PROPERTY AND NATURAL LAW
by
Felix Alluntis

The purpose of this work is to discuss whether or not the right to private property is based on natural law, and, if the answer is affirmative, whether the institution of private ownership as a general system is demanded or merely permitted by natural law. There is some confusion in this matter. Most modern scholastics admit the natural character of the right to private property and consider a general system of private ownership not only permitted but demanded by natural law.[1] However, there are authors pertaining to the same scholastic tradition who either deny that the right to property is based on natural law since, they say, it is founded on *ius gentium,* or affirm that private ownership is allowed but not prescribed by natural law.[2]

The work will include six main sections: I) notions of private property, right to private property, and natural right; II) arguments in favor of private property; III) analysis of their natural or positive character; IV) theological excursus; V) scope of the arguments; VI) exegesis of certain Thomistic texts, which are apparently the source of the confusion that exists among some neo-scholastics.

[1] Cf. Irenaeus González Moral, *Philosophia moralis* (Santander: Sal Terrae, 1960), p. 441.

[2] Austin Fagothey, *Right and Reason* (2d ed.; St. Louis: The C. V. Mosby Company, 1959), p. 451: "There are two opinions, not opposed to each other [?], but differing in the extent to which they are willing to go: (1) The system of private property rests on *ius gentium.* It is at least in agreement with the natural law but not necessarily demanded by it. It is *a* morally acceptable system. (2) The system of private property rests on the *natural law.* It is not only in agreement with the natural law but demanded by it. It is the *only* morally acceptable system." Sister Mary Consilia O'Brien, *Christian Social Principles* (New York: P. J. Kennedy & Sons, 1941), p. 514: "The Natural Law does not demand that possessions be privately held. Neither does it forbid private possessions."

I

NOTIONS OF PRIVATE PROPERTY, RIGHT TO PRIVATE PROPERTY, AND NATURAL RIGHT

Private property is not necessarily individual property. There is also private collective property. The property of labor unions or cooperative property is collective yet private. Public property, whether collective or not, is really the opposite of private property.³ Our discussion is limited to the right to private property of productive goods. Even Marxists admit private ownership of consumable goods.

By right to private property we do not mean "the exclusive right to dispose of an object, its substance, and its use." This Roman, and also Napoleonic, definition ignores another right every man has with regard to material goods, namely, the fundamental right every person has to use the portion of earthly goods necessary for his conservation and the integral, physical, intellectual, and moral development of his personality.⁴ This fundamental right is prior to and distinct from that to private property. It is absolute and inalienable. It remains even after the private appropriation of goods has taken place, and private property is subordinated to it.⁵

Recent popes not only hold that the right to private property of productive goods is "a natural right," "a right given by nature," "a part of the natural law," but also that private property is demanded by natural law; see, for instance, Pius XII, *A.A.S.*, S. II, VIII (1941), p. 231.

³ What many modern authors call institutional property is non-collective public property because it lacks a collectivity as an owner. Cf. R. G. Renard, *La philosophie de l'institution* (Paris: Sirey, 1939).

⁴ Pius XII, *A.A.S.*, S. II, VIII (1941), 231-232: "Every man, as a living being gifted with reason, has in fact from nature the fundamental right to make use of the material goods of the earth, while it is left to the will of man and the juridical statutes of nations to regulate in greater detail the actuation of this right. . . ."

This individual right cannot in any way be superseded, even by other clear and undisputed rights over material goods. Undoubtedly the natural order deriving from God, demands also private property. . . . But all this remains subordinated to the natural scope of material goods and cannot emancipate itself from the first and fundamental right which concedes their use to all men."

Cf. J. Horváth, *Eigentumsrecht nach dem heiligem Thomas von Aquin* (Graz: Moser, 1929); A. Rohner, "P. Horváth's Buch: Eigentumsrecht nach dem heiligem Thomas von Aquin," *Schönere Zukunft*, V. (1929-30), 540-542, 568-569; J. B. Kraus, "Festellungen zu vielumstrittenen Punkten der sozialem Frage," *Ibid.*, 1177-79; F. Alluntis, *Filosofía cristiana de la propiedad* (Habana: Molina, 1960), pp. 1-23.

⁵ Cf. *A.A.S.*, S. II, VIII (1941), 231.

By right to private property we understand "the exclusive power of acquiring and administering (*potestas procurandi et dispensandi*), but not of using, material goods."⁶ The use, as Aristotle already taught in his economic scheme under the inspiration of the Pythagrean axiom, κοινὰ τὰ τῶν φίλων, must remain somehow common.⁷ Our problem is whether the right to acquire property is or is not natural, and whether the institution of private ownership is demanded or merely allowed by natural law. It is obvious that the concrete historical forms of property are not determined by nature. They have changed and continue to change with the social and economic evolution and progress of mankind. Again, the actualization of the right to property is always the result of some human positive act. Only a liberal capitalist would dare to assert that a given form of ownership is natural or that the goods he owns were given to him by nature.

By natural right we mean a right based upon the nature and the properties of things; this is the meaning of natural in the strict sense.⁸ In other words, a natural right is a right based on the natural law, or on our transcendental relations or inclinations, viz., inclinations rooted in our essence or nature. Since everything proper to the essential constituents of man, everything necessary for the exercise of his faculties, everything that is required to live in accord with reason and to attain a goal proportionate to his nature comes under natural law, it is also the object of natural right. We do not limit, therefore, natural law to its first principles. The conclusions drawn from the principles belong also to natural law. Obviously, they do not have the absolute character of the principles, and can be said to belong to secondary natural law.

Is the right to private property a natural right in this sense? The adequate method to answer this question is to analyze the argu-

---

⁶ *S. Theol.*, II-II, q. 66, art. 2.

⁷ *Pol.*, 1263a29-30; St. Thomas, *In Pol.*, Bk. II, 1.4; *S. Theol.*, I-II, q. 105, art 2.

⁸ It must be noted that the scholastics, and also the Fathers of the Church, use the terms "natural," "nature," in a wider and, therefore, improper sense. St. Bonaventure, *In II Sent.*, d. 44, art. 2, ad 4, V. II, p. 109, speaks of nature *simpliciter*, innocent nature, fallen nature, and restored nature. St. Thomas, *S. Theol.*, I-II, q. 85, arts. 1-2, calls original justice natural. H. Lubac, *Surnaturel* (Paris, 1946), p. 449, contends that scholastics had no idea of pure nature. It is true that scholastics used the term "nature" in a broad sense, but the idea of pure nature was not foreign to them. St. Thomas' definition of nature in *S. Theol.*, III, q. 2, art. 1, "nature means the essence of the species insofar as it is a principle of operation," refers to pure nature; St. Bonaventure speaks of nature *simpliciter*.

ments adduced in favor of private property. In so far as they are based or not on natural law, we will be able to conclude that the right to private property is or is not natural.

II

ARGUMENTS IN FAVOR OF PRIVATE PROPERTY

Economic efficiency, social order and peace, the freedom, stability, and security of the person and the family, and the nature of work are the traditional bases for private property. Experience teaches that without private property and without the psychological link that it establishes between effort and recompense, man puts no effort into work and leaves to others the care of the commonweal. Again, if there were no private ownership, and if by chance man should put aside his apathy and set to work resolutely, saving, organizing and putting common capital to production, his efforts would be haphazard, without forethought, security, or method.[9] There would be "confusion if everyone busied himself about everything."[10]

A communist dictatorship could force the citizens to work systematically, but the right of the person and the family to a good life and to adequate, peaceful, and ordered means to achieve it is prior to and independent, to a large extent, of the state. Besides, a communist dictatorship would involve the sacrifice of values without which even the most brilliant results are stripped of human dignity.

Collectivists deny the value of these arguments, for, they say, private property, and not its absence, is the source of social conflicts, which derive from the abuses and economic inequalities of the liberal regime. But we do not defend exaggerated individualism or its abuses. Abuse does not destroy use. A more equitable distribution of goods undoubtedly contributes to social order and peace as well as to efficiency. Experience shows that the management of a private business generally implies a greater sense of responsibility and more initiative and zeal than the management of a public property.

Private property is necessary to protect individual and family

---

[9] *Pol.*, 1261b 33-28; 1263a 27-28; *S. Theol.*, II-II, q. 66, art. 2; *A.S.S.*, XXIII (1891), 663.

[10] *S. Theol.*, II-II, q. 66, art. 2; *A.S.S.*, XXIII (1891), 647.

liberty. Personal and family freedom is correlated to the restrictions existing in the field of private property. If all wealth were in the hands of the state, man and the family would be at its mercy.[11] Metaphysically he would be free, but physically he would be a slave. It should be added that no political democracy, a regime of political freedom, is possible without economic democracy or freedom. An automaton in the economic field can hardly act as a person in the political field. The so-called masses in the economic order are also masses in the political order[12] and cannot constitute an authentic democracy. Political democracy and mass-men are radically opposed, they tend to eliminate each other. No true democracy can flourish, unless the citizens have proper personalities and enjoy true freedom. The system of private ownership demanded by the laws of freedom should not be confused with the liberal capitalistic system; far from protecting freedom, liberal capitalism has very often created a mass of slaves.

The stability and security of the individual and the family are impossible without private property. Pope Leo XIII develops this argument extensively.[13] He starts by pointing out the great difference between man and beast. The latter is limited to the immediate consumption of food under the impulse of the instinct of self-preservation. What exalts man over the beast is reason, which sees an infinity of objects. Man is the master of his actions; he is his own guide and providence under the divine law; he may and must choose the things which he believes useful for the future. He is entitled, therefore, not only to the possession of consumable goods but also to the permanent possession of the means of production.

Private property is a natural consequence of work, which puts a personal imprint on things. By the acts by which man spends the industry of his mind and the strength of his body in procuring the

---

[11] *A.S.S.*, XXIII (1891), 647; etc.
[12] Pius XII, *A.A.S.*, XXXVII (1945), 13, draws the distinction between people and masses: "The people and a shapeless multitude (or, as it is called, 'the masses') are two distinct concepts. The people live and move by their own life energy; the masses are inert of themselves and can only be moved from outside. The people live by the fulness of life in the men that compose it, each of whom —at his proper place and in his own way—is a person conscious of his own responsibility and of his own views. The masses, on the contrary, wait for the impulse from outside, an easy plaything in the hands of anyone who exploits their instincts and impressions; ready to follow in turn, today this flag, tomorrow another." Cf. also J. Ortega y Gasset, *La rebelión de las masas*, in *Obras completas* (2d ed.; Madrid: Espasa Calpe, 1936), V. II, pp. 1155 ff.
[13] *A.S.S.*, XXIII (1891), 643.

fruits of nature, he "makes his own that portion of nature's field which he cultivates, that portion on which he leaves, as it were, the impress of his own personality; and it cannot but be just that he should possess that portion as his own, and should have a right to keep it without molestation."[14] "Even as the effect follows the cause, so it is just that the fruits of the work should belong to the worker."[15]

J. Maritain presents somewhat differently the argument based on the nature of work. Poetic activity or activity concerned with making of things, he argues, is the formal reason of private appropriation since it presupposes the rational nature and personality of the worker. In the metaphysical order every person has a proprietary right over himself and his acts, and this right is the ontological foundation of his right to the ownership of external things. However, the extension of the right the person possesses over himself to the ownership of material goods is achieved by the exercise of poetic activity or work.

> It is of the very essence of this activity to imprint on matter the mark of rational being. Now by virtue of what the work to be done demands for its proper perfection it is in the nature of things necessary that man shall have the fullest control over the material on which he has to work, that the master-craftsman shall have permanent and exclusive right of disposal of the material and of the means necessary for executing the work.
> But this can only be realized through a general system of individual ownership. . . .[16]

The extension of a person's ownership of himself to ownership of external things through work comes about, Maritain adds, by means of habits. Man's productive work is the effect of his personal activity and habit. "The very word *habitus* is significant: one has what the other has not." For this reason "the thing to be made requires that things, materials, and means of work be possessed" by the worker as "a personal right," in "a permanent possession," that befits an agent endowed with intelligence who plans his actions not only for the present but also for the future. Furthermore, the person who plans the work is generally the head of a family and makes provision for his children.[17]

[14] *Ibid.*, p. 644.
[15] *Ibid.*
[16] Jacques Maritain, *Freedom in the Modern World*, trans. R. O'Sullivan (New York: Charles Scribner's Sons, 1936), pp. 196-199.
[17] *Ibid.*, pp. 199-200.

The argument does not necessarily require, Maritain adds, that each person exercising his poetic activity should be the owner of the materials and instruments of production. There can be workers, and governmental officials who do not own the instruments of production but work for the owners of the instruments. In the first case, the wage-earner is considered a member of the other man whom he serves. As such the wage-earner is neither owner nor co-owner of the material on which or of the instruments with which he works. However, his dignity of person is not abolished; the individual appropriation of materials and instruments required for the worker's poetic activity in virtue of his personal dignity "still operates for him on the side of the product, for which the fixed wage is a substitute." As regards government officials, their work is grafted on free work and presupposes it.[18]

[18] *Ibid.*, p. 199. The argument based upon the nature of work has been presented under a third aspect, as follows: Man does not belong to society as a person but as an individual. As a person he transcends society, escapes the absorbing action of society, and is independent of it. For this very reason spiritual faculties, particularly the intellect, which make up the person, are non-social elements; and the fruits of these faculties are not subject to appropiation by society. Since work or production of wealth is an activity of these non-social elements, particularly of the intellect, the fruit of the work belongs to the person, is his property; and it is free from the domination of society. Thus man's personal labor constitutes the undeniable foundation, the metaphysical basis of the natural right of private property. Cf. Ch. J. McFadden, *The Philosophy of Communism* (New York: Benziger Bro., Inc., 1939), pp. 266 ff.

This reasoning is not conclusive. From the disputed, or rather false, principle that man belongs to society only as individual, not as person, it concludes that the person escapes the absorbing action of society and is independent of it. Nobody can deny that the person cannot be absorbed by society; but one can admit that man is social insofar as he is a person and deny the right of society to absorb him. From the fact that the person is not subject to the domination of society the reasoning concludes that spiritual faculties are non-social elements. Again the conclusion is broader than the premises; one can admit that personal faculties are social elements, though not only social elements, without admitting that the person is subject to the domination of society. That private property is anterior to and independent (to a certain extent) of society cannot be based upon the non-social nature of the intellect; for the intellect, far from being a non-social element, is the social faculty *par excellence*. If man is social, it is because he is an intellectual being; if irrational animals cannot form societies in the strict sense, it is because they lack of intellect. Of course, above the activities which refer to social political life, the intellect can and must perform activities which transcend temporal life and reach God Himself, and also activities which refer to personal and familiar life, insofar as the person and the family are anterior to political society with proper and specific ends which cannot be absorbed but respected by society. The independence of the right to private property as regards civil society cannot be based, therefore, on the non-social character of the intellect and its activity.

The foregoing arguments aim to prove that the institution of private property is not only licit and useful but also morally necessary. They condemn the contradictory system which would make the society or the state owner of all, or practically all, natural and artificial goods. As we shall see later, they do not reject public ownership of so-called public utilities and other great instruments of production if economic, social, and political reasons demand such a measure. Another caution concerns the actual distribution and use of private property. The arguments do not favor restriction of ownership of capital to a small minority of the population. Each argument is a plea for a wide diffusion of ownership.

In recent years it has been objected that because of changes in its structure private property has lost its previous validity. The main changes referred to are: separation of ownership of productive goods from managerial responsibility; the existence of insurance groups and social security, which give many citizens the serenity and security formerly dependent on private ownership, however modest. Many citizens now have greater confidence in income derived from work than in income derived from capital, and, as a consequence, they strive to acquire professional skills rather than to become owners of property.

By reason of the separation of ownership from managerial responsibility, public authorities have the task and duty to make sure that the aims pursued by the directors of leading companies are not contrary to the exigencies of the common good. Social security, insurance against unemployment, disease, professional accidents, old age, and premature death, family subsidies, and paid vacations give the worker true juridical titles and, as generalizations of private property, can be considered equivalent to private capital.[19] However, the evolution of the economy does not invalidate the right of property nor the arguments on which it is based. On the contrary, the lawfulness or unlawfulness of certain modern forms of property must be judged according to their subservience or opposition to the functions of private ownership.

Pope John XXIII considers these changes[20] and concludes:

> These aspects of the economy just alluded to have certainly contributed to spread a doubt whether, in the present state of affairs, a principle of the socio-economic order consistently taught and defended by Our Predecessors has diminished in

---

[19] Cf. C. Van Gestel, *La doctrina social de la Iglesia*, Spanish transl. by G. Ferrer (Barcelona: Herder, 1959), p. 184.

[20] *Mater et Magistra*, (New York: The America Press, 1961), pp. 30 ff.

or lost its importance. The principle in question is that of the natural right of private ownership, including ownership of productive goods.

There is no reason for such a doubt to persist. The right of private ownership of goods, including productive goods, has a permanent validity.[21]

The Pope immediately gives reasons why the right of private property keeps its permanent validity: private property is a part of the natural law, "which teaches us that individuals are prior to society, and society has as its purpose the service of man." Free, private initiative is impossible if the "same initiative does not include the power to dispose freely of the means indispensable to its exercise." Without private ownership of productive goods, "the fundamental manifestations of freedom are suppressed or stifled." Modern increase in productive efficiency and a corresponding increase in salaries enables the workers to save and thus acquire property, for the right to property "derives its main force and continuing support from the fruitfulness of work." Private property "serves as an effective safeguard of human dignity, and helps out to shoulder fully his responsibility in every field." Private property "makes for solidarity and security in family life," and also for "the prosperous development of the commonwealth."[22]

III

ANALYSIS OF THE CHARACTER OF THE ARGUMENTS

As already pointed out, the adequate method to decide whether the right to private property is or is not natural is to analyze the arguments given in its defense, and to see if they are founded on the nature and properties of things or on human convention, custom, or law.

It is clear enough that the arguments from freedom, the stability, and security of the person and the family, and the nature of work are based on natural law. Man is endowed with freedom by nature, not by any positive human law. Again, it is his rational nature that imposes upon him the obligation to provide for his own and his family's present and future needs without irrational worries and with serenity and security. Work, or poetic activity which creates

[21] *Ibid.*
[22] *Ibid.*

new goods and radically demands the appropriation of the means of production, is a property of man. In other words, these arguments are based either on the nature or on the properties of man, and consequently are founded on natural law. Furthermore, they prove that private property is not only permitted but demanded by natural law.

With regard to the Aristotelian arguments of efficiency, social order, and peace, there are authors who consider them as purely utilitarian, based on expediency, and valid when restricted to ancient and medieval forms of property,[23] but having little or no application to modern forms.[24] But are these arguments merely utilitarian? St. Thomas does not think so. He uses them to prove not only the utility, but also the necessity of private property: *"quantum ad hoc licitum est quod homo propria possideat. Et est etiam necessarium ad humanam vitam propter tria."*[25] For St. Thomas private property is necessary for human life. The complete reasoning would run as follows: men are so constituted that in a communal system they will not care sufficiently for goods and production nor will they keep the order and peace required by society. Neglect in production and administration, conflicts, and quarrels are effects that will follow with moral necessity from a communistic system. It has been objected that a strong central government could ensure social order, but this objection forgets that man and the family and the rights to life and to an essential economic basis are prior to the state, and that the state is not organized to violate or to suppress but to preserve and protect the rights of the citizens.

It has also been objected that these arguments are based on man's selfishness, greed, and unsociability, that is to say, on his concupiscence or on the disorderly inclinations of the inferior zone of his being. The question narrows down to whether concupiscence is or is not a property of human nature. On this point there can be little doubt. Concupiscence flows from the very constitution of man, from the opposition between the animal and the rational tendencies of his being. Those who contend that concupiscence is not a natural human property, because it is a consequence due to original sin, forget that the gift which Adam enjoyed, the gift of

---

[23] M. E. Borne, "La propriété et son évolution," *Semaine sociale de France* (Chronique sociale de France: Lyon, 1947), p. 81.

[24] J. de Finance, "La propriété, ses formes, son orientation," *Dossiers de l'action populaire* (1934), p. 34.

[25] *S. Theol.*, II-II, q. 66, art. 2.

integrity, that is, the suppression of concupiscence, was not a natural but a preternatural gift. The claim that the existence of original sin can be proved even by reason, the exigencies of the hylomorphic theory, and the supposed dictates of speculative reason concerning the natural subordination that should but does not exist among man's faculties, acts, and habits, is baseless.[26]

A revision of our speculations and theories about human nature would be a better method for explaining our inner conflict than an easy recourse to original sin. What can be disputed is whether or not concupiscence is more intense in the fallen state than in the hypothetical pure state of nature. The fallacy of the statement sometimes made that the right to property is not natural because it would not have existed in Eden is obvious. It assumes that the state of innocence was natural, and it forgets the preternatural and supernatural gifts with which Adam was enriched in being created or shortly after having been created.

With regard to the applicability of the Aristotelian arguments to some modern forms of property, it should be observed that rural property, and even the type of property held by medieval artisans, is still widespread throughout the world. The argument based on initiative and efficiency is valid even for more complicated modern forms of property; of course, some of these cannot be justified at all. In the name of the natural right to property, liberal capitalism has deprived immense masses of such a right, and has created social unrest and conflicts.

From these considerations we draw the following conclusions. Since the arguments justifying private property are not based on human convention, custom, or law, but on the nature and properties of man and his activity, the right to private property is natural, and a general system of private ownership is not only permitted but demanded by natural law.

IV

THEOLOGICAL EXCURSUS

In the preceding section we have touched on two points that belong to theology, not to philosophy, viz., the consequences of original sin, and the existence or non-existence of private property

[26] Cf. R. E. Brennan, *Thomistic Psychology* (New York: The Macmillan Co., 1941), pp. 109-110.

of productive goods in the state of original justice. We have done so, not to justify our conclusions with theological arguments, but because historically the problem of property has been linked with that of original sin. These two theological points need a brief explanation.

As regards the effects of original sin there are three different opinions. A first opinion, long ago abandoned by Catholics, held that by virtue of original sin our natural forces were intrinsically diminished or deteriorated. A second opinion maintains that man in his actual fallen state, prescinding from his restoration, possesses less inclination to virtue and less strength to do natural moral good than in the state of pure nature. Those who hold this opinion do not affirm that natural forces have been diminished intrinsically, or *quoad entitatem,* but only extrinsically, by reason of the obstacles which would not have existed in the state of pure nature.

A third opinion asserts that natural forces have not been deteriorated or diminished either intrinsically or extrinsically; that in both states, pure and fallen, natural forces and the inclination to evil and the difficulty in accomplishing good are identical. According to theologians holding this doctrine, the words of the Council of Trent, *vulneratus in naturalibus,* do not mean that nature was wounded either intrinsically or extrinsically, but merely that by virtue of original sin man lost among other gifts the preternatural gift of integrity; and concupiscence, a natural property of human nature, was unloosed. The distinction between man of pure nature and man of fallen nature would be that of *nudus* (nude) and *nudatus* (undressed).[27] L. Lercher, who follows this opinion, adds that it is the teaching of St. Thomas.[28] The fact, however, is that commentators on St. Thomas are divided into two groups: most Thomists[29] attribute to him the second opinion; others, like L. Lercher and J. B. Kors, O. P.,[30] interpret St. Thomas as a defender of the third theory.

Let us apply the foregoing observations, concerning the relations between the fallen state and the state of pure nature to the problem of whether the right to private property is or is not natural. If

---

[27] Cf. Y. E. Masson, "Nature (Etats de)," *Dictionnaire de théologie catholique,* XI, Pt. I (1931), 38-42.

[28] L. Lercher, *Institutiones theologiae dogmaticae* (2d ed.; Aeniponte/Lipsiae: Rauch, 1934), pp. 480-481.

[29] Cf. Y. E. Masson, *l.c.,* 39-40.

[30] J. B. Kors, *La justice primitive et le péché originel* (Paris: J. Vrin, 1930), pp. 157 ff.

the theory affirming that pure nature and fallen nature are identical is accepted, the Aristotelian arguments in favor of property are based upon a property of our nature, or rather, upon the effects which normally follow from a natural property of human nature, namely, concupiscence. If the second theory is admitted, the traditional arguments would be particularly strong with regard to the fallen nature. Would they also be valid for the state of pure nature? Since even those who think that human nature was somehow wounded by the Fall must admit that concupiscence is to a certain extent natural, and that its suppression or the gift of integrity is a preternatural gift, the answer must be in the affirmative. In other words, theology as a negative norm says that concupiscence is natural to man.

Whether its actual vehemence is or is not due to the Fall is a disputed question. The philosopher must try by rational means to find and determine the relations between our inferior and superior faculties. He knows that concupiscence as such flows from the very constitution of man. Inferior faculties tend naturally to sensible goods, while rational faculties tend to spiritual goods. Further, in the rational faculties themselves different and opposite tendencies may originate with regard to different objects. A natural consequence of these opposite tendencies is conflict, which constitutes concupiscence. Concupiscence is therefore natural to man.

As regards the existence or non-existence of private property of productive goods in the state of original justice, we have said that the scholastics unanimously hold that no private property would have existed in that blessed state. Not all neo-scholastics will agree with this statement. Some of them have attempted to detect a difference of opinion between the Augustinian-Franciscan tradition and the Thomistic teaching.[31] There is no doubt that outstanding representatives of the first school, such as St. Bonaventure,[32] John Duns Scotus,[33] and Ockham,[34] hold the theory of community of goods in Eden. In the Thomistic school we should distinguish between St. Thomas himself and various neo-Thomists.

St. Thomas does not study the problem *ex professo* but touches upon it incidentally while answering an objection in the course of

[31] Cf. M. E. Borne, *l.c.*, pp. 76 ff.
[32] St. Bonaventure, *In II Sent.*, d. 44, a. 2, ad 4, V. II, p. 109.
[33] J. D. Scotus, *Oxon.*, IV, d. 15, q. 2, V. XVIII, n. 3.
[34] W. Ockham, *Breviloquium*, III, 7, p. 85.

his study of the problem concerning the existence of generation in the state of innocence. He writes:

> In our present state a division of possessions is necessary on account of the multiplicity of masters, inasmuch as community of possessions is a source of strife, as the Philosopher says. . . . In the state of innocence, however, the will of men would have been so ordered that without any danger of strife they would have used in common, according to each one's need, those things of which they were masters—a state of things to be observed even now among many good men.[35]

The meaning of these words is apparently clear. He establishes a contrast between the present state and the state of innocence, and says that the difference lies in the fact that in the present state the division of goods is necessary whereas in the state of innocence men would have used possessions in common. Therefore, if the actual division of goods is opposed to the economic regime which would have existed in the state of innocence, the conclusion must be that no private property would have existed in that blessed state. However, a difficulty has been seen in the rendering of the words: *secundum quod unicuique eorum competeret, rebus, quae eorum dominio subdebantur*. Was such dominion exercised jointly or separately? It is our opinion that this difficulty has no foundation. St. Thomas says that the dominion would have been exercised jointly: *communiter usi fuissent*. It cannot be held that he speaks of community of use and not of community of dominion, for the term "to use" may mean not only use of application, but all the activities of which material goods are susceptible.[36] If in this passage use mean use of application, the contrast St. Thomas establishes between the innocent state and actual state would be meaningless.

As regards neo-Thomists there are some, for instance, O. Schilling[37] and T. Tonneau,[38] who are of the opinion that private property is independent of the Fall. Tonneau writes: "We are inclined to

---

[35] *S. Theol.*, I, q. 98, art. 1: "In statu isto multiplicatis dominis, necesse est fieri divisionem possessionum: quia communitas possessionum est occasio discordiae . . ., sed in statu innocentiae fuissent voluntates hominum sic ordinatae, quod absque omni periculo discordiae communiter usi fuissent, secundum quod unicuique ipsorum competeret, rebus, quae eorum dominio subdebantur: cum hoc etiam modo apud multos bonos viros observatur."

[36] *S. Theol.*, II II, q. 66, art. 1.

[37] Quoted by T. Tonneau, *Bulletin thomiste* (Jan. 1932), pp. 605 ff.

[38] *Ibid.*

believe . . . that St. Thomas wished to ignore this concept [that private property is a consequence of original sin] despite the authority of Pseudo-Clement who held it, and he has clearly adopted the solution of Aristotle."[39]

V

SCOPE OF THE ARGUMENTS

The arguments previously adduced in favor of the right to private property prove that this right is natural, and also that the institution of private ownership is an exigency of natural law. They do not prove that the right to property is unlimited, since it is limited by the more fundamental right every man has to the use of material goods. Nor do the arguments prove that the concrete historical forms of ownership or the present distribution of private possessions have been determined by nature, or that all means of production should be privately owned.

Social history reveals a great diversity of ownership forms. God, says Leo XIII, "has left to man and to the institutions of peoples the demarcation of property."[40] Pius XI repeats the same idea, recalling the forms that property has had throughout history. The Pope mentions certain historical forms that are particularly important: "the primitive form among savage and rough peoples," property in "patriarchal times," and "tyrannical types" in the classic sense of the word.[41] He does not go into the problem of whether they were suitable to the common good. He draws a historical sketch presupposing and recognizing the legitimacy of the changing application of an unchanging principle. He hopes that the state will direct the development of the institution of private property, "intended by the Creator of nature in His wisdom to sustain human life," so that it will always fulfill its purpose under changing conditions, rather than create new and intolerable burdens which would hasten its own end.

The Pope could have added other forms of property, especially in regard to money and loans as created by modern commerce, which began at the end of the Middle Ages.

[39] *Ibid.*
[40] *A.S.S.*, XXIII, (1891), 644.
[41] *A.A.S.*, XXIII, (1931), 193.

There arise forms of property that make possible wide separation between ownership and use, as in the forms of capital loan; there arise instruments for the transfer of value which make possible the transfer of property over great distances without movement of goods, thereby avoiding the risk of loss or theft (ex.g., in the fifteenth century remittances of money from Germany to the Roman Curia through the agency of the business houses of the Fuggers). Soon instruments of exchange are developed as means of transferring value over intervals of time; joint ownership is developed, first in the form of shares in mines, then, because of the large capital required for trading over great distances and because of the progressive technical development of industry, share holding ownership in trading and industrial concerns is introduced.

This brings us to the development of modern forms of property, in particular the joint ownership of trusts and cartels in industrial undertakings for the purpose of organization, profit sharing, control, and management. Further developments are forms of property such as proprietary rights in inventions, patents, and trade marks. Not least advanced is the form of property constituted by present-day paper money as a claim to goods resulting from the economic cooperation of a society.[42]

Not all these forms are necessarily ethical. Their justification will depend on whether or not they fulfill the purposes for which material goods should be privately owned. The adduced arguments are a plea for the widest possible diffusion of ownership. Man's rational nature and his actual or potential condition as head of a family give him the right to property. Rational nature is common to all men, and every man has the right to become head of a family. Every worker has a right to the fruits of his work. Personal dignity and economic, political, and cultural freedom, which are guaranteed by private property, must be enjoyed by all. Nobody should be denied the incentives to economic efficiency which private ownership safeguards.

To appeal to the natural character of private property in defense of liberal capitalism, which has selfishly concentrated property in privileged minorities and has denied it to the huge proletarian masses, would be worthy of laughter if it were not so tragic. Of course, the desired expansion of property does not mean that each person or family must possess an equal, or almost equal, share of the national wealth. Such equalitarianism would be utopian. The

---

[42] J. Messner, *Social Ethics*, transl. from German manuscript by J. J. Doherty (St. Louis: B. Herder Book Co., 1949), p. 790.

diffusion of ownership means that personal or family property should be the normal economic condition.

There are different ways of achieving diffusion of private ownership: a salary that permits the worker to save some money,[43] professional organizations, which guarantee social justice,[44] participation in benefits,[45] and co-management.[46] As regards industries which by their very nature must be large, the means to generalize private ownership is co-ownership.[47] Co-ownership may take the form of a cooperative or of ownership of shares, which can be either individually or collectively owned. Up to now, C. Van Gestel remarks, co-ownership has not achieved the expected results. Many workers, in spite of owning some parts of the undertaking in which they are engaged, remain poor, and in time of crisis hasten to sell their shares.[48] L. O. Kelso and M. J. Adler likewise point out that the possession of a few shares hardly changes the economic situation of the proletariate. They add the practical means by which co-ownership can make workers true proprietors.[49] In other words, the fact that co-ownership has not produced the expected results should not make us skeptics as to its potential effectiveness, but spur our minds to think out new and more effective techniques.

Moreover, the arguments in favor of private property do not reject public ownership of the so-called public utilities or even of other large instruments of production, when they "carry with them an opportunity for domination that is so great that it cannot be left in the hands of private individuals without injury to the community at large."[50]

[43] A.S.S., XXIII (1891), 641.

[44] A.A.S., XXIII (1931), 204; *A Code of Social Principles* (Oxford: Catholic Social Guild, 1946), nn. 78 ff; A. Dauphin-Meunier, *La doctrina económica de la Iglesia*, Spanish transl. by A. Arroyo (Valencia: Fomento de Cultura, 1952), pp. 289 ff.

[45] On the different types of participation in benefits, see A. Dauphin, *op. c.*, pp. 199-200; C. Van Gestel, *La doctrine sociale de l'Eglise* (Bruxelles: La pensée catholique, 1952), p. 201; P. André, "L'Enterprise et son évolution," *Semaine sociale de France* (1945), pp. 96 ff.

[46] On the different types of co-management, see C. Van Gestel, *op. c.*, pp. 201 ff.

[47] A.A.S., S.II, XI (1944), 164.

[48] *Op. c.*, p. 210.

[49] L. O. Kelso and M. J. Adler, *The Capitalist Manifesto* (New York: Random House, 1958), pp. 190 ff.

[50] John XXIII, *Master et Magistra*, p. 33.

VI

EXEGESIS OF CERTAIN THOMISTIC TEXTS

Finally, we must interpret certain texts of St. Thomas Aquinas which state either that private property belongs to *ius gentium*, or that property is an addition to natural law, or that the division of possessions is "according to human convention which pertains to positive right." There is no doubt that St. Thomas attaches private property to the *ius gentium* and that *ius gentium*, according to him, is constituted by conclusions derived from the principles of natural law. But do these conclusions belong to natural law? In his *Commentary on the Nicomachean Ethics* he affirms it. In confronting the classification of the Roman jurists with that of Aristotle, who divided the just (δίκαιον) into natural and legal, St. Thomas includes the *ius naturale* and *ius gentium*, a right specifically human, of the jurists in the δίκαιον φυσικόν of Aristotle.[51] He also explicitly says that the conclusions from the principles of natural law belong to natural law.[52]

However, in the *Summa Theologiae*, I-II, 95, 3, he states that both civil law and *ius gentium* belong to human law, but adds that *ius gentium* derives some of its binding force from the natural law.[53]

---

[51] *In I Ethic.*, 1.12: "Est autem considerandum, quod iustum naturale est ad quod hominem natura inclinat. Attenditur autem in homine duplex natura. Una quidem, secundum quod est animal, quae sibi et aliis animalibus est communis. Alia autem natura est hominis, quae est propria sibi inquantum est homo, prout scilicet secundum rationem discernit turpe et honestum. Iuristae autem illud tantum dicunt ius naturale, quod consequitur inclinationem naturae communis homini et aliis animalibus, sicut coniunctio maris et feminae, educatio natorum, et alia huiusmodi. Illud autem ius, quod consequitur propriam inclinationem naturae humanae, inquantum scilicet homo est rationale animal, vocant iuristae ius gentium, quia eo omnes gentes utuntur, sicut quod pacta sint servanda, et quod legati apud hostes sint tuti, et alia huiusmodi. Utrumque autem horum comprehenditur sub iusto naturali, prout hic a Philosopho accipitur."

[52] *Ibid.*: "Dupliciter tamen potest oriri a iure naturali. Uno modo sicut conclusio ex principiis; et sic ius positivum vel legale non potest oriri a iure naturali; praemissis enim existentibus, necesse est conclusionem esse; sed cum iustum naturale sit semper et ubique, ut dictum est, hoc non competit iusto legali vel positivo. Et ideo necesse est quod quicquid ex iusto naturali sequitur, quasi conclusio, sit iustum naturale...."

In the next article, to the question whether Isidore's division of human law into positive and *ius gentium* is correct, he answers affirmatively. The reason given is that one of the properties of human law is that it is derived from natural law, and *ius gentium* fulfills this condition, for it is constituted by conclusions drawn from the principles of natural law.[54]

In I-II, 95, 4, in the answer to the first objection, St. Thomas affirms that *ius gentium* is somehow natural to man insofar as he is rational,[55] although it is distinct from natural law, particularly if natural law is defined as "that which nature taught men and animals," as Ulpian states.

[53] *S. Theol.*, I-II, q. 95, art. 3: "Sciendum est quod a lege naturali dupliciter potest aliquid derivari: uno modo sicut conculsiones ex principiis; alio modo, sicut determinationes quaedam aliquorum communium. Primus quidem modus est similis ei quo in scientiis ex principiis conclusiones demonstrativae producuntur. Secundo vero modo simile est quod in actibus formae communes determinantur ad aliquid speciale: sicut artifex formam communem domus necesse est quod determinet ad hanc vel illam domus figuram. Derivantur ergo quaedam a principiis communibus legis naturae per modum conclusionum: sicut hoc quod est non esse occidendum, ut conclusio quaedam derivari potest ab eo quod est nulli esse malum faciendum. Quaedam vero per modum determinationis: sicut lex naturae habet quod ille qui peccat, puniatur; sed quod tali poena puniatur, hoc est quaedam determinatio legis naturae.

Utraque igitur inveniuntur in lege humana posita. Sed ea quae sunt primi modi continentur lege humana non tamquam sint solum lege posita, sed habent etiam aliquid vigoris ex lege naturali. Sed ea quae sunt secundi modi, ex sola lege humana vigorem habent."

[54] *Ibid.*, art. 4: "Dicendum quod unumquodque potest per se dividi secundum id quod in eius ratione continetur. Sicut in ratione animalis continetur anima, quae est rationalis vel irrationalis; et ideo animal proprie et per se dividitur secundum rationale et irrationale; non autem secundum album et nigrum, quae sunt omino praeter rationem eius. Sunt autem multa de ratione legis humanae, secundum quorum quodlibet lex humana proprie et per se dividi potest. Est enim primo de ratione legis humanae quod sit derivata a lege naturae, ut ex dictis patet. Et secundum hoc dividitur ius positivum in ius gentium et ius civile, secundum duos modos quibus aliquid derivatur a lege naturae, ut supra dictum est. Nam ad ius gentium pertinent ea quae derivantur ex lege naturae sicut conclusiones ex principiis; ut iustae emptiones, venditiones, et alia huiusmodi, sine quibus homines ad invicem convivere non possent; quod est de lege naturae, quia homo est naturaliter animal sociale, ut probatur in *I Polit.* Quae vero derivantur a lege naturae per modum particularis determinationis, pertinent ad ius civile, secundum quod quaelibet civitas aliquid sibi accommodum determinat."

[55] *Ibid.*, ad 1: "Ius gentium est quidem aliquo modo naturale homini, secundum quod est rationalis, inquantum derivatur a lege naturali per modum conclusionis quae non est multum remota a principiis. Unde de facili in huiusmodi homines consenserunt. Distinguitur tamen a lege naturali, maxime ab eo quod est omnibus animalibus commune."

In II-II, 57, 3, St. Thomas identifies *ius gentium* with natural law, proper to rational beings. It is not natural in Ulpian's sense of the term. Obviously, it is not common to men and animals; but it is natural to men, for it is the fruit of natural reason, as Gaius defines it.[56] In the same article, in the answer to the third objection, he adds that, since *ius gentium* contains dictates of natural reason, and is instituted by it, it does not need any special human institution.[57]

In conclusion, according to St. Thomas private property pertains to *ius gentium,* and *ius gentium* is constituted by conclusions from principles of natural law. In some texts he says that these conclusions belong to natural law, or to natural law proper to man. In other texts he includes *ius gentium* in human law. In these last texts he limits natural law to its first principles or has in mind Ulpian's definition of natural law: "that which nature taught men and animals." *Ius gentium* is not constituted by first principles, it is the result of human activity or reasoning; and, of course, it is not natural in Ulpian's sense.

The main points that we should keep in mind with regard to these Thomistic texts are that, according to St. Thomas, who follows Gaius, *ius gentium* is constituted by conclusions drawn from the principles of natural law, and that such conclusions pertain to

---

[56] *S. Theol.,* II-II, q. 57, art. 3: "Ius sive iustum naturale est quod ex sui natura est adaequatum vel commensuratum alteri. Hoc autem potest contingere dupliciter. Uno modo secundum absolutam sui considerationem: sicut masculus ex sui ratione habet commensurationem ad feminam ut ex ea generet, et parens ad filium ut eum nutriat. Alio modo aliquid est naturaliter alteri commensuratum non secundum absolutam sui rationem, sed secundum aliquid quod ex ipso consequitur: puta proprietas possessionum. Si enim consideretur iste ager absolute, non habet unde magis sit huius quam illius; sed si consideretur quantum ad opportunitatem colendi et ad pacificum usum agri, secundum hoc habet quamdam commensurationem ad hoc quod sit unius et non alterius, ut patet per Philosophum, in *II Polit.*

Absolute autem apprehendere aliquid non solum convenit homini, sed etiam aliis animalibus. Et ideo ius quod dicitur naturale secundum primum modum, commune est nobis et aliis animalibus. A iure autem naturali sic dicto recedit ius gentium, ut Iurisconsultus dicit: quia illud omnibus animalibus, hoc solum hominibus inter se commune est. Considerare autem aliquid comparando ad id quod ex ipso sequitur, est proprium rationis. Et ideo hoc quidem est naturale homini secundum rationem naturalem, quae hoc dicat. Et ideo dicit Gaius iurisconsultus: quod naturalis ratio inter omnes homines constituit, id apud omnes gentes custoditur, vocaturque ius gentium."

[57] *Ibid.,* ad 3: "Quia ea quae sunt iuris gentium naturalis ratio dictat, puta ex propinquo habentia aequitatem, inde est quod non indigent aliqua speciali institutione, sed ipsa naturalis ratio ea instituit, ut dictum est in auctoritate inducta."

the natural law, as we understand it. Father Santiago Ramírez, O.P., after an exhaustive study of the texts concludes that St. Thomas' *ius gentium* is our natural law.[58] It should not be translated, therefore, as "law of nations," which regulates the relations among nations. It is a law for individuals, and ought to be observed within nations. The concept of *ius gentium* as law of nations is first found in St. Isidore of Seville, was later adopted by Vitoria, Suàrez, *et al.*, and has become universal in modern times. It may contain some precepts of international natural law, but it is primarily positive. In view of the equivocity of the term *ius gentium*, and because its content, as St. Thomas understood it, is included in the modern concept of natural law, we should drop the older Thomistic terminology and simply say that the right to private property is based on natural law.

Needless to say, the statement that *ius gentium* contains conclusions from natural law presupposes that both premises belong to natural law. If one of the premises were based on custom or positive law, the conclusion would belong to positive law; the conclusion, logic teaches, must follow the "worst part."

There are in St. Thomas other texts dealing directly with private property in which he says that the distribution of possessions has not been induced by nature (*natura non induxit*), that private possession of goods is an addition to natural law, that it is based on human convention.[59] In these texts, again, by natural law St. Thomas means the first principles; the conclusions, he says, are not

---

[58] S. Ramírez, *Derecho de Gentes* (Madrid, 1955), *passim*.

[59] *S. Theol.*, I-II, q. 94, art. 5, ad 3: "Aliquid dicitur esse de iure naturali dupliciter: uno modo, quia ad hoc natura inclinat; sicut non esse iniuriam alteri faciendam; alio modo, quia natura non inducit contrarium; sicut possemus dicere, quod hominem esse nudum est de iure naturali; quia natura non dedit ei vestitum, sed ars adinvenit; et hoc modo communis omnium possessio et una libertas dicitur esse de iure naturali; quia scilicet distinctio possessionum et servitus non sunt inductae a natura; sed per hominum rationem ad utilitatem humanae vitae, et sic etiam in hoc lex naturae non est mutata nisi per additionem."

S. Theol., II-II, q. 66, art. 2, ad 1: "Communitas rerum attribuitur iuri naturali, non quia ius naturale dictet omnia esse possidenda communiter et nihil esse quasi proprium possidendum: sed quia secundum ius naturale non est distinctio possessionum, sed magis secundum humanum condictum, quod pertinet ad ius positivum, ut supra dictum est. Unde proprietas possessionum non est contra ius naturale; sed iuri naturali superadditur per adinventionem rationis humanae."

Ibid., art. 7: "Per rerum divisionem et appropriationem, de iure humano procedentem, non impeditur quin hominis necessitati sit subveniendum ex huiusmodi rebus."

given by nature, but are discovered by reason; they are additions to natural law, namely, to its first principles.

These texts allude also to the actual distribution of goods, which is always due to a positive human act. Such an allusion is obvious in this text:

> Possumus dicere, quod hominem esse nudum est de iure naturali; quia natura non dedit ei vestitum sed ars adinvenit; et hoc modo communis omnium possessio et una libertas dicitur esse de iure naturali; quia scilicet distinctio possessionum et servitus non sunt inductae a natura, sed per hominum rationem ad utilitatem humanae vitae, et sic etiam in hoc lex naturae non est mutata nisi per additionem.

The comparison St. Thomas makes between the distinction of possessions and clothing seems to indicate sufficiently that he alludes to the actual division of goods. He cannot mean, unless he refers to the state of innocence, that nature does not incline us to cover and protect our bodies, but that nature does not supply us with our clothing *(natura non dedit ei vestitum)*; we have to get them by positive acts. It is the same as regards the division of possessions; nature does not assign this particular thing to one person and that particular thing to another.

In fine, there is no opposition between our previous conclusions and St. Thomas' teaching as regards the problem we have discussed. According to him, private property is based on what we call natural law. Furthermore, he affirms that a general system of private ownership is necessary *(necessarium)*, which means that it is not only permitted but demanded by *ius gentium,* by natural law.

8

THE POLITICAL THOUGHT OF TOMMASO CAMPANELLA*

by

BERNARDINE M. BONANSEA, O.F.M.

Boasting that he had been called to reform society, religion, and all the sciences, and posing as a champion of freedom and justice against the social and political evils of his time,[1] Campanella could not fail to include in his ambitious plans of reform a treatise on political science. In fact, his political writings are so numerous as to make up a very considerable portion of his literary work. Their subjects range from particular problems of social and administrative nature to a bold and grandiose conception of a universal monarchy headed by the Pope.

The number and length of Campanella's political treatises and the fact that they were written years apart and with many adverse circumstances make it difficult to reduce his political thought to a unified system.[2] This difficulty is increased by the fact that the

---

* Tommaso Campanella was born at Stilo, in Calabria, Italy, on September 5, 1568. At an early age he entered the Dominican Order and devoted himself to the study of philosophy. In 1599 he was arrested by order of the Spanish government on charges of heresy and conspiracy. Although he never confessed to crime or heresy, he was kept in prison at Naples for 27 years. Released in 1626, he was arrested again and arraigned before the ecclesiastical tribunal in Rome. After regaining his freedom, he spent some time at the Dominican monastery of Minerva in Rome. Fearing further persecution, he followed the advice of Pope Urban VIII and fled to France in 1634, where he was befriended by King Louis XIII and Cardinal Richelieu. He died on May 21, 1639, in the quiet of the monastery of St. James in Paris.

[1] "I was born to defeat the three greatest evils, tyranny, sophistry, and hypocrisy." T. Campanella, *Poesie*, ed. Mario Vinciguerra (Bari: Laterza, 1938), p. 18. Unless otherwise stated, translations are the author's.

[2] Prof. Luigi Firpo classifies Campanella's political works into four groups. The first group includes Campanella's youthful writings glorifying the Spanish government, namely, the *Discorso sui Paesi Bassi* (1594), the *Discorsi ai Principi*

critical edition of Campanella's works is still incomplete, and his political writings, which are known to contain many interpolations by other hands, are perhaps those in greatest need of revision.³ However, we are fortunate to have at hand either a critical edition or the original text of certain fundamental works and on their basis it is possible to reconstruct and evaluate Campanella's political theory. We refer especially to Prof. Luigi Firpo's critical editions of Campanella's *De politica*⁴ and the *Civitas Solis*,⁵ and to the

---

d'Italia (written in 1593 and revised in 1607), and the *Monarchia di Spagna* (1598-1601?). The second group comprises the *Aforismi politici* (1601), the *Città del Sole* (1602), and the *Quaestiones politicae* (1609 ff.), all of which are part of the *Disputationum in quatuor partes suae philosophiae realis libri quatuor*, henceforth to be referred to as *Philosophia realis*. To the third group belong all the writings having to do with Campanella's theory of a universal theocratic monarchy, such as the *Monarchia Christianorum* (1593), which has been lost, the *Discorsi universali del governo ecclesiastico* (1593-95), the *Dialogo politico contro Luterani, Calvinisti ed altri eretici* (1595), the *Monarchia del Messia* (1605), the *Discorso dei diritti del Re Cattolico sul Mondo Nuovo* (1605), the *Discorsi della libertà e della felice suggezione allo Stato ecclesiastico* (1625-26), and the *De regno Dei* (1630). The fourth group embraces some minor works, especially those favoring the French government. They are: the *Antiveneti* (1606), the *Arbitri sopra l'aumento delle entrate del Regno di Napoli* (1608), the *Oeconomica* (1614-15), the *Avvertimenti al Re di Francia* (1628), the *Dialogo politico tra un Veneziano, Spagnolo e Francese* (1632), the *Aforismi politici per le presenti necessità di Francia* (1635), the opuscule *Se al tempo nostro possa e debba trasmutarsi l'impero Romano* (1635), and the *Documenta ad Gallorum nationem* (1635). Cf. T. Campanella, *Aforismi politici*, ed. Luigi Firpo (Turin: Giappichelli, 1941), Introduction, pp. 6-9. Certain dates have been corrected according to more recent discoveries made for the most part by Firpo himself. Although the authenticity of the *Discorso sui Paesi Bassi* has been questioned by Firpo, he admits however that the material is basically of Campanellian origin. Cf. Luigi Firpo, "Appunti campanelliani. XXII: Un'opera che Campanella non scrisse: il 'Discorso sui Paesi Bassi'," *Giornale critico della filosofia italiana*, 33 (1952), 331-43.

³ For detailed information as to the present textual situation of Campanella's political writings cf. Firpo's edition of *Aforismi politici*, loc. cit.; The same, *Scritti scelti di Giordano Bruno e di Tommaso Campanella* (Turin: U.T.E.T., 1949), pp. 263-66; The same, *Bibliografia degli scritti di Tommaso Campanella* (Turin: Bona, 1940), under the title of each political work mentioned in the *Aforismi Politici*.

⁴ The complete title of the treatise is, *Thomae Campanellae, Suae philosophiae realis pars tertia, quae est de politica in aphorismos digesta*. It is part of the *Philosophia realis*, an extremely rare book, published in Paris in 1637. We shall quote *De politica* from Firpo's *Aforismi politici*, where it runs from p. 143 to p. 225. Firpo's edition contains also the critical text of the Italian *Aforismi politici* (pp. 87-142), which is like a preview of Campanella's later treatise *De politica*. The *Aforismi* are preceded by a very enlightening introduction (pp. 5-52), and a discussion on the relationship between Campanella and Hugo Grotius (pp. 53-85). This latter's *Observata in Aphorismos Campanellae politicos* are also included in Firpo's edition (pp. 227-45).

⁵ Cf. Firpo, *Scritti scelti*, pp. 407-464.

Monarchia Messiae, a work that has come down in its original Latin version.[6] This trilogy of works may well represent three phases of Campanella's political thought, as well as three different, although not altogether contradictory, conceptions of the state.

The *De politica* is by far the most important of the three treatises, since it contains Campanella's mature thought and discusses questions of a general character rather than problems arising from particular situations. It is an objective approach to the state in its concrete reality. Although less original than some of his other works, it ranks first among Campanella's political writings. This seems to be the opinion of Campanella himself, who rates it highly and calls it "the foundation of political science."[7]

A work of a quite different nature is the *Civitas Solis* or *The City of the Sun,* a new and original version of Thomas More's *Utopia* built along Platonic lines. The work in itself does not deserve to be taken too seriously as it is a product of Campanella's fertile imagination rather than of solid thought. However, because it is his best-known production and because it is often misunderstood and misrepresented, we make it the object of a special study.

The *Monarchia Messiae* is an important treatise in which Campanella discusses the doctrine of a universal monarchy under the leadership of the Roman Pontiff as its supreme temporal and spiritual ruler. This treatise, together with the *Quod reminiscentur*[8] and the *Discorsi universali del governo ecclesiastico,*[9] a

---

[6] The version was made by Campanella himself in 1618 from the original Italian text of the *Monarchia del Messia,* written in 1605. There are only a few extant copies of the *Monarchia Messiae,* published at Iesi by Gregorio Arnazzini in 1633. For fear that the work might not be well received by the contemporary secular rulers, the Master of the Sacred Palace, Father Riccardi, ordered that the entire edition of 1500 copies be withdrawn from circulation. Reportedly, the book fell an easy prey to rats and worms of the Dominican monastery of Minerva in Rome. Cr. Tommaso Campanella, *Discorsi della libertà e della felice suggezione allo stato ecclesiastico,* ed. Luigi Firpo (Turin, 1960), Introduction, pp. 5-6.

[7] Cf. T. Campanella, *De libris propriis et recta ratione studendi syntagma,* ed. Vincenzo Spampanato (Milan: Bestetti e Tumminelli, 1927), p. 24: "Scripsi praeterea *Aphorismos politicos,* quos deinde in capitula distinxi et politicam scientiam condidi."

[8] The full title of the treatise is *Quod reminiscentur et convertentur ad Dominum universi fines terrae.* The four books that make up the treatise have been edited by Romano Amerio in the following order: Bks. I and II (Padua: Cedam, 1939); Bks. III and IV (Florence: L. S. Olschki, 1955-1960).

[9] Cf. Firpo, *Scritti scelti,* pp. 465-523, where the critical edition of the *Discorsi univerasli del governo ecclesiastico* is contained. The text of the *Discorsi universali etc.* that has come down to us is the abstract of a much larger work

short but valuable document containing practical suggestions for the realization of the author's long cherished dream described in the *Monarchia Messiae,* serves as a basis for discussion of the third and final phase of Campanella's political theory, his conception of a theocratic state.

Other primary sources, such as *Metaphysica,*[10] *Theologia,*[11] *Atheismus triumphatus,*[12] *Monarchia di Spagna,*[13] *De regno Dei,*[14] and especially the *Quaestiones politicae,*[15] an important commentary on the *De politica* and *The City of the Sun,* will also be used. Thus, with the aid of some special studies on the subject,[16] it is

---

which was lost and Campanella himself was never able to recover. He wrote the abstract in question by relying entirely on his prodigious memory. He was so pleased with it that he called it "better" than the lost original. *Ibid.,* p. 265. We shall refer to Firpo's *Scritti scelti* for the *Discorsi universali.*

[10] This is Campanella's most important philosophical work. The original title is *Universalis philosophiae, seu metaphysicarum rerum iuxta propria dogmata partes tres, libri 18* (Parisiis: Apud Dionysium Langlois, 1638).

[11] The MS of this work, *Theologicorum libri XXX,* is preserved in the archives of St. Sabina in Rome. The edition with Italian translation is being cared for by Romano Amerio, who up to date has published ten books in eleven separate volumes. The publication does not follow the original order of the books.

[12] The original title of the *Atheismus triumphatus* was *Recognitio verae religionis secundum omnes scientias contra anti-Christianismum Machiavellisticum.* The present title was suggested by Gaspar Schopp and later approved by Campanella. The edition used in this study is that of Paris (Apud Tussanum Dubray, 1636).

[13] We shall quote the *Monarchia di Spagna* from the edition of Alessandro D'Ancona, in *Opere di Tommaso Campanella* (Turin : Pomba, 1854), Vol. II, pp. 77-229.

[14] The *De regno Dei* is a short political treatise that Campanella wrote to take the place of the *Monarchia Messiae* which had been withdrawn from circulation. It is included in the *Philosophia realis.*

[15] The *Quaestiones politicae* run through pp. 71-112 of the *Philosophia realis* and it is only by mistake that they were inserted before the *De politica.*

[16] Here are the principal studies on Campanella's politics: Rodolfo De Mattei, *La politica di Campanella* (Rome: Anonima Romana Editoriale, 1927) ; Paolo Treves, *La filosofia politica di Tommaso Campanella* (Bari: Laterza, 1930) ; Kurt Sternberg, "Ueber Campanellas Sonnenstaat," *Historische Zeitschrift,* 148 (1933), 520-71; Walther Ducloux, *Die metaphysische Grundlage der Staatsphilosophie des T. Campanella* (Speyr am Rhein: Pilger Druckerei, 1935) ; Norberto Bobbio's critical edition of *La Città del Sole,* with an introduction, pp. 9-51 (Turin: Einaudi, 1941); Gioele Solari, "Di una nuova edizione critica della Città del Sole e del comunismo del Campanella," *Rivista di filosofia,* 32 (1941), 180-97; The same, "Filosofia politica del Campanella," *Rivista di filosofia,* 37 (1946), 38-63. See also Giovanni Di Napoli, *Tommaso Campanella, filosofo della restaurazione cattolica* (Padua: Cedam, 1947), chap. XI, "La politica," pp. 401-428; Romano Amerio, *Campanella* (Brescia. "La Scuola," 1947), "Etica e politica," pp. 171-214; Antonio Corsano, *Tommaso Campanella* (Bari: Laterza, 1961), chap. VI, "Morale e diritto," pp. 189-237.

possible to present an adequate view of Campanella's political thought.

I. THE REAL STATE

Accepting a familiar definition, Campanella calls politics the science of governing a state.[17] It is a science, and not merely an art, since an art may or may not be grounded in sound ethical principles. Politics is in effect a branch of ethics,[18] on which it depends and to which is subalternate.[19] It is a science given to men by God.[20] Hence politics cannot be divorced from religion, for a state without religion is a state that lacks foundation and support.[21]

Since this is the true nature of politics, Machiavelli's theory of state must be discarded as a vicious and pernicious doctrine.[22] No state or empire based exclusively on human prudence or political expediency can last.[23] To build a political system on cunning and mere personal ability, as Machiavelli tries to do, is to show the utmost ignorance of political science.[24]

The state, with which political theory is concerned, is a natural community resulting from the union of several provinces into a

[17] Tommaso Campanella, *Lettere*, ed. Vincenzo Spampanato (Bari: Laterza, 1927), p. 7: "Non mi scema la scienza con la quale si governano gli stati." This statement contained in a letter that Campanella wrote to Ferdinand I de' Medici was apparently overlooked by Treves, who affirms that he could find a definition of politics in none of Campanella's works. Cf. Treves, *op. cit.*, p. 48.

[18] *Metapyhsica*, Pt. I, Bk. 5, chap. 2, art. 4, p. 349a-349b: "Scienta ... moralis dividitur in Ethicam, Politicam, et Oeconomicam: illa regimus proprios mores, Politica Rempublicam et Imperium, Oeconomica familias ... Sed re vera unica scientia est, divisa per nostram imbecillitatem in plures."

[19] *Atheismus triumphatus*, p. 243: "Politica dependet ab ethica tanquam a subordinante."

[20] *Monarchia di Spagna*, p. 163.

[21] *Atheismus triumphatus*, p. 236: "Respublica non potest stare absque religione."

[22] *Metaphysica*, Pt. I, Bk. 5, chap. 2, art. 4, p. 349b: "Machiavellistica politica pessima est, quoniam discordat a primo Rectore, quem ipse non agnoscit, ergo et a toto mundo et a fato: ergo sibi et aliis perniciosa, dum prodesse credit, veluti puerorum astutia, medico et magistro, et patri familias repugnans, perdit eos."

[23] *Articuli prophetales*, in Luigi Amabile, *Fra Tommaso Campanella. La sua congiura, i suoi processi e la sua pazzia* (Naples: Morano, 1882), III, doc. 401, p. 489: "Nullum Imperium aut Regnum sola prudentia politica stetit."

[24] *Atheismus triumphatus*, p. 226: "Machiavellum omnium scientiarum fuisse ignorantissimum, excepta historia humana; et politicam suam non per scientias, sed per astutiam et peritiam practicam examinasse." In his unrestrained contempt for Machiavelli, Campanella calls him "porcus et pecus," *ibid.*, p. 238, as well as "scandalo, rovina, tosco e fuoco di questo secolo." *Antiveneti*, ed. Luigi Firpo (Florence: L. S. Olschki, 1945), p. 49.

kingdom, of several kingdoms into a monarchy, and of all mankind under the Pope.[25] The inner tendency that impels a man to join his fellow men and form a state comes from the First Mind, which disposes things in such a way that a man cannot attain his final end except by living in society.[26] Accordingly, the final cause of the state and the first end of man are one and the same, namely, God, from whom all happiness derives. It is wrong to think that the state exists for the ruler's private good or even for the temporal welfare of the citizens, since wealth and exaggerated freedom lead to tyranny.[27]

Three causes concur to form a state: God, prudence, and occasion. Sometimes the operation of one cause is more evident than that of the others. Examples of this are God, in the formation of the Jewish kingdom, prudence in shaping the Roman empire, and occasion in the establishment of the Spanish monarchy. However, God is always behind all secondary causes.[28] The priesthood takes God's place in the formation of a state; its role is so important that no state can exist without it.[29] Priests should be commissioned to shape and direct the state policy, which rulers enforce, and soldiers and public officers execute.[30]

It is fitting that the Pope, as supreme priest, should have his own army to be used for the preservation of the peace in the world and

[25] *Aforismi*, pp. 145-46: "Naturaliter consociantur quaecunque reciprocum bonum copulat naturale. Igitur . . . septima [communitas] plurium provinciarum in uno regno. Octava, plurium regnorum sub uno imperio. Nona, plurium imperiorum in variis climatibus sub una monarchia. Decima, omnium hominum sub specie humana et Papatu."

[26] *Ibid.*, p. 145: "Mens Prima necessitatis stimulis homines, cum nemo sibi sufficiens esset ad tuendam vitam ab externis internisque malis nec ad speciem propagandam, copulavit in unum fere corpus in quo alii regerent, alii regerentur, alii scientiae agendorum, alii agendis pro communi bono operam darent, mutuisque officiis innumeris, ob innumeras necessitates, sese iuvarent in vita, ad finem propter quem Deus Dominum dominantium creavit hominem ordinata."

[27] *Monarchia Messiae*, p. 78: "Finis reipublicae non est rex, nec eius commoda, nec procerum, nec populi, sed cultus Dei propter regnum aeternum." *Quaestiones politicae*, p. 72: "Finis autem reipublicae est Dei cultus, ut Plato agnovit, non autem rex, aut libertas, aut divitiae: his enim positis finibus tyrannides fiunt."

[28] *Aforismi*, p. 187. Cf. also *ibid.*, p. 176, where Campanella states: "Quoniam dominium hominis est divinae potestatis participatio, nemo potest fundare et retinere imperium nisi vere missus et authorizatus a Deo, vel creditus missus et authorizatus a Deo immediate vel mediate. Religio ergo quae Deo homines religat est causa imperandi."

[29] *Ibid.*, p. 188.

[30] *Ibid.*, p. 189.

the defense of true religion.³¹ To deny the Pope the use of the temporal sword along with the spiritual sword is not only imprudent but also heretical.³² Once the various sects and different religious denominations, as well as all forms of government, have undergone a radical change and lost their right to exist as separate entities, then all men will return to the state of original innocence, a golden age in which there will be one ruler who is both king and priest. He will be chosen from among the members of the senate, a body composed of the best men whose task is to assist the king-priest, that is, the Pope, in governing the monarchy. This is described in the *De monarchia Christianorum*.³³

The second cause in the formation of the state is prudence, a virtue of true kings, in contrast to cunning, the characteristic of a Machiavellian tyrant. Prudence wins even by losing; cunning loses even when it obtains an apparent victory. Prudence dictates laws suitable to all the people; cunning dictates laws that benefit only one man. The commonwealth is best served by the appointment of officers naturally gifted for the particular tasks they are called upon to perform. Material wealth should have no consideration in such appointments. The common good must prevail over the private good. Hence there will be community of goods, culture, and religion. Furthermore, things pertaining to God must have priority over those pertaining to man.³⁴

The third and last cause of a state is occasion, that is, those factors and circumstances that contribute to the acquisition of power over a territory or its extension over a new land. Such factors may be the weakness of an enemy, the dissension among princes in a

---

³¹ *Ibid.*, pp. 193-96.

³² *Ibid.*, p. 175: "Quapropter errant quicunque gladium solummodo spiritualem, non etiam temporalem Papae tribuunt. Sic enim eius Monarchia diminuta esset, cui hoc tutamen deficit, et Christus Deus legislator diminutus esset, quod imprudenter et haeretice affirmatur."

³³ *Ibid.*, pp. 196-98. The *De monarchia Christianorum* was written by Campanella in 1593, when he was in Padua. The MS has been lost, but it is possible to reconstruct its general theme from Campanella's references to the work in his other writings. In Firpo's view, the *De monarchia Christianorum* is "a fundamental work for the understanding of Campanella's complex [political] system." *Bibliografia, op. cit.*, p. 177. In it Campanella expounds "the supreme ideal of his life: the unification of the world under one civil and religious law." Cf. Luigi Firpo, *Introduzione e cronologia premesse al primo volume delle opere di Tommaso Campanella nell'edizione Mondadori, Estratto, 1953*, p. LXIX. In Di Napoli's opinion, the *De monarchia Christianorum* contains the scheme of "a true and proper *Society of Nations* presided by the Pope and having its seat in Rome." Di Napoli, *Tommaso Campanella*, p. 117.

³⁴ *Aforismi*, pp. 198-202.

divided land, corruption of the reigning ruler, and all external evils and vices that lead the subjects to submit to a new ruler.[35]

As to the origin of authority in the state or society, Campanella has no doubt that this comes ultimately from God, who by His very nature is absolute owner of all things.[36] Man can only share in God's power to the extent that this is allowed him by God, to whom all creatures tend as to their supreme and final cause. A man cannot dispose of himself, his limbs, or other men, and much less heaven and earth and the natural elements, in whatever way he wants, but only for the end established by God through natural and positive law.[37]

The person to bear and exercise authority in the state may be chosen in different ways. By nature he is fit to command who excels others in good qualities of soul or body or both.[38] In practice, the selection of a ruler may be made by election, drawing lots, succession, census (polls), or two or more of these methods combined.[39] The best way is when the king is appointed directly by God, rather than be chosen by the people.[40] Yet the system of election is better than mere hereditary succession.[41]

Monarchy is Campanella's preferred form of government, as is evident from his teaching in the *Monarchia Messiae*, where he states

---

[35] *Ibid.*, pp. 203-204.

[36] *Ibid.*, p. 153.

[37] *Ibid.* Campanella distinguishes between *ius, dominium*, and *beneficium*, three acts that correspond to the triple operation *ad extra* of every being. This is in accordance with his doctrine of "primalities" whereby being is a transcendental composite of power, knowledge, and will or love. It belongs to the potential principle (*principium potestativum*) to dominate, to the cognitive principle (*principium cognitivum*) to rule, and to the loving principle (*principium amativum* or *volitivum*) to help others by loving them, speaking well of them, and doing good to them. The *ius* exists among equals, the *dominium* between a superior and his subjects, and the *beneficium* between a possessor and a needy person. *Ibid.*, pp. 147-49. For an understanding of Campanella's doctrine of "primalities" cf. the present writer's study, "The Concept of Being and Non-being in the Philosophy of Tommaso Campanella," *The New Scholasticism*, XXXI (Jan., 1957), 34-67.

[38] *Aforismi*, p. 155: "Natura imperat qui virtute praestantior est; natura servit qui virtute inferior vel vacuus est. Ubi contra fit, dominium violentum est. Praestantia in politicis aut est secundum virtutem animi, aut corporis, aut utriusque. Melius dominatur qui in utraque praecellit."

[39] *Ibid.*, p. 158.

[40] *Monarchia Messiae*, p. 10: "Optimus est si non populorum, sed Dei auctoritate [praeponitur Princeps]."

[41] *Ibid.*, p. 9: "Magis secundum naturam est Princeps unus per electionem, quam per successionem adscitus."

that it is more natural for men to be governed by one ruler.[42] He repeats the same doctrine in the *Metaphysica*,[43] the *Theologia*,[44] and *The City of the Sun*,[45] to mention only some of his better known works. In the *Politica* he discusses this point more specifically and affirms that the government of one man is better in wartime, while the government of many is to be preferred in time of peace. To support his view, he appeals to the Romans, who turned to a dictator whenever a dangerous war threatened, so that he could make quicker decisions for the safety of the country. In time of peace, however, they set up consuls and a senate. All things being equal, the government of one good ruler is better than the government of many good rulers, just as the government of one bad ruler is worse than the government of many bad rulers. But since it is easier to get rid of one bad man than of many, it seems that the government of one bad man should be preferred.[46]

Campanella lays down some good norms to help the citizens in choosing their leader. Any leader of a larger group or society should first prove himself to be a good leader of a smaller community. Thus the ruler of a universal monarchy embracing all mankind should give sufficient evidence that he is a good king. A king, in turn, must first show himself to be a good governor of a province, and prior to that, a good ruler of a town, a village, and his own family. Most important of all, he must have learned how to rule over himself by subjecting his lower appetites to reason and will, and by letting these two higher faculties be directed by God. Thus, Campanella concludes, there can be no good ruler without divine law; otherwise, a ruler would be the scourge of God (*flagellum Dei*) and a hangman.[47]

If a nation is going to prosper and flourish, each citizen must be assigned the task for which he is naturally fit, or there will be chaos and ruin.[48] Who are the real citizens of a state? Campanella's idea of citizenship is somewhat different from notions prevailing both in his time and in our own. For him a citizen is not merely a man

---

[42] *Ibid.*: "Naturalius est hominibus regi ab uno."

[43] *Metaphysica*, Pt. I, Bk. 1, chap. 9, art. 12, p. 85b.

[44] *Theologicorum*, XIV, chap. 6, art. 3. MS referred to in Di Napoli, *op. cit.*, p. 411.

[45] Cf. *Città del Sole*, in Firpo's *Scritti scelti*, p. 412.

[46] *Aforismi*, p. 158.

[47] *Ibid.*, pp. 158-59. See also *Monarchia di Spagna*, p. 107; *Quaestiones morales*, in *Philosophia realis*, p. 13.

[48] *Aforismi*, p. 160.

who happens to be the subject of a particular state or government, but one who resides in the state and does something useful for it. Those who merely live within the state and in no way contribute to its welfare should be called guests, or even the scum of society *(hospites aut reipublicae excrementa)*. Such were, in Campanella's opinion, many members of the nobility at the time he wrote.[49]

To emphasize this, he goes on to say that it is the duty of nobles to defend the nation, while the common people ought to support it, and the learned rule over it and instruct the citizens. Those who do not perform any of these duties should be called scum and drones. On the contrary, mediators between men and God are to be considered as the most honorable members of a society, just as they are its most learned and virtuous men.[50]

Having discussed the nature of the state, the qualities of a good ruler, and the right type of citizen, Campanella takes up the question of law, which he calls a basic requirement for a community.[51] The function of the law in society is compared to what virtue does for the individual. Just as virtue is the norm an individual man must follow in his acts and operations to attain to his supreme good, so law is the norm of acts and operations of a community for the achievement of the supreme common good as decreed and promulgated by the superior.[52] Only God, the state, and those empowered by them can make laws.[53] As a result, there are eternal law, natural law, and divine positive law, all of which are directly from God. Positive civil law is from state authorities, and is a further determination and adaptation of the *jus gentium*. The *jus gentium*, in turn, is the law common to all peoples and is derived, by way of conclusion, from the natural law.[54] Thus all positive

---

[49] *Ibid.*, p. 161.
[50] *Ibid.*
[51] *Ibid.*: "Indiget communitas lege semper."
[52] In his *Metaphysica*, Pt. I, Bk. 5, chap. 2, art. 4, p. 439b, Campanella states: "Virtus est regula conservandi individuum: lex est virtus conservans speciem, id est rempublicam." In *Theologicorum*, XIV, chap. 1, art. 1, he defines law as "regula voluntaria rationis efficacis ad bonum commune per rectorem promulgata." MS quoted in Di Napoli, *op. cit.*, p. 385.
[53] *Aforismi*, p. 162.
[54] *Ibid.*, pp. 162-63. See also *Metaphysica*, Pt. III, Bk. 16, chap. 7, art. 5, pp. 216b-217a. The relationship between the law of nations and natural law is pointed out by Campanella in *Theologicorum*, XIV, chap. 4, art. 1, where he states: "Convenit ius gentium in iure naturali in hoc, quod utrumque est cunctis commune nationibus quatenus rationalibus, et utrumque deducitur ex fundamentis naturalibus; sed immediate ius naturale, gentium vero mediante naturali." MS quoted in Di Napoli, *op. cit.*, p. 388.

laws depend on the natural law, and natural law is simply a participation of the eternal law, which is Christ, the wisdom and reason of God. Stated differently, every law worthy of the name is from Christ as the author of nature and the First Reason.[55]

The eternal law is identical with the divine primalities[56] considered in their relation to the governance of the world. As such, it is immutable and necessarily attains to the end predetermined by God. The natural law is also unchangeable in its primary precepts; however, God can dispense from its secondary precepts when conditions concerning the matter of the law are changed. In such a case God does not act as lawgiver but as Lord.[57]

To be effective, laws must be worded in short and simple terms. They must be few in number and adapted to the customs of the people for which they are made. Laws should not be changed easily, and punitive laws must not outnumber disciplinary laws. A frequent change of laws and an excessive number of punitive laws are indications of a bad government. The best law is that of Jesus Christ.[58]

A final point is Campanella's teaching on the means to be used for the acquisition and conservation of the state, or what in scholastic terminology is called the instrumental cause of the state. This, Campanella says, may be threefold: the tongue, the sword, and money. The tongue is the instrument of religion and prudence, that is, of goods of the soul; the sword is the instrument of the body and all corporeal goods; money is the instrument of the external goods that are useful both to soul and body. Of these three instruments, each one corresponding to one of the three kinds of goods that make up the state, the most important is the tongue; the sword comes in the second place, while money is only an accidental means.

To use the sword alone is the quickest way to establish a state, but, as history teaches us, it is also the quickest way to lose it. By using only the tongue a ruler will succeed in getting control over men's minds, and sooner or later he will also obtain political control. Yet many times preachers pay with their lives for the truth they preach, while their successors acquire a temporal empire by

[55] *Atheismus triumphatus*, p. 107.
[56] Campanella's doctrine of "primalities" of being applies also to God, in whom power, knowledge, and love subsist in the most perfect and simple unity. See n. 37 above for the present writer's article on the subject.
[57] *Aforismi*, pp. 162-63; *Theologicorum*, XIV, chap. 3, art. 1, and XVII, chap. 6, art. 6. MS quoted in Di Napoli, *op. cit.*, p. 387.
[58] *Aforismi*, p. 164.

reaping the fruits of the preacher's campaign. In order to obtain a solid and lasting empire, it is necessary to use the sword as well as the tongue.[59] Thus the tongue seems to be the most effective means of conquering a state, which is best defended by the sword, and best preserved by money.[60]

We have presented the general lines of Campanella's notion of a real state. In the following section we shall present his ideal or imaginary state.

II. THE IDEAL STATE

The City of the Sun, which in its Latin edition appears as an appendix to the treatise, *Politica in aphorismos digesta*, is a fictional dialogue. In it a Genoese Sea-Captain tells a Grandmaster of the Knights Hospitalers about his journey to the island of Taprobane under the equator.[61] While there he met a large group of armed men and women, many of whom understood his language, and they took him to the City of the Sun.[62] The city, in the Captain's report, is largely built on a hill which rises out of an extensive plain, but its rings extend far beyond the base of the hill. The diameter of the city is over two miles and the circumference seven

---

[59] *Ibid.*, pp. 172-74.

[60] *Ibid.*, p. 177: "Ad [imperium] acquirendum lingua, ad defendendum arma, ad conservandum pecunia videntur proficere magis."

[61] The island of Taprobane is now known as Ceylon. In placing Taprobane under the equator rather than north of it, Campanella was apparently influenced by Botero's *Relazioni universali* (Rome, 1591-96), which Prof. Firpo calls "the main source of Campanella's geographic information." Firpo, *Scritti scelti*, p. 407, n. 3. The mistake is due to an error of the ancient maps which led the first sailors to identify Taprobane with Sumatra. In all probability it was Sumatra that Campanella had in mind when he described the City of the Sun. *Ibid.*, p. 408.

[62] Authors are not of one opinion as to the source for this name. It is possible that in calling his ideal republic *The City of the Sun* Campanella was influenced, at least remotely, by the text of Isaias, XIX, 18: "In that day there shall be five cities in the land of Egypt . . . One shall be called the city of the sun"; or by Pliny's *Solis insula* (*Hist. nat.*, X, 2), which the Roman historian places at four-day voyage from India, close to Taprobane. A more direct influence could have been exerted on Campanella by Botero's description of the cult of the sun among the natives of Mexico and Peru, or, as Firpo is inclined to believe, by the *Civitas Solis* or *Paradisus* dreamed of by the Grand Duke of Tuscany, of which mention is also made in Botero's work, *Delle cause della grandezza delle città* (Rome, 1588, chap. I, 2). Cf. Firpo, *Scritti scelti*, p. 408, n. 4. Di Napoli, on the other hand, cites as Campanella's proximate sources for the title of his ideal republic St. Francis' "Canticle of Creatures," where the sun occupies a prominent place, and the abbot Joachim of Flores, who had decreed that his monks should praise creation by singing hymnals to the sun. Cf. Di Napoli, *op. cit.*, pp. 155-56.

miles. Yet, because of the humped shape of the mountain, the area contains more buildings than it would if the city were built on a plain.

The city is divided into seven huge rings or circles named for the seven planets, and each ring is connected by four streets and gates facing the four points of the compass. The city is so built that if the first circle were stormed it would take much more effort to storm the second, and still more to storm the others. Thus anyone wishing to capture the city must storm it seven times.

On top of the hill there arises a splendid temple built in the form of a circle and standing on thick columns beautifully grouped. It has a large dome containing in its center a small dome with an opening right over the altar. There is only one altar, and on it there is nothing but a large globe with the painting of the sky and a small globe with a representation of the earth.

The small dome at the top of the temple is surrounded by several small cells, while larger cells are built behind the level space above the enclosures or arches of the inner and outer columns. These larger cells are occupied by priests and other religious officers.

The temporal and spiritual ruler of the city is a priest called Hoh or Sun, although in our language, the Captain remarks, he would be called Metaphysic. He is assisted by three princes, Pon, Sin, and Mor, names standing for *Potentia, Sapientia,* and *Amor,* that is, Power, Wisdom, and Love. Power takes care of all matters relating to war and peace and the military arts. He directs the military magistrates and the soldiers, and has the management of munitions, fortifications, and the storming of places. Wisdom has charge of the liberal and mechanical arts and all the sciences. He has as many magistrates and teachers under him as there are disciplines to be taught. To foster education, he has had the outer and inner walls of the city adorned with fine paintings and illustrations of all the sciences. Love attends to the improvement of the race by providing that men and women unite to bring forth the best kind of offspring. Indeed they laugh at us for devoting so much care to the breeding of dogs and horses while neglecting the breeding of the human race. The education of children, along with stock raising, medicine, and agriculture, fall also under the care of Love.

Metaphysic treats all these matters with the three rulers, and nothing is done without him. Thus all the business of the state is discharged by the four together, but whatever Metaphysic says is always favorably accepted.

The inhabitants of the City of the Sun came originally from India, as they fled from the sword of the Moguls. Many among them were philosophers, and they decided to lead a philosophic life in common. There is among them a community of wives as well as of property. They hold, in fact, that private property is acquired because each man wants to have his own home and wife and children. This gives rise to self-love. Once self-love is abolished, there remains only love for the state.

They receive whatever they need from the community, and the magistrates take care that no one has more than he deserves. Yet no one is deprived of what is necessary. All young men call themselves brothers; those who are fifteen years older are called fathers, and those who are fifteen years younger are called sons.

They have magistrates called after the name of each of our virtues, such as Magnanimity, Fortitude, Chastity, Liberality, Justice, and the like. Their selection is based on the excellence shown in the practice of the particular virtue they represent. Among them there is no robbery, murder, rape, incest, adultery, or such other crimes as they exist among us. They accuse themselves only of ingratitude, indolence, scurrility, lying, etc., for which they are duly punished.

Men and women wear almost the same kind of garment, which is suitable for war. The only difference is that the women's toga extends below the knee, while men's ends above the knee. Both sexes are educated together in all the arts. They learn the language when they are very young, and they are drilled in various kinds of gymnastics, so that their body is fully developed. They always go barefooted and bareheaded until they are seven years old. They are introduced to different trades, so that each one's talent may be discovered. After the seventh year they begin more serious and more specialized studies by attending lectures, engaging in disputations, and visiting the countryside with their teachers and judges. He who has learned several trades and knows how to practice them well is considered noble and superior to others.

Management for the race is for the good of the commonwealth, and not for the benefit of private citizens. They maintain, in effect, that children are bred for the preservation of the species rather than for individual pleasure. Hence infants are nursed by their mothers until they reach the age of two or more, as ordered by the physician. Then girls are handed over to mistresses and boys to masters appointed by the state. As they grow older, their education is committed to the care of the magistrates, who also have charge of mating the best-endowed male and female breeders according to the rules of philosophy. Women are forbidden under the death penalty to use cosmetics, high-heeled shoes, or gowns with train.

Labor and other duties are so distributed among the inhabitants that each one works only for about four hours a day. The rest of the time is spent in study, reading, writing, walking, and lawful recreation. All citizens are rich because they desire no more than they have; at the same time all are poor because they own nothing in private. They have no fear of death, since they believe in the immortality of the soul and a future reward.

Great emphasis is placed by the inhabitants of the City of the Sun on agriculture, and no piece of ground is left uncultivated. They observe closely the winds and propitious stars, and attach great importance to the science of navigation. They travel abroad in order to become acquainted with other countries and peoples.

In diet, they make a distinction between useful and harmful foods, using them in accordance with medical science. They eat the most healthful foods which vary according to the different seasons of the year. They are very temperate in their use of wine, which is never given to the young until they reach nineteen, unless the state of their health demands it. After their nineteenth year they take it diluted with water, as do the women. When fifty or older the men take wine without water, except when they have to attend meetings. There are very few diseases among them, and for these they have special remedies, many of which are known only to them.

The rulers of the city hold regular meetings to decide on matters pertaining to the public welfare. Judges are constituted by the first masters in each trade. They observe the *lex talionis* or law of recompense and punish serious crimes with the death penalty. Secret confession is practiced in such wise that the citizens tell their sins to the magistrates, the magistrates to the three supreme chiefs, and these to Hoh himself, who offers sacrifices and prayers to God, but only after he has confessed publicly in the temple all the sins of his people. Human sacrifice is practiced on a voluntary basis. A man who volunteers to die for his country is treated with great benevolence and much honor; however God does not require the death of the victim.

Priests, all of whom are over twenty-four years of age, offer prayers and sing hymns to God four times a day. They also observe the stars and note their motions and influences upon human affairs. In most of the cases, it is from among them that Hoh is elected.

The inhabitants of the City of the Sun regard the sun and the stars as living representations of God, which they honor but do not worship. They believe that the world is a huge animal in which men live just as worms live within men. They claim that it is not easy to know whether the world was made from nothing, from the ruins of other worlds, or from chaos; but they hold that it was made and did not exist from eternity. Hence they dislike Aristotle. They admit the existence of two physical principles: the sun as the father and the earth as the mother. Likewise, they admit two metaphysical principles: being, which is God, and nonbeing, which is the lack of being and the necessary condition for all created things. It is their conviction that evil and sin stem from a tendency toward nothingness. Sin has no efficient cause but only a deficient one; it shows a defect of the will in which it resides.

They believe in the Trinity, and say that God is Power, Wisdom, and Love. However, they do not distinguish the three divine persons by name, as Christians do, for they are not acquainted with revelation. They also say that all things are made of power, wisdom, and love inasmuch as they have being; of impotence, ignorance, and hatred inasmuch as they have nonbeing.[63] They know that there is great corruption in the world, and from this they argue to the existence of some serious disorder in the past, but they do not believe that this is due to Adam's sin. They acknowledge the freedom of the will and say that heresy is the work of the flesh. Finally, they teach that the true and holy law is the law of the First Reason.[64]

As was to be expected, many questions have been raised in connection with *The City of the Sun*. Some of these questions concern the general theme of the work in the light of Campanella's entire

[63] This is in accordance with Campanella's theory that creatures are a composition of a finite being and an infinite nonbeing. Thus man is essentially a rational animal, which is a limited entity; but he is also essentially a non-ass, a non-stone, a non-God, and so forth, which is an infinite nonentity. God alone is pure and infinite being. Being and nonbeing concur to make up finite things not as physical components but as metaphysical principles. Moreover, just as being is constituted of power, knowledge, and love as of its primalities, so nonbeing is constituted of impotence, ignorance, and hatred. Cf. this writer's article on Campanella's concept of being and nonbeing cited in n. 37 above.

[64] For this outline of *The City of the Sun* we have used Firpo's critical edition of the Italian text in *Scritti scelti*, pp. 405-464, as well as the English translations by Thomas W. Halliday in *Ideal Commonwealths* (rev. ed.; London-New York: The Colonial Press, 1901), pp. 141-79, and William J. Gilstrap in *The Quest for Utopia* (New York: Schuman, 1952), pp. 317-47.

literary production, and some concern particular issues, such as the practice of the common use of goods and community of wives. There have been interpreters who claim to see in Campanella's ideal republic the model of state socialism and communism, and hold that he is a forerunner of those doctrines.[65] Others prefer to see in *The City of the Sun* a bold conception of a rationalistic state, in which man knows all faiths and religions, including the Christian religion, but accepts none of them.[66] In this view, Campanella's ideal republic would show once more the heretical and rebellious spirit of its author whom the Church never ceased to persecute.[67] The fact that in many of his writings Campanella refers to *The City of the Sun* as a "dialogue on his own state" (*dialogo di propria repubblica*), is believed to lend support to the view that he stood for his own personal rationalistic theory even when he was con-

[65] We refer especially to the study of Paul Lafargue, "Campanella. Étude critique sur sa vie et sur la Cité du Soleil," *Le devenir social*, I (1895), 305-320; 465-80; 561-78. The same study, with some minor additions, appeared also in German under the title "Die beiden grossen Utopisten: T. More and T. Campanella," *Geschichte des Sozialismus in Einzelndarstellungen*, ed. E. Bernstein and K. Kautsky, Vol. I, Pt. II: "Die Vorlaüfer des neueren Sozialismus" (Stuttgart: Dietz, 1895), Sect. IV, 469-506. Lafargue's thesis has been slavishly accepted and reproduced by Andrea Calenda di Tavani in his work, *Fra T. Campanella e la sua dottrina sociale e politica di fronte al socialismo moderno* (Nocera Inferiore: Angora, 1895). The foregoing publications offered to Benedetto Croce the opportunity of discussing the nature and import of Campanella's political reform in his study, "Intorno al comunismo di T. Campanella, a proposito di recenti pubblicazioni," *Archivio storico per le provincie napoletane*, XX (1895), 646-83, where he strongly denies any doctrinal similarity between Campanella's political thought and modern communism. This has not prevented the Russians from portraying Campanella as an early representative of their communistic ideology. Cf. *The Living Age* (New York), Vol. 346 (1934), 453-54, where an anonymous writer, under the heading "A Dominican Communist," reviews a new Russian translation of Campanella's *City of the Sun*, with a commentary by F. A. Petrov and an introduction by V. P. Volghin (Moscow: Akademia, 1934). In the course of his review the writer speaks of the prominent place Campanella occupies in the history of Communism and refers to an article in the *Izvestia*, where A. Djivelegov hails Campanella as a harbinger of Marxist Communism.

[66] This, to mention only a recent writer, is the opinion of Norberto Bobbio, the editor of the first critical edition of the Italian text of *The City of the Sun*. Cf. T. Campanella, *La Città del Sole*, a cura di Norberto Bobbio, *op. cit.*, Introduction, p. 17.

[67] *Ibid.*, pp. 32-33. Similar views have also been expressed by Treves, who believes that *The City of the Sun* represents the last stage of Campanella's dream. The work, in Treves' opinion, is not merely a *Dichtung*, as it has been labeled, but "the logical and necessary consequence of the philosophical premises of Campanella's political system." Cf. Treves, *La filosofia politica di T. Campanella*, p. 54.

templating a universal monarchy under the Pope, as described in the *Monarchia Messiae*.[68]

Neither of these interpretations is acceptable. We believe that a great injustice is done to the author of *The City of the Sun* by those who like to present him as a harbinger of modern socialism and communism or as a champion of a purely rationalistic state theory. There is sufficient textual evidence in Campanella's works to support the contention that *The City of the Sun* is only a "poetical dialogue," as the subtitle of the work indicates,[69] which depicts an imaginary community of men and women *in the pure order of nature*. Following the light of reason but unaided by Christian revelation, they organize themselves into an ideal society where all abuses—with due reservation for some questionable practices to be examined later—are eliminated and all citizens contribute effectively to the common welfare. To prove our point, we shall let Campanella speak for himself and present his case in his own terms. We shall add only those comments and observations that may help the reader to better understand Campanella's thought.

In anticipation of objections that the highly provocative character of *The City of the Sun* would raise among its readers, Campanella wrote a defense of the work to which he refers possible inquirers. This defense makes up the entire fourth question of the *Quaestiones politicae*,[70] and is divided into three articles. In the first article he discusses the truth and usefulness of his political dialogue, while in the second and third articles he deals respectively with the controversial issues of community of goods and community of women. Answering the question whether the work would serve any purpose, since it is hardly conceivable that an ideal state like his could ever be brought into existence, he appeals to the authority of Thomas More, whose *Utopia* served as a blueprint for his own dialogue. Plato is also brought on the scene as the creator of an ideal republic that could not be fully realized in the state of corrupt nature but could have been in the state of innocence. Legislators are likewise known to issue laws that will never be fully observed; yet such laws

---

[68] Bobbio, *La Città del Sole*, p. 16.

[69] Cf. Prof. Firpo's Italian edition of *The City of the Sun* in *Scritti scelti*, p. 407.

[70] The 1637 edition of *The City of the Sun* carries the following remark: "Defensio huius dialogi est in politicis quaestionibus, quarta quaestio, ubi ostenditur esse catechismum Gentilium ad politiam et fidem Christianam pure apostolicam." Cf. Bobbio, *La Città del Sole*, p. 117, note.

serve their purpose, inasmuch as they set a pattern of action to be followed by the citizens in pursuing the common good of the state.[71]

The ideal republic described in *The City of the Sun*, continues Campanella, is not like the Mosaic and Christian laws, which have been revealed to man by God. Rather, it represents the best form of government that philosophers can achieve by the light of reason alone. If in certain matters, such as the community of women, the inhabitants of the City of the Sun differ from the teaching of the Gospels, this is not due to ill-will but to the weakness of the human mind, which considers as permissible certain practices that revelation proves to be faulty. The republic reflects the conditions of a people that is still *in gentilismo*, that is, in paganism, and looks forward to the revelation of a better way of life. They are, as it were, in a state of preparation to Christianity (*in Catechismo ad vitam Christianam*), since, in the opinion of St. Cyril, it is the function of philosophy to prepare the gentiles for the evangelical truth.[72]

These statements are so clear that any doubt as to the real nature of Campanella's dialogue should be out of question. To see in *The City of the Sun* the realization of a naturalistic society that knew but rejected Christian revelation, is to distort Campanella's doctrine completely.[73] It might be objected that he presents his ideal republic as a model also for Christians who have been enlightened by supernatural revelation and restored by Christ to the state of

---

[71] *Quaest. pol.*, p. 101.

[72] *Ibid.:* "Nos autem fingimus illam [Rempublicam] non tamquam a Deo datam, sed Philosophicis syllogismis inventam et quantum potest humana ratio, ut hinc elucescat veritas Evangelii esse naturae conformis. Quod si aliquibus ab Evangelio deviamus, vel videamur deviare, hoc non impietati adscribendum, sed imbecillitati humanae, quae multa putat recte fieri ante revelationem, quae postmodum haud sic se habent, ut dicemus de communitate coniugum; proptereaque fingimus hanc Rempublicam in gentilismo, quae expectat revelationem melioris vitae, ac meretur de congruo ipsam habere, dum quod naturalis dictat ratio observat vitae institutum. Unde sunt quasi in Catechismo ad vitam Christianam, veluti Cyrillus dicit in libro contra Iulianum, datam esse gentilibus Philosophiam tanquam Catechismus ad fidem Evangelicam."

[73] It is true that the inhabitants of the City of the Sun are reported as having some knowledge of Christ, the apostles, the Christian martyrs, Adam's sin, etc. However, such knowledge is vague and superficial and does not amount to a real understanding of Christian doctrine. For them Christ is just one among other great legislators, even though he occupies a prominent place among them.

original innocence.[74] He even expresses the hopes that such a republic may some day, after the downfall of the Antichrist, be established throughout the entire world.[75] These statements, however, which follow almost immediately upon those we have just mentioned, should be interpreted in the light of the entire context and made to harmonize with the preceding doctrine rather than contradict it.

The point Campanella wants to make is that although his ideal republic is what can be best achieved by philosophers who never came in contact with Christian revelation, it represents also the idealization of human nature in its striving for a perfect natural society. By restoring man to the state of original innocence and raising him to the supernatural order, Christ did not destroy human nature, which remains essentially the same even after Christ's redemption. Rather, he made it easier for men to organize themselves into an ideal society that, with the aid of grace and the sacraments, would help them to better attain to their final end, both in the natural and supernatural order. It is in this sense that Campanella can speak in one and the same article and without contradicting himself of an ideal state *in gentilismo,* modeled after Plato's *Republic* and Thomas More's *Utopia,* and an ideal state for the entire Christianity, inspired by the community system of early Christians and the monastic life of religious orders. It becomes likewise understandable how he can say that the Anabaptists, a contemporary religious sect of people living in common, cannot expect to make any real progress unless they decide to accept the

---

[74] Thus Campanella says immediately after the passage quoted in n. 72: "Nos ergo Gentiles docemus ut recte vivant, si a Deo velint non negligi, et Christianis suademus vitam Christi esse secundum naturam." *Quaest. pol.,* p. 101. And a little further in the same article he answers the objection raised against the practical value of his ideal republic by saying: ". . . et si ad tuam exactam Reipublicae ideam pervenire non possumus, haud propterea superflui sumus, dum exemplum ponimus imitandum quantum possumus. At etiam possibilem esse talem vitam ostendit Christianorum in principio communitas sub Apostolis, teste Luca et S. Clemente. Et in Alexandria modus vivendi eiusmodi sub S. Marco observatus, teste Philone et S. Hieronimo. Item vita Clericorum usque ad Papam Urbanum I, immo etiam sub S. Augustino, et nunc vita Monachorum quam tanquam possibilem in tota civitate optat S. Chrysostomus." *Ibid.,* p. 102. Again: "Qui autem ipsam [Rempublicam] negant Aristotelizando, dicunt sub statu innocentiae potuisse servari, non nunc. At Patres etiam nunc servabilem faciunt, et Christum illius status reparatorem." *Ibid.*

[75] *Ibid.:* ". . . ego futuram [Rempublicam] spero post ruinam Antichristi ut in Prophetalibus." Reference is here made to his other work, *Articuli prophetales, op. cit.,* where the theme of his future ideal republic is discussed.

teaching of the Catholic Church and rid themselves of their heretical beliefs.[76]

With regard to the community of goods, Campanella has no doubt that such a system is in conformity with the natural law and that it contributes to the welfare of the state and the citizens. He defends this thesis in the second article of the fourth question of *Quaestiones politicae,* where he argues against Aristotle and all philosophers who stand for the natural right of private property. To establish his position, he makes use of arguments from authority and from reason. Among the arguments from authority he cites statements by Pope St. Clement the Roman, St. Augustine, St. John Chrysostom, St. Ambrose, St. Thomas Aquinas, and others. However he takes some of these statements out of context and twists them to suit his own purpose.[77] He also brings forward the teaching of the Apostles, the example of early Christians and churchmen, and the actual system of community life of the religious orders to show that the community of goods is a much better system than that which allows private property. In his opinion, the relaxation of the law of nature in this respect, especially with regard to the clergy, was made by the Church at a later date in order to avoid greater evils. It amounts in effect to a permission rather than to a real law.[78]

The main reason why private property should be abolished is that this is the only way to prevent abuses that inevitably creep into society once the goods are divided among the citizens. Avarice, which is the root of all evils, fraud, theft, robbery, pride, egoism, jealousy, enmity, and the like are only the most common abuses.

---

[76] *Quaest. pol.*, p. 103: "Dico hanc Rempublicam et seculum aureum ab omnibus desiderari, et peti a Deo, ut fiat voluntas eius in terra sicut in caelo. Non tamen in praxi ob principum malitiam, qui sibi non summae Rationi imperium submittunt. De usu autem dictum et experimentoque probatur esse possibilem: sicut magis secundum naturam est vivere ratione quam sensuali affectu, et virtuose quam vitiose, teste Chrysostomo. Et quidem Monachi id probant, et nunc Anabaptistae in communi viventes: qui si dogmata Fidei recta haberent, in hoc magis proficerent; utinam haeretici non essent, et iustitiam ministrarent, uti nos dicimus; nam exemplum facerent huius veritatis: sed nescio qua stultitia quod melius est respuunt."

[77] *Ibid.*, pp. 104-106. Cf. Di Napoli, *op. cit.*, pp. 392-93, for a short critical appraisal of the texts in question.

[78] *Quaest. pol.*, p. 107: "Concedimus ergo Ecclesiam fecisse posse divisionem permissive potius quam effective, et ex proposito: sed, ut ait S. Augustinus, mavult habere claudos quam mortuos clericos, idest proprietarios, quam hypocritas . . . . Dicimus Ecclesiam posse divisionem facere et permittere illam: et meretrices tolerare ut minus malum, sicuti claudos potius quam mortuos, ut dicit S. Augustinus."

To avoid them, goods must be distributed among the citizens on the basis of their natural talents and abilities. This will also help to uproot the social evils that result from a system based on heredity or an elective system in which ambition plays an important role.[79] In conclusion, the doctrine of the community of goods, affirms Campanella, is definitely according to the law of nature.[80] To hold the contrary is nothing short of heresy.[81] Nor can it be said with Duns Scotus that the community of goods was of natural right in the state of innocence but not after Adam's fall. Original sin deprived man of the goods of the supernatural order, not of those which belong to the order of nature.[82]

Thus, according to Campanella, community of goods is an ideal system for man considered both in the order of grace and the order of nature. Shall we say that his theory is an anticipation of modern socialistic and communistic collectivism? There are no doubt points of contact between the two doctrines, inasmuch as both defend some sort of state absolutism in regard to material goods. However, the doctrinal background and inspirational motive of the two systems, as well as the methods suggested for their establishment, make them far different. The state absolutism advocated by scientific socialism, and especially by Marxist Communism, is a completely materialistic and atheistic conception of society that makes the state the supreme and absolute ruler over the goods and destinies of the citizens. It admits no spiritual or moral values, and controls the citizens, who are almost reduced to insignificant units in the state machinery, by flashing before their imagination the mirage of an ideal temporal happiness that will never materialize.

Campanella's community system, on the other hand, is based on a completely different ideology. It is modeled after the system of early Christian communities and fashioned along the general lines of monastic life in the religious orders, where the abolition of private property is only a means to help the monks detach themselves from earthly goods and attend more completely to the things

---

[79] *Ibid.*, p. 106.

[80] *Ibid.*, p. 105: "Quapropter certo certius est de iure naturae omnia esse communia."

[81] *Ibid.*, p.104: "Quapropter haeresis est damnare vitam communem, aut contra naturam dicere."

[82] *Ibid.*, p. 105.

of the spirit.[83] Furthermore, there is no indication whatsoever in *The City of the Sun* of violence or compulsion in enforcing the laws of the state. On the contrary, everything is done smoothly and in a most reasonable manner, since every citizen is asked to do what befits him best.[84] Briefly, while Marxist Communism attempts to achieve its pure materialistic ends by brutal force, class warfare, and hatred, Campanella's collectivism aims at helping man to better attain the end for which he was created by fostering love and mutual understanding.[85]

A second thorny question that Campanella discusses in his *Quaestiones politicae*, is "Whether the community of women is more in agreement with nature and more helpful to generation, and hence to the state, than the possession of one wife and children."[86] Here he faces the obvious objection, raised throughout the entire history of philosophy from Aristotle to his own time, that the community of women is against the natural law and destructive of marriage, the essential properties of which are unity and indissolubility.

Campanella is aware of the seriousness of the objection and proceeds carefully in his attempt to justify the conduct he ascribes to dwellers in the City of the Sun. To avoid any misunderstanding, he cautions the reader at the beginning that not all kinds of community of women are legitimate, but only the particular type he describes in his political dialogue. There are, in effect, several ways of understanding the community of women. First of all, there is the so-called *concubitus vagus*, whereby a man is allowed to have sexual intercourse with any woman, at any time, with no restrictions whatsoever, as do certain animals. Promiscuity of this kind must be condemned, as it is against man's rational nature and leads to

---

[83] In several places of *The City of the Sun* Campanella portrays the citizens as friars in a monastery. They eat in common refectories while one of them reads aloud (*Città del Sole*, in Firpo's *Scritti scelti*, p. 420); they dress in the same way (*ibid.*, pp. 421-22); their leader and main officers are priests (*ibid.*, pp. 411, 447); regular confession of sins is practised (*ibid.*); young men are called "friars" (*ibid.*, p. 416); etc.

[84] *Quaest. pol.*, p. 106: "Neque enim quis potest recusare dum omnia ratione tractantur, immo amat unusquisque id quod sibi connaturale est aggredi, uti fit in hac Republica."

[85] For a discussion of Campanella's socialism vs. Marxist Communism cf. Benedetto Croce, *art. cit.*, in n. 56 above, and Treves, *op. cit.*, pp. 181-82. Croce's article was published again in *Materialismo storico ed economia marxista* (Bari: Laterza, 1927), pp. 177-223.

[86] "Utrum communitas mulierum sit convenientior secundum naturam ac generationi utilior, quam proprietas uxorum et natorum: ac proinde simul toti reipublicae." *Quaest. pol.*, p. 108, heading of art. 3, quaest. 4.

various abuses. There is another kind of promiscuity, continues Campanella, and this consists in allowing a legally wed man to have sexual relations at certain definite times with a woman allotted to him, as has been the case in certain regions of France and Germany. This system, too, is to be condemned as against the natural law, or at least the divine positive law, for it promotes sensual gratification rather than the good of the offspring.

There is, however, a third kind of community of women, which is the system followed by the inhabitants of the City of the Sun. It consists in matching only the best breeders, who will have sexual intercourse only at the time that is most suitable for generation and within certain age limits. This system, remarks Campanella, does not involve a breach of the natural law and is quite consistent with people who live *in puris naturalibus*, like the citizens in question, who have no knowledge of the divine positive law. Even if such a system were against the natural law, that fact could not be known by reason alone, since it cannot be inferred by way of conclusion from the natural law itself. It can only be known by a specific determination of the positive law, which of its nature is subject to change.[87] Thus the doctrine of the community of women, as propounded in *The City of the Sun,* would become heretical only after the Church's condemnation, and those citizens, whose only rule and guide is the natural law known by reason, cannot be blamed for their conduct in regard to women.[88]

[87] *Ibid.*, pp. 109-110: "Sic nunc dico quod communitas mulierum a nobis posita non est contra ius naturae: aut si est, non potest cognosci a puro philosopho: non enim deducitur per modum conclusionis ex iure naturali: nec determinationis, nisi a longe: determinatio autem variari potest, cum iuris sit positivi." For a detailed description of the three kinds of community of women or *concubitus* cf. *ibid.*, p. 109.

[88] This is substantially the teaching that can be gathered from the following texts: "Communitas mulierum in concubitu non est contra ius naturae, praesertim quomodo a nobis posita est, sed maxime videtur ea congruere propter quod non est haeresis docere illam in puris naturalibus, sed tamen post ius divinum aut ecclesiasticum positivum." *Ibid.*, p. 109. "Quod autem lex sanxit, ut sua sola uxore quisque utatur quamvis sterili, non potest a philosopho facile cognosci naturaliter: propterea ego hoc unum contendo, quod qui instituunt Rempublicam cum tali communitate mulierum, non peccant in naturam, antequam a lege Dei doceantur sic non faciendum esse." *Ibid.* "Manifestum est pluralitatem uxorum non esse contra naturam: immo omnia animalia, excepta forsan turture, pluribus miscentur. Columbus autem soli sorori. Nec quidem in Republica ista, quae ex naturalibus, non ex revelatis gubernatur legibus, id cognosci potest." *Ibid.*, p. 111. "In Republica vero solari fit commissio tam celebris ex philosophia et astrologia, ut generatio sit melior et abundantior: ergo secundum naturam: ergo non est haeresis nisi postquam ab Ecclesia condemnatur." *Ibid.*, p. 112.

Is this teaching inconsistent with the position that Campanella takes in his other works, such as the *Quaestiones oeconomicae*,[89] *Oeconomica*,[90] and *Theologia*,[91] where he proclaims that polygamy is against the natural law?[92] Certain statements of the *Quaestiones politicae*, if taken separately, may seem to point toward a real conflict in his teaching. Yet, if we take a closer look at the context, we will see that the conflict is only apparent. In the works that have just been mentioned, where Campanella treats the doctrine of marriage specifically, he maintains that polygamy is only secondarily against the natural law, so that it is possible for God to dispense from it. In the *Quaestiones politicae* he does not reject explicitly this doctrine; he simply emphasizes the difficulty for the inhabitants of the City of the Sun to discover it by the light of natural reason alone, prior to the positive decree of the Church. That this is Campanella's mind can be inferred from his insistence upon *the state of pure nature* in which those inhabitants are supposed to live, and from his explicit affirmation that the community of women may perhaps be against the natural law, but that this cannot be known by a philosopher as such.[93]

Before closing this section on the nature and meaning of *The City of the Sun* a few observations are in order. The conception of the state that Campanella offers to us in this work is in many respects different from his notion of a real state previously examined. In an ideal state ruled by philosophers who never came into contact with Christian revelation, it is little wonder that some of the beliefs and practices of its citizens conflict with the Christian conscience. A striking example is the system of community of women. Relying almost exclusively on his words, we have shown that the

[89] Cf. *Philosophia realis*, of which the *Quaestiones oeconomicae* are part, p. 174: "sic secundario, et aliquo pacto poligamia adversatur naturae."

[90] *Ibid.*, p. 198. The *Oeconomica* is also part of the *Philosophia realis*.

[91] See, for example, *Theologicorum*, XXIV, chap. 17, art. 22: "Contra naturam poliandria primario, poligamia secundario"; *ibid.*: "poligamiam non esse contra naturam primario sed secundario nec totaliter, meliorem tamen et magis secundum naturam esse monogamiam, et hanc esse secundum Evangelium, illam potius contra Evangelium." MS quoted in Di Napoli, *op. cit.*, p. 396.

[92] The statement of the *Oeconomica*, "Haud propterea damnamus quasi contra naturam uxorum multitudinem, praesertim si quis insterilis copulam impegit, quandoquidem David et Patriarchae plures habuere uxores et concubinas," must be understood in the light of what immediately precedes: "Propterea magis secundum naturam est matrimonium cum una quam cum pluribus . . . Quapropter uxorum multitudo apud Barbaras magis, quam civiles nationes in usu habetur." *Philosophia realis*, p. 198.

[93] Cf. nn. 87 and 88 above.

unchristian sexual mores of those citizens in no way reflect Campanella's own convictions about marriage.[94] He sincerely believes that the Catholic Church is perfectly right in her interpretation of the natural law, and hence in her condemnation of any sort of sexual promiscuity or polygamous practices. However he maintains that polygamy is only against the secondary precepts of the natural law, knowledge of which, in contrast with the knowledge of the primary precepts, cannot be attained by people living in the state of pure nature.

In our judgment this is Campanella's teaching in regard to the community of women as gathered from *The City of the Sun* and his other works where the issue is discussed. Yet, while no doctrinal conflict seems to exist in his manifold approach to the problem, he exaggerates the inability of the human mind to attain knowledge of the natural law. Granting that the secondary precepts of the natural law are not so easy to grasp as the primary ones and may demand a certain amount of training, we believe that the high level of culture achieved by the inhabitants of the City of the Sun, as evidenced from their accomplishments in many other fields, should enable them to understand the evils inherent in sexual promiscuity. Hence we do not agree with Campanella's statement that by the light of reason alone a philosopher cannot know that the community of women is against the natural law.

Another defect in Campanella's political theory is his whole attitude toward private property. He holds for the common ownership of goods in his ideal republic as well as in other works of a more serious nature. Apparently he was firmly convinced that private property is the greatest cause of social evils and that in order to live better and more natural lives men should return to the community system of early Christians. It is the community of goods, insists Campanella, that is in accord with the natural law, and not the system of private property. Needless to say, his community system is inspired by motives that are quite different from those of Marxist Communism. Aside from this he is completely unrealistic in proposing to extend to an entire nation and even to all mankind, as was his lifelong dream, a way of life that has proved effective only in small communities and with a selected group of persons, such as men and women dedicated to the religious life who

---

[94] This should be clear from the texts we have quoted from the *Quaestiones politicae*, and especially from those of the *Quaestiones oeconomicae*, the *Oeconomica*, and the *Theologia*.

embrace it on a voluntary basis and out of supernatural motives. It is inconceivable that the citizens of an entire nation, let alone all mankind, would renounce basic natural rights to their own possessions and submit to the privations that the system of community of goods involves unless forced to do so, as is the case in communistic countries. Heroism may be displayed by a few chosen men and women, not by the community at large. This is what Campanella failed to realize.

It is true that private property can lead to abuses. However such abuses do not suppress the right to private property and its use, when this is demanded by the needs and aspirations of human nature. Abuses call for some control and limitations by the state in view of the common good, inasmuch as private property has to perform a social function; but the institution of private ownership as such must be preserved intact. It is on this basis that Campanella's system of community of goods must be judged as unrealistic and utopian as is his conception of the ideal republic.

In conclusion it may be asked: What is the purpose of *The City of the Sun?* Does the work have any practical value? The first question has received different answers. We believe that in writing his utopia Campanella had in mind the various types of ideal republics conceived by philosophers that preceded him from Plato down to Thomas More and Jean Bodin and that he wished to picture a republic that would be better than those portrayed in the earlier works.[95] He did not, and could not, intend to propose his ideal republic as a model for any state then in existence, simply because the conditions prevailing among the inhabitants of the City of the Sun could nowhere be verified. Nor could he conceive his republic as a substitute for the theocratic state, to be discussed presently, for this is centered on the papacy and presupposes a well-established Christianity. Yet—and this is the answer to the second question—many of the ideas expressed in *The City of the Sun* can have some practical value, inasmuch as they contain the germs of social, political, and educational reforms that would be beneficial to the state. In this respect Campanella may be considered as an original thinker and a forerunner of modern times.[96]

[95] Jean Bodin published his *République* in 1577, while Thomas More's *Utopia* was first published in Latin at Louvain, in 1516.

[96] For the originality and modernity of Campanella's political thought cf. Treves, *op. cit.*, pp. 54-55, where he is called, although with some reservation, "a forerunner of modern democratic theories." Campanella's pioneering efforts in the field of education are discussed by Alfio and Antonietta Nicotra in their

III. THE THEOCRATIC STATE

No matter how ingenious and persuasive the scheme of Campanella's ideal state may be, it could hardly represent his plan of a universal reform that would pave the way for that golden age described in glowing terms by prophets, poets, and philosophers which Christ is supposed to have come to restore. The work that best explains this plan, which was the dream of Campanella's entire life, is the *Monarchia Messiae*.[97] As indicated by its author, the main purpose of the treatise is to prove by arguments derived both from reason and from revelation that the Pope, as Vicar of Christ, is the supreme temporal and spiritual ruler of the world,[98] and consequently, that all other rulers are subject to him in spiritual as well as temporal matters.[99] He does this in a systematic way, beginning with some general notions on the nature of dominion and sovereignty.

The only true and absolute owner or sovereign, Campanella says, is one who can *de iure* and *de facto* dispose of the things he possesses in whatever way he pleases and with no restriction whatsoever. This is dominion *per essentiam* and *per se* and it belongs exclusively to God, on whom all creatures depend for their entire being and operation. On the other hand, an owner *per participationem* and *secundum quid* is one who can dispose of things and men only to the extent that he is so empowered by God.[100] On the basis of this distinction, it can be readily seen that no man is the absolute owner of himself and other beings inferior to him, much less of his fellow men.[101] Nor can he rule over other people merely as a man, but only inasmuch as he is so authorized by God. This may obtain

---

modest work, *Tommaso Campanella* (Florence-Catanzaro: Guido Mauro, 1948). The authors compare Campanella to Rabelais, Montaigne, and especially Comenius. *Ibid.*, pp. 87-94. Campanella's anticipations of modern philosophical theories are discussed in the present writer's studies, "Campanella as Forerunner of Descartes," *Franciscan Studies*, 16 (1956), 37-59, and "Knowledge of the Extramental World in the System of Tommaso Campanella," *Franciscan Studies*, 17 (1957), 188-212.

[97] That Campanella held this work in great esteem is evident from what he says in the preface: "Propterea de messiae monarchia prioribus libris, liber iste connectitur, super omnes utilissimus pluribus causis." *Mon. Mess.*, p. 1.

[98] *Ibid.*, title: ". . . Compendium scripti secundi, in quo per philosophiam divinam et humanam demonstrantur iura Summi Pontificis, Christianorum Patris et Capitis, super universum orbem in temporalibus et spiritualibus."

[99] *Ibid.*, p. 21: ". . . omnes Principes dependent ab eiusdem [Ecclesiae] Capite in temporalibus et spiritualibus."

[100] *Ibid.*, p. 5.

[101] *Ibid.*, pp. 5-6.

either because of certain natural qualities with which he has been endowed by the Creator or because of a special supernatural title. In both cases he will act as a divinized man (*homo divinus*) or a caretaker for God.[102]

Keeping to his principle that the government of one man is better than the government of many,[103] Campanella now goes a step further and says that it is proper for a ruler to possess both spiritual and temporal powers. The concentration of these two powers into one person is beneficial to citizens as well as to the state. It prevents the ruler from becoming subservient to secular princes in order to secure their assistance in time of need, with the consequent danger that laws will be broken. It also helps to keep him from falling prey to heretics and pseudoprophets, who otherwise may overcome illiterate laymen and unarmed priests.[104] Also, citizens are better disposed to obey one whom they know to be their intercessor before God.[105]

That kingship and priesthood can fittingly be joined in one and the same person is proved by the fact that this was the situation of man in the state of natural law and prior to any positive determination. Thus Adam was father, king, and priest of all mankind, and so were all the first-born after him of whom mention is made in the Scriptures.[106] It is not God but the devil who introduced a multitude of kingdoms in the world. This is in opposition to the divine plan which provides for the union of all mankind into one kingdom with but one religion.[107] It is precisely this kind of kingdom that Christ came to restore, as evidenced by the fact that he has given one universal law for all mankind and appointed one man to lead the entire world.[108] The following passage summarizes Campanella's teaching on this point.

---

[102] *Ibid.*, p. 7: "Potest homo naturaliter dominari ac regere homines, non in quantum homo, sed in quantum est a Deo, vero dominatore auctorizatur; accipiens ab eo fundamentum, aut titulum superioritatis, per naturam, aut per gratiam. Hic autem non quatenus homo, sed quatenus homo divinus, imperabit, et quatenus locumtenens Dei."

[103] *Ibid.*, pp. 9-10. See first section of this chapter for pertinent quotations, especially nn. 35 ff.

[104] *Ibid.*, p. 10.

[105] *Ibid.*, p. 11.

[106] *Ibid.*

[107] *Ibid.*, p. 14.

[108] *Ibid.*, p. 19, title of chapter IV: "Iesum Messiam, ac Dominum nostrum, venisse in mundum ad restituendum saeculum beatum, proptereaque dedisse legem universalem, et praefecisse caput universale in toto mundo, super omnes leges et applicationes illarum."

Jesus Christ, God and man, Lord of all things, both temporal and spiritual, established one kingdom (*principatum*) which he placed above all human kingdoms, with a twofold power in the person of St. Peter, Prince of the Apostles, and his successors. When the whole world has been united under this monarchy and all kingdoms and powers that are not totally and absolutely subject to it have been eliminated, and all different religions and sects have been suppressed, then will appear that golden age which Christ came to restore, as predicted by prophets, poets, and philosophers. This age already exists at the present time, even though it does not appear to do so. The Church of God has always been one, and by divine and human right all rulers depend on her head in both temporal and spiritual matters. He [the head of the Church] can give orders to all rulers for some good purpose (*ad aedificationem*), but cannot take away their kingship unless they rebel against God and the universal Church, or become unfit to rule and thus endanger the common good. If the state can do this [in regard to its rulers], so much more can the Pope. Yet neither a king nor the Church as a whole can take any action against the head [of the Church], for the Pope is the father, pastor, spouse of the Church, over whom neither sons, nor sheep nor bride have any power. He can make laws binding all men, just as he can change them; he can guide and correct the actions and the life of his subjects in order to direct them to life eternal.[109]

The same doctrine is contained in the *Theologia*, where Campanella devotes an entire chapter to prove that the Pope is king and priest and has universal power over all the kingdoms of the world.[110] Furthermore, the whole of the *Discorsi universali del governo ecclesiastico* is a practical application of the same principle, which he claims to support with many texts taken from Holy Scripture and, among others, a text taken from St. Thomas's *De regimine principum*.[111]

To add further weight to his theory of a universal papal monarchy, Campanella has recourse to his favorite doctrine of Christ

[109] *Ibid.*, p. 21.
[110] *Thelogicorum*, XXII, chap. 3, art. 7, tit.: "Papam esse regem et sacerdotem super omnia regna mundi in omnibus." MS quoted in Amerio, *Campanella*, p. 202.
[111] Cf. *Discorsi universali*, in Firpo's *Scritti scelti*, p. 469. St. Thomas's text used by Campanella is: "Papa habet potestatem in temporalibus et spiritualibus super omnes reges de iure divino, naturali et positivo." *De regimine principum*, III, 10. It is now commonly agreed upon by commentators that Books III and IV, as well as the last twelve chapters of Book II of the *De regimine principum*, were not written by Aquinas but by his disciple Ptolomaeus from Lucca, bishop of Torcello. Campanella himself was aware of the doubtful authenticity of the work. Cf. *Mon. Mess.*, p. 24.

as the eternal Reason. Christ, the Word incarnate, is God's eternal Reason through which the world has been created and redeemed; hence all things belong to Him by right.[112] When He came into this world, He took on all power in both spiritual and temporal matters, and later gave it to the Church so as to fulfill the prophecies.[113] It is true that Christ, as the second Person of the Holy Trinity had all power over the world even prior to His incarnation.[114] Likewise, there is no question as to the existence of secular powers before the incarnation took place. Yet even these powers were established by Christ, since to be legitimate a power must be based on reason, and Christ is the first essential Reason from which all powers derive.[115] When He came into the world, Christ instituted the Apostolic Church and set it above all secular powers, so that it can direct and control them and help them achieve their end.[116]

That Christ gave to His Church the temporal sword along with the spiritual sword is proved by Campanella in the following way. Since Christ is a most perfect legislator, He must ensure that His law obtains its effect. To be effective, a law must have both a directive and a coercive function. The element of coercion cannot

[112] *Mon. Mess.*, p. 25, heading of chapter VII: "Christum esse Rationem aeternam, et in tempore tandem incarnatam. Ideoque esse Dominum universorum aeternaliter et temporaliter." The chapter begins with the following statement: ". . . assero Christum esse Sapientiam, Verbum, seu Rationem Dei aeternam, per quam creavit mundum et gubernavit semper, et tandem in genere humano instauravit eum cum esset corruptus." To support his statement Campanella brings forth ten arguments from the Scriptures.

[113] *Ibid.*, p. 27, heading of chapter IX: "Christum fuisse Regem in spiritualibus et temporalibus, et ambas potestates assumpsisse, et easdem in Ecclesia reliquisse, ut adimplerentur omnia iura naturalia et prophetiae et expectationes." See also *Theologicorum*, XXIII, chap. 2, art. 4, tit.: "Christum assumpsisse dominium in spiritualibus et temporalibus et harum dignitatum functiones ostendisse in se exemplariter easque in Ecclesia reliquisse." MS quoted in Amerio, *Campanella*, p. 201. The same basic principle is affirmed in the *De regno Dei*, p. 213: "Christus iure creationis est Rex regum . . . et iure redemptionis."

[114] *Mon. Mess.*, p. 28: 'Deus ante etiam erat Dominus in temporalibus et spiritualibus. Ergo Christus cum sit Deus, de iure habet et temporale Regnum."

[115] *Theologicorum*, XXIII, chap. 2, art. 4, tit.: "Christum instituisse principatus saeculares et militiam etiam ante incarnationem suam." MS quoted in Amerio, *Campanella*, p. 201. *Mon. Mess.*, pp. 27-28: "Quoniam Christus est ipsa ratio prima essentialis aeterna: omne autem dominium fundatum est super ratione, ergo pendet ab eo, sicut splendet a sole, et membra a capite."

[116] *Theologicorum*, XXIII, chap. 2, art. 4, tit.: ". . . postea vero [Christus] eis [principatibus saecularibus] praefecisse dignitatem apostolicam ad correctionem et meliorationem, cui etiam addidit potestatem evellendi priores principatus et iudices et instituendi novos." MS quoted in Amerio, *Campanella*, p. 201.

be constituted by the simple threat of hell or of any other spiritual punishment, since men who are truly evil ridicule such things. Hence to enforce His law, Christ must have empowered the Church to use the material sword.[117] It should be clear, then, that the Pope, as the head of the one true Church of Christ, must have inherited from Him all power, both spiritual and temporal, and that he is the supreme ruler to whom all other rulers are subject.[118] To put it in another way, the Messias has established but one reign, and this reign has but one head whose power extends over all men and includes all matters, both spiritual and temporal. Hence all other powers and rights, no matter how they have been obtained, depend on the Pope as the Vicar of Christ.[119]

By attributing to the Pope a direct power over secular rulers even in temporal matters, Campanella goes against an established tradition of Catholic theologians, especially those of the Dominican Order of which he was a member. He does not conceal this fact, but nevertheless he clings to his opinion and maintains that, despite the contrary teaching of the Thomistic school, his is the only correct interpretation of Aquinas's thought.[120]

What is the position of the secular powers in regard to the papal monarchy? Campanella discusses this question in the last part of the *De Monarchia Messiae*. Under the heading of the rights of the emperor and other princes, he writes:

> ... I affirm that the emperor, as the defender of the Church, the body that rules over the entire world in things spiritual and temporal, is also lord of the whole world, but only in temporal matters ... and only insofar as he is the defender of the Church. ... When the emperor's strength fails, each

[117] *Mon. Mess.*, p. 36.

[118] *Ibid.*, p. 45, heading of chapter XII: "Christianismum esse unum et non plures: unumque caput, regem ac iudicem supremum in spiritualibus et temporalibus habere, cui omnes principatus et dignitates subsint per prophetiam, naturam, et propter beneficium principum et vassallorum et universi."

[119] *Ibid.*, p. 65: "Regnum Messiae unum esse unumque habere caput, Dominum omnium in temporalibus et in spiritualibus; et omnes dominorum titulos, sive electionis, sive successionis, sive emtionis, sive iusti belli, a Papa dependere ut Chrsti Dei Vicario."

[120] *Ibid.*, p. 63: "Quapropter ego in Thomistarum choro non potui assentire dicentibus quod indirecte Papa habet potestatem super laicos reges etiam in temporalibus: sed dixi, secundario in temporalibus; in spiritualibus vero principaliter, ut videtur docere Bernardus ... et D. Thomas ...." This statement is contained in an Appendix that runs through pp. 63-64 of the *Monarchia Messiae* in which Campanella defends himself against charges of error. He quotes several texts from St. Thomas to support his own viewpoint.

one of his princes may share his power, but only to the extent that he is so authorized by the Church.[121]

Applying this principle to the specific case of the New World, Campanella defends the king of Spain's right of conquest on the ground that he acted as the right arm of the Messias and his conquests contributed to the defense of the Christian faith and the spread of the Gospel.[122] For him there is no doubt that God was behind the Spaniards in their conquests. However, it is the Pope's task to dispose of, and distribute, the newly conquered territory, which belongs to him by divine right. The invasion of the New Hemisphere was in effect carried out under the auspices of Christ the Messias, who was promised dominion over the entire world. On the other hand, Americans, i.e., the natives of the New World, lead such an irrational life that the Pope is completely justified in punishing them until they return to reason, which they share in common with all other men.[123]

With these statements Campanella concludes what may be called the formal treatment of his theocratic state.[124] However the idea of a universal papal monarchy so dominates his mind that he never misses an opportunity to stress it and add some practical suggestions for its realization. Three works represent his practical approach to the problem of a universal monarchy. One is the *Discorsi della libertà e della felice suggezione allo stato ecclesiastico*,[125]

---

[121] *Ibid.*, p. 74.
[122] *Ibid.*
[123] *Ibid.*, pp. 86-87: "Nunc ex his assero: Proculdubio a Deo missos fuisse Hyspanos ad punitionem alterius Hemispherii per instinctum, sicuti Cyrus, Alexander, Nabucodonosor, Romani, et alii, ac subinde bona certaque iura in natura eos habere contra praefatos Barbaros, hoc est arma propria, et Barbarorum scelera. Itaque quicquid Rex sub auspiciis Christi occupat ad Papam disponere spectat, ab eoque praedictorum Regnorum possessionem, sive, ut dicunt, investituram largiri iure divino certum est, cum enim Messiae mundi Imperium promissum fuerit: et dictum: Gens et Regnum quod non servierit tibi peribit; cumque sit Messias Ratio summa incarnata; et illi Americani contra rationem tam impie vivant, proculdubio potest D. Papa eos iure iudicare castigatione dignos nisi rationi obedierint, cuius capaces participesque sunt naturaliter." For a more detailed discussion of the right of the Spaniards to conquer the New World see Campanella's *Monarchia di Spagna*, especially chapter XXXI.
[124] A more proper term for it is "hierocratic state," i.e., a state governed by ecclesiastics. But since the term "hierocratic" is not very popular, and, on the other hand, the Pope is supposed to head the universal monarchy as the representative of God, we prefer to use the term "theocratic."
[125] Firpo asserts that the *Discorsi della libertà* are to be reckoned among the least known pages of Campanella. Even the date of their composition is uncertain. He places it between 1625 and 1626. Cf. Introduction to the *Discorsi*, p. 8.

which the publisher added as an appendix to the text of the *Monarchia Messiae*, and the other two are the *Discorsi universali del governo ecclesiastico* and the *Quod reminiscentur*. To complete our treatment of Campanella's politics we shall add a brief notice on the contents of these works.

The *Discorsi della libertà* attempt to prove two main points. In the first discourse Campanella holds that there is no greater freedom than under the papal monarchy, and in the second he maintains that it is better to be subject to an ecclesiastical ruler than to a secular prince. In discussing the first point he points out the various types of freedom existing in the papal state: freedom from sin (in the sense that in it there are less sins than in other states), freedom from war, freedom from famine, freedom from pestilence, and finally, freedom from all forms of slavery. He compares this situation with the contrary conditions prevailing in secular states and concludes that nowhere in the world can a man be so free, in the true sense of the term, as in Rome under the Pope.[126] The second point, which is the topic of the second discourse, is stated in the following terms: it is political heresy and theological error to doubt that it is better to be subject to an ecclesiastical ruler than to a secular prince. The reason is that a man cannot lead other men unless he himself is led by God. But we know with certainty that the Holy Spirit assists the Pope in a most special way. The conclusion is therefore evident.[127]

To prove his statement Campanella considers ruler, subjects, and the relations existing between the two in both the ecclesiastical and the civil state. The ecclesiastical ruler, especially the Pope, is on many counts superior to a secular prince. He is a high priest consecrated to God and, therefore, more worthy of respect and more reliable; he is usually more mature and experienced and has a greater learning; he has no wife or children to care for; he is not a warrior, and therefore has no need to levy heavy taxes to support territorial conquests.[128] The subjects of the Papacy ought to consider themselves privileged to be governed by such a wise leader

---

[126] *Discorsi della libertà*, Firpo's edition, p. 36: "Dunque è vero che in nessun imperio di uno principe, nè di molti, nè di tutti si trova viver più libero d'ogni sorte di vera libertà, come in Roma sotto il papato."

[127] *Ibid.*, p. 37: "... è eresia politica ed errore teologico dubitare che non sia meglio sottostare all'ecclesiastico [imperio], sendo certi che l'uomo non può guidare gli altri uomini, se non è guidato da Dio ... Noi sapemo che l'assistenza dello Spirito Santo in abbondanza sopra tutti sta nel papato: *ergo* etc."

[128] *Ibid.*, pp. 37-39.

and appreciate the many advantages they enjoy in comparison with the subjects of a secular state.[129] Finally, there are much better relations between the Pope and his subjects than between a secular prince and his people. The Pope commands with greater authority and his orders are more easily obeyed because of the great veneration people have for him. He is more concerned with their food and defense, and, above all, he administers the state with fairness and justice.[130]

While the *Discorsi della libertà* were written mainly for the benefit of the citizens of the papal state, the *Discorsi universali del governo ecclesiastico* are a confidential report to the Pope suggesting practical ways and means of governing his state, with a view to establishing the universal monarchy described in the *Monarchia Messiae*.[131] These *Discorsi* are much more elaborate and their twenty-four chapters contain the essential principles of what may be termed papal domestic and foreign policy. The topics range from general statements concerning the means of obtaining and preserving an empire, which are but repetitions of what we have seen in the *De politica*, to specific problems of the papal state. "All the mistakes committed by the Church leaders," Campanella asserts, "consist in this, that they believe that the same policy that is good for a secular state is also good for the Papacy."[132] This is evidently wrong, for the secular state and the Papacy are two different types of government, one being concerned mainly with the bodies and the other with the souls of their subjects. One is headed by the Pope who is king, priest, and father, the other is governed by a prince or tyrant; one is built on love and veneration, the other on fear and merciless justice.[133]

To mobilize the whole world and win it over to the cause of a universal monarchy, the Pope need only use a selected group of

[129] *Ibid.*, p. 40.
[130] *Ibid.*, pp. 40-41.
[131] That this was the purpose of Campanella in writing his *Discorsi* is clear from the title and subtitle of the work: "*Discorsi universali del governo ecclesiastico per far una gregge e un pastore. Secreto al Papa solo, con modi non soggetti alla contradizione de' Prencipi.*" Firpo, *Scritti scelti*, p. 467. Furthermore, in his introduction to the *Discorsi* Campanella refers the reader to his *Monarchia Messiae*. *Ibid.*, p. 469.
[132] *Ibid.*, p. 472.
[133] *Ibid.*, pp. 472-73.

religious who are young, learned, and the best in each Order.[134] They will summon a general council, not only of Christians but of all other peoples as well, and discuss with them the truth of our religion by using the logic of Christ.[135] Furthermore, to preserve the unity of the faith, which is indispensable to a universal monarchy, all heretics should devote their abilities to fields of knowledge other than theology, such as astronomy and the mechanical arts. They should be paid for their services. The brightest among them will be sent to the New World, where they have no time to indulge in theological disputes and can acquire fame in some other way.[136]

To foster the cause of the monarchy, it is important that the Pope establish in Rome a council of all Christian princes or their ambassadors so that they can discuss together all matters pertaining to war and peace among Christians.[137] He should also see to it that the balance of power is preserved among the Christian rulers, so that no one ruler can attack another without his consent. Likewise, any attempt to apostatize must be immediately frustrated. Most of all the Pope must avoid calling foreigners into Italy, for fear that heresy may creep in the papal state and his own power be jeopardized and exposed to contempt. Control of Italy is his best assurance of control of the entire world, the aim toward which he should strive with all his power.[138]

The last work to be examined, the *Quod reminiscentur et convertentur ad Dominum universi fines terrae*, is an earnest appeal to all rulers and peoples to join into one great family under the Christian law. Thus they will fulfill the prayer of Psalm XXI which provides the title of the book. The work is divided into four parts, which contain messages to Christians, Gentiles, Jews, and

---

[134] *Ibid.*, p. 474: "Per tirar il mondo alla monarchia universale l'opera dell'eloquenti religiosi basta." *Ibid.*, pp. 474-75: "Di tutti ordini di religione del mondo il Papa deve eligere i piu dotti giovani per predicare la renovazione del secol felice in una gregge e un pastore, e segnarli con un segno suo papale, ma con gli abiti dell'ordini loro, e mandarli a diverse legazioni."

[135] *Ibid.*, p. 475.

[136] *Ibid.*, p. 493.

[137] *Ibid.*, p. 497. The formation of a senate of all Christian rulers in Rome under the presidency of the Pope is the central theme of the *Monarchia Christianorum*. Campanella refers to it frequently in his writings.

[138] *Ibid.*, p. 506: "Quando il Papa sarà signore d'Italia, sarà anche del mondo; però deve procurar ogni via di arrivar a questo." The remaining pages of the *Discorsi universali* are of no particular interest to us. They contain for the most part practical suggestions for the election of the Pope and the appointment of cardinals, archbishops, bishops, and other prelates of the Roman Curia.

Mohammedans. While the general theme is the same, the message to each individual group and composing nation contains points of special interest. In dedicating the work to Pope Paul V, Campanella calls it the epitome and completion of all his studies, for it represents a positive step toward the conversion of all nations under the auspices of the Vicar of Christ.[139] Indeed, it is only through the initiative of the Pope, Campanella states in his message to Paul V, that such a conversion is possible, for all mankind turns to him as to the last anchor of hope.[140] Needless to say, many people do not believe in God and much less in the Pope as His representative, but this pitiable state in which men find themselves itself cries out for the Pope's intervention, just as disease calls for the cure of a physician even though the sick man may not realize the seriousness of his ailment.[141] Campanella ends his message to Pope Paul V with a passionate appeal to him as supreme Pontiff and mediator between men and God to fulfill his duty and call all men back to God.[142]

Being convinced that the return of mankind to God is not possible without divine grace, Campanella prays to God to show His mercy upon men in spite of their sins,[143] and begs the nine choirs of angels for their protection.[144] He also entreats the devils to desist from tempting men, since no benefit can come to them from men's damnation.[145] Moreover he beseeches them—a hopeless task— to recognize their wrong deeds and come back to God, in the hope

[139] Cf. *Quod reminiscentur*, p. 3: ". . . scripsi volumen hoc sat elaboratum, tanquam epitomen et colophonem et finem studiorum meorum, quo omnium nationum conversio facile perficiatur tuis auspiciis, sanctissime Vicarie Christi."

[140] *Ibid.*, p. 31: "Vox totius generis humani clamantis ad te, sanctissime pastor." These are the initial words of Campanella's message to Pope Paul V.

[141] *Ibid.*

[142] *Ibid.*, p. 34: "Exurge, vigilantissime pastor, qui inter Deum et homines pontem Pontifex facis, qui mediator inter nos et Deum, ministerium tuum imple, et caetera omnia adiicientur vobis. Hanc igitur humani generis sequentem legationem perlectam aggredere, et coram Deo, cui proximus es, ipse fungere. Nos in atrio sanctuarii expectabimus, donec tu Moyses noster, imo Melchisedech noster, responsum salutare reportes et iuxta exemplar, quod tibi in monte Dei in vertice montium, ad quem confluent gentes, monstrabitur, ita fac."

[143] *Ibid.*, pp. 35-40.

[144] *Ibid.*, pp. 40-42.

[145] *Ibid.*, p. 43.

that because of this act of humility He might restore them to the kingdom they lost because of their pride.[146]

Quite consistently, Campanella proposes in the *Quod reminiscentur* the same basic principles for the church government that he had already stated in the *De regimine ecclesiastico* and briefly summarized in the *Discorsi universali*.[147] Also, when speaking of the need for the Christian rulers to join forces in order to defend themselves from other rulers and subdue them, he restates his own theory that only the supreme Pontiff can be their leader, for he alone, as Vicar of Christ, can command their respect and obedience.[148]

All messages to non-Christian leaders, whether Gentile, Jew, or Mohammedan, center on the idea that it is imperative for them to recognize the Christian God as the only true God and Supreme Ruler of the universe. Until this is done, there is no hope for salvation either for them or for the peoples with whose government they have been entrusted. Thus the *Quod reminiscentur* stands out as momentous testimony of the ecumenical spirit of its author, whose plan of a universal papal monarchy is designed as the fulfillment of the psalmist's prophecy: "All the families of the nations shall bow down in his sight; for the kingdom is the Lord's and he has dominion over the nations."[149] The work with its inspiring messages to the world leaders may be considered as Campanella's spiritual legacy to posterity. It is in the light of the *Quod reminiscentur* and the *Monarchia Messiae* that his political thought must be viewed, for it is the vision of all mankind united into one fold under one shepherd that gives meaning and unity to his entire political system.

---

[146] *Ibid.*, pp. 43-44: "Quapropter convertimini et agnoscite Deum vestrum: sic enim erit ut humilitas regnum solidum vobis resarciat, quod superbia tantopere constituit inane . . . . Vel ergo vestrum studium superbiendi vos admoneat, ut revertamini, unde cecidistis. Quod si non vultis, coniuro vos per Deum vivum, per Deum verum, per Deum sanctum, ut desistatis ab hominum infestatione, nec hanc, quam paramus, reminiscentiam audeatis impedire."

[147] *Ibid.*, pp. 57-60. The fourteen points that make up the article contain, in Campanella's words (*ibid.*, pp. 57-58), the substance of the *De regimine ecclesiastico*.

[148] *Ibid.*, pp. 68-71. In the course of the article reference is made to the *Monarchia Messiae*.

[149] Psalm XXI, 28-29. These two verses, which follow immediately upon the words of Ps. XXI that make up the title of the book, are cited by Campanella as a subtitle of Book II of the *Quod reminiscentur* containing his messages to the Gentiles.

9

TWO INSTANCES OF THE TRIPARTITE METHOD IN MACHIAVELLI

by

JOHN K. RYAN

Since Machiavelli is a representative man of the Renaissance, he has relations of both continuity and discontinuity to his medieval forebears. Certain of his interests are the same as theirs, although his approach to common problems and his final answers are often very different. At the same time it will be found that Machiavelli neither rejects all the principles of such medieval philosophy as he knew nor does he entirely forsake its ways of analysis and synthesis. He introduced a novel and distinctive method into moral and political philosophy, but his mind was fashioned by the logic and methods of the schoolmen and although lacking in the knowledge, width of vision, and concern for the deepest subjects shown by the great scholastic thinkers, he has something of their precision, order, and clarity.[1] Thus he makes clear and careful distinctions, divisions, and classifications, unites both deduction and induction in his argumentation, appeals to experience and fact for confirmation of his conclusions, has effective analogies, and makes frequent use of the argument from authority. It may in fact be argued that he is in some sense more authoritarian than the earlier thinkers on the state and its problems. Usually for him it is the authority of the "uomini grandi," the great princes and warriors whom he studies, as manifested by their practical achievements, that confirms his conclusions. Such things may be illustrated by passages in *The Prince*, the *Discourses* on Livy, and other books.

[1] Cf. Niccolò Machiavelli, *The Discourses*, tr. and ed. Leslie J. Walker (2 vols. New Haven, 1950). In this work Father Walker provides material for an understanding of Machiavelli, including his relation to the scholastics, especially St. Thomas Aquinas, and his use of *De regimine principum* by Aquinas and Ptolemy of Lucca. Cf. I, 84 and II, 293-98. Father Walker does not note Machiavelli's use of the tripartite method.

249

In certain places Machiavelli states his subject of discussion in the fashion of the schoolmen. Thus the title of one chapter in *The Prince* is "Quantum fortuna in rebus humanis possit, et quomodo illi sit occurrendum," that of another is "An arces et multa alia quae cotidie a principibus fiunt utilia an inutilia sint,"[2] and this type of chapter heading is frequent in the *Discourses*.[3] In two instances he makes what appears to be conscious use of the tripartite method of scholastic philosophy and theology.

As is familiar to the student of medieval philosophy, this method of discussing philosophical and theological questions necessitates great knowledge and skill on the part of the writer for its effective use. It requires a thorough grasp of what is involved in the debated issue, a concise but adequate statement of the problem, a fair presentation of opposing arguments, and a clear and convincing development of the master's own doctrine. Finally, it demands that the writer prove his case further by providing satisfactory answers to the opposing arguments. In the three stages of the method there is place for every legitimate form of argument. Inductive as well as deductive reasoning will appear, and there will be appeals to experience and fact. Illustrations and analogies will be drawn from history, literature, and life. Among the schoolmen wide use of Sacred Scripture and of the great names in philosophy and theology is seen as both licit and necessary. In its finished form the method is the result of a long historical development, and this holds not only for its substance but also for its terminology. It is highly stylized and has great value as a means of discussion and teaching, and the best examples of its use have a striking elegance in the sense applied to that term by mathematicians. Being works of art, both of the art of thought and the art of expression, they illustrate that principle of parsimony or economy which holds for thought and things. Hence there is no needless multiplication of words and

---

[2] The titles of chapters 25 and 20 in *The Prince*. The text used here is that in Niccolò Machiavelli, *Tutte le opere*, ed. Guido Mazzoni and Mario Casella (Firenze: G. Barbèra, 1929) pp. 4-51.

[3] Examples of such titles in *The Discourses* are "Whether mild or severe means are more necessary in ruling a large group," "What value should be set on artillery by armies at the present time, and whether the general opinion with regard to it is true," "How dangerous it is for a republic or a prince not to avenge a public or private injury," and "Whether we should put more trust in a good general who has a poor army or in a good army that has a poor general." On the last subject Machiavelli quotes Caesar to the effect that neither combination is worth much.

arguments. "Rationes," the master reasoners may be credited with saying, "non sunt multiplicandae praeter necessitatem."

The long historical process that brought the tripartite method to its perfection in the *Summa theologica* and certain other works of St. Thomas Aquinas is reflected in the typical Thomistic article, and for the purposes of this note on Machiavelli almost any article in the *Summa* can be taken as a paradigm. In *Summa theologica* I, 2, 2, the problem at issue is stated: "Utrum Deum esse sit demonstrabile." There are two possible answers to this problem, viz., (1) the negative answer of those who on one ground or another hold that the existence of God cannot be proved by human reason, and (2) the affirmative answer of those who hold that it can. After the introductory words "ad secundum sic proceditur," arguments for the negative position are stated, and this statement of the opposition's case constitutes the first part of the tripartite method. The arguments are three in number, each of them being introduced by the phrase "videtur quod: it seems that." One argument is that of a species of fideism and holds that since we know God by faith, his existence is not demonstrable by reason. A second argument is the quasi-agnostic assertion that since our knowledge of God is negative, a knowledge of what he is not rather than of what he is, his being cannot be established by reason. The third argument anticipates the Kantian doctrine that we cannot argue from finite effects to an infinite cause.

Persuasive as such arguments may seem, they are contradicted by those who agree with St. Paul[4] that "the invisible things of God are clearly seen, being understood by the things that are made." This opposing doctrine is introduced by the words "sed contra: but on the contrary." The contradiction between the "videtur quods" and the "sed contra" is next resolved by a development of St. Thomas' own doctrine. Introduced by the word "respondeo,"[5] this response constitutes the body of the article and gives the master's own solution of the problem at hand. In the response, conclusion, or corpus of the article under consideration St. Thomas shows how the existence of God is a matter for rational proof. Having done so, he proceeds to the final section of the method where an answer is given to each of the three original negative or opposing arguments.

---

[4] Romans 1:20.

[5] More fully: "respondeo, dicendum." Cf. St. Augustine's "respondeo dicenti" in *Confessions*, tr. and ed. John K. Ryan (New York: Image Books) p. 286, and p. 140.

These answers are introduced by the words "ad primum," "ad secundum," and so on in numerical order. In certain instances formal answer to one or another or even all of the "videtur quods" is dispensed with as unnecessary because sufficient answer to them has already been given in the body of the article. "Et sic patet responsio ad obiecta," St. Thomas[6] sometimes writes: "And thus the answer to the objections is evident."

Machiavelli's use of the tripartite method in *The Prince*[7] is headed "Cur Darii regnum quod Alexander occupaverat a successoribus suis post Alexandri mortem non deficit." This statement, "Why it was that Darius' kingdom, which Alexander had seized, did not rebel against Alexander's successors after his death," holds the place of the "utrum" in a Thomistic article. The opponent's position is succinctly stated by Machiavelli. In view of the difficulties in holding a newly occupied state someone may wonder at this situation. Alexander the Great became master of Asia in a few years and then died. "Donde pareva ragionevole che tutto quello stato si rebellassi: Hence it seemed reasonable for that entire state to rebel." This "pareva ragionevole," Machiavelli's "videtur quod," is brief, as is his "sed contra": "Nondimeno e' successori di Alessandro se lo mantennono; e non ebbono, a tenerlo, altra difficultà che quella che intra loro medesimi, per ambizione propria, nacque: Nevertheless, Alexander's successors maintained the realm, and they had no difficulty in holding it except that which arose among themselves from their own ambitions."

The corpus of Machiavelli's article is introduced by the exact Italian equivalent of the traditional introductory word. "Respondo," he writes, and he continues the scholastic tradition by making a distinction.[8] Kingdoms are governed in two different ways: (1) by a prince and servants who are completely dependent on him, or (2)

---

[6] St. Thomas Aquinas's articles have their own precise terminology and structure. Other scholastic doctors vary in technical terms and also in their use of the tripartite method. The structure of the articles in John Duns Scotus's works is much more elaborate than in Aquinas. Cf. Duns Scotus, *Philosophical Writings*. A selection edited and translated by Allan Wolter, O.F.M., (Edinburgh: Nelson, 1962), and Fr. Wolter's article "John Duns Scotus, 'On the Nature of Man's Knowledge of God,'" *The Review of Metaphysics*, I (1947-48), pp. 4-34. This article is reprinted in part in James Collins, *Readings in Ancient and Medieval Philosophy*, (Westminster, Md.: The Newman Press, 1960) pp. 289-303.

[7] *The Prince*, ch. 4.

[8] One editor notes with approval the clear character of the chapter, the "energetic respondo," and the neat distinction, but does not recognize Machiavelli's scholastic method. Cf. *Il principe*, ed. Plinio Carli (Firenze, 1939) p. 30.

by a prince together with barons who are not completely dependent on the prince but have rank by reason of their ancient blood. These barons have their own states and subjects who recognize them as lords and have a natural affection for them. Where the prince governs through ministers he has greater authority, since throughout the entire realm the people recognize no one but the prince as a superior. If they obey anyone else, they do so in so far as he is a minister and officer of the prince and they have no particular love for such an official. Examples of the two kinds of kingdom are that of the Turk and that of the king of France. Machiavelli then explains why it is difficult to invade and conquer Turkey, and also why, if it were once conquered, it would be easy to maintain the victory. On the other hand, it is easier to invade a country like France—there are always malcontents among the barons who will welcome an invader—but more difficult to maintain the conquest because of loyal barons and their subjects. Ancient parallels are asserted to be found in Spain, Greece, and France under the Romans, since they had to contend with frequent rebellions in those provinces. There had been many principalities in the three lands, Machiavelli states, and as long as memory of their native lords endured among the people the Roman conquest was uncertain. Once the memory of the former princes was gone, the power and permanence of the empire kept the Romans in sure possession.

Machiavelli finds that Darius' kingdom was similar to that of the Turk. After Alexander's quick victory and Darius' death, it was easy to maintain the new realm "per ragioni di sopra discorse: for reasons stated above." Even after Alexander's death, his successors could have lived in ease if they had only remained united. At the end Machiavelli returns "more scholastico" to the original objection and answers it with the words: "Considerato adunque tutte queste cose, non si maraviglierà alcuno della facilità ebbe Alessandro a tenere lo stato di Asia, e delle difficultà che hanno avuto gli altri a conservare lo acquistato, come Pirro e molti. Il che non è nato dalla molta o poca virtù del vincitore, ma dalla disformità del subietto: That is, having considered all these things, no one should marvel at the ease with which Alexander held the Asian state, and at the difficulties that others, such as Pyrrho and many more, have had in keeping their conquests. This does not spring from the great or little power of the conqueror but from the weakness of the subject people." As may be seen, Machiavelli has conformed to the structure of the tripartite method. In his "Cur Darii," "pareva ragionevole," "nondimeno," "respondo," and "considerato adunque," he has equivalents of the "utrum," "videtur quod," "sed contra," "respondeo," and "ad primum" of the scholastics.

The second use of the tripartite method is found in *Discourses* II, 12, where Machiavelli discusses the problem of a prince on whom an equally powerful enemy has declared war. Should the threatened prince take the offensive and carry the war to his rival, or should he stay on the defensive and wait the attack at home? The "utrum" of the article is stated: "S'egli è meglio, temendo di essere assaltato, inferire o aspettare la guerra: whether it is better, when fearing to be attacked, to strike out at the enemy or to await the war at home." The "videtur quod" is made up of three arguments advanced by those who hold that the threatened prince should carry the war to the enemy. All three arguments are based on events in ancient history, one of which is Hannibal's advice to King Antiochus that the Romans could be defeated only in Italy. The "sed contra" is then stated: "Chi parla al contrario, dice che chi vuole fare capitare male uno inimico, lo discoste da casa: Those who speak for the contrary opinion state that anyone who wants to inflict a serious defeat on an enemy should draw him away from home." Two arguments, one from ancient history and one from events in the kingdom of Naples, are offered by those who say that the prince should adopt a defensive posture and await the attack at home. Machiavelli next varies the formula somewhat by adding two further arguments, one for each of the two opposing theories. He then gives his "respondeo:" "Ma per dire ora io quello che io ne intendo, io credo che si abbia a fare questa distinzione: But to say now what I myself think, I believe that this distinction must be made." The distinction is between a country that has its people armed and ready for war, such as the Romans and the Swiss, and a country where the people are not armed and trained to fight, like the Carthaginians, the Italians, and the French.

After discussing the two types and illustrating them with ancient as well as modern instances, Machiavelli brings the body of the article, in which is found his own conclusion and solution of the problem, to an end with a brief recapitulation:

> I therefore conclude again that the prince who has his people armed and prepared for war should always await a powerful and perilous war at home and not go out to meet the enemy, whereas a ruler whose subjects are unarmed and whose country is unused

to war, should always keep it as far away from home as possible. Thus both the one and the other will best defend himself, each in his own way.[9]

Since Machiavelli has considered differences from his own position in the course of his article—for instance, he writes[10] of the argument based on Hannibal's advice to Antiochus, "Nè mi muove in questo caso l'autorità d'Annibale: Hannibal's authority does not move me in this instance"—he does not need to take them up one by one. He could in fact have ended in Thomistic fashion with the words, "Et per hoc patet responsio ad obiecta," and his closing words "Conchiuggo adunque" have something of this character. Here again in working out his solution Machiavelli faithfully follows the pattern devised by the schoolmen: statement of a problem, conflicting views upon it, the thinker's own analysis and conclusion, and answers to the solution advanced by other thinkers.

Although Machiavelli's adaptation of the tripartite method is sufficiently evident from what has already been said, it may be helpful to give schemata showing how his procedure and terminology parallel those of St. Thomas.

Thomistic article	*Machiavelli's articles*	
a) Utrum	a) Cur Darii	a) S'egli è meglio
b) Videtur quod	b) Pareva ragionevole	b) Chi difende
c) Sed contra	c) Nondimeno	c) Al contrario
d) Respondeo, dicendum	d) Respondo	d) Per dire ... che io ne intendo
e) Ad primum; ad secundum ...	e) Considerato adunque	e) Conchiuggo

Hence in these two passages in *The Prince* and the *Discourses* Machiavelli has made expert use of one form of scholastic pro-

---

[9] "Conchiuggo adunque, di nuovo, che quel principe che ha i suoi popoli armati ed ordinati alla guerra, aspetti sempre in casa una guerra potente e pericolosa, e non la vadia a rincontrare: ma quello che ha i suoi sudditi disarmati, ed il paese inusitato alla guerra, se le discosti sempre da casa il più che può. E così l'uno e l'altro, ciascuno nel suo grado, si defenderà meglio."

[10] Hannibal's advice to Antiochus was more correct than Machiavelli knew. He rightly saw that if Rome was to be defeated, it would have to be in Italy, and that the task of carrying the war to the Romans involved enormous difficulties. His greatness is shown by the fact that he overcame so many of the difficulties and came so close to victory.

cedure.[11] Like the scholastics, he is compressed in thought and economical in his use of words. However, it cannot be said that his mastery of matter has equalled that of form. As in much of his reasoning and in many of his appeals to history throughout *The Prince* and the *Discourses,* he is superficial and addicted to oversimplification.[12] This is especially true when he explains why the Greek conquest of the Persian empire was a lasting success. For the complex of causes that brought on the collapse of Persian power under Alexander's attack and contributed to the subsequent success of the Seleucid kings and the Ptolemies, Machiavelli sees only one factor, and it may well have been the least important of those involved. In this chapter, as elsewhere in *The Prince,* Machiavelli's failure is to provide depth and solidity of thought along with ease and clarity of expression.

[11] In this Machiavelli illustrates what others can do with the tripartite method. I have used it twice in modern form, i.e., without traditional terminology, which is incidental to the method, but with all its main divisions. Cf. "Magna Est Veritas et Praevalebit," *American Ecclesiastical Review* CXXXV (August, 1956) 116-24, and "What St. Thomas Aquinas Asks of Us Today," *The Catholic University of America Bulletin,* April, 1962, pp. 1, 2, 8. I have found that students can make an effective analysis and presentation of philosophical problems by adhering to the tripartite method.

[12] A fellow Florentine, Francesco Guicciardini (1483-1540), makes this charge against Machiavelli's discussion of the problem of offensive vs. defensive warfare. Cf. Walker, *op. cit.,* II, 112, 3.

NOTES ON CONTRIBUTORS

Rev. Felix Alluntis, O.F.M., Ph.D., is Associate Professor of Philosophy in The Catholic University of America, where he received the M.A. degree in 1945 and the doctorate in 1949. He has also studied at the Theological House of Studies, Aranzazu, Spain, and has taught at the University of Sto. Tomás de Villanueva, Havana. He is the author of *Filosofía cristiana de la propriedad* (1960), a translation of John Duns Scotus' *De primo rerum principio* (1960), and various articles in English and Spanish journals.

Gilbert B. Arbuckle, Ph.D., is a graduate of the College of the Holy Cross and The Catholic University of America, (M.A., 1954; Ph.D., 1962). His article is a development of a section of his doctoral dissertation.

Rev. Bernardine M. Bonansea, O.F.M., M.A., Ph.D., Lect. Glis., is Associate Professor of Philosophy at The Catholic University of America, from which he holds his doctorate. He also studied at the Pontificium Athenaeum Antonianum in Rome and has taught at Siena College, Loudonville, N.Y. Dr. Bonansea has translated and edited Efrem Bettoni's *Duns Scotus: The Basic Principles of His Philosophy* (The Catholic University of America Press, 1961) and has published various articles in the field of scholastic and renaissance philosophy. He has just completed a large work on *The Philosophy of Tommaso Campanella*.

Prof. Dr. C. J. de Vogel of the University of Utrecht is an authority on ancient and medieval philosophy. She is the author of *History of Greek Philosophy*, 3 vols. (Leiden, 1950-1959), *Ecclesia catholica* (Utrecht, 1945) and of many articles and books. She has lectured at The Catholic University of America and other American universities.

Rev. Leo A. Foley, S.M., Ph.D., holds the rank of Professor of Philosophy in The Catholic University of America, where he received the doctorate in 1946, and is Secretary of the American Catholic Philosophical Association. He has specialized in the philosophy of nature and science and has lectured widely on these subjects. He is the author of *Cosmology, Philosophical and Scientific* (Bruce, 1962), *A Critique of the Philosophy of Being of Alfred North Whitehead*, and numerous articles.

Rt. Rev. Eugene Kevane, M.A., Ph.D., Assistant Professor of Education at The Catholic University of America, studied at Loras College, the Gregorian University, and the Creighton University. He is the author of *An Augustinian Philosophy of Education for American Catholic Schools* (1962) and of various articles.

Rev. Thomas G. Pater, S.T.D., Ph.D., a member of the Library staff and lecturer in the School of Sacred Theology at The Catholic University of America, received the doctorate in philosophy from the Pontificium Athenaeum Angelicum, Rome, and the doctorate in theology from The Catholic University of America. He taught fundamental theology for ten years at Mt. St. Mary's Seminary, Norwood, Ohio.

Thomas Prufer, Ph.D., received his undergraduate degree from the University of Virginia in 1953 and his doctorate from the University of Munich in 1959, followed by a year of post-doctoral work under a grant from the German Academic Exchange Program. A member of the philosophy faculty of The Catholic University of America, he has published in *Philosophische Rundschau* and *International Philosophical Quarterly*.

Rt. Rev. John K. Ryan, Ph.D., Elizabeth Breckinridge Caldwell Professor of Philosophy and Dean of the School of Philosophy, The Catholic University of America, is the author of *Modern War and Basic Ethics* (2nd ed. 1940), *The Reputation of St. Thomas Aquinas among English Protestant Thinkers of the Seventeenth Century* (1948), a translation of St. Augustine's *Confessions* (1960), and other books and articles on philosophy.

INDEX

Adam, 232
Adam, Karl, 77
Adler, M. J., 205
Alcibiades, 28
Alcuin, 102
Alexander, 252, 253, 256
Alfaric, P., 67-70, 75, 77, 91, 94
Alluntis, F., 190
Alquié, F., 9
Ambrose, St., 7, 231
Antiochus, 254, 255
Atoninus Pius, 60
Archilochus, 27
Arendt, H., 9, 11
Aristophanes, 28
Aristotle, 1-4, 6-8, 14, 17, 21, 23, 28, 33, 35-39, 55, 60, 123, 127-132, 143, 179-81, 188, 191, 198, 206
Atheneus, 28
Augustine, St., 6-10, 12, 61-103, 231
Averroes, 4, 5

Becker, H., 66
Bion, 45
Bodin, J., 237
Boethius, 20, 59, 60, 182
Bohr, N., 185
Boissier, G., 63, 65, 92, 94, 103
Bonaventure, St., 60, 201
Bourke, V. J., 62, 76
Boyer, C., 62, 69, 71, 73-76, 93, 94, 96, 97, 101
Burn, A. R., 27

Campanella, T., 211-248
Capreolus, 143
Carneades, 23, 56
Charaxus, 27
Cicero, 29, 30, 38, 39, 48, 58, 81, 84, 85, 89, 93, 94
Christ, Jesus, 52
Chrysippus, 49, 56
Cleanthes, 32
Clement, St., 231
Colleran, J. M., 87
Connolly, T. K., 137-38, 148, 149, 152-58, 167-75
Copernicus, 179
Courcelle, P., 62, 76, 77
Croce, B., 233
Curies (Pierre and Marie), 181
Cyril, St., 229
Cyrus, 40

Dallion, Père, 183
Dante, 6
Darius, 252, 253
Darwin, C., 117
Degli'Innocenti, U., 137, 138, 148, 160-63, 168

Descartes, R., 1, 8-10, 12
Descoqs, P., 143, 161
Dilthey, W., 14, 102
Diogenes Laertius, 28, 32, 43-45
Dittenberger, 41
Duns Scotus, John, 21, 22, 60, 201, 252

Eckhardt, 10
Edmonds, J. M., 27
Einstein, A., 187
Empedocles, 28
Ephrem, St., 22
Epictetus, 24, 50
Epicurus, 28

Fagothey, A., 189
Faraday, M., 185
Fate, 32
Festugière, A.-J., 7, 43
Firpo, L., 221-17
Franklin, B., 185

Gaertner, R., 135
Gaius, 20, 59, 60, 208-09
Galileo, G., 179
Garvey, M. P., 62
Gilson, E., 20, 22
Gourdon, L., 67, 71, 94, 96, 100
Grassi, E., 87
Gregory of Nyssa, St., 180
Guardini, R., 62
Guicciardini, F., 256
Guignebert, C., 68

Hannibal, 254, 255
Harnack, A., 64-71, 97
Hegel, F. W. G., 5, 12, 13
Heidegger, M., 3, 5, 14-17
Heisenberg, W., 187
Heraclitus, 23, 28, 31, 32, 49, 58
Herodotus, 27
Hilary, St., 3
Homer, 26, 37
Horvath, J., 190
Hume, D., 10, 12
Husserl, E., 1, 5, 8, 13, 14, 16-18
Huxley, J., 9

Isidore, St., 207, 209

Jaeger, W., 82
Jamblichus, 42
John Chrysostom, St., 231
John XXIII, Pope, 196
Julian, 41

Kant, I., 10-12
Kelso, L. O., 205
Kepler, J., 179
Kierkegaard, S. K., 13

Klein, J., 9
Klibansky, R., 20, 22
Kors, J. B., 200

Labriolle, P. de, 76
Laelius, 30
Leo XIII, Pope, 81, 193, 203
Leon, 28
Lercher, L., 200
Leucippus, 185
Lévy-Bruhl, L., 68
Livy, 249
Locke, J., 24
Loofs, F., 65, 66, 71, 94
Lucian, 39
Luther, M., 66
Lyco, 28

Machiavelli, N., 215, 217, 249-56
Mannucci, U., 63, 69, 70, 72
Marcus Aurelius, 29, 39, 40, 49
Maritain, J., 194, 195
Marrou, H. I., 88, 95, 98, 99
Martin, J., 72
Marx, K., 10, 14, 236
Mausbach, J., 72, 102
Maxwell, J. C., 185
McFadden, J., 195
Messner, J., 204
Monica, St., 71, 80
Moral, I. G., 189
More, St. Thomas, 213, 230, 237
Mure, G. R. G., 13

Newman, J. H., 81
Nietzsche, F., 10, 13, 14
Nock, A. D., 78
Novalis, 10
Nörregaard, D. J., 75

Ockham, W., 201
O'Donoghue, D., 137, 155
O'Meara, J., 62, 68, 78, 90, 97, 98, 100
Origen, 32
Ortega y Gasset, J., 193

Panaetius, 30, 33, 39, 58
Parmenides, 185
Pattin, A., 137-38, 155
Paul, St., 61, 71, 251
Peirce, C. S., 184
Philip of Macedon, 41
Philoponos, J., 6
Paul V, Pope, 247
Pius XI, Pope, 203
Pius XII, Pope, 190, 193
Plato, 1-3, 20-60, 81, 82, 155, 180, 184, 230
Pliny, 29
Plotinus, 23, 24, 46-60, 68, 74
Plutarch, 40, 43, 58

Pola, M. G., 137
Porphyry, 29, 55, 68
Portalié, E., 62, 70, 77, 90
Possidius, 61
Pseudo Aristotle, 41
Ptolemies, 256
Pyrrho, 253
Pythagoras, 23, 41-43, 58

Rand, E. K., 99
Reinach, S., 68
Rickert, H., 116-18, 123, 135, 136
Riezler, K., 19
Ross, W. D., 37
Rumford, 185
Ryan, J. K., 83, 86, 251, 256

Sappho, 27
Schadewalt, W., 26
Schilling, O., 202
Schuppe, W., 135
Sciacca, M. F., 78
Scipio Africanus, 30
Scotus, John Duns. See Duns Scotus, John
Scotus Erigena, J., 9, 126
Socrates, 3, 28, 44
Seleucids, 256
Semonides, 27
Sigwart, C., 120, 127
Strauss, L., 4

Tacitus, 29
Thimme, W., 66
Tillemont, Le Nain de, 99
Thomas Aquinas, St., 4, 6, 8, 9, 18, 21, 22, 60, 104-36, 137-77, 179, 182, 191-210, 231, 251, 252, 255
Thompson, 185
Thrasymachus, 28
Tonneau, T., 202
Tourscher, F. E., 95
Toynbee, A. J., 102
Tromp de Ruiter, S., 41, 44

Ueuküll, T., von, 87
Ulpian, 207

Van Gestel, C., 196, 205
Van Steenberghen, F., 137-38
Vergil, 78, 92
Victorinus, 71

Webster, T. B. L., 27
Wörter, F., 69, 71, 96
Wolff, C., 24
Wolter, A., 252

Xenophon, 40, 44-46

Zeno, 33, 45, 185

www.ingramcontent.com/pod-product-compliance
Lightning Source LLC
Chambersburg PA
CBHW031412290426
44110CB00011B/347